The Oxford History of the Book

James Raven is a Fellow of Magdalene College, University of Cambridge, a Fellow of the British Academy, and Professor Emeritus of Modern History at the University of Essex. Formerly he was Reader in Social and Cultural History, University of Oxford, and Professorial Fellow of Mansfield College. He is the author, editor, and co-editor of numerous books in early modern and modern British, European, and colonial history, including *Judging New Wealth* (1992); *The Practice and Representation of Reading* (1996); *The English Novel 1770–1829* (2000); *Free Print and Non-Commercial Publishing* (2000); *London Booksellers and American Customers* (2002); *Lost Libraries* (2004); *The Business of Books: Booksellers and the English Book Trade* (2007); *Books between Europe and the Americas* (2011); *Publishing Business* (2014); *Bookscape: Geographies of Printing and Publishing in London before 1800* (2014); and *What is the History of the Book?* (2018).

The historians who contributed to *The Oxford History of the Book* are all distinguished authorities in their field. They are:

ANN BLAIR, Harvard University
SHEILA S. BLAIR, Boston College and Virginia Commonwealth University
JONATHAN M. BLOOM, Boston College and Virginia Commonwealth University
CYNTHIA BROKAW, Brown University
MARIE-FRANÇOISE CACHIN, Université Paris Diderot Paris VII
BARBARA CROSTINI, Uppsala University
JEFFREY FREEDMAN, Yeshiva University
JORAN PROOT, University of Milan
JAMES RAVEN, University of Cambridge
CHRISTOPHER A. REED, The Ohio State University
ELEANOR ROBSON, University College London
DAVID RUNDLE, University of Kent
JEFFREY T. SCHNAPP, Harvard University
GRAHAM SHAW, University of London
M. WILLIAM STEELE, International Christian University, Tokyo
EVA HEMMUNGS WIRTÉN, Linköping University

The Oxford History
of the Book

Edited by

JAMES RAVEN

OXFORD
UNIVERSITY PRESS

OXFORD
UNIVERSITY PRESS

Great Clarendon Street, Oxford, OX2 6DP,
United Kingdom

Oxford University Press is a department of the University of Oxford.
It furthers the University's objective of excellence in research, scholarship,
and education by publishing worldwide. Oxford is a registered trade mark of
Oxford University Press in the UK and in certain other countries

First Edition published in 2023

Impression: 1

The text of this edition was published in The Oxford Illustrated History of the Book in 2020
The moral rights of the author have been asserted
First published 2020
First published in paperback 2022

Published in the United States of America by Oxford University Press
198 Madison Avenue, New York, NY 10016, United States of America

British Library Cataloguing in Publication Data
Data available

Library of Congress Control Number: 2022946819

ISBN 978–0–19–288689–7

DOI: 10.1093/oso/9780192886897.001.0001

Printed and bound in the UK by
Clays Ltd, Elcograf S.p.A.

Praise for *The Oxford History of the Book*

'This book will become an invaluable point of departure for students new to the field, for scholars who need to venture outside their normal chronological and geographical comfort zones, and—as it should be—to that elusive general reader.'

John Feather, *Library & Information History*

'Together, these fourteen essays form a thorough picture of how and why books progressed along the lines that they did. In an age when books are once again experiencing momentous changes, this well-researched reminder of their durability and timelessness is very welcome.'

Eileen Gonzalez, *Foreword Reviews*

'This volume is a cultural biography of the book, taking a global view of its underlying function as a portable, durable conveyor of reproducible information...Other works trace the history of the book, but Oxford's treatment is a deeper, more multicultural, and more visually appealing approach.'

Lesley Farmer, *Booklist*

'This is an excellent compilation on the world-wide history of the book...Put it on your Christmas present list.'

Prof. T.D. Wilson, *Information Research*

'*The Oxford History of the Book* is a seminal and original work of meticulous scholarship'

Midwest Book Review

'A sumptuous production.'

Liz Dexter, *Shiny New Books*

Contents

    Eva Hemmungs Wirtén

14. Books Transformed   342
    Jeffrey T. Schnapp

    Abbreviations and Glossary   361
    Further Reading   373
    Index   391

Notes on Contributors

Ann Blair is Carl H. Pforzheimer University Professor at Harvard University where she teaches early modern European cultural and intellectual history and book history. She is especially interested in the history of intellectual practices. Her publications include *The Theater of Nature: Jean Bodin and Renaissance Science* (Princeton, 1997) and *Too Much to Know: Managing Scholarly Information before the Modern Age* (New Haven, 2010).

Sheila S. Blair and **Jonathan M. Bloom** shared the Norma Jean Calderwood University Professorship of Islamic and Asian Art at Boston College and the Hamad bin Khalifa Endowed Chair of Islamic Art at Virginia Commonwealth University. Jointly and individually they are the authors, co-authors, or editors of many books and articles on various aspects of Islamic art and architecture. Sheila Blair is particularly interested in calligraphy in the Islamic lands and the arts of the book in the Mongol period, and is the author of the prize-winning book *Islamic Calligraphy* (Edinburgh, 2008). Jonathan Bloom is particularly interested in the history of paper in the Islamic lands and Europe, and is the author of the prize-winning book *Paper before Print* (New Haven, 2001).

Cynthia Brokaw is Professor of History at Brown University, Providence, Rhode Island. A scholar of late imperial Chinese history, she specializes in the history of the pre-modern Chinese book. Her *Commerce in Culture: The Sibao Book Trade in the Qing and Republican Periods* is a study of a rural publishing industry, its distribution networks, and its impact on book culture in south China. She has also co-edited two essay collections on Chinese book history, *Printing and Book Culture in Late Imperial China* (with Kai-wing Chow; Boston, MA, 2007), and *From Woodblocks to the Internet: Chinese Publishing and Print Culture in Transition, circa 1800 to 2008* (with Christopher A. Reed; Leiden, 2010).

Marie-Françoise Cachin, Professor Emerita, Université Paris Diderot Paris VII, is a specialist in modern publishing history and the transnational circulation of books. She was for several years in charge of

'Le livre et l'édition dans le monde anglophone', a group researching book publishing in English-speaking countries. Her publications include studies of nineteenth- and twentieth-century presses and Anglo-French literary and publishing relationships and her most recent book is *Une nation de lecteurs? La lecture en Angleterre, 1815–1945* (Lyon, 2010).

Barbara Crostini is Associate Professor in Byzantine Greek at the Department of Linguistics and Philology at Uppsala University, Sweden. She has worked extensively with Greek manuscripts, producing a catalogue at the Bodleian Library (2003) and working on digital descriptions for Trinity College Library, Dublin, and for the online catalogue of Greek manuscripts in Sweden (www.manuscripta.se). Her online edition of a Greek psalter with catena commentary at the Vatican Library was sponsored by the Bank of Sweden through the Ars edendi programme at Stockholm University. She co-curated the volumes *A Book of Psalms from Eleventh-Century Byzantium: The Complex of Texts and Images in Psalter Vat. gr. 752*, with G. Peers, *Studi e Testi 504* (Vatican City, 2016) and *Greek Monasticism in Southern Italy: the Life of Neilos in Context*, with I. Murzaku (London, 2017).

Jeffrey Freedman is Professor of European History at Yeshiva University in New York. He received his PhD in History from Princeton University, his research focusing on communication and the circulation of ideas in Enlightenment Europe, with particular emphasis on the French- and German-speaking worlds. His books include *Books Without Borders in Enlightenment Europe* (Philadelphia, 2012), a study of the Franco-German book trade in the late eighteenth century, and *A Poisoned Chalice* (Princeton, NJ, 2002), a micro-historical study of the genesis, mutation, and circulation of a spectacular news story from the late eighteenth century. His most recent project is a study of fear in Old Regime and Revolutionary France.

Joran Proot researches early modern book history at the University of Milan. He was formerly Andrew W. Mellon Curator of Rare Books at the Folger Shakespeare Library, Washington, D.C., and Director of the Short Title Catalogue Flanders project (STCV), the online bibliography of pre-1801 hand-press books published in Flanders. He is editor-in-chief of the book historical journal De Gulden Passer. His doctoral work focused on Jesuit theatre performances in the period 1575–1773 and the book historical aspects of printed theatre programmes. In his spare time, he studies book design before industrialization.

James Raven FBA is a Fellow of Magdalene College, Cambridge, Director of the Cambridge Project for the Book Trust, and Professor Emeritus of Modern History at the University of Essex. His books include *What is the History of the Book?* (Cambridge, 2018); *Bookscape: Geographies of Printing and Publishing in London before 1800* (London, 2014); *The Business of Books: Booksellers and the English Book Trade 1450–1850* (London and New Haven, CT, 2007 and awarded the DeLong Prize in the History of the Book); *Lost Libraries: The Destruction of Book Collections since Antiquity* (London, 2004), and *London Booksellers and American Customers: Transatlantic Literary Community and the Charleston Library Society, 1748–1811* (Columbia, SC, 2002).

Christopher A. Reed is Associate Professor of Modern Chinese History in the History Department at The Ohio State University, Columbus, Ohio. He specializes in late imperial and modern Chinese history and is the author of the 2005 International Convention of Asia Scholars (ICAS) prize-winning book, *Gutenberg in Shanghai: Chinese Print Capitalism, 1876–1937* (Vancouver, Toronto, and Honolulu, 2004; and Hong Kong, 2005). With Cynthia Brokaw, he co-edited *From Woodblocks to the Internet; Chinese Publishing and Print Culture in Transition, circa 1800 to 2008* (Leiden, 2010). He has published many other articles and chapters on Chinese print capitalism and print communism. He also contributed fifteen entries on Chinese publishers to the *Oxford Companion to the Book* (Oxford, 2010).

Eleanor Robson FBA is Professor of Ancient Middle Eastern History at University College London and runs the AHRC-GCRF funded Nahrein Network for the sustainable development of antiquity, heritage and humanities in post-conflict Iraq and its neighbours. Her research interests focus on the social and political contexts of intellectual and scholarly life in the cuneiform world, and the ways in which the ancient Middle East have been interpreted over the past two centuries. Her many publications on the subject include, most recently, *The Oxford Handbook of Cuneiform Culture* (co-edited with Karen Radner, 2011) and *Ancient Knowledge Networks: A Social Geography of Cuneiform Scholarship in the First Millennium BC* (London, 2019).

David Rundle is Senior Lecturer in Latin and Manuscript Studies, Centre for Medieval and Early Modern Studies, University of Kent. He specialises in Renaissance intellectual and cultural history, in particular using the palaeographical and codicological evidence of manuscripts to spread the circulation of humanist ideas across Europe in the fifteenth and early sixteenth centuries. He also writes on the history of libraries and on the dispersal of medieval book collections in early modern Europe, and is editor of *Humanism in Fifteenth-Century Europe* (Oxford, 2012).

Jeffrey T. Schnapp holds the Carl A. Pescosolido Chair in Comparative and Romance Literatures at Harvard University, where he is also affiliated with the Department of Architecture at the Graduate School of Design. He is co-director of the Berkman Klein Center for Internet and Society and the faculty director and founder of metaLAB@Harvard. Originally trained as a medievalist, his recent publications concern the modern and contemporary eras with a focus on media, technology, design, and the history of the book. His books include *The Electric Information Age Book* (2012); *Modernitalia* (2012); *The Library Beyond the Book* (2014); and *FuturPiaggio: Six Italian Lessons on Mobility and Modern Life* (2017).

Graham Shaw is a Senior Research Fellow of the Institute of English Studies, School of Advanced Study, University of London. He retired from the British Library in 2010, having been Head of the Library's Asia, Pacific and Africa Collections for over twenty years. For the past forty years he has researched the history of printing and publishing in South Asia from the sixteenth to the twentieth centuries. His published works include *Printing in Calcutta to 1800* (London, 1981) and *The South Asia and Burma Retrospective Bibliography (SABREB): Stage 1 1556–1800* (London, 1987).

M. William Steele is Professor Emeritus of Modern Japanese History at the International Christian University (Tokyo), with a Ph.D. in History and East Asian Languages from Harvard University. His work focuses on the social and cultural history of Japan in the late nineteenth century, the period of Japan's modern transformation. His book, *Alternative Narratives in Modern Japanese History* (London and New York, 2003) examined new ways to document and interpret Japan's encounter with the West. He is especially interested in the role of images, including woodblock prints, newspaper illustrations and photographs, the subject of a co-edited book (with Yulia Mikhailova), *Japan and Russia: Three Centuries of Mutual Images* (Folkestone, 2008). His recent publications concern reaction and resistance to the introduction of Western things and ideas into Japan in the 1870s and 1880s.

Eva Hemmungs Wirtén is Professor of Mediated Culture at the Department of Culture and Society, Linköping University, Sweden. She has written extensively on the cultural history of international copyright, the public domain and, more recently, on patents as documents. Her most recent book is *Making Marie Curie: Intellectual Property and Celebrity Culture in an Age of Information* (Chicago, 2015). In 2017, she was awarded an ERC Advanced Investigator Grant for the project 'Patents as Scientific Information, 1895–2020'.

Timeline

*c.*340   earliest surviving papyrus roll from Greece

*c.*300 BCE–150 CE   creation of the Hebrew and Aramaic Dead Sea Scrolls

*c.*300   foundation of the Library of Alexandria in Egypt

268–232   invention of a South Asian writing system dated to the reign of the Mauryan Emperor Ashoka and inspired by the promotion of Buddhism

*c.*200   birch-bark and palm-leaf books used in South Asia

*c.*150   increased use in China of pieces of silk for writing, partly replacing bamboo

*c.*140–87   earliest known surviving fragments of paper (from the Han capital Chang'an (Xi'an, China)

CE

39   Libertas Temple in Rome hosted the first public library

57   earliest known dated document from Roman Britain, a writing board from London

78   most modern dated surviving tablet in cuneiform

79   eruption of Vesuvius, burying Herculaneum including a villa with a library of 600–800 scrolls which continues to be recovered

*c.*90   earliest extant papyrus with a Gospel text (the papyrus used in the mask of a mummy)

*c.*100   earliest fragment of a Latin codex yet found, a small part of an anonymous historical work known as *De Bellis Macedonicis*

*c.*100–200   earliest known Buddhist scrolls on birch-bark produced in the kingdom of Gandhara

105   traditional (but late) date of invention of modern paper by Cai Lun, senior official of the Han dynasty in China

*c.*150   beginning of codex production in the Middle East and Mediterranean, gradually replacing scrolls

192   great fire in Rome and the destruction of books famously described in a letter by Galen

256   earliest surviving paper book, a copy of the Buddhist *Piyujing Sutra*

*c.*300   increased use of parchment in Europe; gradual abandonment of silk as writing medium in China

*c.*350   creation of the Codex Sinaiticus, one of the earliest and most complete Greek bibles to survive

410   sack of Rome by the Visigoths, a major landmark in the decline of the Western Roman empire

610   paper-making introduced from China to Japan

*c.*630 *Etymologiae* (The Etymologies, also known as the *Origines* or Origins) compiled by Isidore of Seville

632 death of Muhammad and transcription of the Qur'anic text began

*c.*650–70 earliest known examples of Sanskrit block-printing, prayers (found at Turfan)

*c.*680–720 approximate dating of the Springmount Bog Tablets, six wooden pages with wax surfaces on which is inscribed a text from the Book of Psalms and considered to be the earliest surviving example of Irish writing in the Latin script; discovered in 1914 in County Antrim, Northern Ireland

*c.*700 production of the Codex Amiatinus, the earliest surviving complete manuscript of the Latin Vulgate Bible

*c.*704–50 earliest extant block-printed text in East Asia, the *Spotless Pure Light Durani Sutra*, in Korea

715–20 the illuminated Lindisfarne Gospels created in the monastery at Lindisfarne, off the coast of Northumberland

*c.*790 paper-making introduced from Central Asia to the Middle East

*c.*800 minuscule script began to replace majuscule in Byzantine codices

*c.*800 creation in a Columbian monastery in Ireland or Britain of the Book of Kells, an illuminated manuscript of the four Gospels in Latin, and one of the most celebrated surviving early medieval manuscripts in Europe

868 earliest dated block-printed book, a Chinese scroll about 16 feet long containing the text of the *Diamond Sutra*

*c.*900–1000 hemp- and other fibre-based paper began to supplant use of birch-bark, wooden panes, and palm-leaves in India; and papyrus, parchment, and waxed wooden writing boards in the Islamic Middle East

*c.*900–1000 oldest surviving talipot manuscripts (Buddhist texts) from north India

932 Feng Dao, a high official of the later Tang dynasty, initiated the woodblock publication of a complete set of the Confucian Classics (completed in 130 volumes in 954)

1000–1 copy of the Qur'an by Ibn al-Bawwab at Baghdad; one of the earliest Qur'an manuscripts transcribed on paper and in a new style of round script

*c.*1000 the regional languages of South Asia began gradually to replace Sanskrit as vehicles for literary creation

*c.*1000 illustration of palm-leaf manuscripts started among Buddhists in eastern India and Nepal

*c.*1030–50 Bi Sheng invented printing with moveable earthenware type in China *c.***1041–8**   earliest known book printed by moveable earthenware type in China

1057   last known Papal Bull issued on papyrus (although certain use of papyrus in Europe continued, notably in Sicily)

1060   earliest known illustrated Jain manuscript, a painted palm-leaf edition of the *Oghaniryukti*

1087   last known papyrus document in Arabic from Egypt

1088   foundation of the Studium of Bologna, Italy, later regarded as the oldest university in the Western world

1204   libraries burned in the great fire of Constantinople

1231   decree of the Emperor Frederick II prohibiting use of paper for official documents in preference to more durable parchment

1234   the first text known to be printed with metal moveable type, a ritual manual, published in Korea

*c.***1240–60**   compilation of the *Speculum maius* (Great Mirror) by Vincent of Beauvais, a summary of the science and natural history known to western Europe

1264   paper production began in Fabriano, Ancona, Italy

*c.***1270–1300**   invention of reading glasses in Europe, probably in Italy

1276   earliest known watermarked paper, from Tuscany

1297–8   Wang Zhen, a local magistrate in Anhui, China, perfected a method of printing with wooden moveable type

1338   earliest known paper mill in France

1377   earliest known serial book printed with moveable type in Korea (a collection of biographies of Buddhist monks)

*c.***1400**   creation in Florence of a book hand, based on Caroline minuscule, which became known as humanist minuscule or Roman script and was later used in Italian printed books

*c.***1400–1530**   production of knotted string *khipus* in the Inca empire and bark and skin codices in Mesoamerica

*c.***1400–1500**   the Office of Moveable Type in Korea produced a series of increasingly refined metal types

1408   *Yongle Encyclopedia*, a massive collation of excerpts from the major works of the Chinese tradition, completed at the command of the Yongle emperor in 11,095 manuscript volumes

1409   Guild of Stationers (from 1557 the Stationers' Company) in existence in London

1418   earliest known book printed by woodblock in Europe

1424   earliest known manuscripts of the hugely popular *Imitation of Christ* by Thomas a Kempis

1446   King Sejong published *Correct Sounds for the Instruction of the People*, which introduced *hangeul*, the Korean phonetic alphabet

*c.***1452**   Gutenberg began printing indulgences by metal moveable type in Mainz

1451   oldest illustrated Hindu paper manuscript, a *Vasantavilasa*, a poem on Krishna's dalliances with the female cowherds

1454–5   Gutenberg used moveable type to print his forty-two-line Bible

1465   earliest known dry-point engravings issued in Germany

1465   printing by moveable type brought to Italy from Mainz by two Germans, Konrad Sweynheym and Arnold Pannartz

*c.***1469–70**   first printing of the *Imitation of Christ* by Günther Zainer in Augsburg

1470   first printing press in Paris

*c.***1470**   gold-tooled bookbindings began to be produced in Europe

1473   first printing press in Cracow, Poland

1476–7   first book printed by William Caxton in Westminster, England

1477   first book with intaglio illustrations published in Florence

1486   grant of the first known privilege to an author, the Venetian Collegio decreeing that Marcantonio Sabellico be free to choose any printer for his history of Venice *Decades rerum Venetarum.*

1492   conquest of Granada and the destruction of the remaining Islamic libraries in Spain

1499   first books with etchings published in Switzerland and Germany

1498   types produced for printing music, in Venice

1500   printing presses working in some eighty towns and cities in Italy and sixty-four towns and cities in Germany

1501   Aldus Manutius introduced italic as a cursive roman typeface, in Venice

1501   terminal date of all earlier printed books in Europe (about 27,000 surviving titles and editions), known as 'incunabula'

1504   first recorded grant of an exclusive publication privilege to an author in France, André de La Vigne, who petitioned the *parlement* of Paris to prevent his work being printed by Michel Le Noir without his consent

1522   publication of Luther's momentous German translation of the New Testament from Koine Greek

1522   first extant print edition of *Romance of the Three Kingdoms*, a hugely popular novel, at the beginning of the great commercial publishing boom of early modern China

1537 legal deposit initiated in France by the Ordonnance de Montpellier, under which a copy of any published book had to be delivered to the king's library

1537–8 the Venetian brothers Paganino and Alessandro Paganini privately printed a text of the Qur'an

1539 first press in the Americas established in Mexico City; suppression of indigenous writing practices

1542 Leipzig University Library opened

1545 publication in Zurich of Conrad Gessner's *Bibliotheca universalis*, a universal bibliography of all known writings in Latin, Greek, and Hebrew

1551 Edict de Châteaubriant, the first French legislation to use the word 'author' as the composer of a text and ordering all printers to include authors' names in all published works

1555 Mughal emperor Humayun returned to India from Iran with calligraphers and book-painters

1556 a printing press set up by Jesuit missionaries in the Colégio de São Paulo at Goa, India

1557 incorporation of the Stationers' Company in London, with attempts at registration of books and imprint requirements

1559 earliest surviving book printed in India, the works of St Bonaventure in Latin

1559 establishment of the Index Librorum Prohibitorum (Index of banned books) by the Vatican

1562–77 the *Hamza-nama*, the most ambitious of the commissions of the Mughal Emperor Akbar, completed in fourteen volumes each containing a hundred paintings

1568 foundation of the Moscow Printing House

1576 earliest evidence of commercial publishing in Korea

1577 printing types in Tamil first cast at Goa

1580–2 publication of the *Essais* of Michel de Montaigne

1580 copy of Christopher Plantin's Polyglot Bible presented to the Mughal emperor Akbar by Jesuits from Goa

1590 Jesuit missionary Alessandro Valignano brought the first printing press with moveable type to Japan

1590 earliest known book auction in the Netherlands

1592 Japanese emperor presented with printed books and a font of metal moveable types seized during the Japanese invasion of Korea

1598 Thomas Bodley began his refounding of the university library at Oxford, which now bears his name; it opened in 1602

1599–*c*.1620   publication of the Japanese 'Saga Books' near Kyoto

1599   first surviving auction catalogue printed in the Netherlands

1604   Cheng Dayue published *Ink Garden of the Cheng Family*, printed in five colours in late Ming China

1605   publication of *Relation: Aller Fürnemmen und Gedenckwürdigen Historien* in Strasbourg, often cited as the first printed Western news bulletin or newspaper

1615   the chaining of books abandoned at the Sorbonne, Paris

1619   Spanish legal requirement to deposit copies of printed materials in the Royal Library of the Escorial

1620s   first print publication (by moveable type) of Murasaki Shikibu's *Tale of Genji*, a landmark in the development of Japanese fiction and Japanese vernacular script, which had circulated in manuscript since its completion in 1010

1627   Gabriel Naudé composed his manual on the building and management of a library

1633   Hu Zhengyan published *Ten Bamboo Garden Manual of Calligraphy and Painting*, considered the finest example of Chinese woodblock colour printing

1640   publication of the *Bay Psalm Book* in Cambridge, Massachusetts, the first book printed in North America

1640   invention of European mezzotint technique in engraving

1649–55   *Ramayana* manuscript prepared for Maharana Jagat Singh of Mewar with 500 large paintings

1662   Printing Act (also known as the Licensing Laws) defines legal copyright in England

1662   Royal Society of London launched its *Philosophical transactions*

1672   burning of the great library of the Escorial Monastery

1676   earliest known book auction in England (the library of Lazarus Seaman).

1684–7   Pierre Bayle published *Nouvelles de la République des Lettres*

1690   first paper mill in North America, at Germantown, Pennsylvania

1694   lapse of the recurrent Printing Acts (Licensing Laws) in England, leading eventually to the recognition of a new press freedom

***c*.1700–1900**   calendric 'winter counts' drawn by the Lakota peoples on buffalo hides in North America

1702   *The Daily Courant*, first English daily newspaper, published

1710   first Copyright Act passed in England 'for the Encouragement of Learning by Vesting the Copies of Printed Books in the Authors, or Publishers, of such Copies, during the Times therein Mentioned'

1712 first Protestant missionary printing press established in the Danish East India Company enclave of Tranquebar on the Coromandel Coast

1714 first Biblical translation printed in an Indian language, the Gospels and Acts in Tamil

1716 first English-language book printed in India, Thomas Dyche's *Guide to the English tongue*

1716, 1721 Japanese shogunal government recognized booksellers' guilds created to protect copyright in Kyoto and Edo respectively

1723 legal codification of the existing French censorship and evaluation system of pre-publication *privilèges*

1725 stereotype printing invented by Scotsman William Ged in London

1726 reprinted Korean morality book translated classical Chinese into *hangeul*

1727 Ibrahim Müteferrika established a printing press, the first Muslim to do so, at Istanbul

1734 Jean-Baptiste le Prince developed the aquatint process

1737 Dutch printing press established at Colombo, Sri Lanka

1739 the imperial Mughal library looted by Nadir Shah and many of its estimated 24,000 manuscripts carried off to Iran

***c.*1747** James Whatman produced first wove paper, in Maidstone, England

1751–77 publication of the *Encyclopédie, ou dictionnaire raisonné des sciences, des arts et des métiers*, generally known as the *Encyclopédie*

1752 rediscovery of the library of Herculaneum

1757 the chaining of books abandoned at the Bodleian Library, Oxford

1758 French printing press established at Pondicherry, India

1760s Liulichang, Peking (Beijing), began its rise to become the largest book market in China between the late eighteenth and early twentieth centuries

1761 first printing press established at Madras (Chennai) with equipment looted from the siege of Pondicherry

1764 Voltaire published his *Dictionnaire philosophique*

1773–82 manuscript publication of the *Complete Library of the Four Treasuries*, a massive imperially commissioned compilation of selected editions of the most important texts of the Chinese tradition

1774 publication of *The Sorrows of Young Werther* (*Die Leiden des jungen Werthers*), the hugely popular novel by Johann Wolfgang Goethe

1774 interpretative decision by the House of Lords, Great Britain, establishing copyright as a time-limited form of protection

1777 French laws limited length of publishers' book privileges

1780 publication of the first newspaper in India (in English), *Hicky's Bengal Gazette*

1787 first printed copy of the Qur'an made by Muslims printed at St. Petersburg

1788 first printing press arrived in Australia

1790 US Federal Copyright Act with term of fourteen years renewable for a further fourteen years

1791 first print publication of Cao Xueqin's *Story of the Stone*, the novel of Chinese elite family life seen as the masterpiece of the vernacular literary tradition

1793 Declaration of the Rights of Genius, passed by the French Convention, copyright laws establishing protection for ten years after the author's death

1793 first translation of Bunyan's *Pilgrim's Progress* into a non-Western language printed at Madras (Chennai) in Tamil

1795 first printing press established in Cape Town

1796 printing types in Gujarati script cast for the East India Company

1796 lithography invented by Alois Senefelder

1798 first paper-making machine patented by Louis-Nicolas Robert at Corbeil-Essonnes, France

1798 first book published by Indians for Indians without direct European involvement, a Parsi prayer-book printed at Bombay (Mumbai)

1799 Governor-General Marquess Wellesley introduced the first press censorship in India

1799 discovery in the Nile Delta of the Rosetta Stone, instrumental in deciphering ancient Egyptian texts

1800 establishment of the Library of Congress

1800 Baptist William Carey established the Serampore Mission Press in Bengal, a pioneer in evangelical publishing in the languages of South Asia

1800 first cast-iron printing press built by Charles 3rd earl of Stanhope

1803 mechanical paper-making machine patented by Henry and Sealy Fourdrinier

1802–18 steam-driven cylinder printing press pioneered by Friedrich Koenig

1805 first royal press in South Asia established by Sarabhaji II, Maratha ruler of Tanjore

1810 *règlement* created the Direction générale de l'imprimerie et de la librairie to oversee the book trade in France, and required a copy of each new publication to be deposited at the Bibliothèque nationale

1810 National Library of Brazil established

1813 stereotype plate first used in the United States

1814 Koenig steam-powered printing press used commercially the first time, to print *The Times* of London

1815–23 production of the first significant modern Western-style book in China using cut-metal Chinese characters (Robert Morrison's bilingual *Dictionary of the Chinese Language*)

1818 first Indian-language newspaper printed at Serampore, the Bengali *Samachar Darpan*

1822 typesetting machine patented by William Church, generally considered to be the first

1822 Jean-François Champollion published his decipherment of the Rosetta Stone hieroglyphs, describing, an ancient Egyptian system that (then uniquely) combined phonetic and ideographic signs

***c*.1823** William Pickering began issuing books in publishers' bindings using bookcloth invented by Archibald Leighton

1824 first book issued by lithography in India, *Treatise on suspended animation* in Hindi and Urdu

1826 Leipzig publisher F.A. Brockhaus used the Koenig press for printing books

1829 the 'typographer' a forerunner of the typewriter invented by William Austin Burr

1832 Archibald Leighton devised the technique for blocking bookcloth on prefabricated binding cases, preparing the way for the mechanisation of bookbinding

1835 first printing press established in New Zealand

1836 foundation of the National Library of Spain in Madrid; foundation of the National Library of India in Calcutta (Kolkata)

1837 Godefroy Engelmann invented chromolithography in France, allowing printing in multiple colours

1838 the American firm, W. & C.B. Sheridan, bookbinders and manufacturers of bookbinding machinery, introduced an embossing machine

1838 electrotype process developed by Moritz von Jacobi to reproduce illustrations, and later to reproduce moveable type

1838 Société des Gens de Lettres founded in France to defend authors' rights

***c*.1840** early rotary press designed by Richard Hoe

1841 first paperback editions published by Tauchnitz Verlag in Germany

mid-1840s paper made from wood pulp began to supplant paper made from rags; rapid progress in the decipherment of cuneiform script

1846   Electric Telegraph Company founded in Britain

1848   Boston Public Library opened, the first large public library in the United States

1848   W.H. Smith opened the first railway bookstalls at Euston station

1848   'book post', a special cheap postal rate for book parcels, established in Britain

1850   British Public Library Act, allowing the creation of public libraries in major towns

1853   Louis Hachette opened railway bookstalls in a deal with the French Compagnie du Nord

1858   first communication via Transatlantic telegraph cable, reducing the communication time between North America and Europe from ten days by ship to a few minutes, and transforming republication times

1858   William Gamble began the electrotyping of Chinese typefaces

1863   William Bullock invented the rotary perfecting printing press

1867   the Société typographique parisienne founded to fight for higher wages and better working conditions in the printing trade

1867   Christopher Latham Sholes and others in Milwaukee produced the first commercially successful typewriter

1869   Maruzen, Japan's first Western-style bookstore and publisher, founded in Tokyo

1869   New York branch of Macmillans opened

1872   Motoki Shōzō set up Japan's first moveable-type foundry in Tsukiji

1873   E. Remington and Sons began production of their first typewriter in Ilion, New York, introducing the QWERTY keyboard

1874   Underwood Typewriter Company, New York, developed typewriter ribbon and carbon paper

1875   first Arabic print-workshop established in East Africa, in Zanzibar

1876   foundation of Shūeisha, the firm publishing Japan's first true Western-style book, a revised translation of *Self Help* by Samuel Smiles

1878   introduction of Remington No. 2, the first typewriter to include both upper and lower case letters with a shift key

*c.***1880**   beginnings of a print revolution in China with replacement of xylography as the primary print technology by lithography and mechanized moveable type, both introduced by Western missionaries

1883   first Carnegie library, funded by the foundation of steel magnate, Andrew Carnegie, built in Dunfermline, Scotland

1883   foundation of the Incorporated Society of British Authors (the 'Society of Authors')

1886 Ottmar Mergenthaler invented linotype hot metal composing machine in the United States, transforming type composition

1886 Berne Convention introduced international reciprocity in copyright protection

1887 Hindu Tract Society established in Madras (Chennai)

1889 American Tolbert Lanston invented the Monotype type-composing system

1891 United States accepted international copyright with the passing of the Chace Act

1893 Underwood Typewriter Company, New York, introduced the front strike typewriter, allowing operators to see the text as they typed, and leading to a huge increase in typewriter sales

1897 establishment of the Commercial Press, to become by 1930 East Asia's largest comprehensive publisher

1898 opening of Peking (Beijing) University, as the Imperial Capital University, the first of China's public universities

1909 establishment of Kōdansha, soon to be Japan's largest publishing house

1910 British Government of India passed a draconian Press Act to curb the production and distribution of seditious literature

1912 foundation of Zhonghua Books, Republican China's second-largest publisher

1920s discovery of earliest cuneiform tablets in southern Iraq; and of tortoiseshell divination books in China

1922 establishment of the Russian state office, Glavlit, marking the official reintroduction of general censorship

1935 IBM introduced the first successful electric typewriter

1931 invention by Stanley Morison of Times New Roman typeface for *The Times*

1935 Allen Lane launched Penguin paperback books

1937 foundation of the New China News Agency

1939 Chester F. Carlson invented xerography

1951 Siemens invented the first ink-jet printers

1952 decipherment of Linear B script

1955 further international copyright system introduced by the Universal Copyright Convention

1957 invention of the typeface Helvetica

1958 publication of *L'Apparition du livre* by Lucien Febvre and Henri-Jean Martin, a foundational text of book history

1959 first photocopiers sold by Xerox

1964 publication of Marshall McLuhan's *Understanding Media: The Extensions of Man*, introducing the phrase 'the medium is the message'

1967 OCLC started as The Ohio College Library Consortium at The Ohio State University; now restyled the Online Computer Library Center

1968 introduction of WorldCat (now online), the largest public access catalogue of books, by OCLC

1967 publication of Marshall McLuhan's *The Medium is the Massage*, punning on 'message'

1969 first use of metadata with MARC (Machine Readable Cataloging)

1969 ARPANET designed in southern California (a forerunner of the Internet)

1970 introduction of the International Standard Book Number (ISBN)

1970 foundation of the World Intellectual Property Organization (WIPO)

1971 establishment of Project Gutenberg, the volunteer-led digital archive, to 'encourage the creation and distribution of eBooks'

1972 first programmable word processor with a video screen introduced

1972 Alan Kay's formulation of the Dynabook at Xerox Parc as a new electronic reading device

1976 first commercial laser printer sold by IBM

1977 first commercial sales of personal computers

1978 *New York Times* transitioned from hot type to phototypesetting (see https://www.nytimes.com/video/insider/100000004687429/farewell-etaoin-shrdlu.html)

1981 introduction of the first mass-produced, commercially successful portable laptop computer

1989 Tim Berners-Lee invented the World Wide Web

1991 World Wide Web publicly launched

1993 the PDF (portable document format) launched by Adobe

1994 Amazon.com founded by Jeff Bezos

***c.*1995** development of print-on-demand (POD) technology

1998 Google launched at Menlo Park, California

1998 several Canadian and US universities founded the Public Knowledge Project to encourage open access and an open-source journal publishing system

2001 Wikipedia established

2001 Creative Commons founded as a US non-profit organization

2003 first commercial sales of 3-D printing machines

2003 'Yoshi' published *Deep Love*, the first cell-phone novel

2004 Google launched Google Book Search and Google Print, soon to be known as Google Books

2004 first e-reader developed

2005 sixteen Dutch universities launched the Digital Academic Repositories (DAREnet), making over 47,000 research papers available to anyone with Internet access

2006 the 'maker movement' developed the library makerspace, offering computers, audio, video, and 3-D printing facilities in addition to traditional resources

2007 launch of Goodreads, a 'social cataloguing' website enabling free searches of its database of books, annotations, and reviews, and generating library catalogs and reading lists

2007 Kindle sold by Amazon

2008 Smashwords Inc., California, introduced its e-book-distribution platform for authors and publishers to convert text files into multiple e-book formats for reading on various devices

2010 Apple introduced the iPad

2011 a group of North American universities formed the Coalition of Open Access Policy Institutions (COAPI)

2015 United Nations agreed what is now known as the '2030 Agenda', aiming 'to ensure public access to information and protect fundamental freedoms, in accordance with national legislation and international agreements'

2016 US Supreme Court denied final appeal of Authors Guild Inc. in copyright dispute with Google Inc. and its Google Book Search

2016 Bookstagram launched

2017 Twitter increased limit of a Tweet from 140 to 280 characters

2018 Apple Books eBook reader renamed as iBooks

2019 Jisc (Joint Information Systems Committee) replaced COPAC (Consortium of Online Public Access Catalogues) with Library Hub Discover

1

Introduction

James Raven

We probably think we know what we mean by a book. It has words, a cover, and a spine. It might carry pictures. If it is a work of reference, it will probably include a contents list and an index. We instinctively think that it will be printed. And we know that books are found all over the world and that they are read. After a moment's reflection about books in our homes or as sardined on the shelves of some great historic mansion, we also realize that many books are unread. Read, reread, or unopened, books make up familiar and often comforting (or reproving) provisions to our lives. And the reading of certain books, at certain times and in certain circumstances, can be life-changing, enlightening, terrifying, and consoling. When you ask what a book is, however, a material image usually comes to mind. Books—the vessels of knowledge, instruction, and entertainment—carry their contents in very recognizable and culturally specific physical forms.

For some years, our traditional understanding of what a book is has been challenged by the advance of digital media. The appearance of portable computers, smartphones, and scrollable texts challenges assumptions about the make-up, effect, and purpose of books. We text (moving it from noun to verb), we use and customize e-books, and we create and ostensibly control our own publications. Popular and academic critics explore contrasts between analogue and digital media, between paper and pixels. Electronic books generate new reading and knowledge experiences—and ones that question not only our under-standing of material forms but also the definition, design, and networking of knowledge.

But there are and always have been other challenges to assumptions about what makes a book. If you are reading these words in the paper, bound form of this book, then you are implicated in the idea of the book as codex. Taken from the Latin *caudex* for 'trunk of a tree' or 'block of wood', the codex is usually defined as a book constructed of a number of sheets of paper, parchment, papyrus, or similar materials. Although the codex is often associated with handwritten books, it has also become universally coupled with printed books in the Western world. Throughout the world, however, and in different societies, past and present, books exist and have existed in many other forms, even though until modern global exchange and understanding, comparisons of forms and functions were not advanced or at least limited to the experience of very few.

This book breaches both barriers to our understanding of the book: the temporal and the geographical. The following chapters move around the world from ancient to modern times, from clay tablets bearing cuneiform impressions to electronic tablets bearing digital signs and images. No such volume can claim comprehensive coverage, but the sixteen contributors, all leading scholars in their respective fields of study, offer fresh perspectives that offer comparative understanding of what a book meant and means in very different societies. The summary timeline which precedes this Introduction gives a graphic sense of unexpected parallels and contrasts in the history of bookmaking and reading around the world. We are still bound by comparatively localized ideas of past writing and publication practices. This timeline compilation of even headline moments in global book history should make us pause.

What this volume shows, indeed, is how the book has been successively remodelled and reformed over time and in different parts of our world. The different chapters illuminate constants and residual forms, key moments of transition, and the coexistence of contrasting functions and materials over long periods. Difference and simultaneity beg their own questions: was a particular type and use of a book developed to supplant and improve an existing form? When developments appear at about the same time in different parts of the world but without apparent connections between them, are they responses to similar grounding conditions, such as demographic and economic growth, the extension or contraction of empire, political and intellectual maturation (or decline), and concomitant reassessments of educational needs?

This collection of essays also highlights unfamiliar areas, many of which beg further investigation. What follows incorporates many findings of recent scholarship, but we have much more to discover and understand about the creation and appreciation of books in diverse regions, including parts of Africa, Central Asia, and the Pacific Rim. In China and Russia, older scholarship on the history of books has yet to be fully recovered and shared in our own times.

Definitions

The history of the book is multifarious and reaches back at least 5,000 years. As new book forms of the digital age help us appreciate, the history of books is not only a history of the paper codex, or indeed of the printed book, but a history of how different peoples in different parts of the world, in different ways, for different reasons, and with very different consequences have striven to store, circulate, and retrieve knowledge and information. The thirty-third century BCE is the supposed age of the earliest surviving object claimed by some scholars to fulfil the definition of a book.

Books, pamphlets, and magazines transmit knowledge by physical form. The message is conveyed by the medium. Books share some of the characteristics of other material goods. Tactility, design, and ornamentation convey meaning even before a book is read. But books also carry texts whose reading conveys intellectual and ideological significance. The connections supplied by marking, writing, and print fall short of the interactive exchanges possible between people not parted by distance, but in many ways books offer a connectedness between originator and receiver. Manuscripts and printed books and periodicals extended and widened the reach of such exchange, an exchange which altered according to the mutations of colonialism, migration, exile, commerce, political independence, and nationalism.

In an age when we might not know what a book is any more, consideration of what a 'text' is and how it relates to its physical, material embodiment can be helpful. We might be further guided by histories that study the consequences of the production, dissemination, and reception of texts in all their material forms across all societies and in all ages. The challenge is comparative: from cuneiform tablets to digital tablets, of a succession and a simultaneity of forms, of scrolls and codices, of Inca *khipus* (or *quipus*), Chinese and East Asian bamboo books and woodblock printing and xylography, Buddhist thanka scrolls, Javanese, Balinese and Singhalese leaf books, and Dakota buffalo hides. Even within the general domain of the codex, map books, music books, scrapbooks, flip-out books, and comic books (and *manga*) suggest the further diversity of genre and form. Telephone books and Filofaxes suggest how quickly new and innovative forms of book can become outdated and unfamiliar within a couple of generations. Above all, we live today with a diversity of digital book forms capable of very different textual composition, handling, encounter, and reading experience. Comparisons are also across different technologies, from clay imprinting, different scribal practices and the encoding of electronic, telegraphic, and then digital data. In all cases, the use and reading of books result from very different motivations. The challenge, of course, is both conceptual and methodological in defining designations of the book and its various materialities.

A basic premise is that whether books are made of a clay, a skin, or a natural fibre, or enabled by a digital screen, central processing unit, random access memory, or a graphics card, they offer a durable, portable, or mobile, replicable, and legible (that is, readable and communicable) means of recording and disseminating information and knowledge. But in considering the function and purpose of books, is the nature or absence of 'publication' determinate? And with the increased complexity of forms of print and print in conjunction with script and illustration, how wide-reaching does our definition of 'book' become? Newspapers, periodicals, and gazettes have long been established as fundamental to the study of the history of books, but do we include simple jobbing pieces such as posters, tickets, or commercial and legal agreements? The answer given by almost all of those pursuing book history has been yes *when* the central concern is one of communication, of the creation and dissemination of meaning originating from a graphic and legible as well as a portable and replicable form. The issue of critical valuation of the text is quite another matter. Even the classification of textual genres complicates the history of books and distances it from literary studies (without there ever being an unbridgeable divorce).

These definitional differences are far from straightforward. Therein lies the fascination of a global and century-spanning history of books. If we think radically, then we might ask whether a person could be a book. Storytellers, teachers, and preachers, ancient or modern, memorize their tales or knowledge and speak or sing to order. Such a person is mobile and in a sense portable; they are relatively durable, they communicate, and (if not exactly replicable) they can be copied by others. Most of us, however, would discount the concept of a person-book because we believe that a book has to be a vehicle for encoded signs that are visually read. But in thinking through the question, we are forced to hone our definitions and begin to realize that many of our concepts are culturally and temporally conditioned. Take, as another example, the book as a digital download or online as read on a screen. The text is clearly mobile in that the reader scrolls through it or otherwise accesses it, and some screens—on smartphones or tablets or laptops—are clearly portable. But what of the fixed-site computer in a library or even on a desk at home? The 'portability' of the material form within which the text is read (however that reading is done) is more like that of a chained book in a medieval library. The mobility of the digital text, moreover, is now more than manual, moving and changing by automated means if desired—and capable of apparently limitless replication. 'Online' books can only be read when their readers are connected to the Internet. With links to other sites, hyper-text books are also liberated from certain conventional modes of textual appearance and reading.

The further result of such questioning is to unsettle our definitions of a 'text' and its relationship to its material form and conveyance. Is it the material that hosts the ideographic system that is the more important, or should we give more attention to questions of portability or of the potential for preservation and re-reading? And what are the consequences of innovations in design? Gérard Genette (b. 1930) followed Philippe Lejeune (b. 1938) in describing the paratext as 'a fringe of the printed text which in reality controls one's whole reading of the text'. He further divided the paratext, and very much in terms of modern and Western books, between the 'peritext'—or the title, epigraph, preface, author's foreword, preliminary remarks, notes, and illustrations, all within the book itself—and the 'epitext' situated outside the book, including correspondence, diaries, journals, and interviews.

A distinctive contribution of the history of books, therefore, is to re-evaluate what makes a text just as much as it re-evaluates what materially makes a book. The meaning that the text conveys is crucially affected by the material form of the book, and as D.F. McKenzie (1931–99) argued in exploring a 'sociology of texts', form actually *affects* meaning. Readers of printed books know that other readers will, essentially, be reading the 'same book', and yet this is a very different sameness considered, if at all, by readers of manuscript books. Changing valorizations of our own time offer insights into how the relationship between book form and the signs conveyed by and within it has changed and is described differently in different ages. Popular reference to a 'text', for example, is currently given new meaning by the sending of a 'text' message, just as worldwide word processing and text messaging have brought about the rejuvenation but also the reconfiguration of the word 'font'. Font (or 'fount') is a word that only thirty years ago needed explanation to those introduced to typography—but now, exactly because of its casual usage, requires even more careful explanation by historians of books.

Revisions to the material form of books are often radical, effecting new meaning. New editions are reset and reprinted and repackaged, and might be translated, given a new critical apparatus or accompanying images, and be much travelled. All contribute to remaking a text among new communities, internationally, even globally and over many centuries and in very different cultural contexts. At each level, the intervention of manufacturers, publishers, or editors might create multiple time-specific relationships between types of text, the work of the same or similar authors, and other communities of books and readers, but it is also possible to chart this broader, cultural history of a single work over time and space. It is what Roger Chartier (b. 1945) has conjectured as the 'biography of a book', following which analogy James Secord observed that books have no 'life' of their own independent from their use. 'Biography' or not, studies such as that by Isabel Hofmeyr (b. 1953) of the appraisal of John Bunyan's *Pilgrim's Progress*, as it was translated and carried around the world and particularly across Africa, have advanced time and space histories of particular works. The history of the book has reinforced the contribution made by micro-histories to our understanding of the past by deepening research into particular texts and their reception, often in highly specific ways. Such history has also, however, expanded horizons by following the publication and circulation history of specific texts as ambitiously as possible, offering global histories of the long-term and far-reaching impact of authors' ideas.

The residual influences of earlier forms also distinguish the design of even 'born digital' books. This 'skeuomorphism' appears, for example, in the way that the majority of online books and e-resources resemble the page-based and paratextual forms of codices, with traditional formatting parameters. Electronic pages are normally available to read sequentially and are skippable by 'flipping' in a reading mode familiar to all users of codices (and in which search engines still offer sequential results). Many electronic journals retain volume and issue structures with contents lists, although many publish on a continuous basis, and, as with e-books, indexes are replaced by word searching—at once more particular but also less capable of generic and guided assistance. The remediating of books and of print in the digital age questions anew what knowledge is, how it is created and transmitted, and what it looks like.

Different Compasses

Comparisons with other parts of the world offer a particular re-evaluation of the history of European and 'Western' book production and distribution and the means by which readers and clients received texts. Comparative studies of early modern Asian printing practices and the intricate and correctable xylography of China, Korea, and Japan are especially rewarding, notably including study of the interplay between the commercial and the intellectual and between city production and country distribution. That nation-states have largely framed European and Western bibliographical studies is understandable in terms of literary and linguistic interests and of simple practicalities, but it remains a problem for historians. However much print is identified with the cultivation of different vernacular languages and with campaigns and protests that helped advance modern state formation, in many other ways, the nation is a misleading geographical unit for the history of print. The political (not always linguistic) unit was the obvious enabler for retrospective national bibliographies (published as short-title catalogues), but books circulating within that unit were and are international commodities.

Activity in book history is now worldwide. Fresh and innovatory writing and research projects are devoted to the history of the book in China, India, South and Central Asia, Africa, and South America, in addition to regions long associated with bibliographical and book historical studies. Of particular interest is the reassessment, in terms of interaction with manuscript production and woodblock and other printing methods, of the first wave of globalization of European moveable metal type printing technology from the late sixteenth century and primarily from Spain, Portugal, and then France, the Netherlands, and England to Mexico, Peru, Brazil, and elsewhere in the Americas, but also to many different parts of Africa, and to India, China, Japan, the Philippines, and diverse communities in Southeast and East Asia.

But such geographical breadth and comparative study has been a long time coming. Most of the pioneers of modern book history in the 1980s studied Europe and North America in the age of print. Robert Darnton (b. 1939) in his seminal 1982 essay 'What is the History of Books?' proposed that 'it might even be called the social and cultural history of communication by print'. By the early 1990s, courses in book history, centres for the history of the book, and multi-volume book history publishing projects advanced in Britain, France, many other European countries, the United States, and Australasia. Within a decade or more, medievalists and palaeographers, drawing on earlier research and often very different approaches, also led collaborative projects in publishing and broader book history, often nationally conceived. Scholars from different disciplines have increasingly used the designation of 'the history of the book' to advance more capacious questions about the past meaning and function of books. They have pursued fresh perspectives, promoting, in particular, an interdisciplinarity that extends and revises older methods and conclusions.

By themselves, analytical bibliography, critical theory, reading history, library history, and bibliographical history, widely conceived, all answer different types of question and are motivated by different impulses and epistemological concerns, but they are deepened and given greater critical acuity by their collision. In many ways, the most creative aspect of the resurgence in book history has been to bring together in conversation and collaborative scholarship a diversity of participants. These include cultural and social historians, literary scholars and critics, those concerned with the theory and practice of textual editing, bibliographers, codicologists, palaeographers, epigraphers, philologists, rare books' and special collections' librarians, book conservators, linguists, and translators, historians of science, of ideas, and of art, anthropologists, archaeologists, and specialists in media, communications, and graphic communication studies. However different their methods, the different interpreters of books study texts as the products of collaborative human agency acting on material forms. Together with language, those material texts and the information their signs encode are the most powerful tools available to write a history of meanings.

Such an agenda also firmly locates the history of books within the remit of history, contributing significantly to aspects of the history of class, ethnicity, gender, and emotions, and suggesting revisions to the history of ideas, revolution, local and national politics, faith and belief, and diplomacy, among other interests. Contributory research, of and within, the material book, and in a range of extra-textual sources, informs fresh histories of censorship, copyright, the economics and geographies of publishing, the networks of distribution, and the uses of libraries. Book history has also notably expanded the types of source analysis offered in histories of reading and reception. The history of the production, circulation, and influence of books intersects with and advances histories of ideas and of religious belief and practice, the social history of knowledge, and histories of sociability and of intimate personal behaviour.

Despite these new developments and research relationships, printing continues to dominate published book history, but print—word and image—is far from the only means of graphic communication used to convey messages. Texts might be impressed, imprinted, inscribed, written, drawn, stencilled, block- or letterpress printed, engraved, stereotyped, lithographed, or photographically or digitally reproduced. As an example—and one strikingly at odds with the emphasis of many late twentieth-century histories of the book—historians of the great majority of centuries of book production in regions that now comprise India, Pakistan, Nepal, Bangladesh,

Sri Lanka, Malaysia, Indonesia, and the Philippines (and other parts of South and Southeast Asia) are historians of the transmission of manuscript texts. Scribal productions were the only written texts until the mid-sixteenth century; they remained the preferred texts in South Asia until the early nineteenth century, almost three centuries after Catholic missionaries brought the first printing press with separately cast printing types to western India. Many more ancient texts in Sanskrit survive than those of equivalent age in Latin and Greek.

More broadly, although cultural historians and bibliographers of great distinction, including Darnton, McKenzie, and Chartier, wrote pioneering studies in aspects of book history in the 1980s and 1990s, literary scholars subsequently exercised significant impact on its development. In the late twentieth century, objectives and techniques in literary criticism diverged. As new theoretical approaches advanced in literature departments across Europe and the Americas, some refugees from high theory harnessed their more historical interests to an emergent 'history of the book'. More recently, however, a much broader range of approaches in literary scholarship and textual criticism has also contributed to historical study of authorship, publishing, and reception. In addition to extended work on the traditional corpus of canonical texts, canonicity itself attracted greater interest. A literary canon, and especially what has been both positively and negatively termed the 'Western canon', is the body of books, art, and music accepted generally as the most influential in shaping culture. Histories of books assist with the identification and analysis of 'popular', 'minority', and specific 'genre' literature, together with research in women's, gender, queer, and ethnic studies. Histories of books recover the non-canonical—or what the critic Margaret Cohen has called, with teasing historical implications, 'the great unread'.

More recently still, a more comparative book history has extended non-European, extra-North American, and postcolonial perspectives. Certain givens in the history of books are most usefully pursued in a comparative perspective. The need to understand the economics of book production, for example, applies to book history in all ages and places: how a book was financed, why and how an individual or community met the costs of labour and acquisition, and what explains different levels of demand. New histories offer global comparisons in ways that are still in their infancy, but also impossible without the secure underpinnings of accumulated, specialist, local, and national bibliographical and archival research. At the fore are questions about transoceanic as well as transcontinental book production, circulation, and reception, and about the localized creation and widely dispersed transmission of knowledge.

The term *shuji* (書籍 in traditional Chinese and Korean) has been adopted as a translation of the 'book' of European and American histories, and carries sufficient inclusivity to describe, for example, unbound papers bearing written *or* printed characters. More specifically, since at least 1000 CE and the Song dynasty, the word *banben* 版本 has been used to distinguish different, but usually printed, editions of an essentially unchanged text. Etymologically, the term is associated with a prized form of bibliographical learning, not least because of the privileged connections required to access and accumulate esoteric knowledge of rare books—and their resale value. Very obvious is a sense of difference in the balance between the material and the ideological and an emphasis on sacral and spiritual value in a modern intellectual world largely unmoved by religious and existential issues. As a result, the language used to describe books and their appreciation in East Asia highlights a perception of books that is only partially consonant with Western book history.

In another respect, a primary incentive for global histories of the book is to break free of national, imperial, and otherwise political geographies. In rejecting these older and pragmatic organizing units of study, new histories pursue the linguistic, aesthetic, oceanic, and postcolonial perspectives of what are manifestly *livres sans frontières*, books without borders. Sometimes, less obviously, these are also *livres sans lecteurs*, books without readers, where the historical human experience of books concerned an awareness and even use of books that did not involve reading them.

The 'global turn' in book history advances histories of knowledge that took their inspiration from the challenges of early modern and Enlightenment Europe—of changes in the organization of knowledge, the circulation and impact of ideas, the intellectual and social history of libraries, and the global transmission of European cultures. The ways in which the accumulation of knowledge is offset by loss parallel the balance between advances and constraints examined by histories of the book. In an increasing number of case histories from different parts of the world, the focus of study is on displaced, subsumed, and corrupted oral cultures or (with a much more open-minded analysis of printedness in its various forms) on previously written languages. In addition, historians of the book are examining creatively composite cultures in which imposed and invented languages and traditions have their own positive contribution.

Ultimately, these fresh agendas in book history speak to our current digital, globalized, and yet intellectually and ideologically fragmented and often mutually uncomprehending world. Western and non-Western comparisons in particular probe our understanding of the distinctions and overlaps, say, between commercial and non-commercial and institutional and private publishing, of the role of book and non-book printing by moveable type, woodblocks, engraved plates, or other processes, and of the relative efficiencies of different production, distribution, and even reading practices. Study of Asian woodblock printing, for example, complicates more triumphalist histories of the European printing press by suggesting that the casting, composition, correction, and painstaking redistribution of type is not always the most economically efficient method of printing.

Taken together, the histories of books in different parts of the world contribute to a remarkable range of new scholarship from the history of newsgathering and international journalism to the global history of particular works and of technological and knowledge transfer. Book history research informs, revises, problematizes, and nuances broader narratives of practice, behaviour, and representation, including diverse histories of subversion, revolution, reformation, and conquest. Research on book production, circulation, and reception has been conspicuous in recent explorations of the history of ritual, language, humour, and emotions. An understanding of the transformative power of the book and especially of print and indigenous written texts has contributed largely to debates about the invention of traditions, the imagining of communities, colonial encounter, post-colonialism, and subaltern studies.

Debates and Challenges

In the development of modern book history, the main examples of the fusion of different approaches were the foundational *L'Apparition du livre* of Lucien Febvre (1878–1956) and Henri-Jean Martin (1924–2007) and later essays by Darnton, McKenzie, and Chartier, among others. In different ways, their approaches sought to bridge the early theoretical as well as bibliometric emphases of French and Continental contributions with the long tradition of collection-based bibliographical and empirical scholarship in the Anglo-American world. In the latter, British-led enumerative and retrospective national bibliography accompanied meticulous analytical bibliography and an emphasis on economic and material conditions. All contributors sought an understanding of the *historical* circumstances of textual production, circulation, and reception. Examples range from the close reading of the work of monastic scribes to an understanding of the careers of stationers, printers, and magazine and newspaper editors and proprietors. Investigations of the economics of publication and the workings of the literary marketplace vie with studies of patronage and censorship, the distinctions between commercial and private publications, and the multiplicity of readers and reading experiences. Some of these distinctions between different agencies in book production, dissemination, and reception are embedded in models of circuits and cycles, and many foundational accounts of book history incorporate illustrative diagrams. Modelling, often called agent-based modelling, variously affected the early conceptualization of the history of the book as a field of study, even though models are always more contingent and modifiable than prescriptive. As Darnton was the first to acknowledge, models are nothing but the servant of new thinking, even though they are servants who organize thought, directly assist in archival and evidential interpretation, and encourage bolder and more provocative conceptualizations.

As is more recently apparent, particular conceptual questioning applies to book history in China, where interest in 'Western' book history has increased, together with fresh comparative study of China's own and very different history of book production and its social consequences. Some past scholars of Chinese book history, such as the French sinologist Paul Pelliot (1878–1945), the American Thomas Francis Carter (1882–1925), and Zhang Xiumin 张秀民 (1909–2006), variously used research about European printing, while Febvre and Martin offered a tentative understanding of the history of the Chinese book. New methods and research, however, benefit from the deep traditions of Chinese literary learning. We might also claim that late nineteenth- and early twentieth-century developments in East Asia chimed in intriguing ways with book studies in the West. A very limited awareness of British, North American, and European developments was likely, but more certain was a similar national pride and perspective that encouraged the preservation and cataloguing of old publications in relation to national language, philology, and literature.

Bibliography, as developed in Britain and North America from the late nineteenth century, explained the book in terms beyond those of the messages conveyed by the text. All texts, new bibliographers demonstrated, were understandable as collaborative creations where the 'medium', to anticipate a later characterization of material form, was the product of social interventions, even when restricted to a limited corpus of English classic editions, downplaying the importance of the production of *all* texts. At the same time, late nineteenth-century Chinese scholars like Ye Dehui 葉德輝 (1864–1927) began putting notes together about the history of books and book production. The Chinese practice of listing book titles, and most influentially so at dynastic junctures, dates back nearly 2,000 years, accompanied from the twelfth century by *banben*, differentiating editions of an essentially unchanged, usually printed text, but this was very different to the descriptive bibliography of the fuller Anglo-American type. Although working within different traditions, the East Asian pioneers were contemporaries of many founders of Anglo-American bibliography. From their youth, these men began making lists and advancing forms of enumerative bibliography: Edward Arber (1836–1924), Charles Evans (1850–1935), Henry Robert Plomer (1856–1928), Alfred W. Pollard (1859–1944), Edward Gordan Duff (1863–1924), Ronald Brunlees McKerrow (1872–1940), and Walter Wilson Greg (1875–1959). The younger generation of modern Chinese bibliographers included Nagasawa Kikuya 長澤規矩也 (1902–80), a Japanese scholar of classical Chinese literature, teacher of library science, and one of the greatest authorities on Chinese rare books and editions of Chinese classics printed in Japan.

Inescapably, the history of the book connects to our fast-changing media world. In many ways, new technologies challenge our assumptions about what books are and were, coupled with the transformative research potential of digital humanities. As a conclusion to an anniversary piece for the Bibliographical Society in 1992, McKenzie predicted that '"the book" and its history will become something more than the history of books'. The history of the book now features in debates about digitization and the future of the book, contributes to comparative social histories of knowledge, and helps shape the writing of intellectual history.

As explored in the final essay in this volume, books of the digital age enable the encoding of and a new interactivity with information and knowledge, and extend metafiction and narrative techniques. Changes to modes of reading are equally transformational. Digital books offer revisions and tests to our consideration of sign and character design and recognition, the composition and comprehension of the page, of what a 'page' is and where it ends, of the complexity of 'paratexts', and of the variety of our reading practices and motivations. How might we now measure reading and reader response, where we find new and different evidence—much perhaps overwhelming in quantity and ephemerality—from feedback reviews and information such as Goodreads, digital reading group records, Amazon order histories, and easily accessible and monitorable school and university reading lists?

Many physical books were and are, of course, never read at all, and the majority of the copies of certain misconceived editions are pulped and destroyed, but what is now the digital equivalent of the unread and the destroyed? Loss, deletion, and redundancy take on different and challenging meanings.

Allied questions confront us. What is the future of the public and institutional library in the age of makerspaces, hackerspaces, and a 'shared knowledge economy'? In the world of digitized texts and of Google Books, we are challenged not only by questions of the archiving and retrieval of knowledge through 'books', but of what copyright is and of the implications of Open Access, licensing agreements, and inequitable information supply. Authors, publishers, and readers confront new forms of global pirating, of how censorship operates, and of how new technologies change and are changed by commercial, political, religious, and national interests. Publishers are digitizing backlists and keeping books 'in print' to an unprecedented extent. The digital revolutionizes the commercial structure and business models of modern publishing and international conglomerates.

As exemplified by contributions to this volume, the ways in which we think of the book and its history have been revolutionized by what a book might now be. Many commentators associate contemporary 'books' less with their material *form* than with their *function* as a means of communication. The revival and adaptation of such words and concepts as 'icon', 'font', 'table', 'scrolling', and 'the virtual' are cyphers for a reconceptualization of what a book is. Hyperlinked texts, digital editions and the e-book, screen adaptations, audiobooks, and podcasts change the ways in which texts are acquired, transmitted, circulated, read, interrogated, searched, and stored. Authorship identities and rights are made more complex, and automated cross-lingual translation accentuates issues of untranslatability. And in such transformative times, more books are published than ever before, whether through conventional means, print-on-demand, or by the World Wide Web. Facsimile editions of ancient Chinese classics or Mesoamerican codices can be read on smartphones or included in blogs and email attachments; David Mitchell and Philip Pullman (among others) have published short fiction using Twitter, then 140 characters per Tweet; and self-publishing opens to everyone the possibility of publication, uncontrolled dissemination, and unknown readerships.

Definitional quandaries complicate many other types of history, but for the history of the book, uncertainties about material and methodological scope have given a particular edginess to the study—and one much to its benefit. Historians will continue to dispute the *historical* significance of those aspects of book history which appear to marginalize analysis of human actions and behaviours, just as scholars of literature will continue to question the *literary* significance of those aspects of book history which fail to demonstrate how the historical particularities of material forms affect textual meaning.

An important bridge is provided by the history of reading, which, however problematic, often provides the most significant, and sometimes the only significant, historical claim in the analysis of the influence of a text. Reading, self-evidently fundamental to the cultural transactions epitomized by the history of books, offers a history in its own right and one that entails numerous epistemological, methodological, interpretative, and archival challenges. The very act of reading eschews recording—few readers write down what they do in reading. Some readers make marginal notes or doodles, some recall their reading to others or in a diary of reading, but evidence of reading practice, of the precise effect of the text upon its individual recipient, is essentially limited. The history of types of reading and literacies involves consideration of motivations, experiences, skills, aptitudes, places, and consequences, yet the history of reading practices in the reception of texts can also diverge from the history of the engagement with books, where the material object might have been collected, displayed, or otherwise used for symbolic, speculative, aesthetic, spiritual, emotional, sexual, pathological, or other reasons. In certain circumstances and in very different places, ownership of books need not involve conventional reading.

In affirming that there cannot and should not be one type of history of the book, but many types, we discard any rigidly defined 'book history' or '*the* history of the book'. Collaboration between disciplines has been beneficial, but this does not mean that collaboration results in a monolithic idea of what a history of book production and reception might be. Ideographic, pictographic, alphabetic, and other writing systems recording verbal sounds, and graphic signs, script, print, and other technologies determined the manner in which thought was materially produced and consumed. In similar ways, in the digital age, the Internet provides the opportunity but also the boundaries for new modes of social networking and textual formation and reception. The words and ideas conveyed by published texts are the *meaningful* result of the production, circulation, and reading of the material text. In modern times, the history of books has been dominated by discussion of the impact and characteristics of print and also of particular modern forms, such as periodicals and newspapers. Just as important, however, are early books in all their unfamiliar, globally disparate, and challenging forms, books in non-literate societies or societies with differential literacies, and, throughout the world, the continuing and changing significance of manuscripts and written, engraved, and imprinted book forms.

2

The Ancient World

Eleanor Robson

Books existed before the book: that is, many objects and forms carried script before sheets of paper, bound together, became the default portable medium for the long-term storage and transmission of writing worldwide. But we must define our terms carefully: too narrowly, and we risk imposing a false image of the 'proto-book' on a past that had no means of anticipating the invention of the book itself. Define books too broadly, and we risk getting drawn too far into more tangential histories of script, literacy, society, and even of objects and landscapes that are 'read' and convey meaning and consolation.

Ancient Writing

Writing was invented—or developed over the long term—at least four times in world history. Three of those independent starting points, in ancient Egypt, Mesopotamia, and China, each fed into the global book culture that we are part of today. The other, more diffuse starting points, in pre-conquest Mesoamerica, were overwhelmed by that nascent modern book culture almost as soon as their societies came into contact with it some 500 years ago. So while the first three traditions can inform us of how the current state of affairs came to be, the others shed light on how it might have been different.

The three first writing systems were cuneiform signs in Sumer, the Euphrates river plain of southern Iraq; hieroglyphic script along the Egyptian Nile; and Chinese characters down the Yellow River valley. All three systems evolved to communicate, display, or organize information in societies that were increasingly large and complex, stretching the limits of memory and the face-to-face and verbal trust that smaller, simpler communities had relied on for millennia. Wedge-shaped cuneiform on clay has the most clearly documented ante-cedents. It evolved over centuries, if not millennia, from Neolithic accounting systems that used little clay tokens to track traded, stored, or owed goods, and labour, debts, and assets. By the late fourth millennium BCE, accountants were keeping more permanent records by impressing the tokens into flat clay tablets and incising schematic ideograms of what they represented. These objects, which survive in their thousands, mostly from the ancient city of Uruk, *c*.3200 BCE, can claim to be the world's first books. For the original book-keepers not only kept accounts but also standardized school exercises, to help trainees learn hundreds of word-signs and calculate with number-signs in a dozen different metrologies, and perhaps also wrote the very first literature. We will return to what ancient books recorded later.

The precursors of script in ancient Egypt and China are not nearly so well documented, perhaps through mere happenstance of archaeo-logical discovery, or perhaps more likely because those early experi-ments were on media that no longer survive. The earliest known hieroglyphic inscriptions, from a cemetery in Abydos, one of the most ancient cities of Egypt, roughly contemporary with Sumerian Uruk, are carved on bone and ivory and painted on clay pottery. This writing consisted only of numbers and names, and probably quanti-fied the grave goods and labelled their origins. One hundred and twenty-six different signs and variants are known. A few generations later, royal names were also carved into ceremonial objects, while a blank papyrus roll found in another, slightly later tomb, hints at a literate culture in the late fourth millennium wider than the earliest surviving fragments of Egyptian writing would suggest. Similarly, the earliest known Chinese writing—from the city of Anyang *c*.1200 BCE—represents an already sophisticated mature phase of literacy whose only precursors are individual signs inscribed on pottery vessels dating from earlier in the second millennium BCE. At Anyang, writing was used to record the outcomes of divination, royal ceremonial events, and administrative matters, on a range of durable materials from shell and bone to metal and stone. This writing commanded a sign repertoire of over 2,000 characters, representing whole words in heavily pictographic form. One of those characters is the sign *ce*, for bamboo strip book, incontrovertibly indicating that, as in ancient Egypt, there were already other, more ephemeral writing media in use that no longer survive.

The ancient script systems of Egypt, Mesopotamia, and China were all large and complex, perhaps deliberately kept so in order to preserve the status and power of those who had mastered them. Of far greater simplicity and transparency was the ancient alphabet, created by quarry workers in the Sinai desert in about 1800 BCE as a drastic simplification of Egyptian hieroglyphs. Its ease of use and adaptability enabled the ancient alphabet to spread in fits and starts, across languages and cultures from its point of origin on the eastern Mediterranean. In the Middle East, the alphabet only very gradually usurped higher-status cuneiform and hieroglyphic scripts, extinguishing them by the early first centuries CE, and eventually reached far into Europe, Africa, and central and eastern Asia. But new script types did not necessarily involve new media. People wrote alphabetic texts on much the same materials and objects as before.

Ancient Chinese writers in particular experimented with media. Bamboo and wooden strip books, tied together like venetian blinds, become more abundant in the archaeological record of China from the fifth century BCE, while silk—already cultivated at Anyang—started to be written on perhaps as early as the seventh century. Paper made from hemp fibres began to be used maybe as soon as the third century BCE and had definitively replaced heavy bamboo and expensive silk by the third century CE. Variants on Chinese script were adopted in Japan, Korea, and Vietnam in the later first millennium along with block-printing techniques. Hemp paper technology spread westwards too, gradually supplanting indigenous use of birch-bark, wooden panes, and palm-leaves in India and reaching the Islamic Middle East by the ninth or tenth century CE, where it provided a cheap alternative to traditional papyrus, parchment, and waxed wooden writing boards.

The marriage of alphabetic script and paper in ninth-century Baghdad and its environs was a critical development in global book culture. However, looking beyond the confines of Eurasia to the early Americas, archaeologists and historians are discovering a rich array of symbolic systems which challenge comfortable, settled definitions of writing from the Eurasian perspective. Some systems, such as Olmec and Zapotec of the first millennium BCE, or Isthmian of the first centuries CE, are still far from deciphered. Two-thousand-year-old Maya is the best understood of the Mesoamerican writing cultures, while Aztec and Mixtec pictographies are indisputably recorded in books yet, to most scholars, do not constitute writing because of their loose association with spoken language. Even more interesting are the *khipu* knotted string records of the Andean Inca culture, first used just over a millennium ago. For if writing is a technology for recording and transmitting information as much as it is for recording language, and books are simply portable, durable, replicable means of doing so, then we should not exclude *khipu* from the history of the book simply on the grounds of their materiality alone.

What Do Books Do?

The example of the *khipu* suggests that it is unhelpful to limit our definition of 'the book' to objects that comprise a collection of flat surfaces, systematically marked with signs in contrasting colours, and held together by some means that protects them and enables the reader to look at them consecutively. Rather, we might think about function. What do books do? Can we identify objects with similar functionality in past societies?

Books are intended to be portable, more or less, even if some are too heavy to carry comfortably, while others spend their working lives chained to library shelves. They are durable, made to last over years and to travel long distances if necessary. Display inscriptions, therefore, are not books, whether formal public announcements carved into walls or crude graffiti. Nor are single-use ephemera such as potsherds, letters, and receipts. Nevertheless, when collected, attached, and protected by some sort of binding or cover, multiple such objects may become books. The primary function of books is to convey information, ideas, or language through formalized notation (script, loosely defined). Therefore, we should exclude inscribed objects that just happen to be portable, but which serve another primary purpose, such as containers, statuettes, and labels. The contents of books may accrue over time and should remain reproducible (unless deliberately destroyed or mutilated): books should be both legible and copiable even if undecipherable or intellectually obscure to later generations.

Within these functional constraints, books become visible in a huge range of media, from clay to animal skins to plant fibres, across much of world history. Some of those objects were the precursors of the modern book, but many were not. By turning away from the teleological narrative of how the modern book came to be, we can bring into view the diverse and often elegant means by which past societies stored, shared, and protected often complex series of ideas in material form.

Animal, Vegetable, Mineral: Materialities of the Ancient Book

What were ancient books made of, and how did materiality enable or restrict what could be done with them? Some societies exploited existing technologies of making—metal- and stone-working, for instance, or silk production—while others created entirely new media, most obviously, the papyrus sheet and paper. Still other book forms evolved with related technologies: the cuneiform tablet, for instance, was just one of many elements of a clay-based toolkit of bureaucracy and control that developed in the Neolithic Middle East. Not surprisingly, book manufacture depended heavily on the local resources available, but also on social and cultural constraints, leading to quite distinct regional variations as well as some surprising commonalities. Animal skin was never used to write books on in eastern and southern Asia, for instance, while it was a mainstay of prestige manuscripts in the Middle East, Europe, and the Americas. No region of the world preferred stone or metal as primary book media, for obvious practical reasons, while plant-fibre paper was invented at least three different times in entirely unrelated parts of the globe. The following survey of book materialities begins in ancient China, moves westwards across Asia to Europe, and ends in the pre-conquest Americas.

East Asia and Beyond

Animal: Shell, Bone, and Silk

For much of the second millennium BCE, the political and cultural centre of China was the Yellow River valley region of China, ruled by kings of the Shang dynasty. In the fourteenth century BCE, King Pangeng moved his capital to the city of Yin, near modern-day Anyang, where it remained until the dynasty fell to the Zhou in 1046 BCE. Several archaeological excavations since the late 1920s have uncovered huge quantities of tortoise shells inscribed with divinatory writings: hundreds of thousands in total, even if many are now highly fragmentary. On the face of it, inscribed tortoise shells seem unpromising claimants to the title of East Asia's oldest surviving books—and in fact they are rarely discussed in such terms. But if we put aside modern preconceptions of what books should look like, it becomes clear that functionally the inscribed shells of tortoises are very much in keeping with our expectations.

The Shang kings undertook divinations for a variety of reasons: to determine when and how to sacrifice to the ancestral spirits; when and where to organize hunting expeditions; and routinely every ten days to inquire about the well-being of the kingdom. This was not a new practice, but grew out of a tradition of pyro-osteomancy—divination by fire on animal bone—that can be traced back to the mid-fourth millennium BCE, long before the advent of writing in China. In the ideal Shang form of this practice, the diviner took a plastron, the flat shell from the belly of a tortoise, and scraped it clean and flat. He then scarred the inner surface with a series of oval incisions, each about 1 centimetre long and with a circular hole next to it. To perform the divination itself, the diviner or his scribe first inscribed the shell with the date and his name, followed by the question to be posed to the spirits. In the king's presence, he then inserted a red-hot stick into one of the longer hollows until the shell cracked. He might repeat this process, on the same shell or another, numbering the divinations in sequence, and slightly reformulating the question, until the spirits sent an unambiguous answer. The diviner then carved the outcome, 'auspicious' or 'inauspicious', onto the shell, occasionally adding the king's own comments. Later remarks on whether the prediction had come to pass survive only rarely, but it may be that these verifications were usually brush-written in ink, which has since faded away. In this way, the king and his diviners accumulated a reference library of omens and their outcomes as a tool for good governance and correct behaviour towards the spirit world. Once hundreds, or even thousands, of spent divination shells had amassed, they were buried in ritual pits, where archaeologists discovered them over the course of the twentieth century.

Tortoises are not native to the Yellow River valley but live further south, in the Yangtze valley. Inscriptions on the shells themselves, as well as ancient narratives, tell us that they were presented to the Shang court as tribute, by individuals as well as by neighbouring states currying favour. When tortoise plastrons were not available, the diviners resorted to the upper carapaces (although their curved surfaces meant that they were not ideal to work with) or reverted to the old habits of using the shoulder-bones of oxen and other large mammals. Trainee divination scribes practiced how to write by inscribing the blank spaces on discarded shells and especially bones, gradually improving their calligraphy. Typically, young scribes began with repeated copying of the sixty days of the calendric cycle, divided into six ten-day weeks, then moved on to the routine weekly queries for the well-being of the kingdom before following more complex model texts.

Pyro-osteomantic books certainly do not represent the first writing media in China. People had been carving single characters onto pottery vessels and stone objects from at least the mid-third millennium BCE, while in the Shang period, simple formulaic inscriptions also appeared on bronze offering-vessels. Their status as the oldest Chinese books is ambiguous, even if their robust materiality means that they happen to be the oldest that survive. The complexity and sophistication of the script as well as the range of characters in use, perhaps as many as 5,000, demonstrate that writing was no novelty even in the earlier phases of the Shang. (Shifting fashions in script style, as well as the layout of the divinatory incisions, mean that the tortoiseshells can be grouped chronologically even when the ancient dates do not survive.) Although one of the characters in the Shang sign repertoire is the sign *ce* for 'book' and is a schematic representation of bamboo strips tied together by cords, in fact the work of the trainee diviner-scribes demonstrates no prior literacy. Their mistakes in forming, sizing, and ordering the elements of script show that they were not merely transferring well-established skills to a new medium. Nor did the subject matter of their writing exercises ever go beyond the immediate practicalities of divination: we find no draft letters, for instance, model legal documents, or royal proclamations amongst them. So if there was already a bamboo book culture in late-second-millennium BCE China, it operated entirely apart from the divinatory profession, training its own experts in the pertinent techniques of preparation and inscription.

After the fall of the Shang dynasty in 1046 BCE, the new conquerors, the Zhou, continued the tradition of elite pyro-osteomancy for a further two centuries. However, as political culture evolved, the tortoiseshell divination book fell out of favour, while bamboo and silk offered increasing opportunities for writing.

Just as Chinese divination has its roots deep in the Neolithic period, so does sericulture, the manufacture of silk cloth. The earliest survival is a fragment of wild silk fabrics from Henan province in north-central China, dating to the mid-fourth millennium BCE, but representations of silkworms and cocoons in ivory and pottery go back at least a millennium earlier than that. Later, in Shang-era divination inscriptions, the character for 'silk' was a twisted skein of thread. Silk was an important luxury material in the Shang era, not only for clothing the elites, but also for wrapping ritual objects such as offering vessels, whether in divination ceremonies or funerary rites. By this time, silkworms were cultivated widely in northern China, wherever mulberry trees could be grown. The larvae of the silk moth are fed on mulberry leaves for three or four weeks, when they are ready to pupate. They then spin a silk cocoon from their salivary glands over a period of two or three days. At the end of this process, the cocoon is submerged in hot water to kill the pupa and loosen the silk fibre, enabling it to be unwound onto a bobbin. A 5 cm cocoon typically produces a thread over 1.5 km long, which can then be dyed and woven into cloth.

In the seventh century BCE, silk also began to be used as a writing material. No inscribed silks survive from this period, but one ancient literary history refers to a land transfer 'recorded on bamboo and silk' between two dignitaries who lived between *c.*685–645 BCE. Early references such as this one suggest that silk was first used primarily for recording legal documents, sacred records, and other texts of high value whose permanency mattered. It was only from the Han period, in the second century BCE, that people started to use silk for more everyday writings such as letters and literary works.

Evidence for the format and contents of silk books takes two forms: archaeological evidence from the books themselves; and descriptions in ancient writings which have survived through repeated copying over the millennia and are now in modern editions. One of the most exciting groups of finds comes from a tomb near the northern city of Changsha, an independent polity in Han times, and excavated in 1973. The tomb contained around a dozen silk book rolls, dating to the second century BCE or earlier. The books include a history called *Intrigues of the Warring States*, documenting the period *c.*475–220 BCE, a manuscript of the famous divinatory manual *I Ching* 'Book of Changes' which originally dates to the same era, and a copy of the sage Lao Tzu's work on Taoist philosophy and religion, *Dao De Jing*, originally composed in at least the fourth century BCE. All three manuscripts are thousands of characters longer than the received texts of these ancient works as passed down by the copying tradition, hinting at a much richer and varied ancient literary tradition than previously thought.

The Changsha tomb also contained a box containing three silk maps, the largest nearly 1 m square, depicting natural features of the landscape, settlements, roads, and individual buildings such as palaces and military installations. Silk is in many ways an ideal book material. It is light, durable, and easily portable, and it is strong, elastic, and water-resistant. It can be woven or cut into almost any shape required, and for storage it can be rolled around rods and slipped into lacquer cylinders, or folded and put away in chests. In the second century CE, official documents were laid out on rolls roughly 60 cm high and 1.2 m long, but archaeologically attested silk documents are much more variable than this. The text was painted onto the surface with a soft brush using black soot-based inks, as well as reds from powdered cinnabar, a naturally occurring mercury sulphide ore found especially in areas of volcanic activity in south-central Guizhou province. The quality of silk was measured and priced by its weight, the density and fineness of its weave, and the whiteness of its surface. Whatever its quality, however, silk was always relatively expensive, and always difficult to erase. As a result, it was generally reserved for good copies of texts, while bamboo or wood were preferred for drafts. By the third century CE, it had been replaced almost entirely as a book medium by paper, which offered many of silk's benefits without the costs.

Vegetable: Bamboo, Wood, and Hemp

Even though the earliest surviving bamboo books are from the early Warring States period of the fifth century BCE, their use is certainly much older than that. We have already seen that Shang-era diviners had a character for 'bamboo book' in the later second millennium BCE, even though they might not have produced bamboo books themselves. Historical texts about the Zhou Dynasty of the early first millennium BCE mention writings as various as military orders, official documents, and records of sacrifices inscribed on bamboo. In the far north of China, where bamboo does not grow, pale, light, ink-absorbent woods, such as willow and poplar, pine and tamarisk, became common alternatives to bamboo in the early first millennium CE. Over the past century, archaeologists have recovered thousands of bamboo and wood books from hundreds of tombs all over China, typically buried with the officials and scholars who had written and owned them in the millennium or so before the fourth century CE.

It is difficult to overstate the importance of bamboo in ancient China. Bamboo is a fast-growing, easily cultivated plant that is valued for its strength, durability, and hardness, but also for its lightness, smoothness, and flexibility. In Chinese antiquity, bamboo was deployed to make a bewildering variety of objects, from bridges to bows and arrows—and books. But it was not simply a matter of chopping up the canes into appropriately sized slices. First, the craftsman had to scrape off the hard green skin, then split the interior of the cane into even slips, usually about 23–24 cm long and wide enough only to hold one column of script. He then dried out the slips over a fire to preserve them from rot and insect infestation, and to provide a firm writing surface. Each slip was inscribed individually, with a brush and soot-based ink, and bound together only when the whole text was finished. He tied them together at top, centre, and bottom with silk, hemp, or leather to form a continuous surface, knotting the cords tightly but not in general perforating the strips themselves. The resulting book was either rolled like a scroll with the ends of the cords used to tie the roll together, or folded concertina-style and tied to a wooden cover. In either case, the book could be sealed with clay over the knots.

A few examples of the archaeological discoveries give a flavour of the huge variety of texts written on bamboo books and why they survive. When the administrator Shao Tuo died in Boashen, Jingmen province, in 316 BCE, he was buried with the legal cases that he had overseen, as well as bamboo records of Shang-style pyro-osteomancies and *I Ching*-style divinations that he had commissioned in his later years. A century later, a man named Xi, another local administrator, was buried in 217 BCE at Shuihudi in Hubei province. He took with him numerous books that defined him professionally, including several legal tomes, two almanacs, an otherwise unknown handbook called 'The Way of Being an Official', and a history of the Qin Dynasty, by whom he was employed and in which he was mentioned several times.

But within a few centuries, a new technology would replace both costly silk and cumbersome bamboo—and, in time, would render almost all other book media obsolete across the world. The invention of modern paper is traditionally dated to 105 CE, when Cai Lun, a senior official of the Han Dynasty, is said to have presented Emperor He with a paper-making method inspired by watching wasps build their nests. An official history of the fifth century CE records how he pounded together the inner bark of mulberry trees and waste hemp fibre (cultivated since Neolithic times for clothing, rope, and netting). However, the first archaeologically attested fragments of paper are from a tomb in Baqiao, in the Han capital Chang'an (modern Xi'an), that had been sealed up during the reign of Emperor He (140–87 BCE). The Baqiao paper is made from beaten hemp and ramie (an East Asian relative of the nettle) and had been dried on a mat, rather than on a draining screen as in later times. But it, like all the earliest archaeologically attested papers, is blank and was probably used for wrapping, not writing.

By the end of Cai Lun's lifetime, however, paper had become a cheap and convenient alternative to silk and bamboo. *Xu Shen*, a dictionary of Chinese characters written *c*.100 CE, defines paper (*zhi*) as 'a mat of rag fibres (*xu*)', and there are many contemporary literary references to paper, too. By this time, papers were made by dipping standard-sized screens of woven ramie into a vat of pulp and leaving the water to evaporate off. The thin sheets, typically 24 cm square, could be glued together into rolls like silk, and tied together with ribbons. Over the next few centuries, paper-makers experimented with dyes and starches, as well as new fibres such as rattan, jute, flax, and straw, to make more attractive and less fragile writing surfaces. Bamboo was not used until at least the eighth century, as the supply of rattan became exhausted, and it is highly unlikely that cotton or silk were ever raw materials for Chinese paper-making. Ink was typically made of pine soot, vermilion, or cinnabar, like those used for writing on bamboo and silk.

The oldest surviving paper book is a copy of the Buddhist *Piyujing Sutra* from 256 CE. When a cache of bamboo books was discovered in a tomb in 280 CE, the imperial librarian of the Qin Dynasty had them copied onto paper in triplicate, each stored separately. At about the same time, paper manufacture began to spread across Asia, at first existing alongside other book media. For instance, in South Asia, birch-bark and palm-leaf books had first been adopted in the last centuries BCE with the westward spread of Buddhism. But they regularly fell prey to heat and humidity, insects and rodents, and had to be regularly recopied, after which the originals were ritually buried or (for Hindu scriptures) cast into the sacred river Ganges. Paper began to replace traditional writing media in northern Pakistan in the sixth century CE, but only definitively ousted them with the arrival of the Mughals in the thirteenth century.

The Middle East and Mediterranean

Mineral: Clay

In the late fourth millennium BCE, urban living increased slowly but dramatically in the Middle East. As agricultural techniques improved, and the marshes of southern Iraq became increasingly hospitable, people were drawn towards living in densely packed settlements in which specialist production and management skills could flourish, alongside generalist labour. The millennia-old system of tallying surpluses and trade goods with small clay counters evolved, too. By about 3200 BCE, the cities of Uruk in southern Iraq and Susa in southwest Iran were home to two structurally related but visually distinct writing systems, both used to keep account books and to train future accountants. In Uruk it is clear that these men were working for a large central authority, managing grain, flocks, labour, and the secondary products produced by them. Simple receipts and expenditure records were combined into longer-term accounts, tracking commodities over months and even years. Perhaps unsurprisingly, the writing system they used was tied closely to what needed to be accounted for: it was capable of recording goods, quantities, a limited number of verbs, and little else. Essentially, it was language-independent, recording information rather than trying to represent sounds. There was also a system for learning the 1,000-character script, by means of standardized thematic lists: animals, birds, metals and metal objects, plants, official titles, woods and wooden objects, etc. In addition, trainee scribes practised recording and calculating in the twenty or so commodity-specific number bases and measurement systems that were in operation.

Over the next two millennia, we can trace the spread of clay writing technologies, both generically and geographically, and then their gradual decline. By the mid-third millennium BCE, cuneiform could represent the sounds of the Sumerian and (unrelated) Akkadian languages, and was being used all along the Euphrates valley and its environs to write royal inscriptions, legal agreements, hymns, and prayers, as well as its core function to manage the assets of large institutions such as temples and palaces. Within another few hundred years, wealthy families, too, were writing letters, recording sales, loans, dowries, and inheritances. They also trained their young in the rudiments of cuneiform script, while professional literacy remained dominant. In the northern Babylonian city of Sippar, for instance, the chief lamentation priest Inana-mansum brought in jobbing scribes such as Šumum-liši to write individual household documents for the family archive and to teach his son Ur-Utu the rudiments of reading, writing, and calculating in cuneiform. When the house burned down in about 1630 BCE, the now adult Ur-Utu attempted to rescue the most important of his tablets—particularly those that showed his title to the house—but dropped them on the way out, leaving a trail that could be traced by archaeologists 3,600 years later.

Priests, healers, diviners, and scribal teachers wrote ritual instructions, medical recipes, collections of omens, law codes, and mathematical exercises, but rarely collected them into libraries in the second millennium BCE. At this time, these works were written out on clay tablets, if at all, predominantly in order to memorize them, as shown by repeated copying exercises from schools such as House F in

Nippur, in the 1740s BCE. Knowledge circulated primarily through recall, recitation, and performance.

The apogee of cuneiform culture was perhaps the third quarter of the second millennium BCE, when elites as far afield as Cyprus, central Anatolia, southwest Iran, the eastern Mediterranean coast, and even Egypt were using it as a *lingua franca* for long-distance communication, often alongside their own local languages and script practices. In these contexts, most cuneiform tablets bore letters and legal treaties, but some of the literary and scholarly writings of Mesopotamia travelled, too, as well as multi-lingual dictionaries translating Sumerian and Akkadian terms into languages such as Ugaritic, Hittite, Hurrian, and Egyptian. Most famously, the 350 Amarna Letters, found at the site of the pharaoh Akhnaten's capital Akhetaten, document a lively diplomatic correspondence with his counterparts in Assyria, Babylonia, the north Syrian kingdom of Mittanni, and elsewhere, as well as numerous vassal states along the eastern Mediterranean coast. Clay writing technology was also adopted on Crete by *c.*1600 BCE to write the as yet undeciphered Cretan Hieroglyphic and Linear A scripts. By *c.*1400 BCE, Cretans were using clay tablets to write administrative documents in Mycenean, an early form of Greek, in a syllabic and word-based script of about 200 signs now called Linear B. Over 4,000 tablets are known from the Mycenean palace at Knossos, 1,000 from nearby Pylos, and around 500 from sites on mainland Greece such as Thebes and Mycene.

From the late second millennium BCE, the gradual spread of alphabetic scripts on other media, outwards from the eastern Mediterranean coast, eventually led to the decline of clay as the archetypical Middle Eastern writing medium. The collapse of the Assyrian empire in 614–609 BCE put an end to cuneiform culture across most of the vast territories that it had ruled. Buried in the ruined palaces of its erstwhile capital Nineveh were also some 10–20,000 cuneiform tablets bearing works of terrestrial and celestial divination and many other scholarly works. These are often now called Ashurbanipal's library, after the king in whose name they were assembled, but they did not constitute a collection that could be consulted and borrowed. The 'library' is more a hoard of booty, an attempt to monopolize particular types of learning that were considered especially central to imperial success.

Yet clay tablets endured in Babylonia, primarily used by the elite urban communities closely associated with traditional temples, for whom cuneiform literacy was a core element of their cultural heritage. Here, priests and scholars shared works of literature, healing, astrology, and cult within professional groups, still memorizing for the most part but keeping and lending hard-copy back-ups at home, as well as depositing copies as votive offerings to their city gods. The Persian empire flirted briefly with clay as an administrative medium for a few decades around 500 BCE, during the reign of Darius the Great. Two archives of up to 20,000 tablets have been uncovered at his capital Persepolis, in southern Iran, mostly written in the local Elamite language, plus some 800 in imperial Aramaic. However, on his difficult accession to the throne in 485 BCE, Darius' son Xerxes quashed two major rebellions in Babylonia, bringing an end to several major archives there (and presumably the families behind them). The Persian empire then lost its appetite for imitating high Babylonian culture, and imperial production of cuneiform was soon halted. Nevertheless, even in the final centuries BCE, temple priests and scholars in the cities of Uruk and Babylon were still making sophisticated astronomical observations and calculations, recording hymns and rituals, and keeping family legal documents on clay. The last dated cuneiform tablet is a set of astronomical predictions from 78 CE.

Clay emerged naturally as a medium for books, from an administrative culture that was already sealing containers and storerooms with clay bullae and utilizing tiny clay accounting tokens. All along the valleys and plains of the Tigris, Euphrates, and associated river systems, clay was easy to procure and prepare. In the heartlands of cuneiform culture—Iraq, northern Syria, southwest Iran—tablets were made with the same clays as fine tableware, but generally left unbaked, as firing was expensive, unreliable, and dangerous. Sun-dried clay tablets were extremely durable in normal conditions—as evidenced by their long-term survival in the hundreds of thousands. They could easily be recycled by soaking in water at the end of their useful life, and every scribal centre and archive room featured a waterproof recycling bin or clay preparation area. Tablets could be made (and remade) to almost any size, from around a centimetre square up to 30 × 20 cm or more. They were typically inscribed with reed or bone styluses, though precious metal versions were status symbols. But because clay is bulky and dense, as well as prone to breakage, tablets, especially larger ones, were not particularly conducive to long-distance travel. Constraints on size also limited the amount of text they could contain. Nor was clay the optimal medium for accumulating large datasets over time, as surfaces became increasingly difficult to inscribe as they dried out. Not surprisingly, therefore, other media were used alongside cuneiform tablets across the ancient Middle East, from at least the late third millennium BCE.

Vegetable: Papyrus

Parallel to the Mesopotamian development of cuneiform was, of course, the papyrus roll in Egypt. The papyrus reed is native to the marshes of the Nile delta in the Mediterranean, and the swamps of the White Nile in southern Sudan. Its robust yet light and flexible stems can grow up to 5 m high and 40 mm thick, making papyrus an ideal construction material for objects such as boats, ropes, mats, and baskets. By about 3000 BCE, it had also been adopted as a writing medium, although short hieroglyphic texts—such as labels on grave goods—predate papyrus by perhaps a few hundred years.

The standard method of manufacture was to cut the papyrus plant's stem into sections some 20–25 cm long and strip away the hard green outer surface. Thicker stems could be sliced vertically into thin slivers, or peeled in a continuous spiral towards the centre. Two layers of papyrus pith were then laid on top of one other, with the cellulose fibres at right angles to one another, and beaten together on a flat surface. The plant's sticky sap made a natural adhesive, though it could also help to pre-soak the strips before assembling them. The vertically oriented fibres formed the back of the resultant sheet and the horizontal ones the front, which was polished with a pumice stone or shell to make a smooth writing surface. The height of the strips thus determined the size of the object, but one could keep gluing them together to make much longer rolls. Surviving papyrus rolls—which always have their left edge at the centre—are typically anything from 1.5 m to 6 m or so in length, but examples of up to 30 m are known. In relatively dry conditions the cellulose structures of papyrus are impressively resistant to decay, but rot in moister environments. Throughout

Pharaonic times, black ink was manufactured from carbon (charcoal), gum arabic (the sap of the acacia tree), and water, while red ink, used for headings and other highlighted text, substituted the carbon with powdered iron oxide (red ochre or haematite). The ink was transferred to the papyrus surface with a reed brush, made by splitting the fibres vertically along the stem.

· The oldest extant papyrus is a blank roll stored in a cylindrical wooden box, found in an elaborate tomb at Saqqara, the necropolis of the city of Memphis near modern-day Cairo. According to an inscribed label originally attached to another object in the tomb, it belonged to a man named Hemaka, who served as 'seal-bearer'—the highest official in the land—to King Den of the First Dynasty, who ruled in *c.*2950 BCE. However, the earliest surviving inscribed papyri are from a few centuries later. Just like cuneiform in Mesopotamia, Egyptian hieroglyphic script—designed originally for ostentatious display of names, numbers, and objects on high-status objects and monuments—evolved only gradually its capacity to represent whole sentences of spoken language. This mature form of writing continued to be deployed primarily for display purposes, on the walls of tombs and temples, and on open-air rock faces, while the earliest papyri were exclusively administrative in function. For instance, the harbour site of Wadi el-Jarf was constructed on the Red Sea in *c.*2600 in order to provide access to the copper and turquoise mines of the Sinai desert. Here in 2013, excavators found several hundred papyri fragments dating to the twenty-eighth year of the pharaoh Khufu's reign, *c.*2550 BCE, discarded as filler between two huge stone blocks used to seal access to a storage chamber. Some are tabular accounts detailing daily and monthly deliveries of food to the site. Others represent the remains of a work journal kept by one Merer, an overseer of a 200-man gang procuring limestone for Khufu's famous Great Pyramid at Giza, which was already under construction.

The papyrus roll remained an exclusively institutional management tool for several hundred more years. It was only in the Middle Kingdom, in the very early second millennium BCE, that literary and scholarly works, such as mathematical problems and medical recipes, were regularly preserved on papyrus, although it is likely that they had already been circulating in oral form for several centuries before that.

Funerary texts, such as the Book of the Dead, were transferred from tombs and coffins to papyrus only in the sixteenth century BCE.

By the first millennium BCE, if not before, papyrus was exported across the Middle East but remained an expensive commodity outside Egypt. For instance, in the late eighth century, Assyrian crown prince Sennacherib (who would come to the throne in 704 BCE) distributed booty and audience gifts to courtiers after a successful military campaign. While most received several kilos of silver and a few elegant garments, the palace scribe was additionally given two papyrus rolls. Papyrus, however, is rarely mentioned in the cuneiform record; domestically produced wooden writing boards and leather scrolls (both discussed further below) were clearly the preferred alternatives to clay.

The eastern Mediterranean coast, however, had always been much more open to Egyptian cultural influence (and political control). Alphabets, first adapted from hieroglyphs by quarriers writing graffiti in the Sinai desert, spread rapidly northwards from about 1800 BCE. Unsurprisingly, given the environmental conditions, most surviving evidence for alphabetic writing in the Iron Age Levant is in the form of inscriptions on relatively indestructible objects of stone and metal. Yet occasional finds in dry cave sites, such as those at Wadi Murabba'at in the West Bank, show that letters and legal documents were written in local languages such as Old Hebrew from at least the early seventh century BCE. However, it was the enormous Achaemenid Persian empire—which, as already noted, flirted briefly with cuneiform tablets in around 500 BCE—that took up papyrus as a medium of imperial communication and bureaucracy across the Middle East. Papyrus naturally remained the preferred medium in Egypt, both for official and private purposes, in both hieroglyphic and demotic (late cursive) Egyptian as well as the internationally understood Aramaic. But in 1962, eighteen papyri recording slave sales were discovered in a cave in Wadi Daliyeh, in the modern West Bank, where the citizens of Samaria had hidden them ahead of Alexander the Great's conquest of 331 BCE and never returned for them. They attest that wealthy private individuals of the city kept legal records in Hebrew and Aramaic from at least the middle of the fifth century BCE onwards.

The earliest known examples of papyri in Greek are also from the fourth century BCE, including the famous Deverni papyrus, found in a

tomb just north of Thessaloniki in northern Greece. The roll had been
partially burned in the funerary rites, but some twenty-six columns of
text survive, revealing a manuscript written sometime between 340
and 320 BCE of a unique philosophical text composed perhaps a
century earlier. Almost exactly contemporary with it is another
Greek text, a fragment of Timotheus' poem *The Persians*, on a fragmentary papyrus found in Saqqara in Egypt.

The papyrus writing tradition continued in Egypt, and all around
the Mediterranean, well into the first millennium CE. Yet evidence for
classical book culture is mostly derived from historical and literary
sources, with a few spectacular exceptions. When, in 79 CE, Mount
Vesuvius erupted near Pompeii, it also buried the nearby seaside
resort of Herculaneum, including a sumptuous villa, possibly built
for Julius Caesar's father-in-law 120 years earlier. Set in elegant
gardens overlooking the beautiful Bay of Naples, the four-level residence housed a large collection of high-quality classical sculpture and
a library of some 600–1,000 mostly philosophical works on papyrus
rolls. The library had been packed up, ready for evacuation, when the
eruption reached the villa, burying the whole edifice in up to 25 m of
volcanic ash and charring the papyrus into blackened, fragile blocks.
Since the first discovery of the library in 1752, there have been many
attempts to unroll and decipher the more than 1,800 surviving fragments, most recently and successfully using non-invasive digital techniques. The large majority of the texts are by the Greek poet and
Epicurean philosopher Philodemus, who lived a century or so before
the destruction of the villa. But the library also includes writings by
other Epicureans and Stoics, as well as Latin works on rhetoric and
oratory, plus a smattering of Greek mathematics, physics, and geom-
etry. Some of the rolls were originally over 20 m long.

From the first century CE onwards, users started to fold new papyrus
rolls, concertina-style, into compact notebooks whose pages could be
searched much more easily than the traditional format. Glued bindings and covers also made them more robust and usable on the move,
a lightweight version of the wooden writing board that is discussed
further below. The so-called Nag Hammadi library, named after its
place of discovery in northern Egypt, comprises thirteen leather-
bound papyrus codices of 10–17 × 24–30 cm, which had been buried
in a sealed earthenware jar in the desert. Together they comprise a

collection of fifty-two early Christian theological works, written in Coptic Egyptian, in the fourth and fifth centuries CE, perhaps by a nearby monastic community.

Papyrus use—and production quality—began to decline in the fifth century CE, but it continued to be manufactured for about three centuries after the Muslim invasion of Egypt in 639 CE—and increasingly used as a medium for Arabic. But once cheap paper started to be imported from Syria in the late ninth century, it rapidly fell into disuse, exacerbated by the beginnings of local paper-making. Very little Egyptian papyrus was made after the tenth century CE. The last known papal bull on papyrus was issued in Rome in 1057, and the last known papyrus document in Arabic from Egypt dates to just thirty years later.

Animal, Vegetable, Mineral: Substitutes for the Tablet and the Scroll

All other writing media used in the ancient Middle East and Mediterranean worlds can be seen as substitutes for the clay tablet or papyrus roll. The cheapest and most disposable were writing boards and the pieces of broken pottery known to archaeologists by the Greek word *ostrakon* (plural *ostraka*) after the Athenian practice of using them for casting votes to expel (or ostracize) miscreants from the city. Particularly prestigious or high-profile cuneiform texts—boundary treaties, endowments, foundation inscriptions—could all have analogues in stone or high-value metals. But we should probably not count most of these as books, as they were intended to be permanent fixtures in the landscape or built environment, and were not intended to be mobile. At the other end of the scale are two tiny, silver amuletic scrolls, found in a tomb in Ketef Hinnom near Jerusalem. They bear two short passages of Biblical text, in a style of Old Hebrew that can be dated to 600 BCE. Less piously, tightly rolled lead sheets became a popular medium for curses and spells by the fifth century CE and have been found all over the ancient world, from Roman Britain to southern Iraq, written in Greek, Latin, Aramaic, and Mandaic.

At the other end of the social and portability scales were the *ostraka* or pieces of broken pottery. However, people had been scratching or inking writing onto discarded earthenware long before the advent of ancient Greek literacy. In most ancient contexts, the short, ephemeral texts on *ostraka* barely count as books, but in ancient Egypt especially, small fragments of pottery and slivers of limestone were used as disposable notebooks, exercise books, recipe books, and account books from at least the New Kingdom onwards.

While *ostraka* have been found at many Egyptian archaeological sites, the discoveries at Deir al-Medina are perhaps the most revealing. This is the modern name of Set Maat, or 'Place of Truth', the village that housed the craftsmen who built and maintained the pharaohs' tombs in the Valley of the Kings from the eighteenth to twentieth dynasties. The earliest occupation, from about 1550 BCE, is thus a century or so earlier than the clay tablets from Amarna discussed above, and the site was abandoned about 400 years later. Many of the tomb builders and their families were well educated but not particularly prosperous, and so they routinely used *ostraka* for more ephemeral writings alongside the more valuable papyrus for texts that deserved a more elegant medium or which needed to travel long distances or survive the generations.

Waxed wooden writing boards were used in Mesopotamia from at least the twenty-first century BCE, according to references on clay tablets. The earliest surviving visual depictions and archaeological specimens, however, are from the royal cities of Assyria in northern Iraq from the eighth century BCE. They could be up to 25 cm long and composed of up to fourteen hinged leaves, folded and bound so that the wax-covered writing surfaces were protected from accidental damage. Unlike clay, waxed boards could be written on and erased long after manufacture. They were ideal for texts such as ledgers or diaries that had to be compiled over a long period of time, well after the surface of a tablet would have dried out. The boards might also carry texts written far from good sources of clay, such as dispatches from military campaigns. Their easy erasability meant, conversely, that they were less tamper-proof than tablets, so while they became popular for a range of writings, from letters to literature, they were a poor choice for durable records.

Similarly, wooden boards were also inked with hieroglyphs in Egypt, from at least the middle of the third millennium BCE. They were ideal for note-taking and accounts, could be washed clean for reuse, and were more robust than the papyrus roll. Only from the

Greco-Roman period were they waxed and bound as in Mesopotamia, however, and in this form they were used across the literate Old World, as far west as Hadrian's Wall (*c.*85–130 CE). Whether inscribed in ink or impressed in wax, the original writing on archaeologically recovered specimens rarely survives, but the writer's stylus often left indentations in the wood, which can still be read. A recent find of over 400 writing boards in the City of London includes a debt note dated to 57 CE, the earliest dated document from Roman Britain. As in Egypt, the ancient British boards tended to be used for letters, legal documents, school writing exercises, and financial accounts. The writing board continued to be used for similar purposes in some European contexts as late as the nineteenth century CE.

Animal: Leather and Parchment

If the *ostrakon* and writing board were the ephemeral counterparts to the clay tablet and papyrus, the animal-skin roll was a hard-wearing alternative to the latter. There are references to such rolls and roll-makers in Egyptian texts from the mid-third millennium BCE right through to the Ptolemaic period and beyond, but the objects themselves rarely survive. On the one hand, they could be used and reused repeatedly for ephemeral texts, such as accounts and school exercises, but their durability also made them a suitable medium for prestigious and long-lived archival records and library texts. In late-eighth-century Assyria, an official was refused permission to correspond with King Sargon on hide in alphabetic Aramaic, but it is likely that the chancery was fighting a lost cause in trying to maintain cuneiform for this purpose. The Achaemenid empire certainly used leather (as well as tablets and papyrus): in the late fifth century BCE the satrap of Egypt, one Arshama, corresponded on leather with his estate manager while on an official trip to the royal city of Susa in southwest Iran. A century later, in fourth-century Bactria, another Persian satrap, Ahkvamazda, sent similar letters and documents on leather to the city governor of Khulm. In Hellenistic Babylonia, there are regular references to parallel legal documentation on animal skin and clay, with scholarly and literary texts transcribed onto both media and onto writing boards.

In both Egypt and Mesopotamia, it is likely that such scrolls were made of leather that had been tanned—a long, complex, and pungent process involving soaking the hides for a year or more. By contrast, untanned parchment—hide which is only treated to remove the hair, stretched taut, and burnished to create a smooth writing surface—takes only four weeks or so to prepare. Its invention is traditionally attributed to the city of Pergamon (whence parchment derives its name) in modern-day Turkey. In his *Natural History*, Pliny claims that Ptolemy V of Egypt, jealous of the city's prestigious library, which threatened to rival Alexandria's, banned the export of papyrus to Pergamon in 190 BCE, prompting the development of an alternative medium. This story is certainly apocryphal, although it is currently impossible to determine the earliest surviving parchment manuscript, as many ancient historians use 'parchment' and 'leather' interchangeably, and no reliable comparative studies have been done.

In fact, recent chemical analysis of the Dead Sea Scrolls suggests that in the last centuries BCE there might not have been such a hard and fast distinction between leather and parchment as suggested above. The famous scrolls were found in large jars in a series of caves just a few kilometres from the Dead Sea in what is now the West Bank. Nearly 1,000 in number, almost all of them carry Jewish religious texts of some kind, mostly passages of Hebrew scripture and related works, as well as translations into Greek and Aramaic. There were also some private archives and letter bundles mixed in. Most of the rolls, whether leather or papyrus, date to the last three centuries BCE and the first century CE. Debate still rages as to whether they were left there in a single event—hiding the contents of a single library from the city of Qumran ahead of the Roman invasion of 68 CE—or deposited over many generations, as a *genizah* of holy texts no longer in use but too sacred to destroy. While some of the rolls are papyrus, over 85 per cent are made of the skins of goats, calves, ibex, and gazelle. They had been dehaired not with lime—the standard medieval method—but by smearing in an organic material, perhaps dung or vegetable matter, that has left no chemical trace. The hides had been soaked in water from the Dead Sea, and with ink that had also been locally produced.

Parchment-like treatments of hide produced a writing surface that was suppler than either leather or papyrus, and could take ink better, on both sides of the skin, which was then easier to wash off for reuse. However, parchment was not ideally suited to the roll format, as skins had to be cut and stitched together. From the first or second century CE, bookmakers began to fold parchment sheets into eight-page quires, stitching them together to form codices, at about the same time as they were also experimenting with the papyrus notebook. The parchment codex rapidly gained popularity and by the fourth century CE was the dominant form of the book all over the Mediterranean world. It was particularly popular in Christian communities, perhaps because it helped to distinguish their scriptures from the traditional roll format of the Jewish Torah. The *Codex Sinaiticus*, for instance, is one of the earliest and most complete Greek bibles in existence. Rediscovered in St Catherine's Monastery in the Sinai Desert in the nineteenth century, it was written in the mid-fourth century CE. A team of three or four scribes had divided the copying work between them, writing on parchment sheets of roughly 38 × 35 cm, over 400 of which survive. The first part of the manuscript, containing the earliest books of the Old Testament to 1 Chronicles, is now lost.

The Americas

The ancient societies we have considered so far in this chapter all made positive, organic decisions to adopt the paper or parchment codex as a preferred form of the book at some point in their histories, often using it alongside more traditional media for centuries. The peoples of the Americas had no such luxury, however: their books were forcibly removed, denigrated, and destroyed in the process of European colonization over the sixteenth to nineteenth centuries. Nevertheless, over the past few decades there has been a concerted effort to recover, re-document, and re-evaluate these lost American literacies and to rehabilitate them into the global history of the book.

Animal and Vegetable: The Knotted String Records of the Andes

The Andean mountains, running down the west coast of South America, have been inhabited by humans for at least 15,000 years. Societies living there underwent much the same transformations as their

Eurasian counterparts, as small bands of hunter-gatherers grew into larger farming communities which by the mid-fifteenth century CE were ruled by the all-powerful Inca empire. At its height, Tahuantin-suyu, 'The Four Quarters', as it was called in the Quechua language, stretched over 4,000 km from the northern tip of modern-day Ecua-dor in a 40 km band from the west coast down through Peru, Bolivia, Argentina, and Chile. Like any pre-modern empire, it governed a sophisticated complex society, through hierarchies of royalty and nobility, expressing a clear governmental ideology and controlling its population through census, taxation, and an astronomically based ceremonial calendar.

The Inca state managed its human and material assets very closely, by officials who made complex knotted string records, called *khipu* in Quechua. About 600 examples survive today from the period *c.*1400–1530 CE, some from archaeological contexts such as tombs, but many as undocumented acquisitions from the antiquities trade. There are also several depictions and descriptions of *khipus* in use from after the Spanish conquest of 1532, but although the principles of their construction and operation are well understood, no surviving *khipu* can be fully read as if by an Inca accountant.

Khipu cords were spun from cotton or llama hair. This choice of material may have been meaningful, or it may simply have been a matter of personal preference or availability. Colour certainly mattered—many *khipus* show clear regularities in their use of reds, blues, and undyed fibres—but it is no longer known what each colour group signified. Each *khipu* began with a primary cord, to which pendant cords were tied, hanging down from it like washing on a line. Subsidiary cords could also be attached to the pendants, and so on. These structures, too, were meaningful: for instance, grouping herd animals by their owners, and then by their sex and maturity. Decimal numbers were recorded by knotting the cord at regular intervals; about 80 per cent of surviving *khipus* primarily record quan-tifications, and their numerical data is well understood. The remain-der are presumably narrative but have so far proved resistant to interpretation.

Knots could be undone, of course, and cords untied, moved, and unravelled. The *khipu* could be rolled up small for storage, unrolled for operation, or slung like a sash under the wearer's arm and over the opposite shoulder. They were made from readily available raw materials, from the crops and herds that were the empire's staple products, and with a simple drop spindle. They were portable, reconfigurable, and adaptable to a variety of different uses. Archives of up to thirty related *khipus* have been identified, some found together, some identified through similarities and matches in their structure and content. It was common to keep duplicate copies, and for information from smaller *khipus* to be combined into larger ones. One of the largest known *khipus*, with 762 pendant cords, appears to have been organized calendrically, with 730 of those cords grouped into twenty-four clusters of about thirty pendants each. Two other known *khipus* match one four-month section of it.

The Inca *khipu* system may have antecedents that stretch back as far as the seventh or eighth centuries CE, in the form of coloured threads wrapped around ceremonial sticks, and then later a form of proto-*khipu*, without knots. Post-conquest accounts describe messengers carrying letters in the form of *khipus*, and for several decades *khipus* were admissible evidence in Spanish-speaking courts of law. Witnesses describe account-keepers as reading their *khipu* as much by running their fingers over the knots as by visual inspection, and there are some rather obscure descriptions of black and white pebbles and accounting boards used as secondary calculation devices. Colonial governance transitioned rapidly to paper documentation, of course, and the *khipu* fell out of official use in the mid-sixteenth century. Nonetheless, herders in some Quechua and Aymara communities in the Bolivian Andes were still accounting for their flocks with *khipu* well into the twentieth century, while in other villages *khipu* remain central ceremonial garments in the inauguration of village elders, although they are no longer considered as objects to be read.

Vegetable and Animal: The Hide and Bark Codices of Mesoamerica

Human societies have flourished on the isthmus between north and southern America, the region occupied by today's Mexico, Guatemala, and Belize, for many thousands of years. Their peoples have been writing for at least three millennia. The Cascajal Block is named after the quarry where it was discovered in Veracruz, Mexico, in 1999 in an archaeological context that dates it to the so-called San Lorenzo phase of Olmec culture, *c*.900 BCE. Measuring some 35 × 21 × 13 cm and made of serpentine, it displays an undeciphered text sixty-two characters long, composed of twenty-eight different stylized representations of plants, faces, and other objects. We might be tempted to label this object as a book of some kind if it were not more than 12 kg in weight, suggesting that it was not designed for portability. However, this unique and important artefact does open up the likelihood of other forms of literacy in Mesoamerica several centuries earlier than previously thought.

Although most Mesoamerican languages and hieroglyphic scripts— Zapotec, Mixtec, Aztec, and Maya—are attested on stone buildings and monuments and as labels on other objects, there are clear indications that these cultures had both scribes and books from at least the early first millennium CE. In the Classic Maya period (*c*.250–900 CE), for instance, scribes (*ah tz'ib'*—literally 'writers/painters') are shown on pottery vessels, with a conch-shell inkpot and a quill pen tucked into their headdress. They may be depicted as gods, men, or animals, who kneel or sit in front of a folded codex. A scribal workshop has been excavated at Aguateca in Guatemala, with abandoned pigment grinders and shell inkpots, including one inscribed with the name of its owner. This, amongst other evidence, shows that Maya scribes were members of the elite, sometimes even members of the royal family.

However, fewer than twenty Mesoamerican books have survived to modern times, all dating to the fourteenth to sixteenth centuries CE. For instance, one of five or six extant Mixtec manuscripts is the so-called Codex Cospi, written sometime between 1350 and 1520 CE, presumably in central Mexico. It is composed of five bands of deer-skin, sewn together to form a strip 3.64 m long, concertina-folded to form twenty pages of 18 × 18 cm. The manuscript now named the Madrid Codex—one of only four Maya books now known—was made in the late fifteenth century, perhaps in Yucatan. It is constructed from a single strip of fig-tree bark, 6.8 m long and 23 cm high, and also concertina-folded, into pages that are 12 cm wide: fifty-six leaves survive. The writing surfaces of these codices were coated with white chalk, onto which the scribes painted their hieroglyphic texts in black (pine soot), red (haematite), and blue (white clay mixed

with indigo). Codex Cospi, like the other surviving Mixtec manuscripts, gives a long genealogical history, going back centuries, while
the Madrid Codex contains a sophisticated compilation of calendrical,
astronomical, and divinatory material from several sources, by as
many as eight or nine different scribes.

Sixteenth-century European invaders initially saw codices as interesting curiosities, but as Christian conversion campaigns gained
ground they increasingly viewed them as idolatrous. Massive numbers
were destroyed in the decades after the conquests. Local communities
tried to resist: Maya priests continued to perform ritual cleansings of
their divinatory codices, and to take omens from them, as late as 1566.
But the few surviving books of pre-Hispanic Mesoamerica now all
reside in European collections, where they were largely ignored until
their rediscovery in the nineteenth century.

Animal: The Hide Winter Counts of the North American Plains

From at least the seventeenth century CE, and probably also for many
hundreds of years before that, the Lakota people of the North American plains kept community annals, known as winter counts. Originally
farmers on the western shores of Lake Superior, from the mid-
seventeenth century they began to migrate west towards the Missis-
sippi River, in search of buffalo to hunt and to escape conflict with
other Sioux tribes and European incomers. Each *tiyospaye*, an
extended family group of 150–300 people, entrusted to one of their
men the task of memorizing the community's history and to recount
it on public occasions. Each winter he consulted the elders of the
tiyospaye to decide on an image that encapsulated a key event of
the previous year, and added it to a ceremonial list or *waniyetu wowapi*,
literally 'winter record'.

Many Lakota bands named the winter of 1833–4 after a spectacular
meteor shower ('the year the stars fell' or 'it rained stars')—an event that
later enabled the counts to be correlated with each other and with the
Euro-American calendar. But the following year was more typical in that
the keepers made much more diverse choices. Long Soldier, for instance,
named 1834–5 as 'the first year of feather hats', drawing an emblem of
five feathers over two horses. American Horse, however, chose 'war with

the Cheyennes', and depicted it as an arrow fight between two men, one of whom—the Cheyenne—bleeds from his forearm.

The primary historical record was stored in the keeper's memory but could also be copied out on request, accompanied by an oral explanation. Traditionally, winter counts were painted onto deer-, cow-, or buffalo-hide, with the oldest events at the centre, spiralling out anticlockwise to the most recent. In the nineteenth century, however, some keepers copied out their counts onto muslin cloth, sheets of paper, or notebooks for Euro-American collectors, who also transcribed the oral histories that went with them. The tradition died out in the late nineteenth century as the Lakota people were attacked by US government forces and corralled into reservations, but somewhere between fifty and a hundred still survive in national and local museums, each now named for their last Lakota keeper or informant.

Academics have been slow to recognize either *khipus* or winter counts as books, but functionally their relationship between individual and community memory, language, and ceremony is not so different from other, more familiar forms. In many cultures, ancient and modern, the text exists as much in the head as on the page—a scripture or poem learned by heart—or has only a loose association with the sounds of spoken language—early cuneiform, or modern mathematical notation. By shedding expectations of words on paper, we open up the history of the book to a much wider and richer range of cultural experience and expression.

Concluding Observations

Although in retrospect the history of the book may seem like the triumph of the printed paper codex, from another perspective it can be seen as a diverse catalogue of creative, practical solutions to the need to store, transport, and retrieve written knowledge and information. There were, it seems, certain basic needs that constrained material choices wherever books were created and used. The choice of format, simply put, has mostly been between rolled or folded sheets, with knotted strings and clay tablets being the enduring, effective exceptions. However, scrolls and codices are extensible in ways that clay is not, while offering legibility through colour contrast between text and surface that neither tablets nor *khipus* can provide.

Choices of material, whether plant fibres—papyrus, hemp, tree barks especially—animal hair and skin, or mineral clays and terracottas, invariably arise from already well-established manufacturing technologies. As for inks, soot-based black has been the surprisingly universal starting point the world over, for its easy availability, intensity of colour, and erasability when needed. Mineral-based pigments, whether for colour or durability, have always come second. The exact material manifestation of the book thus depends on a balance of different practical and social factors: cost, portability, robustness, durability, reusability, prestige, and sanctity, amongst others. All of these choices have sound economic and cultural bases, and the paper codex has been but one possible outcome.

Equally striking, however, are the social values that ancient and pre-modern cultures worldwide have ascribed to books and their users. Every literate society considered in this chapter supported a class of professional scribes who were not obviously economically productive: they made neither food nor shelter nor goods to trade, and protected no lives from disease, enemies, or predators. Yet all of these communities saw the value in books and the bookish for managing assets and debts, preserving knowledge and culture, communicating with the divine and the spiritual, and creating imaginative worlds far beyond the everyday. Books serve universally to transport community memory through time and space and have done so reasonably effectively in a multiplicity of physical forms for over 5,000 years.

3

Byzantium

Barbara Crostini

The image of Byzantium is largely associated with the production of sophisticated religious art, typically featuring shining gold backgrounds and hieratic figures. In this respect, manuscripts are the next most representative creations after the better-known mosaics of Byzantine churches in Constantinople, Greece, and Ravenna. To look at the history of the evolution of the book in the Roman East is to retrace the mentality behind the luxury products of the Middle Byzantine period, which, in their characteristic appearance, embodied Christian belief in word and image.

This chapter concerns the centuries after the introduction of this new religion and retraces its book culture from its beginning in Roman culture of the late first and second centuries CE to its affirmation during and after the age of Constantine the Great, the eponymous founder in 324 CE of Constantinople, the capital of the East Roman empire. The history of Byzantium, a self-conscious continuation of the Roman empire, ends with the fall of that empire in 1453, when Constantinople itself surrendered to the Turkish advance and finally capitulated.

The struggle with Islam and its secular polity marked the history of Byzantium for the best part of these centuries. Areas of attrition were largely confined to the peripheries of its vast territory, both Eastern (Egypt, Palestine, and Syria) and Western (southern Italy). Through proximity and exchanges, Arab culture and religion exerted a particular fascination. It served both as a model and as a foil for Byzantine rulers. The manner of expressing a cult of the divine by non-figural decoration, for example, appealed to the Byzantine emperors of the eighth and ninth centuries who supported an iconoclast policy, apparently causing the removal and destruction of Christian iconography from churches and other public places. The theory and practice of Christian worship came to be defined by iconoclasm. After that crisis, however, Byzantium's figural identity attracted converts to Christianity in a vast area extending to the Slavic countries and Russia to the north, and Coptic Egypt and Ethiopia to the south. Byzantium's authoritative paradigm was felt not only in monumental artistic creations, but also at the level of book production through the imitation of styles of script and ornamentation.

The Latin West might have acted in alliance with Byzantium against Islamic advance, but linguistic and theological differences, as well as territorial and economic competition around the Mediterranean, undermined attempts at a unified opposition. The popes of Rome were strong supporters of the faction advocating the cult of icons during the Iconoclast controversy, and maintained relationships with key Byzantine players, such as the monastic leader St Theodore of Stoudios (d. 826). That both Greek and Latin handwriting underwent at the same time a parallel transition from majuscule to minuscule is remarkable, and both causes and implications of this phenomenon are still open for further investigation. Books were a means for expressing Christian identity across different cultures. Thus, a characteristic appearance in page layout, presentation of texts, style of ornaments, and the shape of the scripts themselves found evident echoes across book production from different regions of the Byzantine world and its larger sphere of influence. For example, copies of the Gospels were ornamented with full-page author portraits of the Evangelists in Greek, Armenian, Georgian, Syriac, and Slavonic traditions. Such staple elements of book production created a common cultural sphere, broadly coinciding with the current areas of Christian Orthodoxy. What differences remained marked geographical and linguistic divides at the level of detail and style.

The Changing Shape of the Book

Scholars have wondered why the long-established book format of antiquity, the papyrus roll, did not remain uncontested in the centuries leading up to the Middle Ages. Instead, the codex format prevailed, even down to modern paperbacks. Use of papyrus originated in the sophisticated scribal culture of the Egyptians, and its raw materials stemmed from reed-plants along the Nile. The transition to the codex, first made of papyrus and then, as described in Chapter 2, above, derived from animal skins, represented an evolution in the readability and durability of the written product.

Today, the history of the transformation in the appearance of the written page and in material aspects of text carriers attracts special interest as we go through a comparable revolution in how words are presented to readers. Then, like now, questions can be posed as to whether technological innovations should be considered more the product or the promoters of cultural transformations. What are the most significant aspects of this change: practical and functional improvements, such as cost-effectiveness, longer life, easier access to texts, the symbolic value of particular forms, or, finally, the simple inevitability of transformation? We might also ask quite how, where, when, and by whom changes to 'the book', at first presented as alternatives, became the dominant or exclusive format for the transmission of written culture. Scholars have been at pains to stress the gradual nature of this process and to identify several among the concomitant causes behind the phenomenon of transition from roll to codex. An awareness of past transformations and their interpretative history sheds light on our own virtual revolution and on the anxieties that go with it.

The greatest anxiety of all is long-lastingness. Texts are written down precisely in order to endure, yet such ambition, inbuilt in the writing process, is far from guaranteed. Questions of preservation, resilience, and future availability are thus at the heart of any concept of written culture, but despite technological advances offering more lasting forms of written records, chance survivals of ephemera, like unplanned time-capsules, confuse attempts at determining cultural transmission and selecting the legacy to be passed on. One need only think of the heaps of scraps of papyrus and parchment that emerged from excavating the rubbish-dumps of Egypt and Syria, the 'Genizahs'. These designated areas for discarding written materials turn out to be effective places for book storage. Such deposits, including those found in the secluded building (Qubbah) in the courtyard of the Mosque in Damascus, have yielded unexpected information about the cultural components to past civilizations and the close coexistence of different languages, scripts, and religious communities. The accidental survivals from documents meant to be occasional, written for an immediate purpose, and often on recycled supports, can be numbered among some of our most precious sources.

A different matter is that of the lucky escape of the whole collection of philosophical papyri at Herculaneum, where, as noted in the previous chapter, the eruption of Vesuvius in 79 CE had sealed them for centuries. Charred by the volcanic ash, these papyrus scrolls were miraculously still sufficiently preserved for letters to be made out and for new texts to come to light under the patient scrutiny of scholars in the twentieth century. However, before safe techniques for unrolling and photographing these fragile and damaged materials were developed, the eagerness of prying into their secrets sadly led to further, more recent damage. The library of Herculaneum, prevented by *force majeure* from its intended mission of passing on wisdom for generations, unexpectedly resumed its role after a gap of nearly 2,000 years. Contrast the complete disappearance of the most splendid library of antiquity, the Museum at Alexandria. Amid contradictory accounts of its destruction, the library slips off the historical record, together with all its thousands of learned papyrus scrolls. Whether its contents were lost in a sudden cataclysm or dispersed gradually to prevent them sinking into the slowly advancing sea-line, only indirect narratives tell of this treasury of scholarship. Its cultural impact, however, appears indelible, the trauma of its loss replaced by strenuous, repeated attempts at surmising the causes for such loss and the contents of what might have been there. The myth of the Alexandrian Library has proved much more powerful and enduring than its reality. What might seem like a modern psychological search for stability and endurance clearly also underpinned the production of written records in ancient times.

The comparative resilience of parchment largely explains its supplanting of papyrus, but economic concerns and the plant's diminished availability were further considerations in the gradual changeover. The ancients were knowledgeable about different conditions affecting the preservation of books, including local climates. The famous physician, Galen, in a letter entitled 'On avoidance of grief', a text itself newly rediscovered from a single extant fifteenth-century manuscript now in Greece, reviews the hazards that books confront. Galen complains about the unsuitability of papyrus in the marshy area of Rome, claiming that, due to the humid conditions there, 'papyri are completely useless, not even able to be unrolled because they have been glued together by decomposition'. More dramatically, Galen famously describes how a fire that ravaged the city of Rome in 192 CE affected books and their owners:

> ...when his books perished in the fire, Philides the grammarian, wasting away from discouragement and distress, actually died. And for a long time, one after another went out in black garments, thin and pale like mourners. Because they were trusting in the storehouses along the Sacred Way that they would certainly not succumb to fire [...] they were putting trust in them because they did not contain wood— except for the doors—and they were not in the vicinity of any private house, and further, because they were guarded by a military garrison as the district archives of four procurators of Caesar were stored in that place. (Galen, *De indolentia*, 7)

Despite far-reaching preventative measures, Galen continues, destruction by fire struck not just one person or area in the periphery, but the very heart of the city. Fire spread to destroy all libraries on the Palatine, where rare books, 'nowhere else kept', were 'sought out for the accuracy of the text'. These were 'copies of books from many ancient grammarians, [...] also those of rhetoricians, physicians and philosophers'. Galen had wisely taken precautions for some of his own books, which had been copied for him in two exemplars (he had made back-ups). But those books he was writing at the time of the fire, freshly copied in only a single clean version, were lost irremediably. Threats of destruction by fire and concerns about the vulnerability of papyrus in damp conditions tally well with the hypothesis that the use of parchment, eventually combined with the codex form, travelled east from Rome. Against both hazards, fire and water, animal skins proved more resistant and consequently were thought more reliable for the great effort and cost of producing books.

Although Galen's witness belongs to the late second century, appeal is often made to two first-century sources, one Christian and one pagan, attesting to the changing practices in book production. What is probably the earliest passage is found in the New Testament in the second letter of St Paul to Timothy, although neither the date of this work (because of doubts cast on its authorship) nor the exact meaning of the words are agreed upon. Paul asks Timothy to 'bring the cloak (*pheloni*) that I left with Carpus at Troas, also the books (*ta biblia*), and above all the parchments (*malista tas membranas*)' (2 Tim. 4:13). There is much debate over what each of these designated objects might be: is *pheloni* a cloak, or a book cover? Are the *biblia* texts on papyrus, from which the *membranas* are singled out as a sub-category merely because of their different material? Or are 'parchments' chosen for special mention because of the importance of their contents? Another possibility is that the *membranas* should be understood as scribal material, blank notebooks yet to be written, thus bearing no text at all as yet. In any case, why did Paul leave such objects behind? Was it forgetfulness, or transport problems caused by bulk or safety issues? And why did he suddenly need them again? What kind of urgency motivated his epistolary request?

One could imagine that Paul (or the pseudoepigraphical author of this epistle) requested texts for reference (*biblia*) as well as blank parchment exercise books (*membranas*), because, in his new location, he had found the leisure and perhaps also the motivation for composing new works, without having the practical means to do so. Indeed, '*ta biblia*' could designate more specifically the Septuagint written in one tome, perhaps even Paul's own annotated copy, surely necessary as key reference for his writing activity. Alternatively, on the hypothesis that '*membranai*' were portable written booklets, containing preaching notes, they may have been needed to assist the apostle's efforts in spreading the Gospel message. For such an activity, a liturgical (rather than a travelling) cloak might also be appropriate. Despite these terminological uncertainties, the cumulative weight of this passage has lent support to the hypothesis of a connection between the diffusion of the apostle's epistles and the particular format of the parchment booklet. Paul's letter-writing has become strongly identified with the slim, supple pages of portable yet resistant animal-skin gatherings which eventually evolved into full-blown codices. Another interpretative strand identifies Mark's Gospel as the key vehicle for the spreading of the codex format from Rome outwards.

Christian evidence must be balanced with that from a second key source in this debate, the first-century Roman poet Martial. Martial reminds us that codices containing classical texts were also prized for their portability and extolled as economic assets. Nevertheless, the overwhelming number of extant codices is Christian rather than pagan in content. The election of this kind of format for the Christian Bible affirms the involvement of early Christian communities in the spread of this innovative book format. The two revolutions of Late Antiquity, the change from paganism to Christianity and the transition from roll to codex, thus appear closely interrelated.

Whatever the practical or historical reasons that favoured parchment codices over papyrus rolls, by the fourth century codices also came to play a symbolic role. Their materiality was displayed as an evident sign of belonging to a specific culture and religion. In fact, Christian aversion to the ancient practice of writing rolls, whether made of papyrus or parchment, can be interpreted as another sign helping to define the new community against a dominant pagan culture. New community identities were forged from the rejection of established ways of preserving and transmitting texts. This aspect of Christianity's destabilizing force related less to the lower-class origins of its adepts than to the sharp intellectual critique of the rhetoric and philosophy of pagan culture voiced by high-born converts. By contrast, the syntactically simpler and stylistically more direct language of Scriptures emphasized the potential for every human being to attain wisdom and salvation. The more broadly egalitarian attitude of Christians to culture suited booklets made of gatherings that were considered a modest form of literature. Superior to wax or wooden tablets, a set of parchment sheets could be folded and tied together, resulting in a form of proto-codex. The adoption of such booklets in Pauline circles, therefore, as we saw above, not only reflected practical necessity, but also contrasted Christian identity to pre-existent cultures. A distancing from paganism entailed both the rejection and selective assimilation of the writing practices of classical antiquity while Christianity developed its own rhetorical tradition through the writings of the Church Fathers.

An even greater complexity of absorbed and modified practices was operative in the interaction with Judaism. The Jewish community set a standard for religious scriptures that required close scrutiny, especially after the definitive adoption of the Old Testament as an integral part of the Christian canon. Jewish preferences for parchment, exemplified by the booklets discovered at Qumran containing commentary on the

Hebrew Scriptures, suggest cultural continuity in the choice of such materials and formats. Conversely, overt contrast to the Jewish Torah roll may have marked the physical shape of the Christian Bible codex. When, in the fourth century, the Codex Sinaiticus was copied, it stood as an impressive achievement: a pandect of Christian Scriptures, including both Old and New Testaments, manifesting durability, elegance, and authority as an already mature and self-conscious expression of Christian identity.

The Christian Codex

It cannot be a coincidence that the testimony of these extraordinary codices dates from the emergence of Christianity as the official religion under Constantine the Great (after 313). This is not to say that this copy, the Sinaiticus, or any other of the extant early biblical codices, such as the Codex Alexandrinus or Codex Vaticanus, were directly related to Constantine's declared determination to furnish Constantinopolitan churches with bibles, however attractive this hypothesis may be. These early manuscripts reveal their makers' and readers' reverence for the word of God and eagerness for textual study. Large codices were neither especially portable nor yet liturgically framed, because they lacked calendrical apparatuses. Their bulky size and their many parchment folios made them heavy objects. The Biblical Majuscule script employed to write them was certainly both aesthetically pleasing and clear to read, but conventions of word separation and textual transitions were not yet fully developed. Just as our attempts to create digital books have begun with putting a book-page on a screen, so the division of text into narrow parallel columns was not so different from the layout in papyrus rolls. The innovative possibilities of the *mise-en-page* offered by the codex format had yet to be fully exploited. Entirely lacking in figural decoration, these early pandects possess a visual dignity enhanced for us by the mystery of their antiquity. These ponderous books were no longer the agile transmitters of new ideas, as the slender gatherings of Martial and of Paul had once been. Instead, such paradigmatic volumes were emblems of God's presence when displayed at the very centre of a sacred space. They physically embodied a canonical, normative status of the texts within.

Despite these developments, scrolls and rolls continued to be produced in a variety of materials during the Middle Ages, with different techniques of bookmaking simultaneously available. A choice of format was still possible for specific requirements. One striking example is the tenth-century Joshua Roll (Vatican Library, Pal. gr. 431), presenting the biblical narrative of Joshua as a selection of images with extensive captions adapted from the Septuagint text, stretched along a 10-metre parchment roll. Historians have accounted for this unusual format, by that stage, by suggesting that its antiquarian flavour was consonant with the nostalgic enterprises at the court of Emperor Constantine VII Porphyrogenitus (r. 913–59 CE). Constantine inventoried the past in encyclopaedic collections that shaped the identity of his dynasty according to Roman ideals. In such imitative spirit, the Joshua Roll has been considered the medieval facsimile of an ancient roll. In some fundamental sense, the act of copying by exact imitation was the very business of manuscript transmission. Transcribing—carrying over a text from model to apograph, and reproducing at once contents, style of script, and page layout—are essential elements of every single book creation. This attitude, nevertheless, is entirely alien to the modern concept of facsimile, predicated on obsessive accuracy of reproduction, down to faults, with the precise aim of creating a fake. Rather, each medieval copy was approached and regarded as a singular creation. The unusual format of the Joshua Roll at a time when the codex was the established form of the book in a Christian society suggests that its design performed a special function. Given that the Jews were ritually copying the Pentateuch as a parchment roll, the Roll's creators might have adopted this specific format to reach out and promote communication through a common Old Testament narrative. Perhaps even the material making of the Roll required resorting to Jewish ateliers specializing in the confection of parchment rolls, just as later in the Renaissance, experienced Christian painters were enlisted to illustrate illuminated Hebrew Bibles.

Designing the Page: Text Meets Image

The modest variation in shapes and sizes that followed the adoption of the codex format contrasts with numerous experiments and transformations made within its covers. The dimensions of the Greek codex never reached the giant proportions of the Latin 'Atlantic' bibles. The Greek codex stabilized around the quarto format, probably to match the average size of the original animal skins that constituted its structure. Cut to the desired measure, each sheet of prepared parchment was folded in the middle as a bifolium. Each bifolium was layered over a set of similarly sized rectangles of parchment before being sewn together in a gathering. The staple number of bifolia in Greek manuscripts is four, forming a quaternion, a quire of eight leaves. Greek numbers, represented by letters of the Greek alphabet, were sometimes written on the first recto and/or on the last verso of each quire to mark the sequence in which these gatherings, once written, were to be assembled in the codex. This type of quire signatures was used throughout the Middle Ages. Catchwords (words placed at the foot of a handwritten or printed page to assist those assembling the gatherings by anticipating the first words of the following page) were introduced in Greek manuscripts only in the Renaissance. Ruling was applied to individual gatherings according to specific grid-patterns and systems, which can be reconstructed by detecting the impression of the grooves left by the hard point that applied the ruling onto the parchment sheets. The depth of the impression can reveal whether the process was repeated for each sheet or whether one impression was used as ruling for a group of sheets following it. The depth and angle of the furrow can also indicate in which direction the ruling was applied, whether from the verso to the recto or vice versa. French scholars have worked towards a codification of the ruling types and systems, setting protocols for their respective description. Attempts at classification through standardized descriptions were meant to assist the search for provenance and mark significant relations between codices. Results have been disappointing, however. The immense variety of ruling practices defies attempts at systematization. Codicological parameters used to reconstruct provenance and trace production from specific copying centres have thus largely proved unsatisfactory because similar techniques were distributed across widely different locations. Nevertheless, such accumulated data remains part of modern cataloguing standards, and might in the long run yield more significant statistical results.

Better progress has been achieved in the description and classification of Greek scripts. The largely bipartite division between book hands and documentary hands used by papyrologists underpins the growing discipline of Greek palaeography. The latter is a relatively recent branch of philological studies, arising from the need to date and contextualize the physical carriers of a text and retrace the historical details of its transmission. Greek palaeography also imparts skills necessary for reading any text correctly from its ancient handwriting, a task often complicated by the use of abbreviations in manuscripts. The large variety of Byzantine writing styles and their place within particular categories of book scripts have generated sophisticated attempts at retracing coherent patterns of evolution. By detecting influences and cross-fertilizations between styles, we might yet improve our dating and localizing of manuscripts lacking colophons and bearing no other indication of the time and place of copy.

From the fourth to the early ninth century, different styles of majuscule script dominated the page. The Biblical Majuscule, already noted as characteristic of the early pandects, or complete bibles, epitomized hieratic regularity. It is generally regarded as the finest achievement in majuscule writing. Other types of majuscule, such as the Alexandrian and the Epigraphic, survived longer when adopted for titles and liturgical rubrics written as running headers in the margins. The striking style of the ogival majuscule, whether elongated or slanting, gave a more dynamic imprint to the page by the chiaroscuro effects of the pen tracing letters such as mu or omega and alternating thick and thin strokes. It is often compared with the letter shapes adopted by the Cyrillic alphabet, which appear inspired by it. A striking example of this script is the famous manuscript of the *Sacra Parallela* of John Damascene, now in Paris (Parisinus graecus 923). This manuscript is written in two columns and structured by its gold subtitles and annexed marginal author portraits and scenes into sections connected through an index. Although its place of origin is still debated, the orange frames that outline the headpieces are typical of the ink colours found in manuscripts from Palestine. This manuscript exemplifies in its contents the medieval genre of florilegia assembling extracts from earlier works, adapted or partly rewritten to fit the new plan conceived by the compiler.

Commentaries to the Bible known as 'catenae' were also structured as a form of compilation from different patristic authorities. These extracts were juxtaposed less to achieve strict coherence of interpretation than to transmit a variety of possible readings and a wisdom accumulated from the reading notes of past generations. In these cases, the glosses or explanations were arranged on the page in different ways. Some glosses alternated with the main text, offset in a different ink colour or script type. Some manuscripts placed the catenae in the margins, each connected to its lemma by symbolic *signes de renvoi* effectively working as modern footnote references. Other glosses were carefully placed next to the related verse, forming elaborately devised frames of writing around the lines of the principal text. At times, brief interlinear explanations were combined with more extensive marginal commentaries. Such dispositions made novel use of the blank space offered by the margins on the page of a codex, which was accordingly ruled to delimit the written portion. Justification of the edges marked a special compartment for the glosses. Some glosses were even written to form ornamental shapes through the arrangement of their letters. Examples include the columns and birds of the tenth-century multi-volume Niketas Bible, from which three volumes survive (Florence, Laurent. gr. Plut. 5.9, Copenhagen, Royal Library, GKS 6 and Turin, National Library, B. I. 2). Such *marginalia decorata* took their inspiration from the classical *carmina figurata*, in which the content of a poem was made visible through the figurative arrangement of its lines.

Similarly, commentaries could be placed in the margins in the form of images. The *Sacra Parallela* intensively uses the margins of the page as a space for visual commentary, including both narrative images and author portraits. The attribution of this florilegium to John of Damascus, the famous defender of icons from a bilingual Syriac-Greek-speaking area, is significant in relation to this book's presentation. Although its actual place of origin is unknown, its *mise-en-page* suggests a transition between the great majuscule pandects and manuscripts with appended visual commentary in the margins. It places itself deliberately in the tradition of sixth-century illuminated books, in particular the Syriac Rabbula Gospels. The elaborate decorative schemes in the margins of psalters, from the ninth-century Chludov to the eleventh-century Theodore and Barberini Psalters, were carefully planned both in relation to the manuscript's texts, including captions, biblical content, and patristic allusions, and with reference to contemporary events. In the ninth century, such visual programmes

Barbara Crostini

opposed iconoclastic trends explicitly by including images that criticized such policies, but also implicitly by the multiplication of images and their subtle use as visual commentaries on the text. Moreover, illustrated manuscripts affirmed the cult of saints through portraits of holy men and women both in liturgical books and on the margins of biblical and patristic texts. In the eleventh century, images served to highlight controversial issues of the time, as demonstrated by recent work on an elaborate illuminated psalter with *ad hoc* patristic commentary and over 200 illustrations (Vaticanus graecus 752). The images in this psalter seemingly picked up on discussions and debates about the definition of the Eucharist and Roman Primacy. This significant and largely still enigmatic production exhibits the degree of spiritual and intellectual, as well as monetary, investment in the making of a codex. It presents a number of otherwise unknown iconographies devised to match the patristic commentary set in parallel columns with the biblical text. Thus, a study of each of these illuminated manuscripts offers privileged points of entry into Byzantine theology and politics. An understanding of their making recovers a glimpse of the world that produced them which may be more direct than that pro-jected by sources written with a particular agenda in mind—but both texts and images require the right key to decode them.

Images in manuscripts had long performed a range of functions beyond that of enhancing market value together with the aesthetic appreciation of a book. Many full-page illuminations were also intended to function as meditational aids for the reader. In the Rabbula Gospels (Florence, Laurent. gr. Plut. I, 56), the Virgin Mary is shown standing with baby Jesus in her arms under an ornate canopy with sparing but effective use of gold. The Sinai Lectionary (Sinait. gr. 402) includes an impressive full-page standing Christ with his intense look and blue, enveloping mantle set against a full gold background. Like icons, these illuminated pages offered a glimpse of otherworldliness to the reader of the book and inspired personal prayer. Joined with the sacred text, such holy portraits were held close to the reader's gaze, as a painting on a wall could not be. Small-format psalters were specifically designed as personal prayer books, with devotional texts added to the biblical psalms. The didactic function of images as exegesis is particularly evident in the sixth-century Codex Purpureus Rossanensis, now in the Cathedral

Treasury at Rossano in Calabria (southern Italy). The structure of the codex's illustrations not only underscores standard typological exegesis, but further extends the meaning of the text by specific visual details. Passages from the Old Testament written on scrolls held by the respective authors, the Prophets, are set in parallel with corresponding scenes from the New Testament. As in the *Sacra Parallela*, portraits visually mark authorship, drawing attention to themselves and inviting special consideration for this connection in the reader. The specific disposition of each text in separate frames on distinctive backgrounds exploits knowledge about the workings of spatial memory and is configured so as to be more easily recalled by a reader trained in such mnemonic techniques.

The Minuscule Codex

From the ninth century onwards, the minuscule script came to replace the majuscule in codices in order to combine texts and commentaries more elaborately, fit more text within shorter books, and lower production costs. Because a relic of majuscule script lingered on in liturgical books, this virtuoso script took its name from its restricted function and is called Liturgical Majuscule. Its ornamental qualities conferred to the sacred words of the liturgy a character of static, immutable display, together with a sumptuous and exceptional allure. By contrast, the ordinary business of writing, and the increased demands for reading materials, made both East and West practically simultaneously move over to a different, though not unprecedented, writing technique. Minuscule letters were not only smaller, but were also joined together by ligatures that made the act of writing faster, as the scribe had no need to lift the pen from the page. Pens became more flexible, with quills taken from animal feathers. Hands holding such supple pens glided smoothly along ruled lines from which the single letters hung in neat rows. The earliest minuscule scripts, practised at the monastery of St John Stoudios in Constantinople, exhibit a squarish module and are pendant from the line. Documents from this monastery suggest that scribal activity was strictly regulated within the monastic observance. Punishments are listed for scribes who made mistakes in their copying, as well as for monks who were late in returning their books to the library, thus pointing to a self-serving industry and market within the same community. Among the rare, certain evidence for clusters of books copied at the same monastery, the monastery of St John Stoudios at Constantinople stands out, although even in this case the actual range of its local production is disputed beyond the earliest surviving manuscripts. Nonetheless, and however meagre the evidence from other foundations, books clearly played a key role in monastic life, from basic education and literacy to communal readings and liturgy, suggesting localized copying by monastic scribes besides city-located ateliers, probably based in the capital. Among the documented monastic production from Constantinople, the Evergetis monastery, for example, founded by the monk Paul in 1045, produced a number of books signed by its monks that also display homogeneous codicological features.

Besides monastic production, high ecclesiastics of the ninth and tenth centuries formed erudite circles reading and researching ancient texts. Most notably, the Patriarch of Constantinople, Photius (d. *c*.893), in his long and troubled career, produced not only theological treatises, but also a famous compilation known as the *Bibliotheca* or *Myriobiblos*. By summarizing a book from antiquity in each of its 280 chapters, initially for the benefit of his immediate audience, Photius preserves the memory of many ancient works otherwise lost. Stratigraphic study of the only surviving manuscript of this work, now in Venice (Marc. gr. 540), has shown that Photius' notes, assembled initially into booklets, were combined together in this copy from two different models. Detailed reconstruction of the work of its several scribes—six or seven different hands—was combined with codicological analysis of the quires from which the manuscript is composed, showing that the *Bibliotheca* results from the joining of two main parts, assembled for the first time in this form in this codex. Following in his teacher's footsteps, Arethas, bishop of Caesarea (d. *c*.932), also pursued a broad spectrum of interests, with special attention to classical authors. He collected and annotated in his own hand copious manuscripts. Some of these he marked with an ex-libris comprising his name and at times even the place and cost of the acquisition. Other manuscripts are associated with Arethas through the identification of his distinctive hand in the marginal annotations. Arethas also commissioned the copying of texts from a set of scribes, acting as the designer or 'concepteur' and supervising the organization of the books copied for him. As a group, the manuscripts of Arethas exhibit both angular and more flowing minuscule. Some demonstrate rare elegance, with pointy strokes of verticals and obliques jutting out on especially white parchment like small arrows. In other places, dainty heart-shaped leaves elegantly mark initials and line endings. These carefully prepared codices summon up the atmosphere of coteries of learned men intent on enjoying and preserving the classical heritage.

Wide margins, thin parchment, and letters carefully and sparingly written on the page characterize the tenth-century deluxe codices in *bouletée* script. This special canon of writing was defined by the presence of dots (or *boules*) at the end of the letter strokes, conferring to the page a *recherché* appearance often enhanced by gold ink for ornament, titles and initials, and at times even for the text itself. A gorgeous example is the early eleventh-century luxury copy of the Homilies of Gregory of Nazianzus in the Vatican Library (Urb. gr. 15), written almost entirely in gold ink. The ostentatious disregard for economy makes manuscripts written in *bouletée* script look like display pieces with a few lines of text set on the empty page and without any apparent functional concern. By contrast, the need for a more reader-friendly approach in minuscule manuscripts, where the page is packed with denser lines of text, encouraged the development of markers for textual transitions, such as ornamental dividers and enlarged and coloured initials. Such divisions in the *mise-en-page*, subdividing the flow of text and marking its boundaries, were especially useful for compilations of shorter texts, such as collections of homilies or lives of saints. The public performance of these texts, read aloud in churches and monasteries often under inadequate lighting conditions, required these books to be especially legible. Thus, the medieval codex was made distinctive by the style of its dividers, whether rectangular bands or three-sided frames to a 'door' (*pyle* in Greek), typically ornamented by palmette motifs and acanthus leaves in enamel-like colours. The style of initials contributes to both function and character, freely combining cleverly intertwined shapes to creatively interpret the outlines of letters. Initials are constituted of a basic morphology augmented with zoomorphic (dogs, birds, and snakes featuring prominently), phytomorphic (acanthus scrolls and various flowers and leaves), or anthropomorphic (sacred figures or jesters) elements. These distinctive features help in some cases to discern provenance, although oversimplified theories associating specific motifs, such as the fish, or the blessing hand, or even the more distinctive griffins, with specific provincial areas (such as southern Italy or Palestine) have proved less reliable than at first hoped. Clearly, ornamental motifs and styles were widespread and easily a source of mutual influence. The provenance of manuscripts should now be attributed only on the basis of the convergence of multiple factors from the codicological, palaeographical, and art-historical assessment, rather than on a single striking element.

In the eleventh century, a medium-sized legible minuscule of round, regular module became the dominant writing style in Byzantium. It was named *Perlschrift* by scholars because of its similarity with a string of regular-sized pearls extended along the line of writing. Manuscripts executed for Emperor Basil II (r. 967–1025) around the turn of the millennium, notably a psalter (Venice, Marc. gr. Z 17) and the so-called *Menologion* (Vat. gr. 1613), are prime examples of this script at the apex of its realization. Both may have acted as influential models for its widespread adoption. The uniform appearance of the *Perlschrift* and its continued use through the whole of the eleventh century makes the identification of individual hands problematic. Scribes were formally trained in the writing of this canon. Only towards the second half of the century, cursive variants of the *Perlschrift* trickle in, striking a more characteristic note. A faster ductus encouraged the adoption of more inventive letter shapes, ligatures, and inclusions, making room for individual idiosyncrasies. An ongoing phenomenon was also the gradual re-introduction of majuscule letters juxtaposed with minuscule ones. The resulting mixed style was also more prone to individual adjustments, as specific letters could become distinctive features of a hand. These 'scholarly hands' probably belonged to erudites or professionals from the imperial chancery. Such highly learned scribes could break out of the more regular patterns imposed by the prevalent canon of calligraphy, transforming it through individual quirks. By the beginning of the twelfth century, the *Perlschrift* had relaxed into a larger-sized module and had transmuted into a dancing script, all the while retaining its clarity. At the same time, ornamental bands accompanying it left behind the green, blue, and gold palmettes in favour of geometrical (at times compass-drawn) and vegetable motifs outlined in red ink with a paper-cut technique, so that the plain underlying parchment produces the ornamented pattern by means of a see-through effect. Both types of ornamentation were used simultaneously, but the rows of palmette flowers, set in geometrical frames and highlighted in bright colours reminiscent of mosaic or enamel work, remained the hallmark of Byzantine manuscripts. As a result, these distinctive rows of flowers returned in the ornamental vocabulary of manuscripts in the Palaiologan Renaissance of the fourteenth century, when the glory of past empire was intentionally evoked through such imitations.

These developments all occurred within the area of Constantinople; in provincial regions there were more differences. Despite the attraction of the peripheries to the capital and a wish to emulate the capital's sophistication, provincial book production developed in separate ways. A well-studied but far from unproblematic region is that of southern Italy, where Greek-speaking monastic communities continued to flourish in the Middle Ages. This continuity occurred despite the change to Norman and therefore Latin-speaking domination in the region by the twelfth century. Calabria, the Otranto area in Puglia, and Sicily maintained a sustained production of Greek manuscripts with a didactic aim, blending theological and patristic materials with classical authors. Powerful monasteries, such as that of St Saviour *in Lingua Phari* near Messina, and the monastery of Patír near Rossano, were responsible for importing books from Constantinople as models for generating their own production. Celebrated exponents of southern Italian monastic culture include St Nilus, born in Rossano, who, together with some companions, copied manuscripts in distinctive styles of script, small and angular, with intricate interlaced ornaments in pastel colours harbouring naïf-style human and animal figures. Nilus became the founder of the monastery of Grottaferrata near Rome in 1004, where a large library of Greek manuscripts still exists. Puglia had a mixture of small ecclesiastical colleges and larger monasteries such as that of St Nicholas at Casole, with its learned abbot, Nicholas/Nektarius (fl. 1150). Scholia to Homer's epics, as well as more obscure rhetorical and philosophical manuals, were copied for the benefit of teaching and learned reading circles. Several copies of classical texts have also come down to us in the exuberant 'baroque' scripts and heraldic-style ornaments featuring lions and fantastic beasts from the Otranto region.

In examining the copies of these beautiful thirteenth-century books, it is not easy to distinguish southern Italian work from that of the region facing it across the water—namely, Epirus in Greece. Local culture in both areas was characterized by a fusion of Greek and Latin influences in churches and monasteries, and the regional characteristics of the Eastern area are not clear cut. Thus, the production of Epirus merges with that of Thessaly, which in turn echoes manuscript production on Athos (a chapter in Greek palaeography yet to be fully understood). Palestine stands out in the earlier period due to the use of bright colours such as grass-green and orange in the decoration of headbands and initials. Here, too, the Latin occupation during the Crusades made a visible impact on book production. 'Byzantine style' became a sought-after pictorial language, and yet, in its foreign execution, lost some of its spontaneity, as in the Psalter of Queen Melisende (London, BL, Egerton 1139).

The main change in thirteenth-century book production in Europe came with the introduction of paper, at first Eastern-made bombycin or primitive Italian paper, and then the more familiar watermarked paper produced mainly in Italy and Spain and exported all around the Mediterranean. Economic considerations were paramount in this transition, while the survival of books was guaranteed less by the durability of the material than by the creation and distribution of multiple copies, lessening the chances of a text perishing in a single destructive episode. Although the mass-produced pecia manuscripts that were the product of Western universities did not have a precise counterpart in the Greek East, the intensive production of some humanist scribes, such as Andreas Darmarios and his collaborators, cashed in on the demands of scholars across Europe by producing sought-after classical and Byzantine texts in large quantities. The early Oriental paper of many Constantinopolitan codices, sometimes made in larger formats, has a brittle quality that often needed repairs by restorers already in medieval times. The sturdier Western papers can be dated by watermarks that were at times clearly associated with the place of production. These designs, impressed by wire mesh applied to the paper pulp during the drying process, can be detected quite clearly by applying a special sheet of cold light behind the page. Inventories of watermarks can then be used to identify patterns. These repertoires are far from complete, but they usually yield comparable models and approximate dates for the paper—although this date is only vaguely indicative of the chronology for the writing and circulation of the text. In the Renaissance, the use of specific types of paper can even be associated with particular scribes. Many of these scribes, usually *emigrés* from Greece, Crete, or Cyprus, were well-known humanist scholars in their own right. Among the most important known names are Theodore of Gaza, Demetrius Chalkondyles, and George of Trebizond. By cross-referencing their interests with the study of the manuscripts they wrote and owned, we can glimpse their work as erudites and teachers.

Finally, a special type of book, the palimpsest, highlights another strength of the parchment codex—namely, its potential for reuse. Although this technique could be applied to any material written with non-carbon-based ink, including papyrus, it was used primarily with parchment for the recycling of the writing material from larger early codices. This process furnished good quality, second-hand writing parchment in situations where animal stocks were scarce or too expensive, or where the manufacturers of parchment were absent or insufficiently skilled. In southern Italy, for example, where new parchment was often of poor quality—thick and yellow—the re-use of earlier books originating from the Eastern provinces of the empire, especially Palestine and Syria, became common practice. Reuse of parchment is also employed by fourteenth-century Constantinopolitan scribes such as George Baiophoros, operating at the Prodromos Petra monastery. In the Codex Gothoburgensis 1, for example, both southern Italian hagiographical texts and very rare passages, such as one from Arrian's *History*, coexist side by side in the underlying script. Such a combination might be explained if part of the reused parchment came from manuscripts that had travelled all the way back to Constantinople from southern Italy.

Prime candidates for reuse were volumes with obsolete contents and the scripts that became gradually less readable because they were no longer actual, such as majuscules. The more pressing need was to produce books with practical usefulness, such as liturgical service books and catechetical and hagiographical collections employed for readings in churches and monastic refectories. In order to produce a palimpsest, the original ink was washed through a blanching procedure, and the parchment sheets, detached from the original binding, were often turned and folded so that the new script (called *scriptio superior* in the resulting book) was usually applied at ninety degrees from the underlying original text (*scriptio inferior*). Such activity, which to modern eyes seems so reckless, has paradoxically preserved rare ancient texts. Besides early copies of biblical texts, some sensational new discoveries have been made recently, notably that of a new comedy by Menander in the Vatican Library, and of Archimedes' treatises in a manuscript rewritten in the thirteenth century, now privately owned. The Walters Art Gallery and Museum in Baltimore has treated the latter like a patient in intensive care for twelve years, and at great cost, in order not only to secure the extraction of Archimedes' exceptional mathematical texts and graphs, but also to prolong the life of this artefact according to the most modern techniques of manuscript conservation. Although palimpsests crucially preserve ancient versions of extant texts and unique evidence of lost ones, scholars are often frustrated by the difficulties of deciphering underlying faded writings. New photographic techniques and digital enhancement of the remaining ink traces have revived the interest in these chance preservations and increased access to the information they contain. One of the most exciting places of discovery has been the library of the monastery of Saint Catherine on Sinai. Equipped with modern technology, the team of experts at this monastery have discovered, among other things, a surprising amount of yet-to-be-identified texts written in a variety of Oriental languages and including Latin, sometimes in very early scripts.

Readers as Learners: Didactic Strategies

Michael McCormick has stressed the itinerant activities of the first users of bound codices made from parchment. He argues that the portability of the book format found a natural application for doctors, teachers, and for the Christian missionary apostolate. This theory depends of course on how portable the books really were: many parchment codices were bulky and heavy. Doctors, teachers, and missionaries were all educators, however, and with them the codex found its most natural application. A codex could be displayed to an audience when placed on a lectern, it could be read aloud from the same position, it could be read collectively (for example, as a choir book), it could be annotated in the margins and leafed through in rapid succession, and it could be pointed to as a reference even when shut. Bookmarks, often as leather insets, could be applied to the relevant text divisions, so that navigating through material for the purposes of explanation, consultation, and reference yielded more benefits than frustrations. The codex supported knowledge.

Besides the scriptural commentaries already mentioned, school-books in the form of schedographies also survive from the Byzantine world. Such exercises entailed commentaries on set texts, with the student elaborating on the text's grammatical and logical structure before going on to paraphrase and explain the contents. Schooling, perhaps carried on in connection with the activity of copying at a monastic centre and library, incorporated not only standard biblical materials, such as the Psalter and the Gospels, but continued use of classical authors. Homer, for example, maintained a central place in the manuscript tradition. The lore of Homeric scholarship was carried through the centuries in the form of scholia copied in the margins. As late as the twelfth century, the bishop of Thessalonike, Eustathius, compiled books of notes on the Homeric poems, ranging from etymo-logical speculation to grammatical points, and always taking for granted his audience's deep and detailed familiarity with Greek mythology.

The importance of teaching placed the book as a repository of received knowledge at the centre of Christian culture. The work of previous generations in interpreting literature had to be taken fully into account and underpin the advance of new notions and ideas. As a result, the florilegium became the preferred compositional method, where the display of ordered previous scholarship on any topic was the key to claiming capacity for further understanding. Durable books available for consultation during, for example, meetings or church councils, were therefore prized as much as the activities of copying, reading, and storing manuscripts in libraries. Some libraries, such as the Patriarchal Library in Constantinople, were clearly treasure houses of rare classical, voluminous, patristic, and sophisticated scrip-tural codices. A Christian teacher such as the eleventh-century phil-osopher Michael Psellos enjoyed extremely wide-ranging interests. Besides offering basic training in grammar and rhetoric to his stu-dents, Psellos developed lectures on all kinds of natural, scientific, and theological topics. Records of Psellos's classes in the form of notes and short treatises, probably as taken down by his listeners, survive in composite manuscripts or miscellanies. Often, the interests of a single scholar and teacher could result in putting together pamphlets concerning one subject from various separate sources, so that the portable booklet containing one text grew by association with other self-standing units into a larger codicological structure. Unpicking the composition of such codices has been the time-consuming task of much recent scholarship, both attempting to detect the rationale of such clusters (not always obvious) and painstakingly identifying each text, with sometimes astonishing results and new finds.

Further research has examined the layout and illustrative apparatus of Western manuscripts as aids in learning and memorization, exposing medieval theories of cognition that can be fruitfully applied to the products of Byzantium also. Specific techniques of visualization, for example, might lie behind the architectural presentation of materials to be learnt by heart, whether as liturgical recitation in monasteries or as instruction in monastic schools. The best example of such visual aids for the memorization of parallel Gospel passages is the elaborate Canon Tables included in the initial pages to many manuscripts. Set between ornamented columns forming an architectural structure like an open portico, each arcade is individually decorated with different colours and patterns. Thus each Gospel acquires an individual, material identity through being assigned such a table. The variation in ornamental details and colours are consonant with memorization techniques as described in rhetorical treatises. The alternation between illuminated initials and ornamental bands performed a similar function of distinction and emphasis. Readers could then learn a text by picturing its physical layout on a particular page and retain knowledge of it by relying heavily on visual and spatial memory.

The epistemological value of images for the expression and teaching of the Christian faith can be further exemplified by the narrative strips of the Paris Gospels (Par. gr. 74) and the Vatican Book of Kings (Vat. gr. 333). Here, the images extend across the breadth of the written line in the manuscript page, creating a one-to-one correspondence and dialogue between image and text. This mode of presentation is also applied in the eleventh century to manuscripts of classical content, such as the beautiful copy of Oppian's *Cynegetica* now in Venice (Marc. gr. Z. 479). Octateuchs (the first eight books of the

Old Testament) packed with illustrations such as Vat. gr. 747 affirm the virtuosity of Byzantine painting skills in books. Each relies on an intricate network of models but also provides new interpretations that make each manuscript a unique creation. Even a copy of the *Chronicle* by Skylitzes, counter to a tradition of sober presentation of historical narratives, received plentiful and for us curiously eloquent illustrations in a twelfth-century manuscript now in Madrid (Vitr. 26-2). The *Chronicle* manuscript is thought to have been copied at the court at Palermo, Sicily, a safe distance from the delicate matters of Byzantine dynastic succession depicted in graphic and tragic detail in its appealing miniatures. It was for this new context, within the court politics of Roger II (1095–1154), that the illustrative progression of the Madrid Skylitzes was devised. The iconographical choices reflect concern for the political legitimacy even of usurpers, while neglecting more standard Greek-Orthodox concerns such as pursuing a more overtly triumphal account of the victory over iconoclasm.

The Luxury Codex

Patronage behind the production of books is normally associated with the highest echelons of the aristocracy, or ecclesiastical hierarchy, often notably with Byzantine emperors themselves. Most of the highest quality manuscripts are ascribed to the imperial capital, Constantinople, though only rarely is this assumption confirmed by sure signs such as imperial portraits and colophons. Undoubtedly, the illuminated copy of the Homilies of John Chrysostom, now in the Bibliothèque nationale de France in Paris (Coislin 79), was made for an emperor, probably Nikephoros Botaneiates, who is depicted in the full-page dedicatory portrait at the beginning of the manuscript. The illumination features the standing figure of John Chrysostom giving this book to the emperor. Recent studies have attributed a few high-quality products to the provinces, as well. Palestine, for example, hosted many well-trained artists who travelled and collaborated in combinations. In particular, the symbiosis between Greek and Georgian culture, in Jerusalem as on Mount Athos, is evidenced by literary exchanges and translation of texts, as well as in the material details of books. Similarly, the Armenian tradition, built on and inspired by Byzantium, developed its own extensive decorative schemes and characteristic ornaments, and prized the illuminated book as a repository of culture and a sign of faith.

The ornate covers of books, figuratively and preciously manifesting on the outside the essence of their sacred content, enabled them to be fitting objects to be displayed and paraded during the liturgy, confirming the status and attractiveness of the codex form for the faithful. Books as objects or icons have been metaphors used to understand the medieval lavishness of book decoration and the thoroughness of detail concerning their making. Like altar vessels used in the celebration of the Eucharist, studded Gospel books were placed on the altar as part of liturgical worship. Although few precious bindings are extant that are still joined to the original volumes, ivory plaques are indicative of the carving skills dedicated to the representation of holy scenes. Endowed with such spiritual manifestos, the material value of such books was translated into spiritual reverence. A powerful symbol of Christian faith, books were offered up to the divinity as part of communal worship.

Bibles were the primary texts to receive such special treatment. Some Late-Antique copies used a procedure for making the parchment even more luxurious by dying it in purple, so that the darkened surface could accommodate the effect of special ink, either gold or silver. Such is the appearance of the rarest codex of all, the Codex Argenteus, the only extant Gothic Bible (now in Uppsala), but the same procedure was used in Greek books such as the Codex Purpureus Rossanensis, as well as the famous Codex Sinopensis (Paris. gr. 1286) and the Codex Caesariensis (New York, Morgan Library & Museum MS M.874), all datable to the sixth century. A series of purpose-made epigrams and full-page dedicatory portraits reveals the identity of the patron, Leo Sakellarios, as well as gives the names of his brother and of an abbot in the early tenth-century codex, Vatican Library, Reginensis gr. 1. It is frustrating that despite all such documented details, neither Leo nor this monastery (perhaps dedicated to the Theotokos whose figure dominates the dedicatory miniature) are known from other sources. As a consequence, the place of production for this outstanding pandect, presenting an unusual sequence of biblical books, remains unspecified. The quality of its images, as well as a philological study of its texts, has led some scholars to consider it a work from the provinces, maybe even related to the Western world. More central is certainly the production of the Niketas Bible, even though its named patron, too, remains a shadowy figure in history. These volumes combine exquisite prefatory illuminations with the care of writing the biblical text and its scholia in ornamented shapes such as columns, programmatically setting out the importance of the Bible to its patron and his entourage.

The exceptional presence of full-page illuminations in psalters had suggested a division between an 'aristocratic' and a 'monastic' production, the latter characterized by smaller marginal illustrations with a more intensely exegetical focus. Although the grounds for upholding such a distinction too neatly are now contested, examples such as the Paris Psalter (Paris. gr. 139), with its imposing classicizing style, speak of a wealthy commission. David is pointedly a symbol for the Byzantine sovereign, and the personified virtues that hover over his actions and the typological resonances exploited by the illustrator are designed to connect the text of the Psalms both to its prophecy of the advent of Christ, and to its function of moral guidance to the noble reader. A few full-page illustrations powerfully synthesize all these concepts. But a very substantial catena commentary also fills the wide margins of this manuscript, in refined *bouletée* script, poised between elegant display and erudition.

Finally, we should consider the many illustrated editions of a classic of Byzantine spirituality, the *Ladder* of John Climax (Climax means Ladder). On its iconic stairway to heaven, angels and devils fight over struggling souls who climb its steps. Among its many repetitions in numerous media and contexts is a twelfth-century copy from Sinai, Sinait. gr. 418. Every headpiece of this manuscript carries a vignette in which monks are seen enacting struggles for virtue in their daily activities of work and prayer. Another manuscript at Sinai, Sinait. gr. 339, containing the homilies of Gregory of Nazianzus, similarly exploits the space within large rectangular headpieces and the narrative potential of figurative initials. Elaborate scenes allude to the setting or to the content of the homily copied below them. These books—and many more could be added—are not only beautiful creations in themselves, but apparently inexhaustible sources of information about the world and mentality of Byzantium.

Barbara Crostini

The Virtual Codex

The vicissitudes of time have scrambled valuable evidence and created a diaspora of Greek manuscripts across Europe and beyond. Yet we can be sure that the original places of manuscript production were spread across a vast region under Byzantine influence. This area included the eastern provinces of Palestine and Syria, western territories such as southern Italy, different regions in Greece, such as Thessaly, Athos, the Peloponnese, and further influence as far as Russia, Armenia, and Georgia. Later, the maritime powers of Venice, Pisa, Genoa, and especially the islands of Cyprus and Crete, all subject to Byzantine influence, also played a significant role in the preservation of Greek culture and its revival through the western European Renaissance. Manuscripts and their trade were the practical vehicles through which the Greek classical past and the fundamental texts of Christianity, including Greek patristics, continued to underpin European culture, entering the teaching of the early universities and the schools of Greek *émigrés* after the fall of Constantinople to the Turks in 1453.

A great part of the contents of the libraries of Constantinople burned in the fire of 1204. It is estimated that many of the treasures in the Byzantine capital simply perished then, but the interest of the Crusaders in the sacred relics for which Byzantium was famous guaranteed a steady trickle of precious objects and manuscripts towards European cathedral treasuries and other noble houses and collections. The consequences of the 1204 destruction were partly offset by the stability of other great repositories, such as the monasteries of Athos, the monastery of St John the Theologian on Patmos, and the library of St Catherine's monastery on Mount Sinai. Nevertheless, recurrent disasters on a smaller scale punctuate the histories of monasteries and other centres of Greek culture. Among the most famous examples are the fire at the Escorial monastery near Madrid in 1672, the burning of the theological library in Smyrna in 1920, and the bombing of Montecassino in 1944. Of course, not even modern libraries provide perfectly safe environments despite improving standards, and losses continue as a result of decay and poor conservation, besides more spectacular mass destructions in times of war. Nevertheless, cataloguing records are gradually improving in the many

Western libraries that have become home to rescued material and that have benefited from diplomatic gifts and donations from active collectors. At times, entire private collections were subsumed by a public or institutional library, as in the case of the Greek manuscripts from Holkham Hall, given to the British Library and to the Bodleian Library at Oxford in part-payment of death dues. Other times, more modest acquisitions resulting from special circumstances led to the happy retrieval of codices long thought lost. One such was the collection of the Swedish diplomat Johan Gabriel Sparwenfeldt (1655–1727), active in Spain at a time when manuscripts rescued from the Escorial fire entered the book market. Among the largest and most important single deposits of Greek manuscripts are those in the Vatican Library, the Bibliothèque nationale de France in Paris, the British Library in London, the Bodleian Library in Oxford, the Bavarian Library in Munich, the Marcian Library in Venice, the libraries of the monasteries on Mount Athos (despite limitations on access by women), and the State Museum in Moscow. The enterprise of compiling new catalogues according to modern standards of description is still unevenly achieved. More detailed records are being produced as manuscripts are selected for digitization.

Slowly, the digital revolution is coming to the world of Greek manuscripts. Compared with digital study of Greek papyri, the vastly greater quantity of materials offers specific challenges. Nonetheless, hundreds of repositories are following the pioneering digital lead of the Biblioteca Laurenziana in Florence. Many Greek manuscripts in Paris, for example, are now fully available from the Gallica portal. The Vatican Library is also taking giant leaps in placing its collections online. Not only are fully digitized codices consultable from home at any time, but they are available in high-quality specification in colour, opening a new era for detailed palaeographical and art-historical comparative work.

The CNRS Paris-based database of Greek manuscripts, *Pinakes* (https://pinakes. irht.cnrs.fr), is the major reference for Greek manuscripts. It provides key metadata about the contents of the manuscripts, direct links to access the digitalized materials, and information required for further contextualization. The Pinakes Project is also coordinating links between the various sites of manuscript collection and preservation around the world. The tools that this revolution offers, even if still underexploited, are truly exciting: the comparison between two manuscripts on a screen is virtually equivalent to placing two codices now scattered around the globe on the same desk. By doing so, we can see whether objects now separated by geography bear traces that suggest common origins, an earlier housing in the same monastery, or creation by the same scribal hand. By itself, a virtual reproduction cannot tell everything about an ancient manuscript, but it is the best home-based, first-hand experience of these wonderful books. Instead of lamenting further losses, future generations of scholars capable of reading Greek manuscripts and learned in the cultures of Byzantium will enjoy the privilege of reconnecting the historical diaspora of all extant Greek manuscripts into a more coherent picture.

4

Medieval and Early Modern East Asia

Cynthia Brokaw

East Asia has contributed an impressive variety of technologies to global book culture. As in the rest of the world, manuscript-or hand-copying was the earliest method of text production and reproduction. China, Korea, and Japan, even as printing flourished, maintained a highly valued tradition of manuscript publication at least through the early modern era. But, between the seventh and thirteenth centuries, they also invented several print technologies: xylography, or woodblock printing, and earthenware, wooden, and metal move-able type.

Xylography first supported an efflorescence of publishing in medi-eval China, and by the early modern period printing had unquestion-ably become the major form of book production. As China was the leading cultural power in pre-modern East Asia, Chinese publishing and book culture had a profound influence on the book histories of Korea and Japan (and to some extent Vietnam, as well). Woodblock printing, which remained the dominant print technology in the region until modern times, was in origin a Chinese invention. Both Korea and Japan early embraced classical Chinese as the language of gov-ernance and high culture; the Chinese Classics—that is, the discrete body of ancient texts ultimately embraced by Confucians as founts of ethical and political wisdom; and Chinese literary works as models for writing. Thus, East Asia enjoyed, from an early period, a relatively unified language of textual production. Classical Chinese was the *lingua franca*; Chinese texts formed the core of medieval East Asian book culture.

But of course there were differences. Although the major units of East Asian publishing—the government, religious institutions, private individuals or families, and commercial publishers—were the same in each country, the relative importance of these units to the Chinese, Korean, and Japanese book worlds varied considerably. The governments of China and Korea, for example, heavily shaped their respective book cultures, by both sponsoring and censoring text production. But Japanese governments seem to have been largely indifferent to the political uses and implications of print.

And times changed: by the early modern period, Korea and especially Japan had developed vernacular literary cultures largely independent of—and often resistant to—the Chinese textual tradition. Although texts in Chinese continued to be published in both countries, they played an increasingly subordinate role in the newly distinctive Korean and Japanese book cultures of the seventeenth, eighteenth, and early nineteenth centuries.

Technological Innovation and a Shared Book Culture in Medieval East Asia

In seventh-century China, religious institutions—Buddhist and then Daoist—were the first to recognize the potential of woodblock printing for widespread dissemination of texts. The earliest extant printed texts, which were found in Korea and Japan (most likely either printed in China or produced through techniques transmitted from China), are Buddhist incantations (*dharanis*) dating from the eighth century. A magnificent Chinese printed scroll of the *Diamond Sutra (Jingang boruo boluo mijing)* indicates, in the delicacy and precision of both its frontispiece illustration and text, that woodblock printing was already highly advanced by the time of its publication in 868.

By then, family publishers were operating in at least two Chinese cities—Chengdu in the southwest and Luoyang in the north—producing a range of texts for commercial sale: almanacs; dictionaries and rhyme books; works on astrology, dream divination and geomancy; collections of medical prescriptions; biographies of monks; and, above all, sutras and *dharanis*. By the next century, literary anthologies, Confucian Classics, the Daoist canon, encyclopaedias, and works of historical criticism appeared, as well. Kaifeng in the north and Hangzhou in the south emerged, too, as printing centres.

Ironically, it was during a period of political division in the tenth century that a Chinese government recognized the value of printing as a means of disseminating standardized ideologies supportive of state centralization. In 932, Feng Dao (882–954), prime minister of the short-lived Later Tang, recommended the publication of a complete set of the Confucian Classics. Completed twenty-two years later in 130 volumes, this set was the first printed edition of texts that remained, for the next nine and a half centuries, the fundamental expression of Chinese cosmological beliefs and political and ethical values. As such, they eventually became the essential texts of the civil service examination system. Any Chinese male seeking an official position—the most desired status in society—had to have mastered, even memorized, these texts. Their influence on education, government, and society cannot be overstated.

Reunified under the Song dynasty in 960, China entered its first printing boom. Readers gloried in the resulting greater availability of texts. As one official noted:

> When I was young and devoted myself to learning, there were only one or two scholars in every hundred who possessed copies of all the Classics and commentaries. There was no way to copy so many works. Today, printed editions of these works are abundant, and officials and commoners alike have them in their homes. Scholars are fortunate indeed to have been born in such an era as ours.
>
> (Xing Bing, in Li Tao, *Xu Zizhi tongjian changbian.* 2. 60.1333)

Many, however, complained that the easier accessibility of texts cheapened learning (by opening it to lower-status audiences) and degraded the memory training of scholars and officials. At first the government tried to control text output, restricting private publishing and the reproduction of the Classics. The National Academy (Guozijian) was charged with producing correct editions of these texts for the civil service examinations. Local governments were also active publishers, producing histories, gazetteers, literary collections, and practical works on science and medicine, like *Prescriptions Collected by Imperial Benevolence during the Taiping Reign Period* (*Taiping shenghui fang*), published by the Fujian Office of Financial Administration in 1147.

With the relaxation of official restrictions in the twelfth century, private and commercial publishing flourished. Although fifty-one publishing sites have been identified for the Song (960–1279), only a few can be considered major centres: the city of Hangzhou and Jianyang (Fujian); Chengdu (Sichuan); and, in the thirteenth and fourteenth centuries, Pingyang (Shanxi), the only northern site. The most prolific of the Hangzhou shops, the 'bookstall' (*shupeng*) of the Chen family, specialized in the publication of poets of the Tang (618–907) and Song; the shop of the Yin family was noted for its fictional tales and collections of anecdotes. Less productive but more entertaining was the publisher Zhu Gong, who settled in Hangzhou in the early twelfth century in order to 'write books and make wine'; his dual interests in medicine and alcohol were doubtless the inspiration for the two works of his still extant: *Book for Saving Lives* (*Huoren shu*) and *The Classic of Wine* (*Jiujing*).

Jianyang's publishing history spans the eleventh to the seventeenth centuries. With about fifty private or commercial publishers active in the Song and about sixty in the next, Mongol Yuan, dynasty (1279–1368), Jianyang was the largest publishing centre of the medieval period. Publishing operations were based in lineages or lineage branches. The Yu- and Liu-lineage shops produced the best, most carefully collated and edited of Jianben ('[Fu]jian texts') in the Song: editions of the Classics with commentaries, the dynastic histories, literary collections, legal texts, and medical works. Other Jianyang publishers suffered notoriety for churning out examination cribs, collections of examination essays, and editions of the Classics so riddled with mistakes that it became a standing joke that they guaranteed examination failure. Poorly printed on cheap bamboo paper in small and cramped formats, these 'Masha editions' (named after the township in which they were produced) stand in stark contrast to the many fine works published in Jianyang.

Private publishers, temples, and monasteries continued to produce Buddhist texts. In Hangzhou, Jia Guanren ('Official Jia') ran a sutra bookshop that published one of the most beautifully illustrated texts to survive from the Song, *Illustrated Verses by Chan Master Foguo in Praise of the Life of Manjusri* (*Foguo Chanshi Wenshu zhinan tuzan*), as well as an edition of the *Lotus Sutra* (*Miaofa lianhua jing*). Early in the dynasty, two temples in Fuzhou (Fujian)—the Dongchang and the Kaiyuan—each published an edition of the Tripitaka, the Buddhist canon; a third edition, begun in 1132 in Huzhou (Zhejiang), totalled over 5,000 chapters. Such large-scale projects required the skilled management of many scribes and block-cutters, and probably engaged the cooperation of several institutions. Under imperial patronage, the Daoist canon, almost as voluminous as the Tripitaka, was printed for the first time at the Tianning Wanshou Temple in Fuzhou in the early twelfth century.

With the spread of printing and the proliferation of texts, it became easier to build book collections, both imperial and private. Libraries containing both manuscripts and imprints served as official or informal centres for research, encouraging new practices of textual criticism. Textual collation revealed the difficulties of establishing a single authoritative text, enabling reader-editors to assert their authority in choosing between variants and sometimes developing variants of their own. Song scholars edited texts—even the texts of the Classics—creatively, as evidenced in Zhu Xi's (1133–1200) remarkable emendations to *The Greater Learning (Daxue)*.

Aesthetically, the Song is the golden age of Chinese printing. The best Song texts are valued not only for their rarity, but also for their reproduction of the grace and strength of Chinese calligraphy, considered the finest of the Chinese arts.

Manuscripts continued in regular use long after the invention of printing partly because they provided the best opportunities for calligraphic expression. The most ambitious publishers aspired to reproduce this artistry in print; they hired skilled scribes to produce beautiful transcripts of texts and skilled artisans to cut blocks that mimicked the writing as closely as possible. That many Song and Yuan texts list the names of their scribes and cutters indicates the pride they took in their work—although this practice also served as a means of calculating wages.

By the end of the Song, the basic material and visual forms of the Chinese (and East Asian) book were set. The first imprints, imitating manuscripts, were printed paper sheets pasted together and bound as scrolls or in accordion-like folds. Buddhist and Daoist texts often appeared in such bindings, but secular texts began to be bound in codex form, in what was called butterfly binding, with pages fanning out like a butterfly's wings. Each leaf, printed on one side only, was folded in half inward and pasted to the spine of the book along the blank outside fold. A few centuries later, consumers favoured the greater security of thread binding, with the printed leaves folded outward and the free edges sewn together to covers with thread. The resulting fascicles (*ce*) were often enfolded for further protection in a paperboard or wooden case.

Before the twentieth century, Chinese texts were written and printed vertically and right to left. Very often, the columns of characters were separated by lines providing guides for both the scribe and the reader. Two or more registers of text might appear on a page; occasionally multiple 'stacked' texts were printed in one book. Commentary could be printed in the upper margin of a page, in the so-called 'book eyebrow'. Most were interlinear, however, printed in double columns of smaller characters interspersed throughout a text. By the Song dynasty, printing paper was commonly made from bamboo, but might also derive from the bark of mulberry, paper mulberry, or blue sandalwood.

Publishers developed distinctive formats as a means of 'branding' their work: by consistently printing the same number of characters per column and the same number of columns per page and making the margins around the text frame the same size. The upper margin was often widened to accommodate scholars who wished to annotate texts as they read them, however. They also added 'fishtails' (bracket-like markings at the outer edge of the page that often enclosed the book title or chapter number), 'black mouths' (a black column at the upper and/or lower outside edge of a page), and 'ears' (small boxes at the upper right or upper left of a page which sometimes contained a title or chapter number). Such features added visual interest, but also served the convenience of the scribe, cutter, printer, and reader.

Between the eleventh and fourteenth centuries, print technology advanced across East Asia, with many experiments in moveable type. In the eleventh century, Bi Sheng (*c.*990–1051) invented a method of printing with moveable earthenware type. Although it was never widely embraced, the *idea* of moveable type proved a powerful one and, after some early failures, printing with wooden moveable type was successfully used in the late thirteenth century by the magistrate Wang Zhen (d. 1333) to print a local history in about 60,000 characters. But moveable-type printing never became the predominant form. Given the enormous number of fonts required to reproduce thousands of Chinese characters, moveable type was simply not economical. Wooden, and later metal, moveable types were used for texts requiring only a limited number of characters or those funded by wealthy merchants or the government.

Metal moveable type was first developed not in China, but in Korea. As early as the eighth century, Korea benefited from the transfer of woodblock-print technology from China—indeed, the earliest extant printed text in East Asia, the *Spotless Pure Light Dharani Sutra (Mugu jeonggwang dae darani gyeong)*, produced between 704 and 751, was discovered in Korea. As in China, Korean woodblock printing supported the publishing of Buddhist texts, including three versions of the Buddhist Tripitaka produced to enlist the Buddha's assistance against foreign invaders in the eleventh, twelfth, and thirteenth centuries. Over 80,000 blocks from the last of these projects survive today at the Haein Temple.

By the early thirteenth century, artisans at the Korean court were experimenting with metal moveable type. Their first recorded success came in 1377 with the publication of excerpts from Buddhist biographies and histories, the *Monk Baegun's Anthology of Chan Teachings (Baegun hwasang chorok buljo jikji simche yojeol)*. The early rulers of the Joseon (Chosŏn) dynasty (1392–1897) were quick to recognize the value of the technology to governance. As a 1403 edict of King Taejong (r. 1400–18) explained: 'if the country is to be governed well, it is essential that books be read widely [. . .] It is my desire to cast copper type so that we can print as many books as possible and have them made available widely'. Thereafter, the Korean court, the dominant publisher on the peninsula, frequently used metal moveable type, cast with a technique used to make coins. Given Korea's elite reading population and tight government control of printing, most print runs were short, making moveable type an efficient method of production. Tellingly, popular texts in great demand—almanacs, for example—continued to be printed on woodblocks, although manuscript book culture also flourished. As in China, calligraphy remained a highly valued art.

From the early thirteenth century, as elites and rulers used Confucian teachings to strengthen political authority and reinforce social hierarchy, Korea imported and printed Confucian works as well as Buddhist scriptures. But at the same time that the Joseon dynasty was embracing Chinese secular values, one of its most effective rulers, King Sejong (r. 1418–50), developed a phonetic writing system for the Korean vernacular, *hangeul*, that freed readers and writers from the dominance of written Chinese. The twenty-eight symbols of *hangeul* were unveiled in 1446 in *Correct Sounds for the Instruction of the People* (*Hunmin jeongeum*). Repudiated by the elite as a language for the lower orders, *hangeul*, though occasionally employed in rhyme dictionaries, popular Buddhist tracts, and government publications, was not used regularly in printed works until several centuries later, however.

Before the early modern period, book culture in Japan closely resembled the manuscript and woodblock book culture of Korea, with its heavy reliance on Chinese texts and the Chinese language and its engagement with a small number of elite readers. The first books entering Japan were Buddhist and Confucian manuscript scrolls brought from Korea in the fifth century. By the seventh century, the copying of Buddhist sutras had become an organized activity, much of it state-supported through a government sutra scriptorium established in 727 at Nara, the capital. Although printing was known, it was used to produce ritual scripts rather than texts to be read. In 764, the pious Empress Shōtoku (r. 764–70) ordered the insertion of printed Buddhist invocations—a million sheets of them—in miniature pagodas presented to temples around the capital. For several centuries, printing remained a tool of Buddhist ritual, and sutra-copying by hand continued as an important act of devotion. Sutras were often elaborate productions, written on coloured paper in gold or silver ink and including ornamented frontispieces.

Texts meant to be read seriously—that is, political and ethical works, official histories, and government documents in Chinese—were transmitted in manuscript form. Manuscripts in the Japanese written language (combining Chinese characters with a phonetic script) also recorded poetic diaries and anthologies of court poetry. *Monogatari* (prose narratives), popular stories, biographies of famous monks, descriptions of shrines and festivals, and temple histories were reproduced in illustrated scrolls (*emaki*). *The Tale of Genji* (*Genji monogatari*), Murasaki Shikibu's (*c*.973–1014) great narrative of the Heian court, was first produced in this form.

The first evidence that woodblock printing was used to publish texts meant for reading dates to the early eleventh century. The works produced were mostly commentaries on sutras and Buddhist doctrine, and, unsurprisingly, the products of temple and monastery publishing. At first, a single temple in Nara—Kōfukuji, controlled by the powerful Fujiwara family—monopolized printing. Within a century, however, printing spread to other parts of Japan, although Buddhist temples and monasteries continued to be the major centres.

Given the importance of Chinese Confucianism and literary writings to the Japanese elite, it is surprising that such works were not printed until the late fourteenth century, and then only in modest quantities. The *Analects* of Confucius was first published in print in 1364. Over a century later, in 1481, the orthodox commentary on an important Confucian classic, *The Greater Learning*, was printed in Kagoshima, the seat of the Satsuma domain. With little demand for printed texts outside of Buddhist sutras, no full book trade developed. As in Korea, Buddhist institutions played a major role in printing (and in printing secular Chinese as well as Buddhist texts). Unlike Korea, where the central government took the lead in developing new print technologies and sponsoring publication projects, the states of medieval Japan remained largely indifferent to the political uses of print.

The Publishing Boom of Early Modern East Asia

China

After the brilliant flowering of printed book culture in China from the eleventh through the thirteenth centuries, the publication of texts sharply declined in the fourteenth century, a period of brutal civil unrest and rebellion. But in the sixteenth century, during the late Ming dynasty (1368–1644), a burst of new publishing and book-collecting activity, fuelled by rapid population increase, commercial growth, and urban expansion, brought this publishing 'winter' to a close. The demand for books skyrocketed. Book collecting became once again a marker of status. In Ningbo in 1561, a retired official founded the largest and most famous book collection of the early modern period, the Tianyi ge. Wealthy merchants, eager to appear as men of cultivation, quickly developed their own collections.

Commercial publishers soon recognized opportunities for profit. Although the imperial government, particularly that of the Qing dynasty (1644–1911), and private individuals and families remained active publishers, 'printing for profit' dominated the publishing scene. The changed look of books reflected the advance of commercial publishing. Publishers embraced a practice, begun in the late thirteenth century, of printing a 'cover sheet' for each work, listing the title, author(s) and/or editor(s), publishing house, and occasionally the date and summaries of the contents, as an advertisement for the text. Unscrupulous publishers could easily add characters—'new', 'revised', 'expanded', 'illustrated', etc.—to the titles on the cover sheets of works that were in fact *not* new, revised, expanded, or illustrated. A new, more economical calligraphic form was introduced to printing. 'Craftsman's style' (also 'imitation Song style') characters—boxy and rather rigid—lacked the grace and individuality of their Song counterparts, but, as they were easier and faster to cut, they were widely adopted to reduce production costs. Their uniformity also made them easier to read, an extra benefit for publishers hoping to attract as many customers as possible.

In the early stages of the publishing boom, commercial book production was concentrated in just two regions of the empire: the lower Yangzi delta region (and the cities of Nanjing, Hangzhou, and Suzhou), culturally and economically the most advanced region of the empire; and Jianyang, a major publishing centre since the Song. The book collector Hu Yinglin (1551–1602) noted that 'merchants throughout the empire rely on Suzhou and Nanjing for seventy percent of their books and on [Jianyang] for the other thirty percent [...] Putting aside the books these places print, what reaches them from other provinces is extremely little [...] not two or three percent [of all available titles]'. (Hu Yinglin, *Jingji huitong*). The cities of the lower Yangzi delta also functioned, with the capital Beijing, as the major book markets.

The variety of texts produced was impressive. Commercial and private publishers continued to produce primers, dictionaries, the Classics, histories, literary collections, and Daoist and Buddhist scriptures. But they also churned out popular vernacular novels and story collections, dramas, accounts of foreign peoples, travel guides, medical manuals, music, scientific treatises from the West (as well as works by Jesuit missionaries), artisan pattern books, and encyclopaedias including information for daily life, examination preparation, documentary and poetry composition, etc. Growing demand allowed publishers to specialize: the Tang family's Fuchun tang in Nanjing, for example, was known for the publication of plays and drama miscellanies. Texts appeared in more and different editions. *Illustrated Record of Antiquities from the Xuanhe Period* (*Xuanhe bogu tulu*), a catalogue of bronze vessels published first in the fourteenth century, was reprinted in a facsimile edition in 1528 and in five different editions between 1588 and 1603.

The book culture of the late Ming can be characterized, depending on one's tastes, as unusually playful, provocative, aesthetically refined, and irreverent—or as sloppy, 'hucksterish', decadent, and heterodox. Take, for example, the extremely popular *Record of Naked Creatures* (*Luochong lu*), a prolifically illustrated encyclopaedia of foreign peoples. Although written largely in the vernacular, it apes the scholarly style of historical writing. Yet its unknown authors reveal a strong affinity for fiction writing in the freedom with which they invented colourful new 'facts'. When serious bibliographers of the Qing dismiss the work as 'composed of cobbled-together fragments of the various histories along with various collections of apocryphal tales [...] decidedly not to be relied on as a source of information' (Ji Yun, ed., *Siku quanshu zongmu*), one cannot help feeling that they have missed the point. *Luochong lu* is a work of entertainment, imagination, and perhaps some irony, not a serious effort to provide accurate information about foreign peoples.

Late Ming attraction to the entertaining, the new, and the colourful found its fullest expression in two striking material developments in publishing: the heavier use of illustration and the development and refinement of methods of colour printing. Most of the major works of fiction and drama became available in illustrated editions in this period. The Jianyang publishers were famous for the 'picture above, text below' (*shangtu xiawen*) format of their inexpensive editions of vernacular stories and historical romances.

The publisher Yu Xiangdou (*c*.1550–1637), for example, placed a band of illustration above the text of his *c*.1592 edition of the very popular *Chronicle of the Three Kingdoms* (*Sanguo zhizhuan*). Each opened page contained two pictures, one on the verso of one leaf, the other on the recto of the next leaf. The best known of the late Ming Jianyang printers, Yu was a master of self-promotion, claiming authorial credit for many publications most likely not his own. He sometimes included pictures of himself in the guise of a refined literatus in his publications.

Illustrations in these popular works, drawn from a stock repertoire, were often rather crude. But the finest illustrated works of the late Ming were very fine indeed. The *c*.1615 edition of the popular novel *Outlaws of the Marsh (Shuihu zhuan)*, published by the Hangzhou house Rongyu tang, includes two beautifully designed and cut full-page illustrations in each of its one hundred chapters. One of the great painters of the day, Chen Hongshou (1598–1652), occasionally designed woodblock illustrations, including the exquisite prints of the 1639 Hangzhou edition of the much-loved drama *Record of the Western Chamber (Xixiang ji)*.

Novels and dramas were not the only texts to be illustrated. Pictures appeared in technical treatises, catalogues, erotic albums, and painting and calligraphy manuals. With woodblock printing, it was also easy to embed illustrations in the text block. Li Shizhen's (1518–93) influential *Outline of Materia Medica (Bencao gangmu)* was copiously illustrated with pictures of the plants, insects, animals, and minerals he catalogued. *The Works of Heaven and the Inception of Things (Tiangong kaiwu)*, published in 1637 by its author, Song Yingxing (*c*.1590–*c*.1660), provides full-page illustrations of the industrial methods described in the text. Among the more spectacular illustrated texts of the period is a chess manual, *A Shortcut to Weiqi, Finely Edited by the Master Who Plays Weiqi (Zuoyin xiansheng jingding jiejing yi pu)*, produced by Wang Tingna (*c*.1569–1628), the scion of a wealthy merchant family from Huizhou, an area known for its expert block-cutters and fine publishers. Wang, who aspired to membership in elite literati circles, opened his manual with lavish woodcut illustrations of men playing *weiqi* in a large and beautiful garden—his own. The pictures display the exquisite and distinctive pictorial sensibility of the artist, Wang Geng, and the fine cutting skill of Huang Yingzu, from Huizhou's best-known block-cutting lineage. Published by Wang's studio, Huancui tang, in 1609, this work is more a sumptuous display of wealth and refined taste (*weiqi* was a gentleman's game) than a real chess manual. This sort of book was not sold in bookshops, but 'traded' as a piece of cultural capital in the elaborate social rituals of the lower Yangzi delta.

Huizhou publishers and cutters, sometimes working in Hangzhou or Nanjing, advanced the other notable accomplishment of the day: the development of new techniques of colour printing that made the seventeenth century the golden age of the colour print. In 1604, Cheng Dayue (1541–*c*.1616) of Huizhou published a collection of decorative designs for ink sticks using the established 'multiple impression' method, which required printers to apply one colour to appropriate parts of a woodblock, take an impression, and move on to the next colour and the next impression. What made Cheng's *Ink Garden of the Cheng Family* (*Chengshi moyuan*) remarkable was his use of five—rather than the much more common two—colours. This work also included some monochrome images from Western Christian texts, supplied by the Jesuit missionary Matteo Ricci (1552–1610).

Several decades later, another Huizhou native, Hu Zhengyan (*c*.1584–1674), working in Nanjing, perfected a more sophisticated 'assembled blocks' method, which allowed printers to produce fine gradations of colour and to imitate brushstrokes of painting in the admired 'boneless' style (of forms without outlines). This technique required cutting separate blocks for each of the coloured areas of the picture and printing each block in a planned sequence. Hu's masterpiece was the *Ten Bamboo Studio Manual of Calligraphy and Painting* (*Shizhu zhai shuhua pu*). Published in 1640, it contains exquisite illustrations of plants, flowers, rocks, and birds in five colours.

Colour was also used in text printing. The Min and the Ling families of Wucheng, near Hangzhou, specialized in multi-coloured editions of the Classics, histories, philosophical works, and especially literary collections and dramas. Their texts, printed from multiple blocks, used colour to set off commentaries and highlight punctuation. The early-seventeenth-century Ling-family edition of *The Literary Mind and the Carving of Dragons* (*Wenxin diaolong*), a famous work of literary criticism, reproduces text in as many as five colours (black, red, blue, purple, and yellow). A Min-family publisher suggests that aesthetic rather than practical concerns inspired this use of colour:

> In printing of the past, whatever commentary and punctuation there were all printed in black, and readers attuned to aesthetics found [these texts] boring to read. Now we add a separate block, print the Classic and the Commentary in black and the [secondary] commentary in

vermilion . . . The extra spent on cutting is worth it, for now opening the
book is rewarding to the heart-mind.

(Min Qiji, 'Fanli', *Chunqiu Zuozhuan*, in Ye Shusheng and
Yu Minhui, *Ming Qing Jiangnan siren keshu shilüe*, 53–4)

Colour printing achieved even greater aesthetic and emotional
expression by the close of the Ming dynasty in the publication by
Min Qiji (1580–*c*.1661) of a magnificently illustrated edition of *Record
of the Western Chamber*. Almost all its exquisite colour illustrations centre
on objects—a lantern, a compass, a bronze vessel—or on settings—a
puppet theatre, a screen partially concealing a mirror—that emphasize the staged and illusory quality of the drama. The illustrations
dazzle the reader with their beauty, subtlety, and technical mastery,
but they also *interpret* the text. Illustrations here are not simply extrava-
gant add-ons advertising the elegant aesthetic and ample wealth of
their producer and prospective consumers, but also a guide to a
certain haunting reading of the drama.

Min Qiji's masterpiece was published in 1640, undoubtedly for a
very limited, very wealthy elite. Four years later, Manchu conquerors
devastated the lower Yangzi delta region and abruptly brought to an
end the 'decadent' culture of the late Ming. The new Manchu rulers
of the Qing, suspicious of the conquered population and its elite and
eager to assert their Confucian rectitude, were unsympathetic to the
playful, irreverent attitudes and sensual tastes of the seventeenth-
century Chinese book world. The achievements of Qing publishing
and the nature of that dynasty's book culture were very different—
even oppositional to—those of the preceding century.

The map of publishing sites and centres was redrawn. After the
conquest, the lower Yangzi delta sites did regain some stature as
publishing and bookselling communities—Suzhou rapidly and Nanjing and Hangzhou more slowly—but the Qing commercial publishing world was much more decentralized than that of the Ming.
Beijing, and in particular, its great book market, Liulichang, became
the major focus of book production and sale in the empire. Most
strikingly, commerce developed in regions distant from the cultural
and economic centres of the eastern seaboard: Chengdu and Chongqing in the far southwest, Baoqing in the interior of Hunan province,
and Foshan, neighbouring the great port city of Guangzhou in the

south. Xuwan, a market town in Jiangxi province, founded an import-ant publishing industry, with bookselling branches in port cities on the Yangzi river and Liulichang. Several peasant villages in the Sibao basin, in impoverished western Fujian, hosted some fifty household-based printing houses supplying county seats, market towns, and villages of the south with cheap primers, editions of the Classics, medical and pharmaceutical manuals, ritual guides, fortune-telling handbooks, novels, and songbooks.

This expansion of publishing sites in the Qing was spurred by the demographic explosion and migrations of the eighteenth and nine-teenth centuries, which diffused demand throughout the empire, particularly in the south and southwest. The spread of schools, espe-cially those teaching basic literacy, created a larger audience for books. The portability and relative simplicity of xylography made it easy for aspiring publishers to establish operations in the interior. Woodblock printing required none of the elaborate machinery of the European press, but merely a handful of cutting tools and supplies of hardwood, paper, and ink. By the nineteenth century, commercial publishing operated in almost all the provinces of Qing China. Many publishers developed extensive sales networks linking several prov-inces. One Xuwan shop, the Shancheng tang, with shops in Chengdu and Chongqing in the southwest and Liaocheng, Botouzhen, and Liulichang in the northeast, spanned the empire.

A 'mass' readership did not develop in China until the twentieth century, but its groundwork was laid in the eighteenth and nineteenth centuries as more petty merchants, traders, shopkeepers, women, and even peasants joined the reading public. The spread of printing businesses in the interior and the expansion of bookselling routes also gave rural peoples greater access to book markets. A common book culture advanced, based on a large body of texts commercially produced more or less everywhere, although often in cheap, shabby, crudely illustrated, and poorly edited versions. Knowledge of these texts—primers, the Four Books (a collection of essential Confucian texts) and Five Classics, dictionaries, ritual handbooks, pharmaceut-ical collections, medical manuals, fortune-telling guides, almanacs, popular novels, plays, poetry collections, and songbooks—served to integrate populations distant from Beijing and the lower Yangzi delta into the Chinese cultural sphere.

Of course, class and regional variations remained. Abstruse works of scholarship, sophisticated literary works, and costly rare books remained beyond the reach of most Chinese. Works specific to a particular locality, some using local vocabularies, also made readers aware more of cultural difference than commonality. Nevertheless, throughout Qing China commercial publishers played a crucial role in 'spreading culture', as one of them put it, boosting literacy and knowledge of the core texts and stories of the tradition. The size, comprehensiveness, and increasing accessibility of the common book culture served as a powerful integrative force on the eve of China's modernity.

Significant changes in the content of Chinese book culture came not from commercial publishers, however, but from the government and private publishers. The Qing court in particular took the lead in important new publishing projects. To be sure, in the early Ming the imperial court had also sponsored large publications. Three Buddhist Tripitakas and one Daoist canon were published within the first century of Ming rule. In the early fifteenth century, the Yongle emperor (r. 1402–24) initiated the compilation of the *Yongle Encyclopedia (Yongle dadian)*, a huge encyclopaedia of all knowledge. The labour of some 3,000 scholars, this 11,095-volume work was published in manuscript form only.

Later Ming rulers were not as ambitious as Yongle. But the emperors of the early Qing were a very different story, for they had pressing reasons to make their mark on Chinese book culture. Although they also sponsored works in the many languages of their empire—Manchu, Mongolian, Tibetan, and Uighur—as 'barbarians' in the eyes of many Chinese, they felt a particular need to assert their knowledge and control of Chinese culture.

The Kangxi emperor (r. 1661–1722) sponsored three great publishing projects: a fine edition of *The Complete Poems of the Tang (Quan Tangshi)*, to signal his recognition of the golden age of Chinese poetry; the *Kangxi Dictionary (Kangxi zidian)*, to assert his mastery of the Chinese language; and the *Comprehensive Compendium of Illustrations and Books, Ancient and Modern (Gujin tushu jicheng)*, to claim for the emperor, in the spirit of the *Yongle Encyclopedia*, the authority to collect and categorize all knowledge. Bound in over 5,000 volumes, this last work was a technological triumph, printed in the Imperial Printing Office from a font of about 250,000 bronze types and lavishly illustrated with over 6,000 woodcut tables, pictures, and maps.

Kangxi's grandson, the Qianlong emperor (r. 1736–95), made contributions to the book world on an even more colossal scale. Like his grandfather, he sponsored the publication of finely edited master- pieces of Chinese culture, including complete editions of the Thirteen Classics with commentaries (*Shisan jing zhushu*) and the twenty-four dynastic histories (*Ershisi shi*). But his most impressive achievement was the *Complete Library of the Four Treasuries* (*Siku quanshu*), a compilation of the finest editions of the most important texts extant in the empire: the 'four treasuries' referred to the major Chinese bibliographical divi- sions of Classics, histories, philosophers, and belles-lettres. An editorial committee selected 3,461 texts, collected from all over the empire, for inclusion in the *Complete Library* and another 6,793 texts for review. Editing and transcription of the texts took about ten years, from 1773 to 1782. Then, between 1782 and 1787, an army of scribes made seven identical copies of the collection, each comprising about 36,000 volumes; like the *Yongle Encyclopedia*, the *Complete Library* was a manu- script publication. The collators and editors also produced a critical annotated bibliography of the collection, a valuable research tool to this day.

The work of the *Complete Library* fed and fed off the major scholarly movement of the eighteenth century. Appalled by the fall of the Chinese Ming dynasty to the Manchus, scholars of the early Qing had urged a turning away from the frivolous literary productions and empty philosophizing of late Ming scholars towards exacting and profound study of the Classics—the texts that, if only understood thoroughly, would restore ethical and political order (and Chinese rule). Close philological analysis was required, however, to unpack the wisdom of the Classics; and scholars increasingly devoted themselves to textual criticism and research in phonology, historical geography, archaeology, and a host of other subjects in pursuit of this wisdom.

Demand for a wide range of ancient texts in excellent editions to support this 'evidential research' (*kaozheng*) stimulated the private publication, often by wealthy merchants in the lower Yangzi delta, of both facsimile editions and collections (*congshu*) of rare texts that might be organized around a single subject (such as rhyme and phonetics). Devoted bibliophiles like Huang Pilie (1763–1825) built impressive collections, often described in printed catalogues, and opened them to the use of research scholars. Thus, the Qing state and evidential researchers worked in tandem to forge a sober, scholarly book culture very different from the more light-hearted and sensual culture of the late Ming.

Another consequence of government engagement in publishing, however, was perhaps the most vicious campaigns of text censorship in the history of China. Suspicious of the loyalty of their conquered subjects, the Qing emperors remained alert for signs of sedition. The Kangxi emperor, for example, on learning that a history of the Ming contained passages insulting to the Manchus, had executed all the authors, editors, printers, and owners of the work, the local officials who had failed to report its publication, and all the other male members of their families. All associated females were enslaved to Manchu households. Even more effective as a means of weeding out works labelled seditious was the book collecting required to support the *Complete Library* project of the Qianlong emperor. It is estimated that during its compilation, 3,000 works were destroyed—almost as many as were included in the collection itself.

Generally, after the first three decades of the nineteenth century, the quality of woodblock printing declined, despite the occasional appearance of exquisite works like the colour-printed *Illustrated Manual on Goldfish* (*Jinyu tupu*, 1848). A succession of wars with imperialist Western powers and violent civil conflicts, all of which hit the Eastern seaboard very hard, destroyed publishing industries and bookselling networks. The book culture reflected the anxieties of the age. Scholars and officials published 'statecraft' writings providing information about the Western nations and outlining policies to rescue the Qing from their domination, such as the 1844 *Illustrated Treatise on the Maritime Kingdoms* (*Haiguo tuzhi*) by the historian and geographer Wei Yuan (1794–1856). In the 1860s, the imperial court, hoping that vigorous teaching of Confucian values would restore the fortunes of the dynasty, ordered the creation of provincial 'book bureaus' to publish the Classics and other educational texts in inexpensive and accessible editions for sale to schools, academies, and individual students. But the late Qing also witnessed some more innovative and imaginative contributions to its rather sober book culture: novels of science fiction and imaginary travel, like *The New Story of the Stone*

(*Xin Shitou ji*, 1905), which transported the hero of the famous eighteenth-century novel *Story of the Stone* (*Shitou ji*, also *Dream of the Red Chamber, Honglou meng*) to a new, utopian China.

In the late nineteenth century, however, China underwent a revolution in print technology. Lithography and mechanized moveable type, both introduced by Western missionaries and entrepreneurs, gradually replaced xylography as the primary print technology. Woodblock texts continued to be produced, and wooden moveable type remained a popular technology for the production of genealogies (because the number of different characters was limited), but by the early twentieth century, the new technologies—and new genres of print such as the newspaper—had won the day, bringing print now to a mass audience. The port city of Shanghai, entry point for these technologies, became the centre of publishing in twentieth-century China, opening a new era in printing, a reconfiguration of Chinese book culture, and a radical expansion in the reading audience.

Korea

Of the main East Asian countries, Korea enjoyed the most modest advance in publishing in the early modern period. The Joseon court remained interested in improving print technology, and the Office of Moveable Type produced a series of increasingly refined metal types through the fifteenth century. At the same time, however, the government strictly limited the production of books to those of practical administrative or educational use. Economic policies also impeded commercial publishing so that the technological innovations of the fourteenth and fifteenth centuries did not lead to great expansion in publishing, literacy, or demand for texts.

Nevertheless, of all the East Asian countries, Korea cherished the greatest respect, even reverence, for books. The cult of the book in fact partly explains the limits of book production in Korea. Books were honoured as carriers of the highest values and constant principles. Studying books was regarded as the most sacred pursuit of a civilized person. The sixteenth-century primer *Secrets to Successful Teaching of Children* (*Gyongmong yogyol*) ordered students to kneel down and join their hands in a gesture of respect in front of their books. A premium was put on the reprinting of old texts that had proven their value over time rather than the rapid production of new titles. Korean literati sometimes expressed disapproval of new works flooding out of early modern China.

The cult of the book, together with political and economic forces, retarded the kind of lively commercial publishing that developed in China and Japan. Until the nineteenth century, the government dominated the production of texts, printed by metal or wooden moveable type and then distributed to local officials for replication and dissemination in woodblock-printed form. Individual readers also made hand copies from printed texts. Korea, like China and Japan, enjoyed a mixed moveable-type, woodblock, and manuscript book culture throughout most of its early modern history.

Book contents changed slowly. The Joseon court produced editions of the Chinese Classics and Confucian writings for examination study, collections of Chinese poetry, morality books promoting Confucian values, the Chinese dynastic histories, encyclopaedias, and a variety of practical manuals on medicine, agriculture, and military strategy. Local officials published gazetteers, compilations of information about the population, products, history, and culture of the specific regions under their jurisdiction. Elite families often privately printed their genealogies to document family lines and ensure correct transmission of ritual protocols, as well as reproduce the writings of distinguished ancestors. Monasteries and religious associations continued to produce Buddhist texts. Individual scholars and Confucian academies, flourishing in the late Joseon era, also published literary collections and textbooks.

More significant, however, were hints of a fledgling vernacular book culture. Take, for example, the publication history of the *Illustrated Guide to the Three Relations* (*Samgang haengsildo*), a collection of exemplary tales of filial piety. Originally published in 1434 at the command of King Sejong to educate his people in Confucian virtue, the first edition was in classical Chinese, with over 80 per cent of the tales taken from Chinese history. Literati translated the text orally into the Korean vernacular to illiterate audiences, using its lavish illustrations to help them understand the stories. By the end of the century, Sejong's successor published an edition that included mixed Chinese–Korean vernacular paraphrases of the stories in the 'eyebrow' margins

above the Chinese text. Within a century, editions with *hangeul* paraphrases were appearing, and in 1726, the first edition that translated
the classical Chinese into *hangeul*. Sequels to the text, published in
1514 and 1617, reversed the ratio of Chinese to Korean tales, so that
Korean examples of filial piety predominated; and in the 1617 sequel,
the vernacular translation was moved down to the main part of the
page, no longer subordinated to the Chinese. The history of this text,
a product of the Joseon court, suggests both a developing Korean
literary tradition and a growing audience for texts in the vernacular.

Equally telling is the trajectory of the Korean novel. In the sixteenth
century, Chinese vernacular novels were imported to Korea. Despite
the often-expressed disdain of the male elite for such texts, they
became quite popular. Although novels did circulate in Chinese
editions (and would have been read by literati in that form), they
also came to be transmitted in handwritten Korean translations and
adjusted for Korean tastes and social mores. For example, the Korean
vernacular version of the Chinese romance *The Fortunate Union* (*Haoqiu
zhuan*), introduced to Korea in the early eighteenth century, bowdler-
ized the original, emphasizing the obedience and chastity of the
heroine over her heroism. The readers of these Korean translations
of Chinese novels were women within elite households, including the
royal household. They played an active role in the transmission of the
texts; the transcription of such texts was often part of a girl's education, and personal copies part of her dowry. Married women also
transcribed and exchanged these works. Thus the circulation—and
transformation—of works like *The Fortunate Union* reveals both the
growth of literacy among elite women and the development of a
vernacular book culture increasingly independent of China. Indeed,
by the early seventeenth century, the reading audience had expanded
to the point that Korean authors began producing new novels that,
although drawing on Chinese stories, were written in their own
vernacular.

This expansion in Korean reading audiences further stimulated
commercial publishing in the last full century of Joseon rule. Although
the earliest evidence of commercial publishing dates to 1576, it was
not until the nineteenth century that publisher-booksellers printed
primers, rhyming dictionaries, editions of the Classics with Korean
explanations, letter-writing manuals, medical and pharmaceutical

guides, ritual handbooks, and fiction. Most works were published in Chinese, but titles suggesting a broad audience, like the *Outline of Strategies for Rescue from Famine, Newly Printed* (*Singan guhwang jwaryo*), a guide to methods of avoiding starvation during years of famine, or *The Housekeeper's Compendium* (*Gyuhab jyongsyo*), were printed either bilingually or in the vernacular only. Bookshops, however, were still rare. Stores devoted to the sale of books alone—and well-produced Korean imprints in Chinese—existed only in Seoul, the capital. In the provinces, books—usually cheap editions in the vernacular—were sold in makeshift stalls along with other merchandise.

As in Qing China, the nineteenth century proved a period of political decline, exacerbated by increasing pressure from imperialist powers. In fact, the development of a commercial book market was possible only because the government was too weak to maintain its oversight of publishing. But the century was also the beginning of Korea's modern print revolution. Western-style mechanized moveable-type technology was introduced to the country around 1880 and used to support the beginnings of independent publishing, promoted by both political reformers and Christian missionaries, until the annexation of Korea by Japan in 1910 abruptly constrained this development.

Japan

While early modern Korea enjoyed a mild expansion in the scope of publishing, Japan's publishing boom more closely resembled the explosion of print in China, with its origins in an increasingly monetized economy and urbanized society. The book culture that emerged in early modern Japan, however, was, while not completely independent of Chinese influence, most vibrant in its assertion of Japanese difference.

Stimulus for the late-sixteenth-century development of printing came from two unlikely sources. In 1590, the Jesuit missionary Alessandro Valignano (1539–1606) brought the first moveable-type printing press to Japan. Before the machine was destroyed in the persecution of Christianity in the early seventeenth century, it was used to print about one hundred titles, including the *Tale of the Heike*

(*Heike monogatari*), in Romanized transcriptions of Japanese. Then, in 1592, during the Japanese invasion of Korea, troops seized both the printed books and a font of metal moveable types, presenting these treasures to the Japanese emperor. The following year, Japanese craftsmen succeeded in publishing an edition of the Chinese *Classic of Filial Piety* (C: *Xiaojing*; J: *Kōkyō*) from this font.

A transformation in the technology, content, and scope of Japanese book culture followed. The Jesuits, by printing Japanese works (albeit in Romanized Japanese), introduced the notion that Japanese writings were worthy of wider dissemination; and the imperially sponsored Japanese craftsmen, by printing secular works in Chinese, brought textual production out of the monasteries and temples, demonstrating a broader potential for print. Recognizing this potential, the future shogun, Tokugawa Ieyasu (1543–1616), and the emperor both commissioned the manufacture of large fonts of wooden moveable type for the printing of Chinese secular texts and chronicles of Japanese history. Private publishers also embraced the new technology. The physician Oze Hoan, for example, printed four Chinese medical texts between 1596 and 1597. Publishing activity using both woodblocks and wooden moveable type increased in the half-century from the founding of the Tokugawa shogunate in 1600. For the first time, print editions of Japanese classical literature appeared, including five editions of *The Tale of Genji*. The shogunate, interested in promoting Confucianism as the state ideology, saw that editions of the Four Books and other Confucian Classics were printed. These works often included 'reading marks' (*kunten*) to guide Japanese not fully literate in classical Chinese through the texts. Many new titles, 'books written with a view to being printed'—letter-writing manuals, guidebooks, and new works of fiction—appeared as well.

Annotation and illustration of difficult texts in both Chinese and Japanese made many works accessible to broader readerships. Most of the new books, including *The Tale of Genji*, were enlivened with woodblock illustrations added to moveable-type text. Particularly striking, both aesthetically and technically, were the 'Saga books' (*Sagabon*) published between 1599 and about 1620 in Saga village, near Kyoto, in a collaboration between a famous calligrapher, Hon'ami Kōetsu, and a merchant-connoisseur, Suminokura Soan (1571–1632). Almost all the *Sagabon* were Japanese texts reproduced largely in the

Japanese syllabary (*kana*) and printed in moveable type. The fluidity of *kana* calligraphy presented a serious challenge to type-cutters working in wood. The *Sagabon* solved the problem by extensive use of ligatures to capture the beautiful flow of Hon'ami's calligraphy. Intended for elite readers in the imperial capital, some *Sagabon* were printed on high-quality coloured paper and decorated with mica. The most famous of the series, an edition of *The Tale of Ise* (*Ise monogatari*, 1608), was the first secular Japanese work to be illustrated.

Nonetheless, partly because of the challenges of printing *kana* in moveable type, publishers, particularly commercial publishers, effectively abandoned use of that technology by mid-century. Prohibitively expensive capital investment was required to create the enormous fonts of metal types needed to print Japanese and Chinese. Wooden type was cheaper, but split easily and shifted in the frame. By contrast, xylography allowed frequent small print runs, a production strategy that suited the still relatively slow market of the mid-seventeenth century. And calligraphy and glosses were easier to cut and print on woodblocks than on moveable type.

Much as in China, the early modern publishing boom in Japan was a *commercial* phenomenon. The relative stability of the early centuries of Tokugawa rule enabled economic, transport, and urban development. Commerce flourished, and merchants, although ideologically subordinated to the samurai elite, influenced social mores and literary taste, as the work of two great authors of the period, Ihara Saikaku (1642–93) and Chikamatsu Monzaemon (1653–1725), reveals. The spread of schools, even to rural villages, and improved rates of literacy helped create larger reading audiences and a greater demand for books. Educational works became one of the publishing staples of the day.

The seventeenth- and eighteenth-century commercial book trade centred on the two major cities of central Japan: Kyoto, the imperial capital, and Osaka. In the late eighteenth century, the centre of gravity shifted northward, and commercial publishers in the shogunal capital, Edo, dominated the market.

Yet, as in Qing China, publishing operations also spread to provincial towns (usually the seats of local lords or *daimyō*) such as Nagoya, Kanazawa, Mito, and Wakayama. By the second half of the Tokugawa era, about fifty publishers operated from these smaller sites, publishing works of local interest. On occasion, their publications were distributed more widely, through ties with publishers in the major cities. In the early nineteenth century, for example, the Nagoya publishing house Eirakuya Tōshirō produced *Sketches of Hokusai* (*Hokusai manga*), a collection of drawings by the great *ukiyoe* artist Katsushika Hokusai (1760?–1849) that enjoyed widespread fame throughout Japan.

Books published in the major cities circulated throughout Japan via the well-maintained highways of the Tokugawa period. These books included old staples—Chinese Classics, Chinese poetry collections, and Buddhist sutras—now often printed with glosses, notes, and guides to pronunciation to aid the less-educated customer. But publishers competed vigorously to bring out new titles and new genres of texts: poetry, fiction, drama, primers, moral tracts, encyclopaedias, tourist guides, maps, medical texts, agricultural and craft manuals, handbooks for flower-arranging, and official directories. By the mid-seventeenth century, the volume of works published was so great that booksellers began issuing catalogues to their customers. The *Catalogue of Publications for Public Utility* (*Kōeki shojaku mokuroku*), produced by a consortium of publishing houses in 1692, listed over 7,000 titles. By at least the early nineteenth century, some publishers specialized in niche-market publication, producing, for example, only cookbooks, flower-arrangement manuals, mathematical treatises, or popular educational works.

Tokugawa book culture, even more than that of the roughly contemporaneous Qing dynasty in China, appealed to a widening population of readers. Literates (and, through oral transmission, illiterates as well) enjoyed what one scholar has called a 'library of public information', a common store of general knowledge and detailed, specific information about Japan as a place and a polity. Thus, the 1690 *Illustrated Encyclopedia of Humanity* (*Jinrin kinmōzui*, 1690) defined about 500 professions in nine different categories. Books advertised as 'treasuries' of information provided standard knowledge and instruction on a range of skills: letter-writing, poetry composition, cooking, spell-casting, tea-ceremony ritual, and healing. *Everybody's Treasury* (*Banmin chōhōki*, 1692) contained lists of Japanese emperors and leading political, military, and religious figures, the annual ritual calendar, a list of objects used in the tea ceremony, and much else besides. Much of the information was too sketchy to be of real practical use, but *Everybody's Treasury* offered an overview of 'what everyone should know'.

Tourist guides, various and popular, reveal a passion for tourism— armchair or real—in Tokugawa Japan, linked perhaps to the shogunal requirement that even the most distant *daimyō* visit his capital once a year. *The Traveling Sparrow's Guide to the Provinces* (*Shokoku annai tabi suzume*, 1687) took a traveller through the network of roads that connected the major cities and tourist sites, with information about distances, travel times, road conditions, portage fees, and accommodation. *The Excellent Views of Kyoto* (*Keijō shōran*, 1706), by the Confucian scholar Kaibara Ekiken, guided readers through seventeen walking tours of Kyoto and its environs. This guide for 'ordinary people' was written in simple Japanese, offering phonetic aids for many characters. Works like *A Self-Guided Tour to Kyoto Shopping* (*Kyōto kaimono hitori annai*, 1831) or *A Bundle of Personages from the Yoshiwara* (*Yoshiwara hito tabane*, 1680), a listing of the courtesans of the pleasure quarter of Edo, served tourists with more specialized interests.

Exceptionally popular, too, were directories of the shogunate government. Known generically as 'mirrors of the military' (*bukan*), these works, frequently revised, were printed in tens of thousands of copies annually. At first the 'mirrors' focused on the *daimyō*, the regional lords subordinate to the shogun, providing detailed information about each: rank and title, family and genealogy, residence addresses, insignia, and domain agricultural productivity. In 1659, the compilers of these directories also began to include information on officials in the Tokugawa bureaucracy, emphasizing not their personal lives and status, but their specific functions within government. The huge number of *bukan* published, and their commercial profile, suggests an audience that included not just *daimyō* and members of government, but also merchants seeking well-connected prospective customers, aspiring officials, tourists—and many readers simply interested in the power relationships of the shogunal government.

By the end of the seventeenth century, prose fiction came to dominate Japanese literary production, although dramas and poetry (including Chinese poetry) remained in demand. Lively stories of urban, often mercantile, life enjoyed greatest popularity. Saikaku, son of an Osaka merchant, wrote satires of *nouveau riche* merchants (in *The Eternal Storehouse of Japan, Nihon eitaigura*, 1688) and contemporary sexual mores (in his story of the erotic escapades of a fallen court lady, *Life of an Amorous Woman, Kōshoku ichidai onna*, 1686). Many other writers, less talented than Saikaku, churned out similar works. By the late eighteenth century, enterprising commercial publishers in Edo, now the centre of the literary world, seized opportunities to develop new genres of fiction satirizing official life or providing behind-the-scenes stories of the Yoshiwara pleasure quarter. The Edo publisher Tsutaya Jūzaburō (1750–97), for example, began by selling guide-books to the pleasure quarter, but eventually built up his business by expanding his booklist to include tales of the Yoshiwara. Often presented as a series of colloquial dialogues, Yoshiwara fiction was frequently issued in small, cheaply produced formats to attract a non-elite audience.

Printed picture books (*ehon*), another distinctive feature of Tokugawa Japanese book culture, were viewed as much as read. Produced on a wide variety of subjects, they featured pictures and a little text—captions, poetry, or short essays written in fine calligraphy. Originally monochrome, *ehon* were printed in colour in the eighteenth century, using techniques introduced from China.

Best known are the albums of *ukiyoe*, prints of *kabuki* actors and courtesans that vibrantly conveyed 'the floating world' of the Edo pleasure quarters. Some were anthologies of poetry or, more rarely, proverb collections or Buddhist narratives. Like the Chinese, Japanese printmakers made painting manuals and erotic albums of 'spring pictures' (*shunga*). They also produced many site-specific picture books, depicting, most famously, the stations of the Tōkaidō highway connecting Kyoto and Edo, views of Mt Fuji, and scenes from Edo. Shiba Kōkan's *Account of a Western Journey* (*Saiyū ryodan*, 1794) includes illustrations of a Dutch ship in the Nagasaki harbour. Some *ehon* sketched mundane scenes from daily life—although there is nothing mundane about Kawamura Kihō's *Leave Joys and Sorrows to the Brush* (*Kafuku ninpitsu*, 1809), with its beautifully rendered but horrifying scenes of domestic violence, illness, beggary, and unwanted pregnancy. Other picture books, like Koikawa Harumachi's *Master Kinkin's Dream of a Luxurious Life* (*Kinkin sensei eiga no yume*, 1775), told stories, including some narrative text on each picture. These are the forerunners of modern Japanese *manga* or cartoon books.

The government was largely unsuccessful in shaping or disciplining this lively book culture. After the early years of Tokugawa rule, the shogunate took little interest in publishing texts. It did attempt to censor certain types of works. In 1630, the shogun banned the import and reproduction of works by missionaries, in line with the proscription of Christianity. Also prohibited was the publication of works treating the victory of Tokugawa Ieyasu and his son, criticism of the shogun, and government scandals. In the early 1700s, the shogunate outlawed the publication of works on current events, illicit calendars, erotica and accounts of the pleasure quarters, gossip about the behaviour of samurai—in essence, everything but works of Confucianism, Buddhism, Shintoism, medicine, and poetry. But these efforts at censorship proved inconsistent and generally ineffective, falling far short of the Manchu Qianlong emperor's 'literary inquisition'.

More effective restrictions came from the booksellers' guilds, the first established in late seventeenth-century Kyoto. Others followed in Osaka, Edo, and Nagoya. Formed originally to regulate the commercial book trade, the guilds protected a kind of copyright, ensuring that no publisher could reproduce the contents or format of a text published by another house without mutually acceptable compensation. At the same time, however, the guilds practised some degree of self-censorship, often bowing to government prohibitions. Nevertheless, censorship remained ad hoc and poorly enforced. Even when imprints were successfully removed from the market, forbidden texts circulated in hand-copied editions. The relative freedom of publishing in Tokugawa Japan allowed the flowering of a lively, often racy, urban popular book market.

This is not to say, of course, that serious works of scholarship and philosophy had no place in Tokugawa book culture. Japanese intellectuals continued to be interested in developments in Chinese thought. Chinese Classics, new Chinese Confucian works, and Buddhist sutras in Chinese continued to be both imported to and published in Japan. Confucian thinkers such as the great Ogyū Sorai (1666–1728) published their own works of philosophy. His *Distinguishing the Way* (*Bendō*) was eventually published in China over a century after its first appearance in 1717. But there was also intellectual resistance to this engagement with Chinese ideas and Chinese texts. During the eighteenth century, in reaction against slavish worship of

Chinese culture, a group of scholars, led by Motoori Norinaga (1730–1801), celebrated the achievements of the Japanese literary tradition. The 'National Studies' (Kokugaku) advocates produced commentaries on Japanese works like the *Records of Ancient Matters (Kojiki)* and *The Tale of Genji,* arguing that these and other native texts revealed a spontaneity of feeling and a 'sorrow at evanescence' (*mono no aware*) that distinguished them from Confucian writings. By the end of the Tokugawa period, the growing popularity of National Studies even influenced the ways in which books were catalogued. Japanese texts, previously demoted to a miscellaneous category after Chinese works, began to be given greater prominence.

All of these developments reveal an early modern Japan enjoying a varied, vigorous, and socially expansive book culture, one that embraced elite scholars determined to advance a distinctively Japanese literary culture (as well as those absorbed in the Confucian controversies current in China), village-dwellers interested in practical education and the most up-to-date technical guides, newly prosperous merchants and townspeople eager to travel and enjoy the pleasures of fiction and picture books, and a broad public of readers curious about the organization and functions of Tokugawa rule.

In the late eighteenth and nineteenth centuries, as in China and Korea, pressures to engage economically, politically, and intellectually with the West initiated a gradual transformation in both the content and technology of Japanese book culture. Those pressures were negotiated first through exchanges with Dutch merchants (the only Europeans allowed to trade with Japan) living on an island in Nagasaki harbour. Dutch books were known in Japan as early as the seventeenth century, when they were regularly presented as gifts to the shogun. By the next century, interest grew in these largely scientific works, and a school of 'Dutch learning' (*Rangaku*) developed to study them. In 1771 the Japanese physician Sugita Genpaku was shown a copy of J.A. Kulmus's *Anatomical Tables* and, impressed with the accuracy of its illustrations, began work on a translation. In 1774, the *New Book of Anatomy* (*Kaitai shinsho*) was the first work of Dutch learning to be published in Japanese. It further stimulated interest in European medical and scientific learning, and, by the time Japan was 'opened' by Admiral Matthew Perry in 1853–4, interested Japanese were relatively familiar with some facets of Western knowledge.

Japan, in contrast to China and Korea, suffered relatively lightly as a victim of Western imperialism. Within fifteen years of the country's opening, the decaying Tokugawa regime was overthrown and replaced, in the Meiji Restoration of 1868, by an imperial state determined to hold its own against the West (in part by embracing many European and American institutions and technologies). The immediate impact on the book world was a much more efficient system of censorship adapted from the French model. Publishers were required to seek pre-publication permissions from the government, not the booksellers' guilds. And this requirement was strictly enforced, as a series of new laws tightened restrictions on what could be published.

In contrast to its predecessor, the Meiji government also took the lead in introducing new genres and technologies of print, establishing in the year of its founding an official newspaper or gazette to publicize government decrees. Metal moveable type had been reintroduced to Japan in the mid-nineteenth century, but it did not become the dominant technology until the 1880s. Again, the government played a newly important role, establishing an office for the casting of lead type for the printing of official publications. Although some wood-block publishing persisted, particularly for the printing of Buddhist sutras, Japan had entered the age of modern book culture.

5

Medieval Western Europe

David Rundle

In 1207, in the hall of the castle of Fanjeaux, 20 miles west of Carcassonne in southwest France, gathered two groups of religious enemies. On one side stood representatives of the *soi-disant* 'Good Christians', the Cathars considered by their opponents to be heretics or even worse. On the other side were members of the Catholic Church, including a priest from Castile, Dominic de Guzman. The men came together to present their dispute before a set of judges, and each side was called upon to provide a book clearly setting out the tenets of their faith. For the Catholics' part, they selected as the best expression of their beliefs a work recently composed by Dominic. The judges, asked to assess rival claims about the divine, turned to divination for an answer: they arranged for a fire to be lit in the centre of the hall and the books to be thrown on it—if they burnt (they reasoned), then their contents must be merely mortal. The book of the Cathars went up in flames but Dominic's went up out of the flames, jumping from the fire. Amazed at what they saw, they ordered it to be thrown back in only for it to leap out once more. The same happened a third time; some say it jumped so high and was so hot that it hit a roof-beam and singed it, but itself remained undamaged.

In subsequent decades, the nature and availability of books was transformed, partly as a result of Dominic's own actions. This tale, however, encapsulates a paradox apparent in the long period and extensive region surveyed in this chapter: that the book was an essential tool for rational debate, but that its power went beyond reason. This was an age when a book could work miracles: the book was so much more than a container for words inscribed on pages.

David Rundle

This history, of course, is written from the point of view of the victors of the theological struggle in which Dominic was embroiled. Across the millennium, Catholic Christianity and its language— Latin—dominated. That faith had its rivals: there were times following the fall of the Roman empire when the survival of the religion looked in doubt, besieged by invaders, first pagan and later Islamic. The map of Latin Christendom never matched the contours of Europe. The last pagan kingdom, Lithuania, converted in 1386. In the Iberian peninsula, though Islam lost most of its ground by the middle of the thirteenth century, Granada remained an Islamic stronghold until 1492. That loss suffered by the Prophet's faith was more than compensated for by the fifteenth-century success of the Ottomans further east in the lands bordering on the north of the Mediterranean—invasions that resulted in the final collapse of the Christian Byzantine empire as its Western co-religionists watched, incapable of uniting in a crusade. Within the swathes of land which were Roman Catholic, at least in name, there was the dispersed presence of Jewish communities. There were also internal divisions among Christians, as seen not only with the Cathars but also, later, by the fifteenth-century success of the Hussites in Bohemia. Cultures beyond Catholicism certainly prized the written word. There is no equivalent for the Roman alphabet of the potential for the letter shapes themselves to express the wonder of divine creation— something found in Ibn Muqla's reform of Islamic calligraphy; nor was there the same expectation of preserving all religious material after its useful life had ended, as there was in the Jewish tradition of *genizah*. Fundamental, however, to the dominant tradition of the Latin West was the placing of particular value on the written word and on its primary portal, the book.

The written word wielded power in part because of the rarity of the skills required to comprehend it, let alone compose in it. In the later Middle Ages, books were produced in increasing quantities for increasingly diverse audiences, but even then, as earlier, in Christendom, literacy was always the reserve of the few. This situation contrasted with Judaism where, at least in theory, every adult male was expected to be able to transcribe the holy texts. It was also a situation that continued to pertain in England in the early eighteenth century: most people were incapable of signing their names. If we move back from that date just 300 years, we find that reliable estimates are difficult to extrapolate from the incomplete and incidental evidence available: some optimistic assessments would have about a third of England's population being in some way literate; a soberer guess puts the rate of full literacy closer to one in ten. Those contrasting figures partly reflect complexities of definition. The ability to sign does not necessarily demonstrate wider skills of writing or reading; at the same time, an inability to mark the page with more than a cross does not categorically disprove a capacity to read, even perhaps to a level of some fluency. What is certain is that there was substantial variation and some of the factors affecting that are clear. You were more likely to be able to write if you were a man, not a woman, and if you were one of the minority who lived in a town, not in the countryside. Even if you were an urban male, the probability remained that you would be illiterate, unless you were fortunate enough to have been born towards the end of our period into a good family in Florence, which probably had the highest rates of literacy in Europe. Both a result of and a reason for the increase in literacy in that city was the development there, and elsewhere in northern Italy, of education in the vernacular. In other places and at other times, school meant Latin, and instruction was primarily intended for boys who were going to enter the church. The bond between learning and religion remains in English, latent in the double meaning of clerical (contrast 'clerical assistant' with 'clerical garments'). The implication is that those who came to gain some facility in reading and writing in their mother tongue may not have had access to the *lingua franca* of communication shared across Europe. Only a minority of the small minority who were literate were so literate to the level of being literati.

Readers were few, but writing was everywhere. You might not have been able to decipher the letters, but you would have been hard pressed to escape encounters with texts. Words were written on wooden markers or chiselled on stones in your local graveyard, and painted on the walls of your parish church. They were carried in your purse, as the legend—the literal meaning of which is 'what must be read'—on coins. They might travel close to your flesh, as short texts stored in amulets to bring good fortune and ward off evil. Written records were also a technology of control, the documents held by landowners defining the dues they claimed from those who lived on their land—and so writing was, for some, an object of hatred, a symbol of oppression, to be destroyed when the opportunity allowed, as during the Flemish peasants' revolts of 1323–8, the Jacquerie rebellion in northern France that began in 1358, and England's Peasants' Revolt of 1381.

Lettering was applied to many objects. On a wax tablet, a text could be drafted and then removed by heating, leaving the surface smooth and ready to be reused. Also generally ephemeral in its intended use was the birch-bark on which texts were written (usually, as on wax, with a stylus) in eastern Europe, from the Baltic to the Ukraine. In contrast, the comparatively short-lived practice in Viking lands in the late tenth and eleventh centuries of engraving and colouring runes on stones was consciously monumental, as was the tradition of epigraphy in the Latin West. A lasting record could also be committed to parchment: in English legal practice, an agreement might be written—twice—on one sheet which was then cut in two so each party had a copy; a simple guard against forgeries was to make the cut with a jagged line looking like a set of teeth, and thus comes our word 'indenture'. Sets of records on individual pages might be sewn together and stored as a roll. Of all the vehicles for the written word, however, the structure which ties together multiple sets of leaves and places them within a protective cover—in short, the book—had, in Christendom, a privileged status. An element of this is purely pragmatic, turning the leaves being less cumbersome than unfurling and furling a scroll. Practicality, of course, could be trumped by higher considerations. In Jewish communities, while whole Bibles were produced as books, the traditional design for a synagogue's Torah (the five books of Moses that open the Bible) was as a scroll, the care required in handling it having the virtue of being a ritual of respect for the text's holy nature. There was, throughout this period, no parallel use of multiple formats for Christian scripture, and so the material volume and its contents became synonymous: the Good Book was both text and object.

The artisans who created manuscripts of the Bible were often conscious of the need to make their product worthy of the veneration the text should inspire. It could be said that they were working with unpromising raw materials. In an Anglo-Saxon riddle from the tenth-century Exeter Book (so-called because it was given to that cathedral by its first bishop, Leofric), a voice speaks from beyond death (here, in Richard Hamer's translation):

> Some enemy deprived me of my life
> And took away my worldly strength, then wet me,
> Dipped me in water, took me out again,
> Set me in sunshine, where I quickly lost
> The hairs I had. Later the knife's hard edge
> Cut me with all impurities ground off.
> Then fingers folded me; the bird's fine raiment
> Traced often over me with useful drops
> Across my brown domain, swallowed the tree-dye
> Mixed up with water, stepped on me again
> Leaving dark tracks. The hero clothed me then
> With boards to guard me, stretched hide over me,
> Decked me with gold . . .

The enemy is a parchment-maker, killing an animal and preparing its skin. The riddle does not say what animal—sheep, goats, and cattle were all used, with the most highly prized surface being known as uterine vellum, suggesting it came from a stillborn or neo-natal calf (the term vellum—related to English 'veal'—is sometimes reserved for parchment from calves, but medieval sources do not insist on the distinction). The poem's description of the preparation is brutal but also understated: to remove the follicles, the washed skin had to be soaked for days in a solution, usually of lime but sometimes of urine. In twelfth-century Toledo, there is also talk of dog excrement being employed. The parchment was then scrapped smooth, as the riddle describes. The poem goes on to imagine the sheets being compiled into gatherings or quires, and the scribe drawing lines on the page, using a quill of a feather (the 'bird's fine raiment') into which is poured ink, usually made from oak-galls—that is, growths on the bark caused by insect larva (thus 'tree-dye'). From these earthy elements, a book is born. It is beautified: the 'hero' is the binder who uses wood ('boards') and leather ('hide'), finished with a gold plaque. This last detail tells us it would have been a special volume. The riddle ends by giving a hint of what it was:

> Say who I am, useful to men. My name
> Is famous, good to men, and also sacred.

The 'me' of the riddle has been transformed from the carcass of a beast of the field to something holy, a manuscript conveying God's word. The metamorphosis—from creature to creation in touch with the Creator—was, in an earlier, eighth-century Latin riddle, perceived as nothing short of an apotheosis: 'before the voice in us sounded without saying a word, but now we express words, without having our own voice'.

The corporeal origins of parchment are sometimes said to be the reason for one of the basic coordinates of the book. Take a book—the one you are reading now will do—and look at its shape. It seems unremarkable precisely because we are culturally conditioned to conceptualize 'book' as being this way: a rectangle, taller than it is wide, its breadth in the region of three-quarters of its height. Of course, we can immediately think of volumes that do not meet that norm—and those books speak to us through their unusual shape. Why, though, should books in the Western tradition have come to be this particular rectangular style? The argument has been made that, because the hide of an animal is longer than it is wide, making best use of the parchment it provides will invariably create a rectangle of similar proportions. While this is true, it does not dictate an 'upright' orientation. There are other factors that influence the preference for the long-established format: ease of reading—lines too long are more difficult to follow; ease of handling—there are limits to what is comfortable to hold and manoeuvre; and strength of binding—the broader the page, the weaker the hold of the spine will be. Those factors give a rationale explaining why proportions designed for parchment manuscripts remain standard centuries later (whether they should remain so when 'the page' is virtual and seen on screen is an open question). At the same time, it is incontrovertible that the book-shape we take as read, so to speak, is a legacy of a manuscript culture in which the codex was unmistakably carnal, the flesh made Word.

The words applied to the supple surface of the transformed skin could themselves be made to speak of their precious nature. The Anglo-Saxon riddle talks of black ink being applied to the page, but in the most sumptuous of manuscripts, the lettering would be in silver or gold or sometimes both. This might be applied only to individual words—the name of the Lord Himself—or to short sections, but in the early Middle Ages, whole texts were sometimes treated in this way, often written on parchment that had been dyed purple. Such lavish presentation had been derided in the fourth century by the Church Father and translator of the Bible, Jerome, but it found favour as an expression of royal magnificence at—for instance—the courts of Theoderic (king of Italy, 493–526), of Charlemagne (Holy Roman Emperor, 800–14), and of the Ottonian emperors of the tenth and early eleventh centuries.

The fashion fell into desuetude in later generations, though it was not unknown in Renaissance Italy, when there was also a parallel practice in some of the highest-grade manuscripts of writing text in gold on deep blue, as in the title pages of the magnificent eight-volume Bible, with Nicholas of Lyre's exegesis, commissioned from Florentine craftsmen by Manuel, king of Portugal (1495–1521) for the Hieronymite monastery at Belém (produced in the 1490s, these codices remind us that the arts of the manuscript did not die with the dawn of print). The relative decline of purple and the rise of blue are both evidence that there is a cultural history of individual colours, in which perceived status is autonomous of, but related to, its financial value. Shades of blue were known in the early Middle Ages, but from the thirteenth century particular prestige was associated with the bright hue that came from lapis lazuli, partly because its one known source was the Sar-e-Sang mines of what is now northeast Afghanistan, and so, like the presence of gold on a page, it spoke, to those with eyes to see, of the pecuniary investment which had been committed to the production. It also reminds us that the flecks of paint on the folio can bear witness to trade transactions spanning continents.

Long-distance contacts providing the costliest materials possible were not the only route to a sumptuous page. Two of the masterpieces of Insular book arts—the Lindisfarne Gospels and the Book of Kells—were made beautiful by the calligraphy of their scripts in simple black ink and their intricate illuminations in pigments from plants and minerals that were largely available locally (the theory that either of these employed lapis lazuli is now discredited). More generally, the painted pages of manuscripts are what, perhaps, most capture our twenty-first-century imagination—and frequently are what constitute the main source of monetary value on the rare books market.

Full-page miniatures, borders, and historiated initials do comprise some of the supreme productions of medieval art, but they were rarely intended to dominate the book of which they were part, and never were its sole *raison d'être*. A better sense of balance might be achieved by considering one particular tradition of miniatures, those which depict the event of the book being presented to its patron. There are some early examples of such scenes—for instance, in the Vivian Bible presented to Charles the Bald (king of West Francia, 843–77) in 845—but they proliferate in the later Middle Ages and take on a canonical form. They depict the person presenting usually on his knees (nearly always 'his', though an exception involves the poet Christine de Pisan (1364–*c*.1430) before the French queen, Isabeau of Bavaria). The person receiving the volume tends to be seated, sometimes with others standing in attendance. The centre-point is the book itself, caught at the instant when it passes from the donor to the recipient. Often included is the very codex which was to be presented, with the miniature providing a sort of future perfect, expressing the aspiration of the author for their work, as mediated through their illuminator. What is noticeable is that, while very few imagine the book being read by the patron—a famous example from 1372 shows the royal valet Jean de Vaudetar in an uncomfortable pose, on one knee, holding open at head-height the *Bible historiale* to be perused by a seated Charles V of France (1364–80)—the customary portrayal involved the manuscript being handed over shut. What the artist promotes is not his own artistry but what might well have been the most expensive part of the book, its binding, sometimes pictured in these miniatures with admirable attention to the detail of its fittings.

This is to say that a book need not be opened to be resplendent. While the basic format of a sturdy binding was a set of wooden boards covered with leather, it could be adorned further. The desire to protect the surface could dictate the addition of metal at the corners or as bosses studded on the cover, so that, when open at a lectern, the leather would not be rubbed. In some instances, this was taken much further and a 'treasure binding' considered suitable for the contents was provided, replete with precious metals and jewellery. One example of this is the Berthold Missal, so called after the Abbot, who commissioned it for his abbey of Weingarten near Lake Constance, probably around 1215. It is a lavishly illuminated manuscript, made all the more luscious by its cover of silver, gilt silver, gold filigree work, 101 mounts for gems, semi-precious stones, and enamel work, and with plaques of the four evangelists around a central plaque of a seated Virgin, the Christ Child on her lap. In other cases, the centrepiece might be an inlaid ivory relief, a form of art with ancient Roman precedents and with Byzantine influences. A fashionable alternative from the twelfth to the fourteenth centuries was to have complete panels of enamel work in the style for which Limoges was famous. To return, though, to the Berthold Missal, what makes its cover more unusual is that in it were also seated tiny relics of saints. Its status as a reliquary provided a further reason for the object to be venerated, but, as will already be clear, that added impetus was rarely thought necessary: the book was designed so that it was worthy of respect and of wonder in its own right.

One of the rationales for the expenditure that could be lavished on such volumes is revealed in a letter which Boniface (d. 754), the West Saxon missionary to the Germans, sent back across the Channel. In it, he thanks Abbess Eadburh for books she had sent him and asks her to continue her good deed by having written 'with gold' the Letters of St Peter, to inspire 'honour and reverence of the holy scriptures before the eyes of the worldly when I preach'. In the Latin, the term 'worldly' is *carnales*: those given to the flesh and yet to be converted but who, Boniface believes, will be persuaded to appreciate the spiritual through awe of the physical, by seeing an object itself carnal glisten with gold. The book does not simply record what is holy—it is a gateway to the sacred.

Such were the intrinsic elements—from the preparation of parchment to the design of its outer cover—which could ensure a manuscript declared its value. In addition, there are extrinsic factors of where and how it was kept. Reverence could be expressed by placing the volume in a book shrine, a *cumdach* in Ireland, where the practice was at its height in the eleventh century.

A *cumdach* was a wooden or metal casket decked, like a treasure binding, in silver and with jewels, a reliquary in which a manuscript was preserved and also transported—including into battle, with the hope that the enshrined Holy Word would bring victory. The enclosing of the book is taken to its extreme in the medieval references to a manuscript being buried with its owner. In the eleventh century, the chronicler Adhémar of Chabannes claimed that the first Holy Roman Emperor Charlemagne had been laid to rest in 814 in his imperial chapel at Aachen (Aix-la-Chapelle), sitting on a gold throne and holding on his knees 'a gold Gospel book'. Adhémar is not a reliable source, and the identification of the book with the Vienna Coronation Gospels is a much later invention. The authenticity of such detail, however, is less important than Adhémar's assumption that his readers would find it plausible that a precious codex might become a grave good. Higher purposes than reading could be envisaged for a book.

A similar conclusion can be drawn from the size of some volumes. The rationale for the basic shape of a book is to make it convenient for the eyes to read and the hands to hold it. There are exceptions to these conventions. Ease of handling was certainly not in the minds of the creators of a near-complete copy of Jerome's Vulgate Bible, which is known as the Codex Amiatinus (because, for most of its life, its home was the abbey of San Salvadore on the slopes of Monte Amiata in Tuscany). It was made at the beginning of the eighth century in Northumbria and then transported south. Its journey over almost the whole length of Europe must have been a significant undertaking: the volume stands at over 50 cm high, its pages are 34 cm wide, and it weighs 34 kg. Contrast this with the Psalter of St Rupert, founder of Salzburg. Constructed in France a century after the Codex Amiatinus, its dimensions are 37×31 mm, shorter than a thumb and about as thick as two fingers. Neither of these was designed for easy perusal. The Codex Amiatinus was undoubtedly intended to be an authoritative record of its text, a storehouse of holy knowledge rather than a volume for daily use. St Rupert's Psalter, meanwhile, is undeniably easy to carry, but its diminutive size suggests it would have been carried not for study itself but as a talisman or as a prop for prayer.

It was natural that the impulse to veneration concentrated on what was considered to be God's revealed Word, but the practices spilt over into some secular texts. A late example concerns an early manuscript, a sixth-century volume of the legal code established by the Emperor Justinian, which was the foundation text of the medieval tradition called civil or Roman law. The manuscript goes by several sobriquets, one being the Codex Florentinus, because, from 1406, it was in the ownership of the city of Florence, and there was kept, with other documents considered precious, in a silver casket—the 'Holy of Holies'—in the chapel of the town hall, the Palazzo Vecchio. It was provided with a new binding covered in a velvet chemise considered suitable to honour 'the most sacred laws'; access was restricted to only the most favoured scholars. The reasons for this treatment lay in its text and its venerability, combined with its history: the Codex Florentinus had been the Codex Pisanus, held in the rival city and taken to Florence in triumph when Pisa fell to them. It was, in other words, a piece of war booty, and thus a trophy.

In contrast to this example, the literary and historical texts of ancient Rome very rarely were shown similar respect, at least until the fifteenth century. This is not to say that the Middle Ages spurned classical literature. On the contrary, a range of pagan works were well known: to mention only the most famous, the poetry of Virgil was used in schools, and Cicero was considered an authority for his oratory and philosophy. It is true that, after the collapse of the Roman empire, many texts were lost and the process of depletion continued for centuries. Because parchment was an expensive commodity, a seventh-century member of the monastery of Bobbio in northwest Italy decided that rather than have new folios prepared for a copy of the commentary on the Psalms by the Church Father, Augustine, the leaves of an old manuscript should be rewashed to remove its original text. It was through this act that the lone surviving witness to Cicero's masterpiece *On the Republic* was expunged. The destruction was not complete: traces of the text under the reused material (or what is now known as a palimpsest) were rediscovered in 1819 by the Vatican Librarian, Cardinal Angelo Mai. The fortunes of that work demonstrate how precarious a text's life could be when it survived in only a single copy—and also, therefore, how important monks as scribes and librarians could be for the preservation of pagan culture. When, in 1416, the Florentine humanist, Poggio Bracciolini, saw at the monastery of St Gallen (a little south of Lake Constance), the complete text of Quintilian's guide to oratory, which was unknown until that point in medieval Europe at large, he berated the monks for having locked it away and ill-treated it; surely, instead, he should have thanked them for having kept the work alive so that it was there for him to 'discover'. The manuscript Poggio saw survives:

it is an unadorned copy in a clear book hand made in the eleventh century and studied soon after by one of the brothers of St Gallen.

Such an example helps to remind us that most of the codices discussed so far are unusual. Most date from the earlier centuries of the Middle Ages, and most are Biblical books, often of exceptional quality—for it is often the exceptional that survives. They do, however, reflect elements of the construction of the codex that dominated through the millennium we are surveying and suggest how the book was capable of having a social status which made it much more than an inert conveyor of words: the book itself speaks. It is sometimes assumed that with the increased presence and increased variety of manuscripts in the later Middle Ages, the authority of the codex declined, but this can be overstated. The mystique of the manuscript did not die.

Many factors explain the spread of the book in later medieval Christian Europe, but a basic cause was the fundamental technology of the page. Before parchment became the most common support for writing, the favoured surface was papyrus. As described in Chapter 2, the papyrus plant was associated primarily with Egypt, but it also grew in Sicily. Its use as a writing support for administrative documents was not unknown in early medieval Europe, and Sicilian papyrus still supplied the papal chancery into the eleventh century. Early in the following century on the same island, a material was known which was reminiscent of papyrus and so came about the name by which we know it, paper.

The oldest known Christian manuscript to be constructed, in part, from paper is a late tenth- or early-eleventh-century Mozarabic Breviary at the abbey of Silos (south of Burgos in Castile), but the material was imported. At this time, on the European continent, the expertise to produce paper—the basis of which was the treatment of cloth rags in water—was known only in Islamic al-Andalus. It was only during the Reconquista that places of paper production like Játiva, in Valencia, fell into Christian hands. By the time of Játiva's capture in the 1240s, paper-making was probably taking place in Italy; the place and date usually credited with being the first is the small town of Fabriano (in the Marche, near the border with Umbria) in 1268, but it may well have had predecessors and it may also have started its manufacturing slightly later. What is clear, though, is that by the fourteenth century

Fabriano had become a renowned centre of production, in part because the process was refined to make the paper sturdier; it was also given a watermark, intended to signify who had produced it. Others imitated these innovations, both in Italy and beyond the Alps. By the mid-fifteenth century, there were paper mills in France, the Low Countries, the German-speaking lands (from Trier in the west to Vienna in the east), and beyond in Copenhagen, Cracow, and Buda—but none north of the European mainland in the British Isles. In England, one paper mill was briefly set up outside Hertford in the 1490s, but there was not to be a continuous tradition of paper-making until the 1580s. That is not to say that the English were without paper: the material was both cheap and transportable, and thus, in contrast with parchment which was made for local consumption, an international trade quickly developed, one which could export paper not only to England but also to Islamic North Africa.

Paper, though, was always parchment's poor cousin. A 1231 decree of the Emperor Frederick II (1194–1250) prohibited the use of paper for official documents: he reasoned that parchment was to be preferred so that imperial decisions were recorded in a format which 'would not succumb to the danger of destruction from old age'. The paper he had in mind, produced according to Arab techniques, may have been liable to disintegration at a speed avoided later through the innovations at Fabriano, but a concern about durability dogged the 'new' material. We might marvel at how many texts on paper have survived from the Middle Ages, but we do so partly because the material feels insubstantial; there is no denying that books made from it are more fragile—as well as less aesthetically pleasing—than codices on parchment. This affected how the material was employed: Frederick's prohibition demonstrates that paper had been put to service in his Italian chancery, and its primary use continued to be for documentary purposes like registers and accounts. In the four-teenth century, however, the clerks who created those documents began to adopt the cheap material they encountered at work for their own private activities, and so there developed a sub-culture of books on paper of practical or literary texts, often in the vernacular. That is to say that some secular professionals for whom literacy was primarily intended for transactions transferred their skill from business to books.

Parchment remained the mainstay of books—that situation only changed when the mechanics of the printing press privileged a less supple surface on which to impress its metal letter-forms, and, even then, for more than half a century copies aiming to be high-grade were printed on parchment. This hierarchy of materials used in handwritten culture continued even after the mid-fifteenth century. In earlier generations, the advantage of paper with its lower quality was that it was accessible to some with financial resources too small to invest in parchment. It was certainly more reasonable in cost: even by 1280, in Bologna, it was one-sixth of the price of parchment.

The development of a lay audience for cheaply produced books is part of wider social change. In terms of location, non-clerical readers were most concentrated in those places with a cadre of administrators and merchants—in short, larger urban settlements. Cities were dangerous and unhealthy places to live, their roads more likely paved with bodily waste (human and animal) than with gold, but they were perceived as places of opportunity and grew through inward migration higher than their mortality rates. For some towns, there was a significant additional source of expansion. The first gatherings of masters and students to follow what we would call higher education took place in the twelfth century. Only some of the first locations endured—Bologna, Paris, Montpellier, Oxford—to become, in the thirteenth century, institutions defined as *studia generalia* or universities.

These few were joined by others, some short-lived, but a marked number across Europe were more long-lasting. In some cases, like Ferrara in the fifteenth century, the local ruler proved keen to promote his city as a centre of higher education for the economic boost it could bring, attracting students from elsewhere. To the trades associated with such an influx of young men—lodgings, taverns, brothels— was added the supply of books. Their education, focused on the lecture hall, required them to follow their master in his explication of particular texts. In addition, the richer (or more assiduous) among them might want to purchase or construct books for their private use. At the same time, constituent elements of a university—the colleges of English universities or Paris, for instance—built up their own collections as libraries. The presence of a university became a stimulus to a local book trade so that, for instance in the ramshackled space of

Oxford's Catte Street, artisans gathered to transcribe, illuminate, and bind manuscripts, or sell them second-hand.

That is certainly not to suggest that to be a focus for the book trade, having a university was essential. Indeed, in the short list of towns where the first agglomerations of students took place, Paris stands out because it was a royal city and international entrepôt: the vast majority of university towns were not so significant. For instance, in Italy—the gateway to the eastern Mediterranean—Venice did not have a university until it annexed Padua in 1405, Milan's university was outsourced to nearby Pavia, and the late-medieval trading giant of Genoa had none. Meanwhile, in England, neither royal Westminster nor commercial London had a university, though the latter was home to the professional education in the common law provided by the Inns of Court. Book production and bookselling occurred, though, in all these cities in the later Middle Ages. What made Paris unusual and such an important hub for the book trade was that it combined the elements of commerce, secular bureaucracy, ecclesiastical centre, and higher education within its confines.

The rise of the university was interconnected with another contemporaneous innovation, best exemplified by the city of Toulouse. It was in its region that the Catholic church was on a crusade to extirpate the Cathar heresy, and one of the stratagems was to imitate the universities which had grown organically by founding one in the city with the intention that its graduates would assist the papal cause. The University of Toulouse was created in 1229 and supported by a papal bull of 1233. Its professors were largely drawn from members of a new religious order created only a few years earlier, whose first house was in the same city and whose founder was the Castilian priest whose book triumphantly flew from the flames at Fanjeaux, Dominic de Guzman—it was the Order of the Preachers we know as the Dominican Friars. The friars' official title reflects Dominic's intention that his 'brothers' should be different from monks by being urged to travel and to give sermons. This was not the only new order of friars: in the same period, in Italy, Francis of Assisi established his, and others were to follow. With them, the book needed to travel. In a monastery, books could be stored in a cupboard in the cloister (an aumbry, from the Latin *armarium*) or in a chest or—a late medieval innovation—be chained to desks in a dedicated library room. Friars' convents could have such spaces: indeed, it was for them that the first two libraries of Renaissance Italy were designed—that by Michelozzo for the Dominicans of San Marco in Florence (1436–43) and Cesena's Biblioteca Malatestiana, housed in the town's Franciscan convent (built by Matteo Nuti and completed in 1452). More fundamental, however, to the orders' purposes was that each of their members could have with them books on their tours of duty as preachers. Thus, manuscripts of sermon collections were produced—and in such numbers that it has been claimed that the level of production was symptomatic of 'mass communication'.

The friars' need for portable books also relates to a development at the very heart of Christian culture. Most of the early medieval Bible manuscripts already mentioned in this chapter were not complete texts of the Old and New Testament together in one binding, and we have seen that one of the exceptions, the Codex Amiatinus, was so heavy as to be unwieldy. The single-volume Bible as later Christian cultures knew it was a creation of the thirteenth century, and its success was predicated on two changes of technology. First, the parchment was prepared in such a way as to be very thin—the direct ancestor of 'bible paper'. Second, the script was transformed from stately large letters to a much smaller book hand with many abbreviations in order to fill more text to the page. The result was a codex that was undeniably thick—it could number over 700 folios—but was portable and suitable for private use. Quite how an individual volume might have been employed is usually a matter of speculation: in some volumes, the script is so microscopic as to strain the eye unless read with spectacles (themselves a late thirteenth-century Italian invention); in many, the accuracy of the text is not high. Perhaps an owner, already familiar with the Biblical canon, needed a copy less for close consultation than as an aide-mémoire, or a spur to devotion or, indeed, as a charm intended to keep them safe: for some, it may have had the value of a reference work; for others, of a talisman.

The new layout of bibles left little space for frequent full-page miniatures, and illumination was often confined to initials and borders at the start of each book in both Testaments. This did not inhibit some illuminators' inventiveness, and there was a particular trend in full Bibles and Psalters, as well as manuscripts of secular works: the introduction of illustrations, seemingly disconnected from the meaning of the text, that were weird, grotesque, and sometimes downright rude. Out of the border grew monstrous animals with brightly coloured human faces, and in the lower border were scenes made to shock or amuse. In the Rutland Psalter, a knight with a lance charges a snail; in the Macclesfield Psalter, a man can be seen deftly projecting his urine into a cup; and in several holy books, another man is being shot up the anus with an arrow. Scholars of the late twentieth century became fascinated with these images and provided several theories to explain them. There may, on occasion, be bilingual word-play: the presence in the Latin of the letter sequence *-cul-* might explain the repeated presence of backsides (*cul* in French). We might see in their playfulness an element of the carnivalesque, a licensed undermining of the authority of the text. In addition to these inter-pretations, we could also think of them this way. Even an eye trained to focus on the written word could not avoid being drawn to see the whole page, and to realize that in its layout, the written space is a small proportion of the whole: the marginal is the majority. In effect, the text is cloistered, a rectangle within the rectangle of the page, its dark hue hemmed in by whiteness enlivened with colour. Those who were able to discern meaning from letter-shapes may be intent on contem-plating higher things, but they cannot forget that beyond lies a weird world of earthy realities and hallucinatory imaginings, there to delight, to distract, and to defy them. The page itself serves as a metaphor of a culture of the Word within a majority illiterate society.

The implication of this perspective is that the incongruence of the images gave them a salutary purpose, reminding readers of their privileged position at the same time as providing occasion for a wry smile or maybe even fleeting temptation. In other words, the literate could not be unaware of their minority status, recognizing that others lacked the direct access to the knowledge available to them. Their own responses to the page, however, were not always confined to what we would define as reading. After all, those illuminations themselves demand a process of interpretation different from that of apprehend-ing text—one which could be available to those who had not been to school: the unlettered could be visually literate.

There is striking evidence of another form of interaction with the page that goes beyond our understanding of reading. It is provided by some late medieval Books of Hours and other volumes intended for private devotion. The increase in ownership of Books of Hours in the fourteenth and fifteenth centuries was so substantial that it encouraged—as happened with only a few other types of books—the development of production for a speculative market. Some were created in the Netherlands specifically for export to English booksellers. Most of those which followed that route and survive bear the evidence of Reformation disrespect; decrees by Henry VIII in the 1530s demanded the removal of references to the pope and to Thomas Becket, newly considered a troublemaker rather than a saint. In some manuscripts, though, there are signs of earlier interventions, with, for instance, the face of a saint or the sign of the Cross so rubbed that they are now indistinct. This damage is the result not of vandalism but of a ritual rubbing with fingers or kissing with lips as part of one's prayers. It is defacement by devotion. Similarly, the corners of some folios are blackened with the ink smudged—a sign that it has served something like the function of rosary beads. At times, the way a patch of the illumination shows signs of having been dampened may be the effect of sweaty fingers but, on occasion, it may be from tear-drops falling on the page, as the believer roused themselves to religious fervour. All these habits point to the book becoming part of the apparatus of worship in which the reading of the text was not necessarily the primary function; it served its use by acting as a focus for a process of contemplation which was visual, tactile, and overwhelmingly emotional as much as it was mental.

These practices may echo what book-owners saw in church, with the priest kissing the missal at specific points in the Mass (a ritual which continues in some form into the twenty-first century when, at the Eucharist, the celebrant kisses the page of the Gospel). The engagement of men and women with their Books of Hours, however, takes us into the household where habits of prayer varied according to gender. Some of the manuscripts in which rubbing has occurred were identifiably marked or repaired by female hands. One such is a Book of Hours made at Bruges around 1410 and owned in England by a 'mistress Trygg'. It has been noticed that it includes not only signs of rubbing but also, on some leaves, stitch-holes from which hang a thin piece of silk, covering the image; perhaps mistress Trygg herself picked up her needle to add these demonstrations of her devotion. Men were also excluded from another ritual use of books:

the arrangements around child-birth. During their labour-pains, mothers-to-be were encouraged to invoke the name of St Margaret of Antioch, patron saint of pregnancy. Some also wore as a girdle a parchment roll on which were written prayers to the saint; similarly, a woman might be encouraged to touch or kiss a manuscript of Margaret's life, or it would be placed on her belly.

Such devotional—some would say superstitious—uses of the book in pursuit of life and the afterlife were obviously not relevant for those secular volumes made for edification or entertainment. Even with those, however, we should be careful not to assume that they were solely implements for solitary study. Silent reading was, by the late Middle Ages, established practice, but, in a courtly context, reading was often not undertaken alone. There are fifteenth-century examples of the practice which, for the early modern period, is called 'facilitating', where two men would sit in a chamber, reading and explicating together a text. Similarly, in the hall of a high-status house, a book was often the centrepiece of an evening's proceedings, being read aloud to the prince and their court. So the French chronicler and poet Jean Froissart describes himself reading his romance, *Meliador*, before the warrior count of Foix, Gaston Phoebus (1331–91). He conjures up a scene in which a silence fell among the courtiers as he declaimed, broken only by the interested questions of his host. Those interruptions mark this type of event out from its precedent, the custom in monastic refectories where one of the brothers would read the Bible to his fellow monks while they ate their dinner and listened without a word. Both habits, though, remind us that there was a cluster of practices which have been termed 'aurality', the art of engaging with a book via listening. Reading aloud was not confined to the class-room or the lecture hall.

In the examples just cited, those who heard the text could as well have picked it up and studied it themselves. In other cases, though, an oral recitation could introduce a book to those who were not trained in reading. This might be in a domestic setting, an evening by the fireside where the husband reads to his wife, sometimes in company with her female friends—an example from fifteenth-century Norwich is recorded because the husband explained the text as he went through it, introducing heretical thoughts which resulted in his being taken to court. The role of the wife need not be that solely of the listener. The church often relied on mothers to direct their sons to learn to read, even if they could not do so themselves. This could lead to marital dispute, as had happened to the family of Theodoric (1007–86), a future abbot of St Hubert near Liège; his biographer tells how his mother, 'though she was completely ignorant of letters', was convinced her son should go to school and, in doing so, incurred the wrath of her husband. There were many women like Theodoric's mother, before and after her—as well as those who were themselves more literate than their husbands. The wider relevance of these examples is that a community—whether it be as small as the family unit or a larger group bound by a shared faith or habits—could be literate without requiring all its members to be so. Cultures of literacy embraced the unlettered, who could respect the skills without mastering them. What is more, we can posit that the respect, perforce, was mutual: the literate had to recognize the expectations placed on the book by those who might not be able to read the words but to whom it was no less powerful for that.

The prizing of the book certainly had some paradoxical effects. This chapter opened with a scene in which manuscripts were thrown onto a fire. Few that received such treatment escaped unscathed in the way that Dominic's did. In his culture, however, there was an imperative not only to protect some books, but also utterly to destroy others: what was intended to be the preserve of truth could not be allowed to be a propagator of error. The later Middle Ages did not invent book-burnings, and there were centuries to come when the flames licked higher and with more regularity, but there are plentiful examples from this period. They were not confined to the destruction of heretical works like those of the Cathars. When Granada finally fell to the Catholic Kings of a newly united Spain, its bishop, Francisco Jiménez de Cisneros (1436–1517), oversaw the burning of thousands of copies of the Qu'ran, though he extricated a few hundred Arab scientific manuscripts for the University of Alcalá. In other cases, a text's morality rather than its religion so offended that it had to be purged with fire: the poetry of the Sicilian humanist, Panormita (Antonio Beccadelli, 1394–1471), in which he did not blush to describe all sorts of sexual acts, was burnt in public in the squares of the Italian cities. It did not stop the circulation of the work.

The ostentatious destruction of these books averred their power to be dangerous; to decrease their number acknowledged and enhanced the value of those that remained. Those who stoked these fires were sometimes also participants in another late medieval fashion, that of collecting books. Not only did institutions gather substantial libraries, but so did private individuals, princes of the church, or their lay counterparts. 'Substantial' deserves definition—in comparison to the possibilities created by print, these were small: the French royal library of the late fourteenth century, assembled primarily by Charles V, had a little over 1,200 books, and that was outsize for its day; the collection of the English noble, Humfrey, duke of Gloucester (1390–1447) which, at a rough estimate, was at most half that size, was more typical of what a prince with reasonable resources and inclination could achieve. However limited this may seem, for some contemporaries this first stage in the post-classical history of bibliomania caused anxiety. They wondered whether such amassing of books masked an owner's failure to engage with them intellectually. The Italian scholar, Petrarch (1304–74), asked what the point of a library could be without reading. He assumed his question brooked no answer but, considering what we have seen in this chapter, we might feel in a position to give a partial response to him. A library need not be an active hive of study in order to announce the owner's recognition of the importance of knowledge, just as an individual book need not be read to be the focus of respect or veneration. The paradox remained: the book was the essential weapon of rational debate in part precisely because it held power beyond reason.

6

Renaissance and Reformation

James Raven and Joran Proot

In a letter dated 12 March 1455, Eneo Silvio Piccolomini, the future Pope Pius II, confirmed rumours about a wondrous innovation:

> What was written to me about that marvellous man seen at Frankfurt is entirely true. I have not seen complete Bibles but only a number of quires of various books [of the Bible]. The script is extremely neat and legible, not at all difficult to follow. [You] would be able to read it without effort, and indeed without glasses. (trans., Martin Davies, in 'Juan de Carvajal and Early Printing' *The Library*, 6th ser., 18: 3 (1996), 196)

This brief passage is very helpful to our knowledge of the history of the book in the West, even though it went unnoticed until the second half of the twentieth century. 'That marvellous man' was almost certainly Johannes Gutenberg of Mainz, and Piccolomini provides an approximate date for one of the greatest achievements of early modern Europe: printing with moveable type, a technology which allowed the rapid reproduction of large numbers of books. Visitors to the Frankfurt fair were shown several leaves from sections of the Bible, assuredly in large folio and opened in a double spread. Each page of Gutenberg's Bible carried two forty-two-line columns of Latin text rendered in a large and formal script—printed with moveable type. It is clear from Piccolomini's letter that the printing of the Bible was unfinished, yet the project was sufficiently advanced to exhibit considerable parts of it. When its printing was fully completed is uncertain. One whole forty-two-line Bible was said to be dated by its rubricator as 1456, but this copy has been missing since the Second World War.

The letter is important because so much about the introduction of moveable type remains mysterious. Experiments probably began a decade or more before the printing of the great Bible when Gutenberg abandoned his idea of manufacturing medals for pilgrims and mirror periscopes for viewing relics, and turned to the mass production of paper or parchment forms which claimed to ease the buyer's passage through purgatory. Manufacture of these blank 'indulgences' required the replication of writing by mechanical means. It was a perfect subject for the use of moveable type on a manually operated printing press. The success of indulgence printing prefigured Gutenberg's large-scale and iconic production of Bibles.

Europe's first letterpress printer quite possibly knew something of the centuries-old printing in East Asia, using woodblocks and moveable cut characters, and would have heard of, if not seen, recent experiments in copperplate engraving in Germany. Gutenberg was certainly familiar with the block-printing long used in Europe for trademarks on sacks and decorative designs on altar cloths (among other devices). The design of his press might well have been inspired by the wooden screw of local wine presses. So much of this early history is speculative, and even the method used by Gutenberg to make his innovative type is uncertain.

Early Printing

Gutenberg's Bible and how it came into being leaves us, then, in spite of all research efforts thus far, with more questions than answers. We do not know what his press exactly looked like, nor the composition of his ink that left such an intensely black impression on paper and vellum. The basic idea behind printing with moveable type, however, is fairly simple: it involves a press, type, and an appropriate ink. In this letterpress printing, a font (or fount) of type comprised a set of all the characters of one size and type design (notably black letter, from the 1460s, roman, and then italic), usually cast in the necessary quantities to fill the compositor's pair of type-cases (trays divided up to separate out and store the different characters), and including numerals, ligatures, abbreviations, and punctuation. For each character, a punch-cutter created a steel punch showing the face of the letter in reverse. The punch was then struck into a block of copper. This was the 'strike' which after adjustment became a matrix or concave mould into which was poured melted alloys to cast the pieces of type, known as 'sorts'. The face of any piece of type was the surface inked to impress its shape upon paper. In the sixteenth century, type was made from an alloy mostly comprising lead, tin, and antimony. Tin and antimony lower the melting point of lead alloys, and in addition antimony increases the hardness of type, minimizes shrinkage, and sharpens the definition of the face.

Of the printing process, the basic methods were these. A sheet of paper was dampened (for better ink absorption) and pressed onto an inked surface consisting of moveable type. Each time a sheet was printed, the type was inked again and the next sheet was printed, until the entire print run was ready. Then the type was cleaned and re-distributed into the type-cases waiting to be reused for another printing project. This process is known as relief printing. It still remains unclear how this was exactly done by Gutenberg, because we only have samples of the ink and the paper in the form of printed books. Presses from the fifteenth century do not survive, and there are only very few samples of type left from that period (and even these cannot be dated exactly). In Gutenberg's case, we know neither who designed the punches for the type nor how the sorts were cast. But one thing is absolutely clear: it was a hugely difficult and expensive undertaking. Everything had to be developed and tested for the first time and on a large scale.

The design of new type based on handwritten script (and where early French Gothic bastarda contrasted with Italian roman type) proceeded at a swift rate. Fonts for vernacular printing in Czech, for example, were cast from the 1470s (with influential diacritical marks), and the first books in Romanian printed in cyrillic type date from a printing house in Brașov, Hungary in the 1520s. In addition to languages, different typefaces were also adopted for different genres. Humanist scholars promoted the 'littera antiqua' as a combination of the classical epigraphic *capitalis quadrata* for the capitals, on the one hand, and the Carolingian minuscule, created in the eighth century in the Carolingian Renaissance, for lower case, on the other hand. Scholars have argued that this letter was accepted because of its good readability and because it was easy to write. Konrad Sweynheim and Arnold Pannartz, founders of a press in Subiaco, south of Rome, used a type which showed characteristics of both the traditional black letter and the humanist minuscule, called *gotico-antiqua* or *fere-humanistica*. When they moved to Rome, they introduced a type that rendered more faithfully the characteristics of the humanist minuscule. After its place of origin, it was thenceforth called 'roman'. Some parts of Europe also called roman 'antiqua', and the labels 'medieval' and 'old-style' were employed to indicate roman types dating from the late fifteenth century, especially those used by the Venetian humanist Manutius. South of the Alps, roman type swiftly replaced black letter in the majority of texts, both in Latin and in the vernacular, by about 1525.

North of the Alps, type design evolved more slowly. In Spain and England roman largely replaced black letter for all but chapbooks between about 1550 and 1575, and in France during the second quarter of the sixteenth century. Many texts used a combination of types, including in the Low Countries where roman type became standard in Latin publications by about 1540, but where publications in the vernacular black letter predominated until the late 1660s. In the northern Netherlands—the Dutch Republic—some genres retained black letter until the mid-eighteenth century. In the Catholic southern Netherlands, the acceptance of roman was more rapid—notably for literary and state publications, and by the last quarter of the seventeenth century for devotional and topical publications such as news reports. By contrast, in Germany and other language regions such as Latvia, printers and their clients cleaved to black letter types, such as Fraktur and Schwabacher, at least for vernacular texts until the twentieth century (and its sudden, politically directed suppression). Italic, a cursive roman introduced in 1501 in Venice by Aldus Manutius (1449–1515), was soon copied by many other type-cutters and founders, including in Lyon 1502, in Paris in 1507, and in Germany in 1510, in Basel in 1519, in Latin books produced in the southern Netherlands in 1522, and in 1533 in Denmark. A thrifty letter because it uses less space than roman or black letter, italic allowed the production of more compact books. For a brief period (*c.*1525–35), italic was used more often than roman in the southern Netherlands, but the great Antwerp printer Christophe Plantin (*c.*1520–89) expressed a preference for roman because of its readability. By the end of the sixteenth century, printed italic was established in the secondary but critical role it maintains to this day, for textual emphasis, citations, references, and other special cases.

Relief printing also involved other processes. Woodcuts, using often crudely incised blocks, accompanied letterpress printing for centuries, particularly for ballads and chapbooks. Many woodcuts travelled between printers. The first illustrated book printed in France used woodcuts from Basel, and some of the first printing in Portugal used woodcuts and engravings from Germany. Intaglio printing (or the incising of a printing plate) advanced from the 1430s. In contrast to relief printing with paper impressed upon inked moveable type, intaglio comprised several methods of working, but principally etching and engraving, and usually on copper plates. In etching, the plate was covered with a waxy ground, resistant to acid. Marks were made in the ground using a pointed etching needle or an *échoppe*, a tool with a slanted oval section, and invented by Jacques Callot in Lorraine in the 1610s. The marks were turned into hollows by bathing the plate in acid. Once the remaining ground was cleaned off, ink was forced into the hollows of the plate, and its surface wiped clean. The ink marks in the hollows made the print. Most intaglio printing, particularly for pictorial work, was first etched and then completed with a burin (a hand-held steel tool used to engrave metal or wood), thereby combining the relative cheapness of etching with the finish of engraving. It is often impossible to recover exactly how the plate was worked, and for this reason such prints are often simply referred to as 'engravings'.

Market demands also supported new practical possibilities in the printing of images, including maps, portraits, emblems, and elaborate script by copperplate engraving, then by etching, and later, by a half-tone or 'mezzotint' process creating subtly different tones between black and white. The transformation in the character of books was well under way before Gutenberg's enterprise, but print dramatically enhanced the changes: the extension of vernacular literature, the gradual (but not entire) reconfiguration of production centres and personnel away from the clerical and monastic, the eclipse of bespoke publication and clientage by the speculative and the commercial, and the expansion of non-elite custom. In most cases, customers did not have long to wait for their book to be produced, but a large quantity of books had to look for customers. One copy of a text for one customer was replaced by multiple copies for an unknown market.

Developing Trade and Practices

The new printing processes changed the ways by which European books reached readers. Before printing with moveable type, as earlier chapters have shown, books were usually reproduced in small numbers, often one by one. Those wanting to own a copy of a text had to reproduce the text by themselves or order a copy. For a book as voluminous as a folio Bible, the undertaking could take an entire year. Total costs were great, but by receiving interim payments to buy materials and to support him, the scribe minimized risks that any customized manuscript book would not eventually be bought. In the era of moveable type, this business model had to be fundamentally rethought. The main purpose of printing was to produce larger numbers of copies, print runs normally ranging between a few hundred and a few thousand. For pragmatic reasons, printers counted in reams—typically packs of 500 sheets—or in parts or multiples of reams (250, 750, 1,000, and so on), but variants were common also. For any book project, start-up costs began with investment in equipment and a printing house large enough for at least one press, the type and other materials, and to dry and then store the printed sheets. Printing always was a capital-intensive trade with a slow return on the investment cycle.

Within the printing house, at the very beginning of the printing process, a copy text was prepared for the compositor who 'composed' or set the text type by type, word by word, and line by line, on a hand-held composing stick. Lines were placed in an assemblage of a block of type that would become a printed page. The compositor adjusted each line by means of small word spaces one or more 'points' wide, resulting in the text block appearing as a perfect rectangle with visually straight left and right edges (what we now call 'justification'). Headlines with running titles and page numbers were added to the top of the page and so-called direction lines at the bottom of the text. Lines of type at the bottom might contain catchwords (described in an earlier chapter) or signatures (letters and letters-with-numbers) to indicate the gatherings for inspection by the trade, the stationer or bookseller, then to verify the completeness of the copy, and then for the book binder. The gathering of the printed single sheet of paper once folded, trimmed, and cut, comprised the pages of the book.

To achieve this, the composed pages were organized in a specific sequence on the imposing stone and locked up into a chase (the frame holding the set pieces of type) so that after printing and the folding of the sheet, the pages appeared in the right order. A proof sheet was printed and mistakes corrected before the printing of a full run of the first or 'outer forme', which covers the so-called recto side of the first sheet (the side that faces the reader before the page is turned). The verso (overleaf from the recto) required the composing of another forme, the 'inner forme'.

At the beginning of the sixteenth century, the composition of one page of a folio Bible required about 5,000 pieces of type. Because each forme consists of two pages in folio format, the total number of moveable types to set one forme added up to about 10,000, and double this number for the printing of both sides of a sheet. This preparatory work could easily take up several days, depending on the skills of the compositor and the difficulty of the text. To make this investment worthwhile, a minimum number of copies had to be printed. Outlays included equipment, labour, storage, and handling, but paper invariably proved the most expensive running cost, followed by ink. Even so, the leather inkballs and the costly moveable type itself needed to be replaced regularly. Doubling a print run involved not only redoubling the amount of paper and ink, but also the labour needed to print all copies and to dry and to store them. Five hundred copies of a folio Bible of 1,000 pages, for example, required 15 square metres of storage space and weighed more than 2.5 tonnes. Above all, the process hugely protracts the point at which any return on the investment can be achieved—the time at which the books produced can be sold. Until the very last sheet of the very last forme is printed, all copies remain incomplete and unsaleable.

For the printer-stationer, and all those involved in financing the publication of a printed book, it was therefore of the utmost importance to make a correct evaluation of the market and not to print off more copies than could be sold within a reasonable time. In theory, a printer might set aside the composed type until the need arose to produce more copies, but in practice this was viable—in terms of space and economics—only for rather small works or parts of relatively brief texts such as single-sheet almanacs, reused or adjusted for a new year, and taking up no more than a few formes. Type is not only very heavy to store, but if kept as 'standing type' in stored page blocks or even formes, it is obviously unusable for other jobs. The whole point of moveable type was that it could be broken up again after one printing job and redistributed in the type-cases so that it could be reused for another one (however inefficient this process actually is when compared, say, to printing by the carving and storage of wood-blocks in East Asia).

Instead of tying up valuable resources in standing type, therefore, printers preferred to print editions in conservatively estimated quantities and, if sales proved successful, to print a further edition afresh. This strategy was followed from the earliest days of printing. Of all steady-sellers, the *Imitation of Christ* by Thomas à Kempis (1380?–1471) probably provides the best illustration of this tactic. The four-part spiritual treatise dates from 1427, and its popularity was immediate. After its first printing by Günther Zainer in Augsburg sometime before 1470 as a work in folio format, the book was reprinted at least 745 times before 1650. In all, thousands of editions have appeared in a multitude of forms and formats. In prose or in verse, illustrated or not, in a wide variety of languages and in a wide range of scholarly and other editions, innumerable adaptations, variants, and versions have been printed and continue to be so.

Paper is the constituent we know most about. The many hundreds of European paper mills required a constant high volume of water for power and for the washing process. In collecting rags to break down and effectively recycle their fibres, each mill produced a unique paper identifiable now by the wire-lines, chain-lines, tranche files, water-marks, and uneven structures created in the production process. The sheets of paper, made from organic materials, responded to the changing conditions in which they were stockpiled. It explains the robustness in different climatic and storage conditions of the rag-based paper of printed books before the early nineteenth century (when experiments were begun first with straw and then acid wood pulp). Another consequence was that in addition to the variation in size even within one stack of paper, the different absorption qualities of different papers and changing humidity in the printing house results in different ink-to-surface impressions and even in the dimensions to printed text blocks from one copy to another within the same edition. Product diversification extended further with printing on vellum and the use of an increasing range of different sorts of paper. Numerous improvements in paper manufacture included in the late seventeenth century the so-called Holländer, creating more quickly finer pulp, as well as larger moulds to make two sheets of paper, side by side. Recent research also confirms that between the 1470s and 1540s, paper used for printing gradually became much thinner.

Because, at least in principle, and largely triggered by religious surveillance during the Reformation, many national, civic, or guild authorities required imprints on each publication, a set line or two of type for the imprint could be kept apart and transported to the next publication. If needed, only the date of publication had to be altered. Between 1600 and 1615, the Ghent printer Gaultier Manilius often reused his imprint on the title pages of octavo editions in the vernacular. The imprint is conspicuous by its combination of three different typefaces: roman type for the name of the city, *civilité* for the printer's name, and black letter for the actual address and the name of his premises. The use of *civilité*—a cursive black letter invented in the late 1550s—is especially striking because of its rarity in seventeenth-century imprints. In combination with Manilius' printer's device depicting a white dove—referring to the name of his printing house—it provides his publications with a distinctive and recognizable 'brand' mark. Fust and Schöffer were the first to use a printer's device (in the colophon of their *Biblia Latina* of 1462) as twin shields hanging from a tree branch. Notable subsequent and celebrated printers' devices include the dolphin wrapped around an anchor used by Manutius in Venice from 1501, the pair of compasses that referred to Plantin's motto in Antwerp, 'labore et constantia' (labour and constancy), and the winged turtle of Henrick van Haestens, first in Leiden, 1596–1620, and then in Louvain, 1622–9, and accompanying his motto 'cunctando propero' (hasten by delaying).

The mid-fifteenth-century production of printed indulgences, missals, Bibles, and other religious artefacts proved very profitable. Secular printed texts (especially by dead classical writers) followed almost immediately. Others were quick to copy Gutenberg, despite efforts to keep the technology a secret. By 1470 printing presses worked in some fourteen European cities. Ten years later, 110 towns and cities published printed books. For about fifteen years, however, printing with moveable type remained a largely German undertaking, with the work of Gutenberg in Mainz joined by the printing of Johann Fust and Peter Schoeffer. The first printers in Italy were also German: Ulrich Han in northern Italy, Konrad Sweynheim and Arnold Pannartz in Subiaco monastery near Rome (before moving to Rome and then, in 1469, to Venice). Nicolas Jenson, from Tours in France, also migrated to Venice. Given the commercial vibrancy of northern Italy, printing businesses readily flourished on Italian soil. By 1500 printing presses worked in about eighty towns and cities in Italy and sixty-four towns and cities in Germany. By 1501, there were at least 10,529 separate editions originating from Germany and 10,576 from Italy. In Venice alone, one hundred printing offices and 268 individual printers flourished between 1481 and 1501, producing some two million copies of books.

The first successful press in Florence operated from within the San Jacopo di Ripoli convent of Dominican nuns, who were sometimes employed as compositors. This was also the first Florentine press to produce a substantial and varied corpus of works. There was nothing particularly unusual about a monastic printing office in the decades before 1500. Such presses produced mainly liturgical or theological work for monastic communities. Among precious early records from the Ripoli press is the *diario* or business ledger, which details its financial backers and loans for the initial start-up capital and also documents the day-to-day operation of the press, with detailed schedules for the printing of works, as well as print runs, distribution and sales patterns, pricing fluctuations, and purchases. Besides such locally inspired operations, the role of the immigrant printer proved crucial. German and Dutch printers in particular spread the new technique to France, Spain, England, and eastern and northern regions of Europe. Success was offset by early obstacles and failures: many presses were short-lived and many printed editions proved slow sellers and offered poor returns for the heavy investment involved. In 1634, two dozen Polyglot Bibles remained for sale from the 1,200 copies printed by the great Antwerp press of the Plantin-Moretus family some sixty years earlier between 1568 and 1573.

Even in major cities, few presses worked to capacity in the first centuries of printing, and the printing of jobs—that is, small non-book items of print for commercial, social, or political purposes (a very large proportion of which no longer survive)—was always prioritized on account of the assured custom and tie-over income it provided.

The basic historical profile is of an unrelenting extension of printing presses across Europe and, surprisingly rapidly, their arrival in the colonies, even though the vast majority of reading material for the colonists of the New World continued to be imported from Europe. A printing press operated intermittently in Mexico City from 1539, in Lima from 1581, and in Boston, Massachusetts, from 1638. Again, however, any portrayal of the 'progress of print' has to be qualified by a recognition of the shakiness of the business model of many early modern presses and also of the continuing importance of scribal production and distribution. In the first decades of the press, printed books were not necessarily cheaper than manuscript copies; there was a very well-developed method to produce manuscript books, and new markets had yet to be opened, notably by advertisements and catalogues. Once printers had invested in material, they needed to decide on what to print, for it was (and still is) crucial to select the 'right' text and book to print. The financing of publication, prefiguring the development of what we now call a 'publisher', evolved in different ways by the combination of printers, stationers, and merchant patrons to the advance of publishing booksellers by the seventeenth century. We should also remember that the earliest printed books often mixed techniques. While the main text was printed, rubricators still had to add so-called rubrics and large initials with colour, often red or blue. This marking of initial capital letters and sometimes headings was known as rubrication. Certain continuities acted as constraints. The most notable continuity was the technology of the letter printing press. The Gutenberg printing press and type introduced a technological regime that was to last until 1814, although there were developments in type cutting, the making of paper and ink, and engraving and binding techniques. All these were important in reshaping printed products, but the basic hand printing press remained the only method of printing books, ballads, chapbooks, and derivative printed forms such as newspapers until the nineteenth century. Basic printing press processes and printing house practices changed little before the advent of steam-driven presses. Further restructuring of the book trade concerned distribution and new forms of print such as news-sheets and periodicals. Book-trade development was led by population growth, greater market and economic activity, and the transformation of living practices. If Gutenberg had returned to Mainz in 1800, however, he could have resumed work in printing houses with virtually unchanged printing processes. The only substantial difference was that over time methods had gradually become quicker and cheaper.

Paper-making similarly remained dependent on the collection of rags and on water-powered and manually operated mills, and (despite certain developments in the late seventeenth and early eighteenth centuries in beating and other manufacturing techniques), the main changes to the production of paper came with the increase in the number of mills. Many mills, for obvious water-based reasons, remained at some distance from publication centres, such as the ancient mills of the Valle delle Cartiere of Toscolano Maderno (near Verona), and Brescia, which continued to supply quality paper for the great printing presses of Venice (and elsewhere). Other paper mills were sited closer to presses, such as those in Beaujolais and the Auvergne, not too far from the first printers of Lyon, and those at Prądnik Czerwony, established near Cracow in about 1493.

Although some copies were bound for direct sale, before the mid-eighteenth century most books traded between booksellers changed hands unbound, leaving the ultimate purchaser to select his or her own binder and binding preference. Books for personal devotion (Bibles, psalms, books of hours) were sometimes beautifully bound and therefore often ended up in collections. It is difficult to ascertain which portion of a certain edition was bound, particularly as the remaining known examples may not be representative. Plantin shipped some of his emblem books in bindings to the Frankfurt fair, but most volumes traded at the fair remained unbound. Many incunables (books printed before 1501) have been rebound and 'improved' by past owners and librarians. We have only a few surviving examples of original basic or intermediate bindings (the so-called 'reliures d'attente', meant to protect a book in the short term and to be replaced by a more substantial binding of the owner's choice in due course). Small books, often for immediate consumption, were sometimes just stab-stitched. Examples include chapbooks, pamphlets, and book sale catalogues, but also many Shakespeare quartos and other, more substantial publications.

Volume and Distribution

Charting the advance of the volume of publication is more challenging than identifying the setting up of presses in different parts of the world. Many scholars supply sombre health warnings to 'bibliometrics', but not everyone attends to them. The enlargement of the book trade can be generally plotted by the increase in the publication of separate titles, but estimates based on title counts are no sure indication of the total volume of publication given the extreme variation in the size of print runs.

Comparative production figures range from a hundred (or fewer) copies of privately printed curiosities to 10,000-copy editions of popular dictionaries and grammars and even larger editions of Bibles, missals, and prayer books. Archival evidence of printing house activity offers some measure of the volume of production, but this is available only for a minority of titles. Most printing accounts and business records are lost. Publishers and printers frequently refreshed popular or poor-selling publications by the insertion of new title pages, a practice that further confuses edition tallies. Title counts, which are nationally based and for new publications, also ignore the wider ongoing trade in books both old and new, including imported and second-hand books. If it were possible to produce a snapshot of all books and magazines circulating in any given year, it would reveal a mix of new and old, foreign and home-produced, finely bound, incomplete, and damaged.

Yet another reason for caution is that the commissioning and transmission of texts through scribal publication, well established by the fourteenth century, multiplied as a result of civic, business, financial, and bureaucratic needs and with the increase in written correspondence. The interaction of the scribal with the printed word and image is a critical feature of early modern Europe. Greater authority is often associated with the coming of print. The printed text and certificate seemingly offered greater authentication than the scribal, but in many cases actual authority was not given to a printed document until its blank parts were filled in by pen or it was signed and otherwise validated by written marks or words. The manufacture and use of registers and ledgers similarly expanded with the advance of printing, much, perhaps, as the use of paper has hugely (and apparently paradoxically) increased in the digital age. Both printed and scribal activity required the proliferation of paper mills and output from the late seventeenth century. In addition, increased demand for musical notation and specialist scripts resulted in larger font design and casting, printing and non-Western script, and calligraphy.

Nation-states frame European and Western bibliographical studies (and continue to do so in eastern and central Europe, where many bibliographical archives have become newly available or have received fresh attention in recent years). This is understandable in terms of literary and linguistic interests and of simple practicalities, but it remains a problem for historians. However much print is identified with the cultivation of different vernacular languages and with campaigns and protests that helped advance early modern state formation, in many other ways the nation is a misleading geographical unit for the history of print. The political (not always linguistic) unit was the obvious enabler for retrospective national bibliographies (published as short-title catalogues), but books circulating within that unit were and are international commodities. Even national histories of book and print production need to be accounts of book exchange in and out, of the trade in books, of the different books in circulation and read at any one time, irrespective of where they were originally printed or sold.

Identifying the origins of many early printed books is also beset by problems. For example, in order to escape censorship or seizure, the imprints of many editions declared that they were printed in the Netherlands when they were not, and many that *were* printed in the Netherlands stated that they were printed in France or Germany, or elsewhere. By putting Den Haag (The Hague) in their imprints, publishers in France might escape censorship; similarly, Catholic editions printed in the Dutch Republic often used an Antwerp or Louvain imprint to avoid criticism, but also to emphasize their Catholicism. Even under censorship, in other examples, the main sources of early Romanian-language printing were Wallachia and Moldavia, whose products travelled to Transylvania. Romanian-language volumes appeared in Vienna and Buda. In these and many comparable cases across Europe, false imprints continue to offer enigmatic bibliographical puzzles. The shrewdest printers even 'borrowed' existing imprints from unsuspecting colleagues.

The broader issue is the travel of books and print. Attention to the transnational requires consideration of the transmission of texts, of how bibliometrics might move from production to circulation. Across early modern Europe, the distribution of books, one of the mechanics of cultural transaction, underpins the ways in which frontiers for the written and printed word, vernacular or otherwise, were both created and breached. Continuing scholarship traces, for example, the Russian and Eastern destination of books from the Netherlands, Amsterdam, and The Hague, and the German links forged with St Petersburg and the Baltic towns.

Medieval, usually bespoke, book production and trade centred on monastic and university centres. But late fifteenth-century stationers and printers used the great fairs of Europe as important trading and distribution centres for progressively commercial wares. The earliest record of a printer-publisher trading at the fair at Frankfurt-am-Main dates from 1478. Other fairs operated recurrently at Paris, Lyon, Vienna, and Nuremberg, although early modern Parisian publishers relied on relatively local distribution and rarely sent representatives to the Frankfurt fair, unlike publishers in Venice and Antwerp. The Frankfurt fair contracted in the early seventeenth century, and the Leipzig fair became less international (if, by the end of the century, still advertising the 'Latin' book trade in law, medicine, and theology). Competing urban centres and sharply increased vernacular printing by the end of the seventeenth century stimulated semi-national publishing regions and long-distance book-trading circuits with a deepening social penetration of print. Of many examples, the regular routes of indefatigable small book pedlars through France, Savoy, and Italy were traced by the social historian Laurence Fontaine. Basel and Lyon remained especially active, while Amsterdam's publishing developed during the seventeenth century, also exemplifying the complex and sometimes unexpected currents of publishing history. There is, for example, clear evidence of supply by booksellers across the Low Countries to meet the increased demand for print from the Counter-Reformation Church. Not only did important Antwerp printers like the Moretuses and Verdussens print Roman liturgical books and vernacular devotional Catholic literature, but so too did printers in the Protestant North such as the Elzeviers, Blaeu, Schipper, the Huguetan brothers (émigrés from Lyon), and the cartography specialist van Loon.

Great cities boasting many printers and publishers by the end of the sixteenth century, led by Paris, Venice, Amsterdam, and Antwerp, were major distribution centres, but so also were other cities on major European crossroads. The Kobergers of Nuremberg kept stocks with distribution agents in Venice, Danzig, Hamburg, Basel, Frankfurt, Lübeck, Prague, Augsburg, Amsterdam, Vienna, Lyon, and a dozen more. As Anton Koberger had extolled in a printed advertisement that accompanied the more than 2,500 copies of his great *Nuremberg Chronicle* of 1493: 'Speed now, Books, and make yourself known wherever the winds blow free'. In what might be described as the 'Hansa model' of book marketing, merchants travelled to fairs and other marts selling to other wholesale merchants, making use of numerous factors, licensed itinerant salesmen, and warehousing facil- ities along both established and developing trade routes. Books— many exported as sheets and packed in barrels—travelled in a net- work connected to the great freight routes. Key overland routes included the Amsterdam to Breslau route and the Iter Italicum, the two-way route from Poland to Rome used by clergy, diplomats, scholars, and students. The Polish bibliographer, Jan Pirożyński went so far as to argue that the effect of the Iter Italicum book route limited the much vaunted influence of England, the Low Countries, and France in the Polish Renaissance.

Printing was introduced to Poland, in Cracow, as early as 1473 (by an itinerant Bavarian printer), and at least 7,000 different editions were printed in Cracow and the other towns of Poland-Lithuania in the sixteenth century. Even though the Polish book industry was less developed compared to the printing houses and publishing booksellers of Italy, the Low Countries, and France, Polish presses nevertheless played a vital part in supplying print to central and eastern Europe. The earliest books in cyrillic type were printed in Cracow and then in the Balkans before the seventeenth-century ascendancy of the Moscow Printing House, founded in about 1568 and then reopened and more effectively productive from 1614.

From the mid-sixteenth century, Poland further exemplified a production centre that also constituted an important market for books. Similar interplay developed in Hungary, Bohemia, and Moravia a little later (most early Hungarian books were printed in Cracow and Vienna). The Polish market is graphically reflected in the surviving inventories of booksellers and merchants (which include, among many examples of imported texts, thousands of Protestant books printed in Polish in Königsberg). Polish booksellers imported and distributed books that were produced in Europe's leading printing centres. There was a similarly growing demand for imports of printed matter in Scandinavia, where, for example, the Danish printer Henrik Waldkirch (active 1598–1629) established important connections to the Frankfurt fair and to Basel. For all the attention to a golden age of English letters from Shakespeare to Milton, the English model was not dissimilar to the Scandinavian, being far from self-sufficient in printed and especially scholarly book production before the end of the seventeenth century.

In sustaining this pan-European development, booksellers' catalogues, issued and used by both wholesalers and retailers, were originally the sole vehicles for the advertisement and promotion of booksellers' wares. By the late seventeenth century, the catalogues were very widely available, but were also only part of a broader commerce in print where distributional success limited as well as promoted new printing and publishing initiatives. Correspondence networks also increased hugely, encouraging the printing and transport of printed texts but also long-distance scripted exchanges of knowledge. The network built by Henry Oldenburg (1619–77), first secretary to the Royal Society in London, for example, stretched from Breslau and Danzig to Styria, Carinthia, and the Balkans (as well as to remote extra-European settlements).

Publishers attended so closely to distribution because of the commercial need to sell quickly and prevent competitors from saturating the market. With major capital tied up in unsold expensive printed materials, it was usually necessary to sell as quickly as possible the whole edition in which so much was invested. Fresh capital was also required to undertake the next big project. The only development concerned the use of back-lists, with volumes stored in depots at international fairs. When an especially urgent sale was required, discounting also proved critical. In mainland Europe, the greatest of the international booksellers maintained permanent warehouses at the fair cities of Leipzig and Frankfurt and swapped, sheet for sheet, printed materials with other publishing booksellers (a practice known as Tauschhandel). Established trading circuits in southern Germany extended their reach, much in the same way that the printers and publishers of Venice, dominant in Europe by 1500, developed far-reaching trading alliances and networks. As we know from his letters to the English diplomat and scholar Thomas Bodley, the London printer and bookseller John Bill not only issued his copies of Frankfurt catalogues but also travelled to the fair, then at the height of its fame as the central book mart in Europe. There is every reason to think that similar exchange practices, if on a more modest scale, operated between other leading booksellers.

Sale and commercial exchange were not the only means of distribution. At times when large collections represented a great proportion of the overall book market, books travelled as gifts, as the pawns of religious contest, and as trophies of war. Royal deaths, for example, brought the dispersal of great libraries like the Corvina of Matthias of Hungary and the great collection of Zygmunt August of Poland. The *Reconquista* in Spain, the advance of the Ottomans in the Balkans and Central Europe, and the Reformation and Counter-Reformation caused widespread upheaval in the book market. Private, institutional, and monastic libraries, from Tunis to Pozsony, were pillaged or broken up and sold. Stockholm's royal library gained hugely from the looting of the Thirty Years' War, while the bibliographical price Sweden paid for the abdication of Queen Christina in 1654 was her eventual transference of thousands of manuscripts and books to the Vatican library. Much other pillaging during the Thirty Years' War paradoxically rejuvenated the exchange of ancient books and manuscripts. Crates of books crossed the mountains of western Europe and sailed down the Danube and the Rhine (and there are scores of other major redistributive examples). This does not, of course, diminish the impact of war or religious struggle on the sale of books. Few gluts or dearths after conflict or pillage have been without their commercial beneficiaries, and booksellers (and book-buyers) are certainly not excepted from this.

Many critics, such as the philosopher Gottfried Leibniz, feared the consequences of a great deluge of books, of literary devaluation by unbridled commercial publishing. Alarm at the popular helps to explain the obsession with order in architectural statements in both internal and external library design, and the contradictory tensions in Enlightenment Europe, seen at quite humble levels as well as grand ones, between the worship of literature and the desire to set up boundaries to reading, to exclude those who could not be trusted to read 'properly'.

It is also salutary to consider demand for print not as demand for reading but as demand for objects viewed as worthy of possession. Printing did introduce the luxury book edition that was not to be read. As pointed out by Eugenio Garin long ago, we have to give attention to the number of books shelved and not read; displayed and talked about, but not read; fought over and sent round Europe as booty, but not read. Histories of books and print must encompass all aspects of possession and exchange, and it is probable that the increased production of books—and of exceptional editions—by printing increased the proportion that remained unread.

Notwithstanding the relative standstill in printing technology, printed output nevertheless advanced. Early printing Leviathans commanded numerous presses such as those of the Aldine press of Manutius in Venice, of the Officina Plantiniana of the Plantin-Moretus family in Antwerp, and of the Cromberger family in Seville. At its peak in 1574, the Plantin printing house maintained sixteen presses, with up to a dozen operating at any one time between the 1620s and 1730s. Following new market activity and in many regions a mini-consumer boom in the late seventeenth century, many other European printing houses increased the number of presses they operated on-site. The typical workshop, however, operated only one or two presses.

These considerations highlight a further, little discussed aspect of printing house regimes. At least until the economic developments of the late seventeenth century the majority of presses never worked at full capacity. Early modern printing houses were busy, noisy, and dangerous places (many printers and apprentices suffered from lead poisoning), but the demand, at least for book production, was not always sufficient to keep them all working all of the time. Until the late seventeenth century most presses worked at undercapacity or at least under very uneven work patterns in which surging demand for a particular publication (and resultant shared work between printers) was offset by long periods of reliance on jobbing work. For at least the first two centuries of printing, demand for printed book publication would have proved insufficient to keep presses working, even if the manually operated wooden printing presses had been remodelled to increase productivity (and as eventually enabled by the iron presses after about 1800, allowing the introduction of steam-driven presses after 1814). This was as true in London and Paris as it was in Russia. In St Petersburg and Moscow, for example, the number of printed items published in the reign of Peter the Great (1682–1725) was more than double that of all titles printed in Russia before 1682, but more than 60 per cent of this new printing actually comprised state and legal documents. In London, despite regulations restricting the number of presses and despite petitions from those eager to set up new presses, the productive capacity of the city's printing trade probably changed little before the English Civil War. Analysis of the day-to-day economics of an early modern printing house also confirms an important broader conclusion: 'print culture', an overused and problematic term, is about more than books, about more even than periodicals and newspapers. It is about all products of the press, of print considered in the widest sense of the term: of printed labels, forms, indentures, advertisements, bills, receipts, tickets, and all manner of lists, including for laundry.

Most printers from the fifteenth century to the nineteenth century and throughout Europe also depended on the regular income afforded by jobbing work. Printers printed sheets, not books. The sheet work that did not comprise pages for books and periodicals ranged over many different sorts of commissions. These orders for certificates, blanks, tickets, and much more besides, provided crucial tie-over income in fallow times and valuable training for apprentices, as well as promotional displays of printers' craftsmanship. The printing of so many thousands of different 'blanks' further complicates simple assertions about the primacy and authority of print. Numerous printed items ranging from receipt slips to certificates of residence and employment were forms left largely blank to be filled in by pen and ink. As with Gutenberg's indulgences, final authority resided less exclusively in the print of the form than in the empowering penned-in details and signature.

Effects

Charting the progress of printing town by town across Europe has its challenges, but more problematic is the evaluation of the impact of that printing. Modernity, it is often asserted, arrived with gunpowder, the compass, and the printing press. The success of the introduction of printing by moveable type, and also by engraving and other intaglio processes, followed on from the recovery of the population after the Black Death of the fourteenth century and the concomitant greater movement of peoples and modest increase in discretionary and disposable income (which increased demand for consumables). Print undoubtedly transformed politics, religion, commerce, and intellectual, linguistic, and cultural life, but is it really possible to speak of a 'print culture' in early modern Europe when so much continued to depend on oral communication? Much of what was read was also persistently *written* not printed, especially in the form of graffiti, ledgers, and letters. Many texts, especially in the early years of printing, circulated in manuscript before appearing in printed editions. Consequently, as earlier chapters have suggested, the history of books and writing before the introduction of print offers insight into cultural and communication practices that transcend the technological difference between script and print—and especially as printing also encompassed the reproduction of cut, engraved, and printed images as much as of printed words.

The most obvious perspective in the history of printing is that of transformation, of the revolutions brought to individual mental worlds as much as to collective politics, commerce, or devotion. As several generations of historians have demonstrated (with differing emphasis and insistence), printing encouraged and enabled both the organized transmission and the personal understanding (and misunderstanding) of new intellectual, political, and religious propositions from the Protestant Reformation and Catholic Counter-Reformation to secular Enlightenment and American and French revolutions. Nevertheless, change in the practice of communication is subtler than often appears. Emphasis on new technologies can disguise a broader historical context in which material objects—namely, books changing from script to print—are socially highly specific.

In this history of books we should of course remember that relatively few people in fourteenth-century Europe engaged directly or extensively with written words and numbers. If needed at all, basic literacy and numeracy enabled labourers to mark down numbers of livestock or products, or create simple calendars. Some tradesmen and craftsmen required more advanced literacy or numeracy, but their proficiency remained well below that of clerks and clerics, whose activities depended more perceptibly on counting, reading, and writing. Given that knowledge of Latin was often demanded, 'literacies' might be a better skill description than 'literacy'. Even so, much was memorized, and the oral continued to dominate the written. From northern and western to eastern and southern Europe, print is rightly associated with linguistic consolidation and with the orthographic and syntactic distinction and standardization that were key components in the formalization of national languages. Before the coming of age of dictionaries and popular grammars in the mid- to late eighteenth century, however, popular linguistic development resulted as much from day-to-day verbal exchange between migratory peoples and from secular and religious oral performance as from the direct influence of written and printed texts. The reading of texts reached the ears rather than the eyes of the illiterate during great upheavals such as the Reformation and rebellions such as the Fronde in France (1648–53), in the form of pamphlets (and, later, newsletters) that were often read out loud to the people.

The material forms of the printed book also had clear antecedents. Gutenberg's Bible enterprise created heavy tomes that in many ways resembled huge twelfth-century manuscript lectern Bibles. After the increased popularity of smaller hand-held Bibles in the fourteenth and early fifteenth centuries, lectionaries (large collected readings from Scripture) returned to favour. Lectionaries were read on many different occasions and certainly not simply in monastic refectories. Gutenberg and his rivals and successors exploited huge market opportunities in the Rhineland and Netherlands, where the vast manuscript lectern Bibles were hugely expensive to produce. More than eighty editions of the Latin Bible were printed by letterpress before 1500. The early option to have the first printed Bibles manufactured on vellum proved an unanticipated success, and one that highlights continuities. Gutenberg's Vulgate Bible, with forty-two lines on each page, followed a format made standard in thirteenth-century Paris. Books of hours, similarly growing in popularity from the early fourteenth century, offered printers a physical template for innovative design and decoration. With their selection of religious and liturgical texts, these books commanded notable demand among monied and devout women and, at least in their simpler, unilluminated form, increased custom among those of modest wealth. Such demand boosted the market for print, but it also encouraged different typographic design paradigms, with clear differences, quite aside from the different sizes and formats of books, between the layout of Latin and roman and of vernacular and gothic texts.

At first, little appeared to change in the use of books following the introduction of printing by moveable type and the increased use of woodcut illustration and intaglio printing from the mid-fifteenth century. A Bible, psalter, or prayer book might be glimpsed in church or on the deathbed. Some men and women read the occasional ballad or advertisement, and, according to one's lot, papers and small parchments referring to trials, military service, or the supply of food and other necessities. Many children learnt to read by use of ABC hornbooks—small printed sheets of letters and numerals protected by a covering of translucent horn so that these hand-held primers could be reused down the generations. For most men and women, however, knowledge related to the natural world, to practical skills and handed-down lore, and depended more on observation, listening, and memory than on material texts.

By 1650, the world had changed, and especially in urban communities. Now, many more men and women directly or indirectly encountered the multiple products of the printing house. Print, however, must not be confused with, or at least restricted to, books and what we usually think of as 'publications'. By the mid-seventeenth century, only a minority of Europe's population confidently read pamphlets, newspapers, and books (even including Bibles, prayer books, and hymnbooks). An especially refined minority engaged with works of great learning, fastidious devotion, or sophisticated entertainment. The small books that most people encountered were probably almanacs and prayer books. Books remained expensive and most common people could not afford to buy them. As described in the next chapter, libraries only began to open up to the public in the seventeenth century, and then only for specific groups of clerics, the intelligentsia, or nobility.

Nonetheless, between 1450 and 1650, the impact of books, printed and manuscript, deepened and diversified, but the contours of this development over time were uneven and complicated by the vagaries of printing and publishing history. During these three centuries, technological and production constraints counterpointed developing market demands for printed staples (Bibles, prayer books, psalters, almanacs, religious and instructional primers, chapbooks, ballads, and prognostications) and for new and evolving types of production (legal, geographical, maritime, military, and other secular guides and compendia, as well as early news books). Certain step-changes were a consequence of the unblocking of obstacles to market take-up and especially the reduction in the number of civil wars in western and central Europe after the 1650s and, later, transport changes from the 1670s.

The outpourings of agitators and the attacks and defences of printed pamphlet and propaganda warfare had sustained both urban and peripatetic, clandestine printers from the earliest years of the Reformation to the Thirty Years' War and beyond. International peace remained rare, and wars and skirmishes continued to interrupt long-distance book traffic, but within many states the late seventeenth-century calming of civil and religious confrontations brought new if socially uneven market conditions. These offered new possibilities for spending on non-essential items, among which books and print were increasingly prominent. Greater domestic stability, however, also encouraged new censorship and regulatory procedures. Many impositions appeared with claims that they were intended to prevent a return to the internecine horrors of recent times, but many also protected monopolistic trading by leading publishers (and notably in England where the Stationers' Company technically policed all copyright registration). New restrictions, of both pre-publication censorship (as in France) and post-publication censorship (as in Britain) curtailed expression, dictated where production took place, and encouraged clandestine printing but had no overall restraining effect on the expansion of the volume and the market for different kinds of printed material. As the distribution of printed material became easier, the networks of intellectual exchange that had flourished from the early sixteenth century, and continued through the most difficult years of turmoil of the late sixteenth and mid-seventeenth century, attained an unprecedented reach. Private publishing, financed by the patronage of individuals and institutions, also increased but was increasingly eclipsed by new forms of commercial popular literature spreading across Europe from an increasing number of production and distribution centres.

Reading and the Impact of Print

The relegation of scribal culture has been implicit in many histories of the early modern book. The historian Elizabeth Eisenstein, for example, radically extended the narrative of the modernizing impact of printing by arguing that the sixteenth-century press fomented intellectual, scientific, political, and religious revolution. The Eisenstein thesis, which has been as influential as the 'communications circuitry' model developed by Robert Darnton at about the same time, rested on three main propositions: that the printing press revolutionized first the volume of textual production; second, the speed of that production; and third, the nature of the text itself. The volume of printing was palpably far greater than the written output of scriptoria, as was the rapidity of printed manufacture that enabled faster dissemination and more effective—and vituperative—debate.

The third claim of the 'technological determinist' thesis was the most crucial and the most contentious. The reproductive quality of printing that effected the communications revolution resided in an unprecedented textual fixity that gave new authority to the published word and new certainty to debate. A reader in Prague might read and discuss a near-identical text with a reader in Lisbon in possession of a copy of the same printed edition. No longer might the text vary according to the style and aptitude of the scribe and suffer from a real or presumed unverifiability and rely, as a result, on supportive oral transmission. This 'communications shift' further codified images, visual aids, and signs, leading to what Eisenstein described in a leading chapter title as the 'features of print culture'. Standardizations, linguistic fixity, the revivification of scholarship and interest in ancient languages and the Classics, and translation into vernacular languages—most significantly, translation of the Bible—all epitomized a printing revolution. Technology interacted with new forces in religion, politics, and science to produce (among a vast array of other publications) Lutheran and Calvinist tracts, Copernican treatises, and printed editions of Pliny, Galen, and Aristotle.

One observation, not generally made, is that the discussion between readers and authors encouraged by print, and sometimes continued by printed commentaries, might, more often, be conveyed by written correspondence. Such letter-writing greatly increased during the sixteenth and seventeenth centuries and added to the interrelationship between script and print. The resultant intellectual ferment invites questioning of how print and script interacted with oral communication but also rests uneasily with social histories from below, where more precise study of the interaction with the printed word is required. Intimate social histories most effectively question emphasis on the 'fixity' of the printed text, and they do so by evaluating the experience of reading. While printing technology might allow texts to be replicated more quickly, in greater numbers, and with unprecedented technical stability, no meaning is given to a text until it is read. In this sense a book and a text is an unstable cultural object. The evidential basis of the effect of reading, of ascertaining how and why reading was done, is hugely problematic. Questions of reading abilities and aptitudes relate to age, gender, social and economic circumstances, environment, and even light and posture, but the history of reading practice also requires an understanding of motivation. Consumers revisited texts and effectively remade them by their different readings. Differences in interpretation were made not only between different people of different genders and different competences (affected by intelligence, education, skill, and incentive) but by the same person revisiting the text on different occasions, at different ages, for example, or for different reasons.

Reading, self-evidently, made printing and the acquisition of books both dangerous and revelatory. Certain occurrences are evident, from the dissemination of humanist learning and the fine production of maps, charts, and reckoners, to the creation of a vast informative literature of the street and field. In its replication of ballads, ABCs, chapbooks, and firebrand pamphlets and news-sheets, the printing press did prove a progressive force. Astronomy, botany, medicine, natural philosophy, and geography were obvious beneficiaries of the printing house and its attendants, the master printer, the highly skilled compositor, and the learned proof reader (sometimes in combination). Printing boosted use of vernacular languages and effectively standardized and determined them, directly changing literacies and boosting simple literacy levels (if not always creating a vast new population of readers, and not always leading to the codification of spelling: standard written Slovak, for example, did not develop until the 1780s). New areas of expertise were created, and information exchange speeded up and diversified. The press indirectly changed popular understanding by reshaping the interplay between the written and the oral. Above all, the immediacy of the printed word was seen, heard, and feared.

As Reformers insisted, readers searched for salvation by means of the direct word of God. They searched in the vernacular and in defiance of the Vulgate Bible, essentially the Latin of St Jerome. The sixteenth-century domestication of the printed Bible in modern languages was new in extent but not in origins. Followers of John Wycliffe in the late fourteenth century anticipated the central feature of Reform, investing the immediacy and intelligibility of the vernacular with a further authenticity derived from Greek and Hebrew and declared to be superior to the Vulgate. With revolutionary scale, print carried and personified truth (and later rationality) over superstition. In 1516, Desiderius Erasmus published his Latin edition of the New Testament to rival the Vulgate, and translated from the original Greek. Erasmus provided the basis for Luther's German translation of the Bible. As many as eighteen editions of parts of the Bible in German were printed between 1466 and 1522, the date of Luther's publication of the New Testament in German. The earlier German Bibles, often also adorned with large woodcuts, had been translated from the Vulgate (with sections rivalling the incomprehensibility of parts of the Wycliffe Bibles). More than fifty editions of Luther's New Testament were printed between 1522 and 1529. Luther completed his entire Bible in German in the autumn of 1534, most of it translated from the 1494 Soncino Hebrew Bible. On the printed woodcut title page of the New Testament, God is depicted leaning over the text with the motto (as translated): 'God's word remains forever'. The New Testament was translated into French in 1523, Dutch in the same year, Danish in 1524, Swedish in 1526, and Finnish in 1548; the whole Bible was issued in Dutch in 1526, in French (from the Vulgate) in 1530, in Swedish in 1541, and in Danish in 1550. Printed commentaries poured forth. During Luther's lifetime, his own books and pamphlets were published in German in more than 3,700 editions.

Printed books thus vastly enhanced the effect of translation. Textual differences were often minute, but as daunting and high-profile claims about printed variants ensured, tiny differences in translation and emphasis supported momentous doctrinal dispute. Many productions were also magisterial printing house efforts, in which accuracy and the beauty of design proved significant attributes. The Complutensian Polyglot Bible, by Francisco Ximenes de Cisneros, was finished in mid-1517 after three years of printing. Modelled on the Hexapla of Origen, this immense polyglot edition arranged the Greek, Vulgate, and Hebrew texts in six parallel columns, together with complex apparatus and keyed letters to notes. The Antwerp Polyglot was printed by Plantin in eight volumes between 1568 and 1573, incorporating Syriac, as did the Paris Polyglot of 1645. The fourth such Bible, 'the London Polyglot', completed in 1654 by Brian Walton at the press of Thomas Roycroft, has been mooted as the most distinguished as well as the most substantial product of the British press in the seventeenth century.

Print filtered language, but it also broadcast radical and seditious images. The prominence of images and decoration increased rather than diminished because of printing. In early printed books the intervention of scribes and illuminators remained crucial, further complicating the history of print-with-script. Rubrication proved too difficult to insert in early printed Bibles, and compositors created blank spaces for later attention (something which also related to inherited standards of book design). To assist, Gutenberg printed eight sheets of instructions for rubricators. Indents were similarly left for inscribed initials, before woodcuts found renewed favour, notably affecting the evolution of page design in almost every type of publication from Bibles to chapbooks. The social historian Bob Scribner championed the historical importance of visual and oral communication alongside printed words, which he believed to have been overestimated in the dissemination and impact of the Reformation. But he also insisted on the complexity of such media. Visual propaganda works at several levels; printed illustrations needed to be read as a system of signs whose semiotics required careful decoding. Luther's 1522 New Testament paraded hundreds of woodcuts, mostly as formulaic initials, but at least the first 3,000 copies printed also included notoriously idolatrous images of the Pope. We still need to know more about why and how people read in the Reformation, but the visuals that accompanied the lettered text were evidently powerful. Here were *livres sans frontières* with a geographical as well as an intellectual unboundedness that impelled authorities to invent bans on books and on the movement of printers.

The quest for illumination over ignorance was as public as it was private, and the reaction to the pernicious power of print was as much about its effect upon crowds and congregations as it was about individual readers and deviants. The threat of publicly supported doctrinal error, of a frenzy of ideas let loose, was still more alarming than individual error. The invasive, subversive, and heretical power of print provoked churches and states into punitive action, from the burning of books to the creation of lists of banned books and a battery of regulations and penalties against authors, publishers, distributors, and the printed words themselves. For four centuries after Gutenberg, the rate and manner of selling books continued to be curtailed by two different types of obstacle: by regulation imposed by church, state and town government, and guilds, and by the constraints of transport infrastructures.

Contraband books and literary undergrounds have been the subject of many distinguished studies. First, and most obviously, printing and pre-publication regulation was introduced by ecclesiastical and national authorities and by trade and guild regulation from within the industry. Censorship and policing, and to some extent guild authority, followed not an economic but a political time-frame, with varying effectiveness at different periods and locations. France, Spain, and Italian states, including Venice, variously adopted direct control over censorship and the policing of the press, and were subject to the constant attentions of the church.

Post-publication policing took many forms. In reputation at least, the *Index Librorum Prohibitorum*, established by the Vatican in 1559, dominated censorship in Europe. The *Index* curtailed distribution, forced underground transmission, and remains an unavoidable part of any study of bookselling in the Catholic realms. Its influence contributed largely to the demise of the Frankfurt book fair, further undermined by a book commissioner sent by the emperor and by a successive Book Commission that suppressed Protestant publications. In the sixteenth century, Frankfurt handled about twice the volume of books traded at Leipzig; by 1700 the figures were reversed. Nonetheless, Leipzig was never to be as international in character as Frankfurt. Protestant realms developed similar censorship and introduced brutal curbs to the publication and transport of print, especially across borders. In England, the Low Countries, and northern Europe, press regulation was largely, although never entirely, devolved to guilds or trade companies also maintaining commercial monopolies and regulating employment conditions and entry to the trade. Confusion between or conflation of a state policing and a private property protection role was evident in the advancement of patent holders and formal and informal cartels. In the more corporatist model, different crafts adopted different regulative and trading functions. The supremacy of the Stationers' Company in England in the late sixteenth and seventeenth centuries can be compared with the mighty Guild of Binders in northern Scandinavia, where bookselling largely comprised the sale of imported books, unbound. The binding trade took responsibility for import and regulation of printing and publishing from 1620, at the zenith of Swedish international power, until the second half of the eighteenth century. The powerful binders in Lithuania and the Ukraine, who also specialized in the crucial foreign book trade, exercised similar authority.

Many early modern town governments also imposed limits to trade in books and publications, although protection was often more from economic than ideological concern. The distinction between wholesale and retail was often reinforced by civic laws which forbade those who were not freemen of a town from selling by retail. For many sixteenth- and seventeenth-century merchants, native and alien, and certainly including the producers and sellers of books and print, the rounds of the fairs and markets held outside the jurisdictions of the towns were increasingly successful sources of business. In central and eastern Europe, such constraints endured for a further century or more, with many changes and interruptions during an often volatile political history.

Alongside essentially trade regulation, the revolutionary possibilities of printed knowledge provoked further restrictive controls following on from the Thirty Years' War, the Fronde, the English Civil War, and indeed almost every rebellion and war of the late seventeenth and early eighteenth centuries. The French government developed a system of pre-publication *privilèges* (codified in 1723 which also often offered permissive critical assessment). In contrast, in England the punitive Licensing Laws (technically, the Printing Acts) operated for most years between 1662 and 1695 in conjunction with the first and only appointment of a Licenser and 'Surveyor' of the press, charged with seizing hidden presses and seditious literature. In many parts of Europe, effective censoring, both before and after publication, remained with local rather than far-distant authorities. But print also encouraged a very different mode of revolution, as provocative but not easily repressed by simple bans or restraints on publication and circulation. The vastly increased geographical and social penetration of print created different modes of textual engagement. Encounters with print spanned the development of specific methods and fashions in book collection and the formation of libraries to different modes of reading and the evolution of different cognitive processes.

As a result of printing, European books metamorphosed from elite luxuries into diverse, popular, and more generally available commodities. The distances travelled by books are not perhaps a surprise, given that by the fifteenth century, manuscript circulation was extraordinarily far-flung. For at least two centuries, cargoes of written books had travelled by land and water as part of increasingly sophisticated international trading networks, focused on urban, religious, and university centres.

What astonishes is the rapid advance of the social as well as geographical penetration of print, enabled by the development of new production, trading, and transport techniques and initiatives. The commercial transformation responded not only to new technological, commercial, legal, and political opportunities, but also to shifting incomes and to increasing and changing literacies. Changes, however, were unevenly paced, with checks and constraints as well as productive spurts and underlying, gradual advances.

A growing cast of craftsmen and commercial operators mediated between writer and reader. By the end of this period, private proprietary libraries with membership by subscription, together with commercial circulating libraries, offered new modes of access to print as well as new social spaces for reading and discussing ideas and gossip. The locales of printing and bookselling gained a reputation as places of information exchange. Buyers, borrowers, and browsers swapped news that was informative, practical, and sometimes scurrilous. A growing market for print specifically created for women paralleled sharper divides between reading societies and libraries established with women in mind and those excluding women. But print also bridged gender distinction as much as it encouraged it. For all the emphasis at the end of this period upon magazines and practical, domestic books for women, at the same time both sexes were attracted to broadly based periodicals, religious publications, essays, playbooks, and travel guides (among others). Advancing publication combined, by the mid-eighteenth century, with the growth of a literary infrastructure of reviewing and criticism to span but also to foment confessional and political difference. The increase in the number and range of correspondence networks further supported the translation activities that underpinned many publishing ventures. This triumph of print translated into profit. Many books proved valuable commodities, and privilèges, patents, and copyrights were granted and created and sold to protect property interests in publishing more than they guarded the intellectual or economic rights of authors or even the licensing concerns of state and church. Conversely, many booksellers and publishers failed in a high-risk industry where so much capital was tied up in expensive paper that, for the unsuccessful, mouldered in the unsold editions stacked up in the warehouse.

7

Managing Information

Ann Blair

Books convey texts, and texts convey meanings. As described in earlier chapters, many different types of book have circulated and updated information since ancient times. In the modern age, the easy and understandable elision of books and literature, especially of celebrated imaginative literature, tends to obscure the contribution of books to the promotion, understanding, and creation of basic, useful, and essential knowledge. Informational genres range from the short and enumerative to extended narratives, such as pedagogical texts, biographies, histories, or scientific treatises. The collection of information takes place not only in the contents of books, but also in institutions such as libraries, archives, and museums, devoted to accumulating books and other materials which they make more or less accessible.

The accumulation and transmission of written information is a centuries-old goal of many cultures throughout the world. The importance of textual knowledge to the exam-oriented Chinese administrative service and cadre has been illustrated in Chapter 3, while many other ancient peoples used writing to convey information vital to the governance and civic well-being of their societies. Buddhist sutras ranged from Singhalese palm-leaf books to the block-prints of Tibet and Mongolian *thangkha* scrolls; later Mesoamerican and Aztec peoples fixed calendric and mathematical calculations and collective memories of names and places on long paper codices and deer skin rolls as well as the knotted cords called *khipus*. Such information was the private but also often the public concern of the literate and those able to hear and memorize oral accounts. Alongside the power of oral tradition, the survival of books has played a crucial role in the transmission of culture, making possible in particular the recovery of texts after a period of neglect. From ancient Greece and Rome, large works of history and natural history (such as Livy and Pliny) have come down to us today, but many more such works were lost, including the *Pinakes* of Callimachus, a vast bibliography of Greek writings based on the holdings of the Library of Alexandria, of which we have only a few fragments. In East Asian cultures, the long continuity of the Confucian Classics masks the loss of texts which did not become canonical. Elsewhere, pre-Columbian Aztec and other Mesoamerican codices perished, although their combination of pictography, ideograms, and phonetic symbols was partially transmitted in some colonial manuscripts. Recent rediscoveries, for example of 'lost' books in Ethiopia, continue to broaden our awareness of the scale of textual destruction.

The word 'information' entered English usage in the fourteenth century (and in French and German in the eighteenth century) and first designated a process of informing, as in an educational or a legal context; it also came to designate the content and particular knowledge conveyed in such a process. The word has been in use ever since, but not with the frequency or valence that we give the term today. Our notion of living in an 'information age' defined in important ways by new digital technologies has developed over the last fifty years especially. When historians apply the term 'information' to earlier periods in search of parallels and contrasts with our current categories and concerns, they do so loosely and use 'information' for convenience, roughly to designate reports supposed to be truthful or useful that could be spread in various media. Information can be transmitted orally or by gestures, through objects or rituals, but writing—of texts and images, in manuscript and print—has long been the dominant medium for the creation, storage, and retrieval of information. The information challenge most characteristic of the European Middle Ages was the limited distribution and availability of information, even while the scholars involved in interpreting and composing large works also suffered from the difficulties of managing extensive source material and thus experienced 'overload'.

During the European Middle Ages, religious and legal doctrines were codified, and the study of canonical texts prompted debates and commentaries, generating informational works of many kinds. The term 'encyclopaedia' is commonly applied to a number of medieval works that gathered knowledge considered essential across multiple disciplines, ranging from the *Etymologies* of Isidore of Seville in the seventh century to the *Speculum maius* of Vincent of Beauvais (*c.*1255), which at over 4.5 million words was not surpassed in size until more than 300 years later. Although 'encyclopaedia' is a modern term that historians of the nineteenth century projected back onto medieval books, it remains a handy way to refer to books designed to make available in one place material drawn from many sources. Medieval encyclopaedic works were valued for the textual excerpts they provided at a time when access to books was a rare privilege. Medieval florilegia and encyclopaedias gathered quotations and summaries from other books as a valuable substitute for direct access to hard-to-find sources. In a few cases, in fact, medieval collections of authoritative quotations comprise our only record of ancient passages that were otherwise lost.

The nature of the information challenge began to change in the sixteenth century, when complaints about an overabundance of books became commonplace. Contemporaries blamed printing for a constantly accumulating mass of books. Historians also point to concurrent cultural movements which fuelled an explosion of new information, including the humanist recovery of ancient sources, voyages that expanded the geographic reach of European colonization and trade, the competition of new philosophies with the legacy of traditional ones, and underlying all these trends, an abiding ambition to integrate and make coherent sense of all these different inputs. Many of the solutions deployed to manage this information explosion had roots in the medieval period, but the printing of books (together with a plethora of small-job printing of forms and the like) helped to make them familiar to readers of many different genres, both learned and vernacular. Some solutions were paratexts within books, finding devices such as tables of contents and alphabetical indexes, or visual tools, such as tabular displays or images with captions. Others were books about books that served as guides to finding or assessing texts of interest, including bibliographies, library catalogues, booksellers' and auction catalogues, and periodicals containing book reviews.

Institutions played a crucial role in prompting these publications and in facilitating access to information. From the mid-seventeenth century, European bookshops and institutional and personal libraries increased rapidly in number and scope as sites for knowledge creation and exchange. Learned societies, informal gathering places such as salons and coffeehouses, and expansive epistolary networks were all characteristically early modern responses to the outpouring of books of information, each generating distinctive kinds of printed and manuscript sources.

Overabundance: The Growth in the Number and Size of Books

Historians bemoan the loss of many, perhaps most, ephemeral imprints from the early modern period, and celebrate the recovery of cheap print. Fragments of otherwise lost works have been found in the bindings of books where they were used as endpapers once they had no value beyond the paper they were written on. Sixteenth-century imprints can also be discovered unexpectedly, such as the religious pamphlets that were found in the floorboards of a Delft house under renovation in 1989; they had been hidden because they were dangerous to own in a climate of political and religious conflict. But many early books displayed significant physical and cultural durability. If books were bound they were durable, and most bound books retained cultural value long after their first circulation. Although we know little about the market in used books, surviving copies of early modern books often carry signs of multiple owners and readers across many decades, before the rise of the rare book market in the eighteenth century made them worth collecting simply because they were old. As a result, books accumulated: unsold in printers' and booksellers' shops, and once purchased, whether they were read or not, in personal collections or more formal institutional libraries.

Early modern users of books experienced a real explosion in the availability of books. We know of some 27,000 incunabula printed by 1500, each in a print run of at least a few hundred copies. After 1500, book production continued to grow, both in the number of editions produced and in the size of print runs—1,000 copies is generally offered as a reasonable estimate for print runs between the sixteenth and eighteenth centuries, although particular cases involved both larger and smaller print runs. These books had a massive cumulative impact—in particular in the creation and diffusion of knowledge and information.

Complaints about the overabundance of books targeted both the steady production of new books and the overall accumulation that resulted. The great humanist Desiderius Erasmus (1466–1536) complained in his comment on the adage 'Festina lente' ('Make haste slowly'), first published in 1525, about the 'swarms of new books' being printed which enticed readers with the promise of novelty away from true learning formed from reading ancient authors. Printers 'fill the world with pamphlets and books [that are] . . . foolish, ignorant, malignant, libellous, mad, impious and subversive books; and such is the flood that even things that might have done some good lose all their goodness'. Of course Erasmus voiced this complaint in a printed book in which he drew wisdom from ancient sources—one of those few 'good' books designed to stem the tide of bad ones, which he entrusted to renowned humanist printers (first Aldus Manutius of Venice, then Johann Froben of Basel) to produce. Similarly, in 1545 Conrad Gessner of Zurich (1516–65) complained of both the 'silliness of useless writing in our time' and of the 'harmful and confusing abundance of books' accumulated over a century of printing. He, too, did so in one of his many publications, his *Bibliotheca universalis* (1545), a universal bibliography of all known writings in Latin, Greek, and Hebrew. Gessner had in mind not only the impact of printing, but also the great loss of books suffered after the decline of the Roman empire. Gessner's project to gather information about all known books was designed to forestall any such catastrophic loss of learning in the future. The early modern abundance of books thus had dual roots—in a new technology for multiplying books, to be sure, but also in a cultural imperative to multiply and accumulate books in order to guard against loss. The complaints about overabundance did not trigger serious measures to reduce the production of books; instead they motivated new kinds of books and new features in books to facilitate finding one's way within an ever-increasing body of texts.

Some of these genres and their textual and paratextual features (such as front matter and back matter) developed from medieval antecedents, but they were transformed by printing, which facilitated and incited a constant growth in the size of informational books. Reference books—that is, books meant to be consulted rather than read through—survive from as early as the thirteenth century, including alphabetized works like dictionaries, and works like florilegia excerpted other books to spare the reader the need to read those books directly. Among the first books to be printed was a medieval Latin dictionary, the *Catholicon*, first composed in 1286 and printed by Gutenberg in 1469, then reprinted thirty times before 1500. A thirteenth-century florilegium, the *Manipulus florum* by Thomas of Ireland, was printed twice, in 1483 and 1494. Shortly after 1500 each of these medieval works had been eclipsed by a larger reference book of the same genre: the *Dictionarium* of Ambrogio Calepino, which soon became a bestseller (a term used by historians of this period for works which appeared in at least one edition per year) for over a century, and remained a 'steady-seller' (a term for works with at least five editions in thirty years) for a further hundred years after that; and the *Polyanthea* of Domenico Nani Mirabelli, which remained in print down to 1686. Printing facilitated and even drove this kind of expansion. Whereas the thirteenth-century *Catholicon* weighed in at around 700,000 words, Calepino's *Dictionarium* started in 1503 with 850,000 words and had almost doubled in size by 1546 to 1.5 million words. Through successive editions, the Calepino acquired both new entries and new material in existing entries, including translations into multiple languages (up to a total of eleven different languages by 1590). By 1681, it had grown by the same amount again to about 2,350,000 words. Meanwhile, the *Polyanthea* almost sextupled in size from its first edition of 430,000 words to seventeenth-century editions totalling 2.5 million words.

Large books were of course more expensive than smaller ones, because they involved more labour and more paper—the latter comprised a major expense in any book (as it still does today). Yet printing made it more economical than ever before to produce large books. With good sales, a large book could generate strong profits, because the profit margin was generally greater for more expensive books. But each new edition of a reprinted work of any kind needed to find buyers who would choose it over used copies. Furthermore, a new version of the text could justify being granted a new privilege guaranteeing the printer protection (within the relevant jurisdiction) from a competing edition. For these reasons, reprinted books often boasted on the title page of new features, such as a new or newly augmented index, or a newly corrected or expanded text. Although some of these boasts were exaggerated, books that sold well indeed tended to become larger in successive editions.

The enlargement of the text in successive editions was common across many other genres than dictionaries and florilegia. The *Essais* of Michel de Montaigne, for example, grew substantially across three editions, and the title page of the *Essais* of 1588 explicitly stated that the text was enlarged by one-third over the earlier edition of 1580–2. That expansion warranted a renewal of the privilege, thus preserving for the printer a monopoly on printing a work that he knew to be lucrative. Since Montaigne had invested some of his own money in the publication of the *Essais*, sharing the costs and the risk with the printer Simon Millanges of Bordeaux, he was no doubt aware of the financial benefits of expanding his *Essais*. Indeed, he composed more additions for a subsequent enlarged edition, though he died before it appeared in 1595. His intellectual heir Marie de Gournay saw it through publication, working from the copious manuscript annotations Montaigne had made for this purpose in his personal copy of the 1588 edition (in the so-called 'Bordeaux copy' which is still extant and has now been digitized).

Intellectual factors also fuelled the growth in the size of various types of books of information. In natural history, for example, the number of species of plants and animals soared between 1480 and 1630, first from the recovery of ancient sources, like Dioscorides on plants and Aristotle on animals, and second from travel reports of explorers to the new world and the observations of travellers to the Levant, Asia, and within Europe. As a result, works of natural history became longer, with more information for each species under discussion and with many more species to discuss. The number of known plant species increased by six times between 1550, when the 500 species in Dioscorides constituted the best learning on the topic, and 1623 when Caspar Bauhin described 6,000 plant species in his *Theatrum botanicum*. Early modern humanists and naturalists also worked hard to match species described in books with actual specimens observed and drawn or collected in exotic locations or even transplanted live to grow locally in botanical gardens.

As knowledge was re-evaluated in these books, some species long reported in ancient and medieval texts were abandoned, in some cases only after heated disputes, in other cases quietly by reclassifying or omitting them. For example, the survey of plants and animals in the *Hortus sanitatis* first published in 1491 included an image for the 'leonthophonus' or 'leucrocuta', reported in ancient authorities and medieval bestiaries as a beast from India, part hyena, part lion. However, in 1551 Conrad Gessner, the bibliographer and naturalist from Zurich, only mentioned the term as a variant name for the hyena. Gessner still cited the ancient sources without explicit critique, but he did not consider the animal worthy of its own chapter or an image. The leucrocuta was effectively dropped henceforth from the roster of quadrupeds as a result.

Images played a key role in many informational genres. Printed images were diffused more widely and more consistently than the images in a manuscript, but they could be just as fanciful as medieval images. Conversely, medieval images could also be reproduced quite exactly through the technique of pouncing, which involved poking holes along the edge of the original and transferring the outline onto a blank space by sprinkling coloured dust through the holes; the technique was used, for example, for reproducing highly prized illuminations. Nevertheless, several early modern scientific works included images of a scientific quality far superior to any medieval antecedents. The reasons for this development are complex, and include a new attention to empiricism across many scientific fields, and a related new trend to stake reputation on accuracy. Printing amplified these effects by diffusing work broadly: authors making claims about the accuracy of their images could be criticized for errors, or conversely praised for accuracy by many more readers than before. Authors seeking to include high-quality images in their books incurred extra expenses in securing specialists to make the drawing on paper, to transfer the drawing to a woodblock or a copper plate, then to carve the wood or inscribe the copper. Printing a woodblock image did not involve any extra expense in itself, but copper engraving required the use of a special press that applied more pressure than the usual press used for printing text and images set in relief; hence considerable extra expense was involved although engraving allowed for a higher level of detail and finish. No images were printed in colour in Europe until the eighteenth century, but colour could be added by hand, at the expense of an individual buyer, either following a model provided by the author's draughtsman to ensure optimal accuracy, or without such a model for more decorative purposes.

Printers and authors employed various stratagems for offsetting the expense of images. They sought patronage for the images especially, offering, for example, to dedicate a copperplate to a donor by inscribing his name on the image. To those who paid the most money, printers promised images of more prestigious topics or images positioned more prominently in the book. Printers also made multiple editions from the same set of images. Froschauer of Zurich printed the four very large volumes of Conrad Gessner's natural history with detailed text accompanying the images. But Froschauer also printed Latin 'picture book' editions containing the images and minimal text, and German translations with an abridged (and modified) text along with the images.

Gessner's new versions targeted different kinds of readers from his original. These readers were less learned but nonetheless appreciated the images, and they were more numerous too, given that the Latin picture books appeared in two editions and the German versions appeared in three or four editions, while Gessner's original editions were not reprinted. A printer involved in a project like Gessner's might also tap yet another market by publishing a small-format edition of a large illustrated book, as Isingrin of Basel did for Leonhard Fuchs's history of plants. This required carving new versions of the images at the appropriate size, but the great initial expense of making the image from life could be further amortized by selling a much less expensive version, too.

Like Andreas Vesalius or Leonhard Fuchs, who produced carefully illustrated books of anatomy and plants in the middle of the sixteenth century, Gessner prided himself on illustrating his natural histories with high-quality images drawn from life. When Gessner went botanizing in the mountains near his hometown in Zurich, he brought with him a draughtsman who could make an image of the plants they found in the wild. But Gessner did not travel to all the places from which he reported observations and species. Instead, he relied on his extensive correspondence with scholars all over Europe who sent him information, specimens, and images. Given the multiple relations of mutual obligation, respect, and concern for reputation that bound together this sub-community of naturalists, Gessner implicitly trusted these contributions. He used the broad diffusion of his printed works to thank those who had sent him materials and to encourage other readers to contribute. In his natural history of birds, for example, Gessner especially appealed for examples from Spain and Scandinavia. Although Gessner was a Protestant whose works would normally be banned in Catholic countries, many censoring bodies made exceptions for works like Gessner's considered to contain useful information. Trusted Catholic scholars could apply for permission to read books like Gessner's in copies that had been purged of dangerous passages, including any mention or praise of Protestant authors whose names were blotted out in censored copies. Thus, Gessner could rightly have hoped that his work would reach learned readers in Spain, although no Spaniard featured among his correspondents.

Other feats of learned publication include the Polyglot Bibles that presented the texts of the Hebrew Bible and New Testament in as many early versions as possible, displayed so that they could be compared passage by passage on the same page opening. The Complutensian Polyglot of 1522 printed texts in four languages—Latin, Greek, Hebrew, and Aramaic—and the Antwerp Polyglot of 1572 added Syriac. The Polyglots of Paris, 1645, and London, 1657, further expanded the corpus to include texts in Arabic, Samaritan, Ethiopic, and Persian. These sets of six- to eight-folio volumes printed in multiple different alphabetic fonts were only possible with funding from deep pockets like those of Cardinal Jimenez de Cisneros in 1522 and of Philip II of Spain in 1572. Just as munificent was the French treasury administered by Cardinal Richelieu. Even so, each one of these projects nearly bankrupted the printers involved, including Christoph Plantin (1520–89), the greatest printer of his day (and much discussed in the previous chapter). The early modern Polyglots remain more impressive in the size and complexity of their layout than their modern counterparts.

Tools for Managing Text: Layout and Paratexts

Publications conveying very different types of information were often at the forefront of the innovations in layout and paratexts that we associate with the 'modern book'. Across all genres, the title page and table of contents, which were only occasional trappings of medieval manuscripts, became standard in most incunabula (that is, books printed before 1501). They served an important purpose in highlighting the special features of each book in order to attract buyers. Foliation (numbering just the front or recto of each page) then pagination (numbering front and back), typically in the upper right of the page, provided a method of easy reference within the book, to which other finding devices could refer, such as tables of contents, indexes, and lists of errata. By contrast, the signature numbers in the lower right of about half of the pages of an early printed book were not used for reference, but were there to guide the printer and binder in putting together the folded sheets into a book.

The shift to print also brought with it losses, in particular in the use of colour. In a well-produced medieval manuscript, colour served not only for decoration and illustration, but also to highlight breaks between sentences, paragraphs, and sections of the text. As noted in the previous chapter, incunabula were often designed to be completed by rubrication of capital letters at the beginning of sections, for example, but after 1500 colour disappeared. Two-tone printing (in red and black) was technically possible, but expensive, because it involved printing each page twice, with each ink colour applied separately. It was thus principally restricted to highly decorative title pages. Instead printers relied on layout to achieve aesthetic effects, by tapering lines at the end of a section, and practical ones, using variations in font type and size, printed lines and printed ornaments generally known as dingbats, and the distribution of blank space to highlight divisions in the text and guide the reader's eye.

Not all of these books emphasized readability. In the early editions of Montaigne's *Essais*, each essay was laid out in continuous text—in one instance for over 210 pages. Paragraphing consisted of just one extra blank space between successive sentences, and the text was interrupted only by Latin quotations that were italicized and sometimes printed in verse form. Nevertheless, by the seventeenth century, modern paragraphing, by moving to a new line, had become standard in all texts and was introduced in Montaigne's *Essais* as well. We have little explicit evidence of how readers experienced differences in layout, but they clearly had to adapt when shifting from one book to another. Large reference books especially developed elaborate systems of layout with special symbols to indicate a cross-reference, or the level of each section within the hierarchy of textual subdivisions. Books of information grew larger in size under pressures of marketing new editions and because of the growing quantities of information authors sought to include. Printers increasingly packed more words on a page, narrowing the spaces between lines and the margins between columns. Even while printers abandoned the many abbreviations common in medieval manuscripts and incunabula, over time they generally managed to fit more and more words on a page. Doing so helped to minimize the cost to the reader, but could threaten readability, and hence the need for enhanced techniques of layout.

Reference books were also at the forefront of innovations in finding devices to facilitate rapid retrieval of information. Alphabetization was present in a variety of medieval texts, such as dictionaries or lists of plant and animal species, and in the alphabetical indexes devised for various large and encyclopaedic texts, following the model of the concordances to the Bible first composed simultaneously in at least two different religious orders in the second half of the thirteenth century. In the Middle Ages, however, indexes were a tool known only to an elite of scholars. Printing played a crucial role in familiarizing a broad range of readers with alphabetical arrangements. Several kinds of reference books were alphabetically arranged, especially dictionaries, bibliographies, and works of natural history. And printed books of all kinds contained alphabetical indexes, even from the first decades of printing. Early printed indexes, following medieval models, were often only approximately alphabetized, through the first two or three letters of a word. In an important move towards a more modern practice, in 1545 Conrad Gessner advocated strictly alphabetized indexes: he provided many such himself, along with advice on how to index, by cutting the material to be indexed into slips of paper that could be held in place with temporary glue and rearranged until the list was complete and properly alphabetized. By contrast, a common method of alphabetizing in the Middle Ages involved making lists of words in the order of their appearance in text, sorted into sections defined by the first two letters of the word. One such example, the draft of a biblical concordance, has been found surviving within the endpapers of a later binding. Every later round of copying could improve the level of alphabetization further, but the preference for alphabetizing only the first few letters was no doubt linked to the practical costs of alphabetizing more thoroughly, especially when expensive parchment was the only available writing surface for the purpose.

Manuscript indexes referred to book and chapter divisions in the text: these were independent of the layout of any particular manuscript, and thus an index to a text could circulate independently of any particular copy of the text being indexed. Although this versatility of the medieval index was very handy, printed indexes straightaway referred to folio or page numbers which were instead unique to that edition. In the case of large pages, the index could also specify a section of the page by the use of guide letters (A, B, C, and so forth) printed at intervals from the top to the bottom of each page, or by numbering columns instead of pages. This form of reference guaranteed that the reader would not have to search an area greater than a page or section of a page. It is also possible that by making the index unique to each edition, the printer hoped that his index would serve as an incentive to buy that particular edition. Early indexes often opened with a brief explanation of how to use them, suggesting that readers were not expected to be familiar with the tool. In a preface to one of his indexes, Theodor Zwinger wisely pointed out that the user should look in the index under different synonyms for the same concept, showing that he was aware of a problem that is still today familiar to anyone wondering which terms to use in a search on the Internet.

Alphabetically arranged books invited immediate consultation even without using an index. In works of natural history, which compiled information on many different kinds of plants and animals, an alphabetical arrangement was common, even if some authors apologized for choosing this order for convenience rather than attempting to devise a 'natural' order. Alphabetical order was also the norm in bibliographies, as François de La Croix du Maine explained in his French bibliography of 1584, in order to avoid the delicate task of assigning precedence among authors if they were listed according to some other system. But authors of informational works also experimented with other types of order. One historian has identified early modern encyclopaedic works structured in over a dozen different ways, including following the order of the Decalog or of the days of Creation, known as hexameral order. An explicit rejection of order was another option favoured by early humanists, modelled on ancient authors like Aulus Gellius who claimed to have arranged his *Attic Nights* fortuitously. Erasmus also praised the variety of the miscellaneous order he chose for his *Adages*, which formed a large folio with more than 4,300 Greek and Latin sayings with commentary. Although the book was too big to be browsed effectively, it could be consulted thanks to the presence of multiple alphabetical indexes.

At the other extreme, Theodor Zwinger (1533–88) arranged his vast collection of examples of human behaviour according to a division of topics of his own devising, which he represented by branching diagrams of the kind especially associated with the sixteenth-century pedagogue Petrus Ramus. Zwinger designed the order differently in each of the three editions of his *Theatrum Humanae Vitae* (1565, 1571, 1586) which grew from 1.5 to 4.5 million words. We know of one learned reader who complained that Zwinger's order was excessively complex and advised using the alphabetical indexes to find things in his book instead. In a further enlargement of Zwinger's work made suitable for a Catholic readership in 1631, Laurentius Beyerlinck abandoned the systematic arrangement and Ramist diagrams of Zwinger's original and simply alphabetized the headings of the work. But Beyerlinck also supplied an alphabetical index so that readers could locate the many proper names and themes which were buried within a heading; he opted for a single index that combined material that Zwinger had indexed separately, such as proper names, headings, and 'memorable words and things'. Johann Heinrich Alsted's *Encyclopaedia* (1630) was arranged according to the disciplines, including a number of fields for which Alsted coined the term and the concept. He, too, opted for a single alphabetical index to make the large four-volume work easy to consult.

The branching diagram was probably the longest-lived form of visualization of information and was geographically widespread. In Europe, the branching diagram was used in the Middle Ages to outline sermons and also by readers in marginal annotations to follow a complex argument. In China, where the notion of *tu* encompassed both images and diagrams, branching diagrams appeared only rarely, to interpret specific passages in textual commentaries between the thirteenth and fifteenth centuries. Diagrams were used instead in Confucian writings to describe the place of humans in the cosmos, and their interaction between heaven and earth. In ancient India and South Asia, equivalent diagrams are rare, however, and date mostly from the introduction of lithography in the 1820s.

There is no evidence of any direct imitation between such productions, East and West, and each appear to draw on different traditions. In the late sixteenth century, the Paris professor, Petrus Ramus, advocated the roughly dichotomous diagram as a way to lay out any topic in order to retain it in memory; although Ramus's system was controversial, it inspired the spread of these diagrams to all kinds of fields. For example, Theodor Zwinger's book of advice on travel (*Methodus apodemica*, 1577) consisted mainly of Ramist diagrams outlining principles of travel in general, recommendations for different kinds of travellers, including merchants and doctors, and the main attractions of each recommended city. But branching diagrams in this period were not all inspired by Ramism, and they endured well beyond the decline of Ramus's popularity after the mid-seventeenth century. The branching diagram featured especially in charts of the disciplines, most memorably in d'Alembert's 'system of human knowledge' that accompanied the beginning of the publication of the Enlightenment *Encyclopédie* in 1751.

Alongside the dichotomous diagram, the tabular arrangement was another long-running form of visual aid, especially favoured to represent history synoptically. Some medieval manuscripts had transmitted tables for the ecclesiastical history first composed by Eusebius in the fourth century, but these were not always included in the earliest editions. Christoph Helwig's *Theatrum historicum*, first published in 1609, offers one of the most elaborate tables of history which extends from Creation in 3947 BCE to a present which moved forward across multiple successive editions down to 1666 (with an English translation in 1687). Historical information in Helwig's table accumulated not only across the passage of centuries, but also through the multiplication of major political entities in Europe and of the many different fields in which developments needed to be recorded (including various facets of religion and theology, but also law, medicine, philosophy, and the academies—in multiple sections added for years after 1610). Some chronologists of the time were also concerned about integrating the history of other major civilizations like China and India into the Christian timeframe.

Informational books in the sixteenth and seventeenth centuries experimented with colourful titles (including 'margarita' or 'pearl', 'theatre', 'garden', and their equivalents in other languages), and with many different arrangements and ways of representing them in textual and visual layouts. By the last decades of the seventeenth century the 'dictionary' as a title and a format—alphabetically arranged though possibly also indexed—became the dominant model for the explosion of reference works across a wide range of fields in the eighteenth century. Voltaire was one of many eighteenth-century figures who complained about all those dictionaries. The fact that Voltaire did so in an article in his own bestselling *Dictionnaire philosophique* (first published in 1764) shows that the genre had become indispensable to his contemporaries and to him, just as printing had become indispensable by 1500 for all those who complained in print about an overabundance of printed books.

Tools for Managing Books

In devising the features of printed books that helped readers find what they sought inside a book, authors and printers (and those who worked with them, including editors, compositors, indexers, and helpers of various kinds) drew in part on medieval techniques which they developed and diffused more widely. But overabundance also posed the problem of finding the books in the first place to suit one's needs, and there were few medieval examples of tools to aid in that process. The jurist Giovanni Nevizzano of Asti noted the problem already in 1522 that 'the multitude of books removes the ease of finding them'; as a remedy he published an inventory of law books gathered during his travels to different libraries. Awareness of overabundance prompted the development of new genres that helped readers know about, select, and obtain copies of books that matched their interests. These books about books included library catalogues and bibliographies, which had medieval antecedents, and new genres which did not, such as booksellers' and auction catalogues, lists of libraries, books of advice on the knowledge of books, and periodicals devoted to book reviews.

With the greater availability and affordability of printed books, libraries grew in size and in number throughout the early modern period. Whereas in the Middle Ages the large libraries were mostly ecclesiastical, with a few princely collections, during the early modern period individuals could accumulate significant collections, while princes could develop stunning ones. A typical French magistrate in the late fifteenth century owned about sixty books; a century later Michel de Montaigne reported owning 1,000 books; and in the early eighteenth century Montesquieu, another famed French magistrate, owned 3,000 books. Great book collectors of the Italian Renaissance, like Niccolo Niccoli (who died in 1437, before the invention of printing) and the Medici, formed libraries of wide renown that exist to this day; these libraries were not public by modern standards, but they were open to visitors and scholars, who could only be impressed by their often lavish books, buildings, and decor. In the seventeenth century exceptional collections ranged from the private library of the Parisian scholar Jacques Auguste de Thou with 6,000 books in 1617 to the library of the Duke August of Braunschweig, which in 1666 housed 30,000 volumes comprising 130,000 items—the large discrepancy stemming from the fact that the library often bound two or more separate books together when they were of similar format and topic. Beyond these exceptional collections were numerous ordinary ones, such as the professionally oriented collections of lawyers, doctors, clerics, and teachers, and the libraries of the wealthy, which often favoured books in history, science, and belles-lettres.

Forming a significant library became such a widely shared goal among the elites that Gabriel Naudé composed an advice book on the topic in 1628, in which he recommended buying a wide range of books and decorating the space modestly. Naudé exemplified a new line of work for learned men by serving as librarian to French noblemen, including the French magistrate Henri de Mesmes (d. 1650) and Louis XIII's prime minister Cardinal Mazarin (d. 1661). Other noteworthy thinkers who worked as librarians before 1800 include, among many others, Gottfried Wilhelm Leibniz, David Hume, Immanuel Kant, and Johann Wolfgang von Goethe. Mazarin in any case ignored Naudé's advice on modesty and formed a lavish collection of 40,000 books at its height that also included paintings, statues, and coins. Today's Mazarine Library in Paris descends from that collection.

Book ownership as a display of prestige and vanity was not unique to early modern Europe. Seneca had complained of the pattern in ancient Rome. But the wide appeal of competitive library-building in the seventeenth century has left durable traces that we can see today in institutions like the Mazarine Library in Paris or the Herzog August Bibliothek in Wolfenbüttel, in many other surviving rooms and buildings, and in the books themselves in these extensive collections, which included beautifully decorated texts and expensive bindings, particularly those stamped with the coat of arms of their owners. A new kind of book also highlighted these ambitious new libraries when, in 1644, Louis Jacob de Saint-Charles published a description of the greatest libraries of Europe. Many collectors aspired to be included, judging from a later complaint that Jacob de Saint-Charles had puffed up some of the libraries he mentioned to flatter their owners.

During this period of rapid expansion of educational institutions, including the large network of Jesuit colleges and the foundation of new Protestant universities especially in the German-language area, many institutional libraries were formed in educational settings, but also for the new houses of Counter-Reformation religious orders. These libraries typically comprised one large room with shelves of books arranged by discipline and tables amid the shelves, on which the books could be read even if they were chained to the shelving, as they often were. Chaining was abandoned gradually throughout the early modern period, as early as 1615 at the Sorbonne in Paris or as late as 1757 at Oxford's Bodleian Library. Libraries were typically off-limits to students, but served teachers and clerics who in some cases were also allowed to borrow one or two books to take back to their quarters. Library growth was not uniform throughout the early modern period, and some institutional libraries declined. Many libraries had little budget for new acquisitions and therefore relied on donations, but meanwhile might suffer from thefts and from sales of books to raise money. In England, for example, the closure of the monasteries during the Reformation destroyed many medieval collections. In addition, the 300 books donated to Oxford by Duke Humphrey in 1444 had been sold off by 1550, and the library fell into disuse. Thomas Bodley refounded the library starting in 1598, drawing on his own wealth and encouraging donations by keeping and displaying a parchment register in which the names of benefactors were entered for all to see. He also hired a librarian, Thomas James, who published a catalogue of the newly named Bodleian Library in 1605. This was the first printed library catalogue.

A printed library catalogue could be put to use beyond its initial purpose of providing information about the holdings of a particular library. For example, the preface to the printed Bodleian catalogue of 1674 noted that it could allow the reader to 'compile an index of books...which will aid him in his personal study', whether or not he had access to Bodleian Library itself. In addition, that same printed catalogue served as the basis for a catalogue of the Mazarine Library in the late seventeenth century: manuscript annotations in an inter-leaved copy of the Bodleian Library catalogue indicated which books were present in the Mazarine and added on the blank inserted pages the details of the books owned by the Mazarine, but not the Bodleian. In a similar way today, libraries often rely for cataloguing on the entries made by a central national cataloguing system which are shared electronically.

Early modern library catalogues were also more detailed and versatile than their medieval antecedents. Medieval library cata-logues typically consisted of shelf-lists or inventories meant for the use of the owners rather than to help readers identify and access books directly; to use a book in any case required the help of an authorized person who mastered the collection. Only a few medieval library catalogues offered sophisticated features like an alphabetical list of books, such as that at Dover Priory Library containing 440 books, or a union catalogue spanning multiple libraries, such as in the thirteenth-century *Registrum Angliae*, a collective catalogue of English Franciscan libraries. Early modern library catalogues were often also kept in manuscript only, but many featured at least one form of alphabetical listing. The most sophisticated catalogues experimented with thematic indexing of the contents of books, akin to a modern subject catalogue. For example, the catalogue of the Stiftsbibliothek in Zurich under the librarianship of Conrad Pellikan in 1543 included four different ways of listing its collection of 752 books: an inventory by volume size and order of acquisition (typical of medieval catalogues); an alphabetical list by author; and two topical lists—one by discipline, another by commonplace heading, in which each book was assigned to one or more topics to which it was relevant (forming a total of about 440 topics). In this way the catalogue could guide a reader to a book that he had not already known about but that would likely be of interest.

In their most sophisticated forms, therefore, library catalogues served some of the purposes of a bibliography. Conversely, the great works of early modern bibliography by Gessner were inspired by Pellikan's catalogues of the Stiftsbibliothek. Gessner arranged his *Bibliotheca universalis* of 1545 alphabetically by author. He used the author's first name rather than the last, as was common at that time, but he also provided an index of last names corresponding to each first name on the list, and he included details about the contents of each book when possible. Gessner's policy was inclusive, even of 'bad' and 'barbarian' books, inspired by the ancient dictum attributed to Pliny the Elder that 'there is no book so bad that some good cannot be got from it'. Gessner also mentioned lost works of which no copies had yet been found, notably to aid in recovering them. But the *Bibliotheca* was only the first part of a more ambitious plan, which Gessner carried out in the *Pandectae* (1548) and *Partitiones theologicae* (1549): a universal subject index of all those books listed in the *Bibliotheca*, arranged by discipline and within each discipline by topic (although he failed to treat medicine, perhaps because it posed a greater challenge since it was the area in which he had specialist-knowledge). None of these large folio volumes was reprinted, but Gessner's *Bibliotheca* inspired sequels in Latin and imitations in the vernacular, and frequent references to it as a model bibliography, even into the eighteenth century. However, Gessner's vision of a universal topic index did not find notable imitators until the modern period with the *Mundaneum* begun in 1895 by Paul Otlet and Henri La Fontaine as an attempt to classify all knowledge using index cards.

In compiling his *Bibliotheca* in 1545, Gessner was very conscious of the utility of printers' catalogues that listed recent publications. These small and utilitarian imprints, probably left unbound along with other forms of advertisement of new books in flyers or broadsides, very rarely survive from the early modern period, so when Gessner copied out lists of books printed by each of a dozen learned printers in his *Bibliotheca*, he gives us unique insight into a kind of information that was available at the time, though it is now mostly lost. The sales catalogues which have come down to us are the larger catalogues of the Frankfurt book fairs held each fall and spring. The Frankfurt printer Georg Willer started printing a catalogue for each fair in 1568, and these catalogues were produced regularly down to 1792.

Willer's catalogues were organized by field and by language, and within the theology section by religion (Lutheran, Catholic, Calvinist). No sales catalogues included prices because these were not fixed in this period, but varied with the circumstances of each sale. The printed book fair catalogue was of use to booksellers who came to trade, but also to individual buyers like the French scholar Jacques de Thou, who annotated his copies of the fair catalogues with asterisks to indicate the books he wished to buy.

In addition to new books traded at the Frankfurt fair, older ones also continued to circulate commercially, although we have little information about how second-hand books were sold or marketed before the rise of the book auction. The first surviving auction catalogue was printed in the Netherlands in 1599, just a few years after the first well-documented auction took place, in 1596. In England, auctions started in 1676 and in France, in about 1700. Probably only a fraction of auctions produced a printed catalogue in advance announcing what would be for sale, but those catalogues became a widely valued tool for information about books. To give an extreme example, the major book collector Hans Sloane, who bequeathed his massive collection to the British Library at his death in 1753, owned 700 book auction catalogues. The most precious auction catalogues are copies in which the prices at which items sold were entered in manuscript annotations. Booksellers holding the auctions could sell multiple copies of such annotated catalogues after the fact, which helped inform readers of the most recent prices fetched by various works. Auction catalogues typically called attention to the fact that the books on sale had been owned by a person of social or scholarly standing because this made the books more attractive; indeed, contemporaries complained that auctioneers also included items that had not in fact formed part of the estate in question, simply to get the books sold. Amid the vast abundance of books, buyers thus valued the judgment of earlier book owners whom they respected.

By the late seventeenth century, advice about books could also be purchased directly, in new kinds of books about books—periodicals comprising book reviews and bibliographical manuals of *historia litteraria* produced in German universities. In his bibliography, Gessner had explicitly deferred any judgment about books to his readers and sought only to be exhaustive in listing books. Bibliographies of works in a particular language or nation or discipline tended similarly to be as inclusive as possible within their designated scope. The *Bibliographia parisina*, for example, published a list of all books printed in Paris each year starting in 1645, but bibliographies could also be selective, to include only 'best books' on a topic and to avoid 'bad books' such as those perceived as religiously suspect in a given context. Nevertheless, even selective bibliographies did not focus on a detailed appraisal of individual books.

In this respect, the book review came to meet an important need and spread rapidly among the learned periodicals that were founded in the last decades of the seventeenth century. Most of these early periodicals were monthlies available by subscription or in bookshops. Some periodicals were created by more or less formalized learned societies which advocated a collaborative framework for the creation and dissemination of knowledge. The Royal Society of London launched its *Philosophical transactions* in 1662, devoted to reports of experiments held in London, letters from members, and a few book reviews. The *Journal des Sçavans*, the *Acta eruditorum*, and the *Weekly Memorials for the Ingenious*, were all founded soon thereafter, between 1665 and 1681. The *Nouvelles de la République des Lettres*, edited by Pierre Bayle from 1684 to 1687, and then by various successors down to 1718, consisted entirely of book reviews.

The reviews often included excerpts from the books in addition to a summary and assessment, and provided these in translation when the book under review was in a foreign language. For many readers, such reviews stood in for reading the book itself. Reviewers themselves were sometimes criticized for not reading the books carefully, and in some cases these complaints might have been well founded. For example, Giovanni Lami in the *Giornale de' letterati d'Italia* (1710–40) typically discussed only the beginnings of books; and Albrecht von Haller wrote 9,000 reviews in thirty years once he took over as editor of the *Göttingische Zeitungen von gelehrten Sachen* in 1747.

The knowledge of books (*notitia librorum*) featured as a subject of university teaching and academic treatises, especially in the German-language area. Daniel Georg Morhof's *Polyhistor* (1688, augmented in 1708) offered advice about how to read and take notes, but also assessments and summaries of a large number of recent books in various disciplines; these could serve as reading recommendations, as well as substitutes for the books when students could not access them directly. Similarly, Adrien Baillet's *Jugemens des sçavans* (1685) comprised a large collection of his judgments about books in eight volumes which he claims to have started for the use of his son. In his preface Baillet explained the importance of selecting among books with good judgment because overabundance had reached truly dire proportions: 'We have reason to fear that the multitude of books which grows every day in a prodigious fashion will make the following centuries fall into a state as barbarous as that of the centuries that followed the fall of the Roman Empire'. Like authors writing 150 years before him, Baillet suggested that he could reverse the ill effects of overabundance through the guidance he offered his readers.

Much had changed since Erasmus' day. In using French, Baillet did not reach the sort of international audience achieved by Erasmus who wrote in Latin, and yet Baillet gained a much larger readership because of the growth in literacy in the interim and because French had acquired a special status as a language mastered by the educated throughout Europe. By the late seventeenth century the Republic of Letters also featured new institutions devoted to the discussion of books and ideas, including periodicals, but also salons where women often played a leading role as arbiters of taste, coffee houses which typically excluded women, and formal and informal academies. The exchange of letters, already visible in Erasmus' abundant correspondence in the early sixteenth century, criss-crossed large swathes of European society in ever denser patterns owing to a postal system which functioned on major routes with about the same speeds as today (but more slowly in the winter months). We can catch some insight into the circulation of ideas and advice about books by letter and conversation thanks to the many editions of correspondence and 'table talk' by learned contemporaries.

These genres were successful because ordinary readers of books felt they could find in them models and inspiration for their own ways of navigating an increasingly complex world of information. Books remained the crucial tools for managing information even while contemporaries complained about their overabundance. The finding devices, techniques for visual presentation, and various kinds of 'books about books' developed between about 1500 and 1700 formed the core of the information management methods which have been in use since then and are often still visible in the electronic era.

8

The Islamic World

Sheila S. Blair and Jonathan M. Bloom

Islam is a culture of the word. For Muslims, the major miracle of the faith is that God sent down a revelation in Arabic to the Prophet Muhammad in the early seventh century of the Common Era. Because of the sanctity of the revelation and the desire to record it faithfully, writing and books have always played an extraordinarily important role in Islamic culture, which has spanned a millennium and a half from the eighth century to the present around the globe from southern Spain and North Africa to Indonesia and beyond. This chapter traces the rich history of the development and production of books across this broad chronological and geographical spectrum not only as written texts, but also as physical objects that shed light on important social and intellectual questions such as the change from the oral to the written, rates of literacy, identification of readership, the roles of illustration and illumination, collecting, preservation, and libraries.

Principles of Arabic Script

Virtually all books produced in the Islamic lands were written in Arabic script, which was adopted for almost all of the languages used in the areas to which Islam spread. Like Hebrew and Syriac scripts but unlike Greek and Roman, Arabic is written from right to left, although curiously the numerals reflect an older system and read in the opposite direction, from left to right. This right-to-left orientation dramatically affects layout, for readers always begin at the right side of the page. Codices, the nearly ubiquitous format adopted for books in the Islamic lands, therefore open in the opposite way to how they do in the West.

Like Greek and Roman scripts, Arabic script is written with individual symbols for letters. Whereas in an alphabetic language, these characters denote both consonants and vowels, in the system used for Arabic (what linguists call an *abjad*), the characters represent consonants (and long vowels), leaving the reader to supply the appropriate short vowels. Furthermore, whereas many scripts have two forms, one with the letters of a word written separately and another with them connected in a cursive script, Arabic script has only one in which some letters always connect within a word. Therefore, these letters change their shape depending on their position within the word (initial, medial, final, or independent). These forms are interrelated, and their position in relation to the baseline (a hypothetical ruling on which the letters 'sit') can vary, depending on where the letter connects to the preceding or following one.

Early writers of Arabic adopted a script used for older languages in the region that had only eighteen graphemes or forms, not enough to represent the twenty-eight distinct phonemes or sounds used in the Arabic language. The same grapheme can therefore be employed in Arabic to represent as many as five phonemes, and so early writers sometimes added diacritical marks to distinguish the different sounds represented by the same form. This flexibility allowed Arabic script to be adapted for a host of languages with other sounds merely by adding extra diacritical marks to the eighteen graphemes. For example, to indicate the sound *p* used in Persian, scribes simply modified its voiced partner *b* used in Arabic by increasing the number of subscript dots from one to three. In this way, the eighteen letter shapes used to write the twenty-eight phonemes of the Arabic *abjad* were expanded to cover the thirty-two phonemes used in Persian and Turkish, the first two languages to adopt Arabic script. Using the same kinds of transformations, this versatile system was modified to transcribe scores of other languages belonging to many different branches of the linguistic tree, from the Berber languages of North Africa to Javanese. Muslims in medieval Spain wrote their native Romance tongue in Arabic characters in the script known as *aljamiado*.

Early Manuscripts of the Qur'an

To ensure accuracy and disseminate the divine message, Muhammad's companions and followers began to write down this oral revelation as a book known as the Qur'an (Arabic القرآن *al-qurʾān*; literally, recitation). Exactly when this process began has been a matter of lively scholarly debate, but opinion is now coalescing around the view that the transcription of the Qur'anic text began soon after the Prophet's death in 632 CE, perhaps even during his lifetime. Looking at fragments of early Qur'an manuscripts helps us understand the transition from an oral to a book culture.

These early Qur'an manuscripts, which exist mainly as single folios or groups of folios, are all codices transcribed with a reed pen and iron-gall ink on parchment, generally assumed to be sheepskin (rather than the calfskin used in Europe). The pages are often large (average size 33×24 cm), usually in portrait format (taller than they are wide), and always with a single column of text written in a distinct style of script whose verticals slant up to the right. This style of script is known as *ḥijāzī* (literally, from the Hijaz, site of the holy cities of Mecca and Medina within the region on the west side of Arabia where the Qur'an was revealed).

One of the manuscripts from this early group, sometimes dubbed San'a' I because at least thirty-two folios from it were discovered in this city in the Yemen, is a palimpsest. The parchment has been carbon-dated to the first half of the seventh century. The original text contains slight verbal variations and a different ordering of the suras, or chapters, from the standard compilation of the Qur'anic revelation. These disparities suggest that the earlier text on San'a' I belongs to a recension different from that said to have been codified under the third caliph 'Uthman (r. 644–56). After this text on San'a' I was erased, another text was written in the same style by at least two different hands following the canonical version of the text, in which the suras are arranged roughly in descending order of length (with the exception of the short opening sura, *al-Fātiḥa*). Curiously, the original text on San'a' I was more elaborate, with decorated footers indicating that 'this is the end of sura such-and-such', dashes to separate verses, and even some diacritical marks for short vowels. This arrangement contradicts the common assumption that older is always simpler and that elaboration was strictly linear.

These early Qur'an manuscripts in *ḥijāzī* style were expensive to produce. They each required some 17–18 square metres of parchment obtained from a flock of sheep to transcribe the entire Qur'anic text of some 75,000 words, about the same length as the New Testament. Yet at the same time, several features show how novel these manuscripts were. The script adapts the *scriptio continua* of Late Antiquity in which spaces between letters and words are equal. The *ḥijāzī* style is unevenly written and unevenly spaced, with lines extending to the very edge of the parchment. The number of lines per page varies, and different writers often used different styles within the same codex. These physical traits indicate that these books mark the beginning of a tradition that was still fluid. The largest of these Qur'an manuscripts in *ḥijāzī* style seems to have been made for use in public settings, where the text would have been recited. Thus, the manuscripts functioned as aide-mémoires for people who had already committed the text to memory. No evidence survives to indicate whether the leaves were sewn together and bound or simply kept in portfolio-like covers.

Over the course of the eighth century, scribes gradually standardized format, page layout, script, and other features to produce a more uniform codex. Scripts became more upright and rectilinear, with letters evenly spaced over the page, sometimes with elongated horizontal strokes (Arabic *mashq*) to fill out lines or emphasize repeating letters. Letters were laid out with precise proportions in relationship to a horizontal baseline, and the same style was maintained throughout a manuscript. The folios were typically gathered in quinions (quires of five bifolios), an arrangement that can be achieved only by stacking the pre-cut bifolios and thus different from the repeated folding of large sheets used to produce the quartos and octavos standard in Western manuscripts. Other new features also increased the visual appeal and uniformity of these Qur'an manuscripts. Chapter divisions became the norm. Wide margins set off the text, which was sometimes framed with a box. Illumination increased in quantity and variety, typically executed in gold, red, blue, and green. Members of the ruling elite of the Umayyad dynasty (r. 661–750) may well have commissioned some of the largest examples (average size 40–50×30–40 cm). Datable to about 700 CE, these manuscripts appear to relate to the state building programmes sponsored by the caliph 'Abd al-Malik (r. 685–705), his son al-Walid (r. 705–15), and their governor al-Hajjaj to disseminate a public image and affirm dynastic prestige.

By the ninth or tenth century, the vertical format used for many early Qur'an manuscripts was abandoned in favour of a horizontal, oblong ('landscape') format. Like the earlier copies, these oblong Qur'an manuscripts are still transcribed on parchment, but the folios are smaller (about two-thirds the surface area of folios in the *ḥijāzī* style), usually with an odd number of lines per page (typically three, five, seven, or nine—far fewer than the twenty-five or so used in the vertical manuscripts). These oblong Qur'an manuscripts are often divided into thirty volumes (Arabic *ajzā'*; sing. *juz'*), perhaps so that one volume could be read daily during the holy month of Ramadan. The script is commonly called *kufic* (after the city of Kufa in southern Iraq, although again not all manuscripts in this script were produced there). These copies were still intended to be used by people who already knew the text by heart, as the calligraphers left the same spaces between letters as between words and sometimes divided words arbitrarily between lines. Indeed, the anonymous calligraphers seem to have exploited decorative principles such as elongation to make patterns at the expense of legibility. For example, a calligrapher might stretch out the letters of a line so that the same shapes fell below those in the line above and both lines would end with the same letter. Or the calligrapher might arrange the text so that similarly shaped letters descend gracefully on a diagonal axis across the page.

Various devices are used in these *kufic* Qur'an manuscripts to make the text handsomer and easier to consult. Marks for vocalization can be added in red and black ink, and some diacritical marks may be included to distinguish homographs (letters sharing the same basic shape). A pyramid of dots often indicates the end of individual verses, a heart shape (resembling the numeral 5 in Arabic) marks the end of five verses, and a circle (resembling the dot used to indicate 0) marks the end of ten verses. Decorative bands might sandwich the opening or closing spreads of text in each volume. In addition, the beginnings and ends of the individual volumes often have decorated pages, dubbed 'carpet pages' because of their geometric designs. They served as guardians of the sacred text, akin to the ornamental pages in contemporary Insular manuscripts such as the Book of Kells or the Lindisfarne Gospels.

The individual volumes of these oblong Qur'an manuscripts were typically encased in box bindings comprising leather-covered boards and a 'wall' of leather attached to the lower board to protect the edges of the text block. The box was held closed by a thin leather strap fixed to the lower board and attached to a peg set into the upper cover. The leather boards were sometimes blind-tooled with patterns similar to those used to decorate the text itself, although no surviving manuscript preserves its original cover. Extant covers are decorated with designs of twists, braids, and knots not unlike those used to set off the opening spreads of text. A new type of information makes it easier to date these oblong Qur'an manuscripts: several have endowment notices inscribed on them. A codex now in the Chester Beatty Library, Dublin, for example, was endowed by one 'Abd al-Mu'nim ibn Ahmad to the Great Mosque of Damascus in AH Dhu'l-Qa'da 298/July 911 CE. This date provides a *terminus ante quem*, and it is usually assumed that the manuscript was commissioned shortly before this date.

The Transition to Paper

Because of the sacred nature of the text, Qur'an manuscripts are inherently conservative, and for many centuries parchment remained the support on which to transcribe the divine revelation. In contrast, a major change took place in the production of books containing texts other than the Qur'an. From the late eighth century, scribes copied these books using carbon ink on paper, introduced to the eastern Islamic lands from Central Asia. Paper, which had been invented in China many centuries earlier, was adopted enthusiastically by the Abbasid bureaucracy which needed to administer a vast empire that stretched from the Atlantic to Central Asia. The availability of this new material, which was light, less costly than parchment, and pro-ducible anywhere with a sufficient supply of water, led to an unpre-cedented explosion in book production on virtually all subjects from history and science to cooking and popular literature.

We get a good sense of how widespread book production became from Ibn al-Nadim (d. 995 or 998 CE), a bookseller in Abbasid Bagh-dad who compiled the *Kitāb al-Fihrist*, which he himself described as

> an index of the books of all nations, Arabs and non-Arabs alike, which are extant in the Arabic language and script, on every branch of knowledge; comprising information as to their compilers and the

classes of their authors, together with the genealogies of those persons, the dates of their birth, the length of their lives, the times of their death, the places to which they belonged, their merits and their faults, since the beginning or every science that has been invented down to the present epoch: namely, the year 377 of the Hijra [987–8 CE].

Ibn al-Nadim's book comprises ten discourses arranged thematically and chronologically. The first six deal with Islamic subjects (Muslim, Jewish, and Christian scripture; works on grammar and philology; history, biography, genealogy, and the like; poetry; theology; law and Traditions of the Prophet (*ḥadīth*)). The other four discourses cover secular subjects (philosophy and the secular sciences; legends, fables, magic, conjuring, and the like; the religious doctrines of the Hindus, Buddhists, and Chinese; and alchemy).

The popularity of these subjects derived in part from the translation efforts sponsored by the Abbasids in Baghdad. The caliph Harun al-Rashid (r. 786–809) and his viziers, a Persian family called the Barmakids, began to have Greek philosophical and scientific works translated for their library, often dubbed the *Khizānat al-Ḥikma* (Treasury of Wisdom). Under Harun's son al-Ma'mun (r. 813–33), this system was institutionalized as the *Bayt al-Ḥikma* (House of Wisdom), likely in imitation of the Sasanian academy at Jundishapur in southwest Iran. The staff included translators (the most famous were members of the Banu'l-Munajjim, a family of scholars, literati, and courtiers), as well as copyists and binders. Although the *Bayt al-Ḥikma* did not survive the orthodox reaction under the caliph al-Mutawwakil (r. 847–61), it became the prototype for several other libraries or scientific institutes known as *Dār al-ʿIlm* (House of Science). The most important library was that founded at Baghdad in the 990s by the vizier Abu Nasr Shapur, which was said to have contained more than 10,000 books on all scientific subjects and had famous grammarians and secretaries as librarians. Other court libraries in Cordoba, Cairo, and Shiraz were equally renowned, and this culture has been described as one of the most bookish societies in the medieval world.

At least forty dated examples of non-Qur'anic books on paper from the early period have survived. These books deal with history, grammar, Arab-Christian subjects (of which several are preserved in the Monastery of St Catherine on Mt Sinai), and other topics. The earliest dated example is a codex on unusual terms in the Traditions about the Prophet Muhammad, *Gharīb al-ḥadīth*, transcribed in AH 252/866 CE, probably at Baghdad (Leiden University Library, ms. 298). The Leiden manuscript, like many of the others, is a small (28×17 cm), vertical-format codex transcribed on a brownish friable paper in what has been called a round book hand. Unlike the rectilinear *kufic* used for Qur'an manuscripts, the script used in these non-Qur'anic manuscripts makes many concessions to readability. Although the letters are written closely together, giving a somewhat crowded visual aspect to the page, the anonymous scribe of the *Gharīb al-ḥadīth* manuscript left more space between words than between unconnected letters of a single word, thereby making it easy to distinguish individual words from groups of connected letters. To further enhance legibility, the text is fully pointed, with diacritical marks added to distinguish letters of the same shape. Long horizontal strokes between connected letters, particularly in the word *qāla* ('he said' used to introduce the Traditions), serve as headings dividing the individual reports. All of these features show that this was a codex designed to be read and consulted by its user, not one recited aloud from memory prompted by a few visual cues.

Scribes slowly adopted this round book hand for Qur'an codices, often the fanciest but also the most traditional manuscripts produced in the Islamic lands. One early example is a very small (12×9 cm) dispersed Qur'an codex with a note in Persian stating that it was corrected by a certain Ahmad ibn Abu'l-Khayqani in AH Sha'ban 292/June 905 CE. The text was still transcribed on the traditional parchment, but within a century or two paper had become standard for Qur'an codices, and with it a suppler and more graceful round script. The single-volume Qur'an codex copied at Baghdad in AH 391/1000–1 CE and now in the Chester Beatty Library (Is 1431) is a landmark in this regard for many reasons. It is one of the earliest Qur'an manuscripts transcribed on paper. It likewise shows the new style of round script, sometimes called *al-khaṭṭ al-mansūb* (the proportioned script), that is remarkable for its clarity, neatness, and flow despite its modest size (17×13 cm; 7×5 in.).

This Qur'an codex is signed and dated in a full colophon (tailpiece) by 'Ali ibn Hilal (d. 1022), better known by his sobriquet Ibn al-Bawwab (literally, son of the doorkeeper). He began work as a house painter and then turned to illumination before becoming a calligrapher, so famous, in the words of the scholar and biographer Yaqut (1179–1229), that he 'excelled all those who preceded him and confounded all those who succeeded him'. Ibn al-Bawwab attests not only to the stature and professionalism of the scribal class but also to its organization into schools. He traced his calligraphic lineage to the Baghdadi calligrapher Ibn Muqla (885–940), and Ibn al-Bawwab himself related a story about how successfully he could imitate his predecessor's hand. Once when he was in charge of the library of the Buyid prince Baha' al-Dawla (r. 998–1012) at Shiraz in southwestern Iran, Ibn al-Bawwab reported that he had found twenty-nine of the thirty parts of a Qur'an manuscript transcribed by Ibn Muqla. They were scattered among the various parts of the library, but a lengthy search failed to turn up the missing volume. Ibn al-Bawwab reproached his patron for treating the work so carelessly and offered to complete the missing section on condition that Baha' al-Dawla reward him with 100 dinars and a robe of honour if he could not detect the forged section. The prince was unable to do so but also failed to reward Ibn al-Bawwab, who instead asked permission to help himself to the Chinese paper kept in the library. It provided him with supplies for a number of years. Assuming this charming anecdote is true, it shows that already by the tenth century there was a ready market for books by famous hands; that one calligrapher could imitate, even forge, the hand of another; and that Chinese paper was available and prized as a writing support.

The story also alludes to the large size of the Buyid library, a report confirmed by the Jerusalem-based geographer al-Muqaddasi (c.945–91), who left a lengthy description of the library that Baha' al-Dawla's father and predecessor 'Adud al-Dawla (d. 993) had built and where Ibn al-Bawwab served as librarian. It was, according to the chronicler who walked around it, part of the ruler's palace in Shiraz, the likes of which the chronicler had never seen in East or West. The library comprised 360 compartments above a large assembly hall; a manager, a librarian, and a supervisor chosen from among the people of good repute in the town oversaw the library. There was, al-Muqaddasi continues, not a book on all the various sciences that was not there. The library consisted of a long oblong gallery with rooms on every side. Attached to the walls of the gallery and the rooms were bookcases made of decorated wood that measured 6 feet high and 3 cubits long. The bookcase doors opened from above, with the books arranged on shelves inside. There were bookcases for every subject and catalogues listing the names of the books, both reserved for people of distinction. Even if somewhat panegyric, al-Muqaddasi's report confirms the care lavished on libraries in the Islamic lands in medieval times.

The opening page of the Qur'an manuscript signed by Ibn al-Bawwab is blank and bears no dedication, so the manuscript may have been made for sale on the open market. By this period most people were Muslim, and there were thus many new readers for the foundational text of Islam. Ibn al-Bawwab included many features to address this new market. For example, he used a different display script for chapter headings and a third script for other incidentals to show that all of this information was not part of the sacred revelation. He separated sets of five and ten verses by heart-shaped and round devices to make it faster to count verses and identify specific passages. He set words further apart than individual letters. He carefully distinguished letters of the same shape from their homographs by a smaller letter written below the main one and included a full set of diacritical marks to indicate short vowels and fully point the text. In addition, he included five sets of double-page frontis- and finispieces detailing such information as the specific recension of the text used and the number of chapters, verses, words, letters, and diacritical points in it. He also added much marginal illumination in gold, sepia, white, blue, and other colours. This manuscript bears out Ibn al-Nadim's description of the rich market for books in tenth-century Baghdad.

Despite the introduction of paper and its gradual adoption for Qur'an manuscripts in the Eastern Islamic lands from the late tenth century, parchment remained the favourite material for many centuries for Qur'an manuscripts made in the Maghrib or western Islamic lands. Many Muslims in this region of Spain and North Africa adhered to a more conservative approach to Islam, and a distinctive style of Qur'an manuscript developed there, as exemplified by a single-volume codex copied by Yusuf ibn 'Abdallah ibn 'Abd al-Wahid ibn Yusuf ibn Khaldun at Valencia in AH 596/1199–1200 CE, now in the Khalili Collection (QUR 318). Like many Qur'an manuscripts from this region, it is a small squarish codex copied using the traditional iron-gall ink on parchment in the distinctive *maghribī* ('Western' script) marked by looped descenders and a different system of pointing the homographs *fā* and *qāf* (the former with a dot below the letter, the latter with a single dot above the letter). Like contemporary Qur'an manuscripts produced in the Eastern Islamic lands, this one contrasts various text and display scripts and uses copious marginal illumination in gold and blue, but it includes additional information such as palmettes indicating the division of the text into sixtieths (*ḥizb*) and even half-sixtieths. The manuscript also has a double-page frontispiece with geometric ornament which resembles that used to decorate contemporary buildings. The proliferation of this type of codex (at least two dozen dated copies are known) coincides with the proselytization of the region under the Berber Almoravid (r. 1040–1147) and Almohad (r. 1121–1269) dynasties, and these revivalist reformers seemed to have created a large market for such manuscripts, which were often commissioned by private individuals, probably for personal use.

Deluxe Books with Illustrations

In the period between the late thirteenth century and the early seventeenth, especially in the lands where Persian was the literary language, artists and patrons transformed the book into a major medium of artistic expression in which paper and calligraphy were combined with illumination, illustration, and binding to produce some of the finest examples of book art made anywhere at any time. Although some earlier Arabic books had been illustrated, the main stimulus for this extraordinary development seems to have been increased contact with China and Europe, the result of transcontinental trade under the Mongols, who had conquered much of Eurasia in the early thirteenth century. The first illustrated books contained epic poetry and history, as such books became a means to connect the present with the past, both real and legendary, thereby helping to legitimize the Mongol rulers who lacked any Islamic authority, whether as descendants of the Prophet (the Shiʿi position) or as those elected by consensus of the community (the Sunni position).

Many of these books contained the Persian national epic, or *Shāhnāma* (Book of Kings). Around 1010, the poet Firdausi had collected stories that had been recounted orally for centuries into a 50,000-couplet epic. The earliest surviving manuscript of his text dates from two centuries later: an incomplete copy dated AH 614/1217 CE discovered in the National Library in Florence. The manuscript has fine illumination but no illustrations and is too polished to be the first example of the poem to have been written down, but the early written history of the epic is still debated.

Copies of the text proliferated *c*.1300. The finest—dubbed the Great Mongol *Shāhnāma* and probably made for the Mongols' Persian vizier Ghiyath al-Din at Tabriz in the 1330s—exemplifies the new role of illustrated books in this period. Conceived as a monumental two-volume codex with some 300 folios, it probably had at least 200 illustrations, of which only fifty-eight are known to have survived, scattered in a handful of museums and collections around the world. Each full text page contains thirty-one lines of text in six columns within a written surface measuring 41×29 cm. The pages have been remounted but must have been significantly larger, probably folded in half from a full-*baghdādī* (110×70 cm) sheet of paper, the size standardized during this period and used for the largest thirty-volume copies of the Qur'an penned by famous calligraphers who worked in tandem with named illuminators. The full-*baghdādī* sheets represent the limit of the mould a single paper-maker could lift from a vat. The sheets made during the Mongol period are also some of the finest, smoothest, and whitest ever produced, perfect surfaces for exquisite calligraphy, illumination, and illustration.

The paintings in the Great Mongol *Shāhnāma* generally occupy one-third to one-half of the written area, but appear much larger in conception and scale. They are some of the most dramatic renderings of these scenes known. For example, the one showing Alexander supervising the building of an iron wall to protect the civilized world from the barbarians depicts the ruler, astride his steed with his head encircled by a golden halo, gazing impassively over the construction carried out by his craftsmen gathered from across the world, as indicated by their diverse headgear and dress. Equipped with hammers, tongs, and bellows, they prepare the molten metal for the wall. Grotesque creatures from Gog and Magog, described as beasts with black tongues and teeth like wild boars, peer over the hills in fascination. The scene, one of a dozen from the Alexander story illustrated in this copy of the epic, must surely symbolize the Mongol sultan's dominion over the world as the 'Alexander of the age'.

From the fourteenth century onwards, an atelier or scriptorium (Persian *kitābkhāna*) producing deluxe books became a standard accoutrement of princes, who commissioned fine copies not just of epics and history but of all the classics of Persian literature as well. A unique document (*'arżadāsht*) preserved in an album in the Topkapı Palace Library in Istanbul (H2153, folio 98a) gives a progress report on the work carried out by such a scriptorium. It was almost certainly addressed by Ja'far Tabrizi, head of the scriptorium, to his patron, the Timurid prince Baysunghur Mirza (1397–1433), governor of Herat and sponsor of one of the finest book ateliers ever known. The report shows the seminal role of book artists, who often prepared designs that were then reproduced in many media, from architecture to ceramics, textiles, and metalware. The *'arżadāsht* mentions, for example, a design for a saddle by the painter Mir Dawlatyar that was copied by another artist, Khwaja Mir Hasan, whose son and a further artist then executed it in mother-of-pearl.

Over the course of the fourteenth century, books came to be produced in smaller formats, but the illustrations in deluxe manuscripts grew larger in proportion to the written surface, such that a manuscript of the poems of Khwaju Kirmani made at Baghdad in AH 798/1396 CE (British Library, ms. Add. 18,113) has paintings that are virtually full-page compositions, independent of the text they illustrate and much larger than the written surface of the text pages. Within the large illustrations, painters shifted the horizon about two-thirds of the way up the vertical composition, with the figures arranged on a flat plane and executed in brilliant opaque pigments.

Illustrations were but one way to glorify such deluxe books. Illuminators added multi-coloured marginal rulings along with headings and rubrics decorated with polychrome floral and geometric designs. The margins of the pages could also be decorated or even illustrated, as in a manuscript containing the poems of the Jalayirid sultan Ahmad (Washington DC, Freer Gallery of Art 1932.30–37), eight pages of which have margins filled with lightly coloured drawings in black ink depicting extraordinary scenes of daily life. Papers themselves were often tinted, usually by immersing the prepared sheets of paper in a vat of dye rather than by colouring the fibres in the vat before making the paper, as was later common in Europe. The inspiration for such coloured supports may well come from Chinese papers, which were increasingly available by the fifteenth century, especially in eastern Iran, as a result of diplomatic missions. Persian authors such as Simi Nishapuri, a librarian at Mashhad in eastern Iran in 1433, wrote treatises with recipes for producing and colouring such paper. In addition to dyeing, paper-makers in Iran also developed techniques of sprinkling (Persian *zarafshānī*) and painting paper with gold.

Luxury manuscripts were encased in elaborate bindings. As distinct from the box bindings typical of early Qur'an manuscripts, later codices from the Islamic lands are usually set in envelope bindings, which have fore-edge and triangular flaps that fold around the text block to rest beneath the upper cover. Most bindings were made of pasteboard covered with leather, often blind-tooled but increasingly gold-tooled, a technique known in the Muslim world as early as the twelfth century. Geometric strapwork designs were typical in the western Islamic lands, whereas bindings from the eastern Islamic lands were often pressure-embossed with elaborate floral motifs. The typical rectangular cover displays an oval medallion in the centre and quarter medallions in the corners. Even fancier bindings were made of 'lacquer', actually pasteboard painted with elaborate scenes and covered with a clear varnish, a technique known again from the late fifteenth century, as on a copy of the poems of Jalal al-Din Rumi made at Herat for the Timurid sultan Husayn Mirza in AH 887/1483 CE (Istanbul, Turk ve Islam Eserleri Müsezi, 1905).

The doublures (the linings on the interior of covers) were elaborately decorated, as well. Some were made of silk cloth and others (particularly in Egypt) of block-printed leather, but the most beautiful were executed in cut-leather (Persian *munabbatkārī*), a technique reportedly introduced in the early fifteenth century from Tabriz in western Iran to Herat in eastern Iran. The cut-leather technique appears already on the doublures of a splendid copy of the six poems by the mystical poet Farid al-Din 'Attar (*c.*1145–1221) transcribed at Herat on highly polished Chinese paper painted with gold landscapes in AH 841/1438 CE for the Timurid ruler Shahrukh ibn Timur (Istanbul, Topkapı Palace Library A.III.3059). The binding features both block stamping and intricate leather filigree. Rather than pressing and moulding with individual stamps or tools, the bookbinders engraved and carved single blocks to produce elaborate images like the fantastic landscape with wild animals shown on the exterior. The doublures are executed in leather filigree, with a stunning array of chinoiserie motifs including a pair of duelling Chinese *qilin*s (mythical beasts) set against a glowing blue ground in the central medallion.

An even more elaborate design was used for the doublures on the 'lacquer' cover encasing a manuscript of Rumi's *Mathnavī* copied for Sultan Husayn Mirza at Herat in AH 887/1483 CE in Istanbul's Museum of Turkish and Islamic Arts (1905). The doublures display large scenes of monkeys, deer, birds, and other creatures cavorting within leafy vegetation, the whole set against a rich blue ground. Such scenes must have been used in albums and workbooks of the type taken to India (see below), where similar scenes were carved in low relief on palace walls, as at the House of the Turkish Sultana erected at Fatehpur Sikri, the capital founded by the Mughal emperor Akbar in 1571.

In order to situate a full-page painting at the appropriate break-line in a poetic text, copyists learned to stretch out the text by copying some verses diagonally so that less text occupied more space and the appropriate line of poetry fell at the top of the page with an illustration. Such pages with diagonal lines of text sometimes begin a folio or two before the illustrated page and thus heighten the reader's anticipation when leafing through the codex. This is the case with one of the most fully documented manuscripts produced in sixteenth-century Iran: a deluxe copy of the *Haft Awrang* (Seven Thrones) made for Ibrahim Mirza, governor of the province of Khurasan in eastern Iran for his uncle, the Safavid shah Tahmasp (r. 1524–6), and a bibliophile who reportedly had a private library of 3,000 volumes. The text is a collection of seven *mathnavī*s (long poems in rhyming couplets) composed by the mystical poet Jami (1414–92). Perhaps planned to celebrate the prince's marriage to Gawhar-Sultan Khanum, the manuscript was something of a mail-order project, as the text was transcribed over nine years (1556–65) in three different cities (Mashhad, Qazvin, and Herat) by at least five calligraphers (Shah Mahmud Nishapuri, Rustam 'Ali, Muhibb 'Ali, Malik al-Daylami, and 'Ayshi ibn Ishrati). The calligraphers, who all wrote in a virtually indistinguishable fine *nasta'līq* script, were interested in variety and visual excitement, setting verses on the diagonal and also switching the direction of successive lines to produce a zigzag effect, as on the last page to the first book of the first poem *Silsilat al-Dhahhab* (Chain of Gold), where the calligrapher Malik al-Daylami stretched out the text so that the triangular colophon would fall precisely at the bottom of the page. To flatter his patron, he transcribed the prince's name and titles in pink and gold: Abu'l-Fath Sultan Ibrahim Mirza al-Husayni al-Safavi. To further show his deference, the calligrapher signed his work beneath his patron's name, using appropriately humble epithets (the poor, the lowliest of his servants, Malik al-Daylami), followed by the date (AH Dhu'l-Hijja 963/October 1556 CE) and the place (the holy, the sublime Mashhad, referring to the shrine city around the tomb of Imam Reza in eastern Iran). Once transcription was complete, the text in this sumptuous codex was further decorated by adding the long headings in the rubrics in different colours of ink, alternating between red, blue, orange, and green.

In order to assemble the seven poems copied by different hands seamlessly into one coherent volume, craftsmen then added copious illumination throughout the manuscript, including gold contour panels and polychrome column dividers, as well as inserting the calligraphed pages into margins of different colours of paper, themselves painted and stencilled in gold with scroll, cloud, and lattice designs. Painters further enhanced the book with twenty-eight paintings, all but the first full-page and usually expanding well beyond the written surface. The large compositions, executed in brilliant jewel-like pigments, display complex arrangements of detailed architectural settings and idealized figures with multiple focuses such that the subject in question is often obscured in the wealth of detail. They represent the apogee of the classical style of Persian painting.

This deluxe manuscript remained a prized possession, although it often changed hands and was refurbished and rebound, at least once from water damage, with the opening and closing folios restored and replaced. In AH 1017/1608–9 CE, the Safavid shah 'Abbas I donated the manuscript to the dynastic shrine at Ardabil, as indicated by multiple seal impressions. Their placement attests that both text and binding were intact when 'Abbas donated the manuscript to the shrine. The codex next passed to the Mughal court in India, as shown by a page added at the end (folio 304b) that bears various seventeenth- and eighteenth-century seal impressions and inspection notes mentioning the emperor Shahjahan (r. 1628–58) and his son and successor, Awrangzib (r. 1658–1707). The manuscript then seems to have returned to Iran, for the first folio has illumination in the style of the Qajar period (1785–1906). At this time the codex was probably rebound with its current 'lacquer' covers with floral compositions against a red ground. The 'lacquer' covers are now attached to a red leather spine typical of late nineteenth- or twentieth-century European bindings. The binding may have been put together in Europe, as the manuscript appeared in a 1926 sale catalogue in Milan. The dealer Hagop Kevorkian acquired it there before selling it two decades later to the Freer Gallery in Washington, DC. Despite its vicissitudes and peregrinations, the manuscript looks much the way it did when it was produced for Ibrahim Mirza in Iran in the mid-sixteenth century, and its repeated refurbishments attest to the esteem that owners and collectors in the Islamic lands accorded to books. Such respect and care given to books over the centuries makes recent political events such as the destruction of the National and University Library of Bosnia and Herzegovina by Serbian shelling during the siege of Sarajevo in 1992 or the burning and looting of the Iraq National Library and Archive in Baghdad in 2003 all the more unfortunate.

Other Forms and Formats

As an assemblage of many hands and many parts, the copy of the *Haft Awrang* made for the Safavid Prince Ibrahim Mirza can be compared to another type of luxury book produced in the Islamic lands from the fifteenth century onwards: the album (Arabic and Persian *muraqqaʿ*, literally, patchwork; also Persian *jung*, literally, ship). Befitting the role of calligraphy as the most esteemed of the arts, the earliest albums were calligraphic. They contain individual specimens by a variety of calligraphers on a wide range of subjects, including Qurʾanic excerpts, traditions, wisdom sayings, pious phrases, sacred names, aphorisms, prayers, letters, treatises, exercises, and more. Most texts are in Arabic, but Persian became increasingly popular.

To make these albums, the single specimens were gathered, trimmed, repaired, and ruled before being pasted on to sheets of backing paper and then attached to the page. In fancier albums made for court patrons, the individual pages were often set into painted and decorated borders, which served to unify the disparate components and compositions. Binders then assembled the folios, sometimes together with pictures, in either codex or concertina/accordion format. The most famous of these albums that were produced in Iran in the fifteenth and sixteenth centuries survive not in Iran, where they were made, but in Istanbul, where they were taken as booty or sent as gifts and incorporated into the Ottoman archives stored in the Topkapı Palace. These albums typically have introductory prefaces written in the ornate prose prized at the time and a style appropriate to the lavishness of the decoration. They offer some of the first evidence for a conscious history of calligraphy, painting, and books in the Islamic lands.

The Mughals, rulers of northern India from 1526 to 1857, commissioned even more splendid albums. They follow Persian models but have alternating spreads of calligraphy and images. Many of the calligraphic specimens are short exercises (*qiṭaʿ*) written by famous calligraphers under the Mughals' Timurid ancestors in Central Asia. The pictures range from portraits, genre scenes, and allegorical, literary, and historical subjects to natural history studies and even European prints that had entered the imperial collection. These spreads were then mounted in lavish borders, often with alternating figural borders around the calligraphic spreads and floral borders around the images. The finest examples were produced for Akbar's son, Jahângîr (r. 1605–27), such as the so-called Gulshan album, much of which is preserved in Tehran's Gulistan Palace Library (ms. 1663).

One page from the Jahângîr album is particularly important for the history of the Islamic book because its margins illustrate various stages of book production. The central field contains a quatrain calligraphed by Mir ʿAli Haravi, a famed calligrapher who had worked for the Timurids and Uzbeks. The margins show six artisans at work. In the upper right, a paper-maker energetically polishes a sheet with a heavy burnisher. In the lower right, a calligrapher seated at a low table charges his reed pen in a blue-and-white ceramic inkwell to continue writing in a codex. Facing him, an artist melts gold by blowing through a rod to intensify the fire in an open container; beside him are his tools for pounding the gold into leaf. At the bottom of the left margin, a woodworker saws a folding bookstand, his carving tools and blocks laid on the ground near him. Further up the left margin, a bare-chested artisan trims the edges of a bound book held in a wooden clamp; several other text blocks are set beside him. In the upper left, a bookbinder, surrounded by awls and other tools of his trade, stamps designs onto a leather book cover on a low table; an envelope binding lies on the ground beside him. The marginal scenes illustrate how the album, from paper and calligraphy to illumination and binding, was a consummate work of art in the Muslim lands.

The accordion album (Turkish: *kökrüklü murakkaa*, literally, 'bellows album') was popular in the Ottoman lands from the seventeenth century onwards, particularly for calligraphic specimens (Turkish *kit'a*; Arabic *qit'a*), which were mounted on pasteboard and covered in leather on one side, with the two edges joined along the long side. The whole album could be spread out in a strip or folded so that two pages could be seen at a time. The texts correspondingly could be read in various ways. The album could contain a single text. Two different texts could be juxtaposed in larger and smaller scripts. Each page could also contain a discrete specimen.

A concertina album in the Sakıp Sabancı Museum in Istanbul (120-0164-KMI), for example, contains twenty-three pages with a single text, the *Qasīdat al-Burda* (Ode on the Prophet's Mantle), composed by the Egyptian poet al-Busiri (1211–94), who is said to have been cured of paralysis when the Prophet appeared and wrapped the poet in his cloak. Whereas specimens of Persian verse are typically written diagonally in the hanging *nasta'līq* script (as in Mir 'Ali Haravi's quatrain in the Mughal album), calligraphic specimens written in Arabic verse or prose during the Ottoman period are typically written horizontally in landscape format, juxtaposing lines of large and small paired scripts. Each page in this concertina album has two lines of large *thuluth* script, sandwiching two lines of its smaller counterpart, *naskh*. The side panels flanking the ends of the shorter lines, sometimes called *koltuk* (under-arm or armchair), are filled with decoration. On the last page of this album, the calligrapher signed his work in the left panel in rhyming prose, *hāk-pāy-i evliyā sayyid 'izzat mustafā* (Dust of the feet of the saints, Seyyit Izzet Mustafa), and added the date in numerals, [1]265, equivalent to 1848–9 CE.

The calligrapher Mustafa Izzet (1801–76) was one of the most prominent in his time. He held various religious and juridical posts under sultan Abdül-Mejid (r. 1839–61), whose imperial monogram (*tughra*) is inscribed on the album's covers. Mustafa Izzet eventually rose to become supreme judge (Arabic *qāḍī ʿaskar*, Turkish *kadiasker*) of Rumelia, head of the *ulema* (the Islamic religious establishment), and supervisor of the affairs of the Prophet's descendants. His career shows the intertwining of the book arts with politics, religion, and even music, as he was an accomplished player of the reed flute, the same material used for the calligrapher's pen.

Despite the courtly tradition of luxury books, the vast majority of books produced in the Islamic lands were much simpler objects designed for daily use. For example, Qur'an manuscripts produced in sub-Saharan regions of West Africa, particularly in the nineteenth century, comprise loose-leaf pages held in a tooled leather wallet that is not attached to the text block, but rather wrapped around it. In some cases, a flap on the cover is folded on the outside and held in place by a cowrie shell and leather thong wrapped around the binding. The wallet, in turn, is held in a leather satchel, said to preserve the manuscript from impurity and protect it from the evil eye, but also used to enhance portability. Made of goatskin, the satchel usually has a shoulder strap and a flap secured by plaited leather thongs.

These nineteenth-century African Qur'an manuscripts are relatively small: the typical sheet of paper measures 22–23×16–17 cm, although some copies are made from sheets half that size or smaller. The sheets are watermarked with the *tre lune*, the distinctive three crescents used by the firm of Andrea Galvani at Pordenone and several other towns in the Veneto in northern Italy on paper made for export to the Ottoman empire, Egypt, and sub-Saharan Africa. Once the Italians had learned the art of paper-making from the Arabs in the thirteenth century, they soon exceeded their teachers, thanks to technical innovations such as wire moulds, watermarks, and the increased use of waterpower. From the fifteenth century, European paper increasingly replaced the local product in most areas of the Muslim world.

Like the format, the script, layout, and illumination in these African Qur'an manuscripts are distinctive. They are generally vertical in format and typically contain fifteen lines of text per page, but the number can vary from thirteen to twenty, sometimes within the same manuscript. In this way, they resemble early Qur'an manuscripts in the *ḥijāzī* style and bespeak a fluid tradition of transcribing the sacred text. Furthermore, in most of these manuscripts a block of decoration follows the opening sura. In Qur'an codices copied elsewhere, such illumination comes before, not after, the opening chapter *al-Fātiḥa*. The effect here is to distinguish this sura from the rest of the text, and indeed it is different. Its seven brief verses stand at the beginning of the revelation. It is the only sura that Muslims must memorize to perform ritual prayer, whose full legal observance requires reciting this chapter seventeen times daily (twice at dawn, three times at sunset, and four times during each of the remaining three prayers). The Fatiha is used in many other ways in daily life as well: as a devotional prayer, a hymn of praise, a supplication, an invocation, a talisman, and an expression of solace or condolence. As the primary prayer and scriptural formula in Muslim communal and personal life, it can be compared to the Lord's Prayer in the Christian tradition. Marking it off here with distinctive illumination at the end of the chapter shows what an important role oral recitation plays in the daily practice of Islam.

These African Qur'an codices are illuminated with a variety of geometric designs done in vivid earth tones of yellow, brown, and red. The typical marginal decorations are circles used to indicate places of prostration (*sajda*) and divisions into sixtieths, themselves divided into eighths, the same divisions used earlier in the Maghrib. The script, too, continues the distinctive style used earlier in the Maghrib. Strokes have a uniform thickness, written with a reed pen whose nib becomes increasingly blunt over the pages. Reed pens, like paper, must have been imported and expensive. Letters follow the characteristic *maghribī* style, with looped descenders and the distinctive system of pointing the homographs *fā'* and *qāf*. Altogether, these West African Qur'an codices exemplify a strong local tradition ultimately descended from *maghribī* styles. It is all the more important, then, that these and thousands of other manuscripts held by private libraries in Timbuktu, Mali, be saved from the destructive raids by Islamist militants in the region.

The esteem given to handwritten books in the Islamic lands was one of the reasons that Muslims were relatively slow to adopt printed books, although they had used blocks to print talismanic scrolls and amulets since medieval times. The primacy of calligraphy in transcribing the Qur'an and other holy texts seems to have discouraged the adoption of printing, and the many calligraphers and scribes also objected vociferously to its use. There were practical obstacles, as well. More individual sorts, or characters, are needed to print Arabic because so many of the letters change their shape depending on their place in a word. Insufficient capital and the relatively high price of books may have played a role, as well.

Nevertheless, the advantages of printing for the rapid dissemination of standardized information gradually came to be accepted in the Islamic lands. Jews and Christians resident in the Ottoman lands had printed from around 1500, but the Hungarian convert Ibrahim Müteferrika was the first Muslim to establish a printing press—his own at Istanbul in 1727. Before it closed in 1742, it had issued seventeen secular publications ranging from printed maps to dictionaries. In most features, the books resembled handwritten ones, with traditional scripts, formats, and bindings, so that when stacked, only experts could separate printed volumes from handwritten ones.

Only in the nineteenth century was printing introduced widely to the Islamic lands. The prime movers were *littérateurs* who came from the old literary and scribal elite, but were also in the vanguard of the new literary and intellectual culture there. For example, Faris Ahmad Shidyaq (1804–87), one of the founding fathers of Arabic literature, started al-Jawa'ib press in Istanbul, which published semi-official Ottoman publications, classical Arabic literature, and contemporary writing, including his own. He introduced running headers, tables of contents, title pages, and cloth bindings, although his attempt at using Western-style punctuation was adopted only in the twentieth century.

Printing the text of the Qur'an faced more obstacles. The Venetian brothers Paganino and Alessandro Paganini had privately printed an edition in 1537–8, probably for Christian missionaries. Rather graceless because the typesetters had difficulty in reconciling the exigencies of setting type on a line with the piling up of letters in Arabic script, the book was neither a commercial nor an evangelical success, and all copies were thought to have perished, until the 1980s, when a single remaining example was discovered in Venice. The first printed copy of the Qur'an made by Muslims was also something of an outside project: it was completed at St Petersburg in 1787 at the behest of

Catherine the Great who wanted to curry favour with Muslims in the newly annexed Crimean Khanate. The text was more accurate than the Paganini edition, but ligatures still presented a problem and the letters were again set rigidly on a flat baseline. Despite its awkward appearance, this edition was more successful, and it was reprinted several times, first in St Petersburg and then at Kazan, the city on the Volga that had been the capital of the Tartar khanate. It is estimated that as many as 150,000 copies were produced, and this edition played an important role in the centuries-long process of creating a uniform text of the Qur'an, something achieved only in the early twentieth century. The edition produced by the Official Printing House at Bulaq, Cairo in AH 1342/1923–4 CE was a watershed, although elements of the oral tradition still prevailed. The text was compiled after a decade of collaboration by Muslim specialists not by collating written fragments, but rather, from oral recitations.

The primacy of the word and the book means that artists from the Muslim lands today create artists' books that play with traditional formats and styles. For example, Lebanese-born Etel Adnan (b. 1925) creates accordion-style books in which she transcribes Arabic poetry and phrases in a deliberately non-calligraphic hand. Algerian-born Rachid Koraichi (b. 1947) makes lithographed scrolls with alternating text and pictures whose signs and symbols evoke magical vocabulary. Moroccan Mehdi Qotbi (b. 1951) uses meaningless combinations of letters to make fold-out books whose running texts evoke the sense of speed in the title 'Plus loin, plus vite' (Further and Faster). Iranian-born Farkhondeh Shahroudi (b. 1962) uses different fabrics to make cloth books in which poems alternate with drawings of veiled women to challenge cultural notions of material substance and subject matter. Iraqi-born Nazar Yahya (b. 1963) produces handmade books with digital prints of Sufi texts about the encounter with the Divine. Most of these artists, who are also poets or novelists, have moved to Europe or America, where there is a wider audience for their art. Neverthe-less, they show that the vibrant tradition of the Islamic book lives on.

9

Enlightenment and Revolution

Jeffrey Freedman

In 1783, in the city of Geneva, a magistrate, a bailiff, and a surgeon broke into the bedroom of a 19-year-old man who had barricaded himself in his room. Drawn there by the complaints of a downstairs neighbour who had testified to seeing blood dripping from the ceiling, the three officials discovered the lifeless body of the young man seated in a chair, the back of his head resting against a wooden partition and his brains scattered around the room. On a night table beside the body lay a small book entitled *Werther, traduit de l'allemand*. The magistrate noted that 'the book was opened', 'its pages covered with blood', and that the young man 'held a pistol in his hand'. A year later, in London, the *Gentleman's Magazine* reported a similar incident. This time, the victim was a young woman, found dead by her own hand, with an English translation of *Werther* under her pillow.

The man in Geneva and the woman in London were only two of the many young people across Europe who apparently took their own lives after reading *Werther*, the short epistolary novel by Johann Wolfgang Goethe. The novel's tragic story of a young, moody, and love-lorn artist, who escapes the pain of romantic heartbreak by shooting himself with a pistol, was reported to have ignited an epidemic of copycat suicides. The threat of 'Werther-fever' indeed seemed serious enough that several states tried to ban the sale of the novel. Although some reports of suicide were almost certainly apocryphal, there can be no doubt that a great many readers of the novel identified closely with its hero. Some signalled their identification by imitating Werther's style of dress (yellow hose, blue waistcoat, and brown boots), others by travelling to the actual locations (the stations of Werther's *Leiden*) at which the story was supposed to have taken place. Such readers seemed ready to efface the boundary between art and reality—much to the horror of Goethe himself, who had intended to write a work of literature (*Dichtung*), not a brief for suicide. Many years later in his memoirs, Goethe described how the reception of *Werther* had dramatized for him the 'enormous chasm' separating authors from their public.

Yet such a chasm had not always existed. European court poets in earlier centuries had written for a narrow circle of patrons, friends, and admirers—readers whom they knew and whose reactions they could predict. The sense of estrangement and loss of control that Goethe described were the characteristic experiences of a new type of author who wrote not for a patron but for an anonymous literary market. The origins of that new type can be traced back to the early eighteenth century and the career of such figures as Alexander Pope in England. By the last third of the century, it was becoming increasingly common for authors of imaginative literature to sell their works to commercial publishers. Goethe released the manuscript of *Werther* to a publisher in Leipzig named Johann Friedrich Weygand. Thereafter, he no longer had control over what became of his work or who read it. As many as fifty translations of the novel into French, English, Italian, Dutch, Spanish, and even Russian were published between 1774 and 1792, in addition to dozens of editions in German. Copies of the novel were sold not only across Europe but also in Europe's colonial outposts—in bookshops from Philadelphia to Bombay. To describe *Werther* as a 'bestseller' hardly does justice to its impact. It was practically a global phenomenon, an early example of what Goethe himself designated 'World Literature'.

Few if any other books published in the eighteenth century were translated as frequently and disseminated as widely as *Werther*. And yet the production, circulation, and reception of Goethe's work exemplified the ways in which the relations between authors and readers were mutating during the last third of the eighteenth century. The strong demand for a work of fiction (specifically, a novel); the multiple, mainly unauthorized reprints and translations that the novel spawned; the ineffectual attempts by the authorities to prevent it from circulating; the frenzied competition among book dealers to profit from it; the small-format editions (mainly octavo and duodecimo) in which it was printed; the empathic, emotional responses it provoked in readers;

and the sense of bewilderment the readers' responses inspired in the author—all of these phenomena pointed beyond the specific case of *Werther* to deep structural changes in the book culture of eighteenth-century Europe and its colonies, particularly in the three largest and most dynamic markets for modern vernacular literatures: the German, the English, and the French.

By contrast, the technologies of European bookmaking remained largely unchanged during the eighteenth century. The far-reaching transformations to which the history of *Werther* bore witness occurred within the framework of traditional artisanal modes of manufacture, a system of production historians describe as the *ancien régime typographique*.

The Book Trade

Goethe's novel burst on the market during a tumultuous period in the history of the European book trade. As recently as the mid-eighteenth century, the book trade in many parts of Europe had resembled a gentleman's club. In Germany, for example, several hundred publisher-booksellers from across the German states would come together twice a year at the Leipzig and Frankfurt fairs to socialize, settle accounts, and swap their editions sheet for sheet. Hardly any money changed hands, and the swapping took place on such a large scale that all the major German firms ended up owning much the same stock of books. It was a system with obvious advantages at a time when publishers were also booksellers and had to operate in conditions of chronic monetary scarcity. But it worked only so long as the sheets exchanged at the fairs were of roughly equal value.

By the time of *Werther*'s publication, that equivalence no longer held. A group of publishers in Leipzig (including Weygand, Goethe's publisher) had managed to acquire a virtual monopoly on the original editions of works by Germany's leading contemporary authors. Instead of swapping such valuable editions against those of other dealers, the Leipzig publishers insisted that their books be paid for in money, at low discounts (just 16 per cent off the retail price), and with no provision for the return of unsold copies. Judged by the traditional standards of conduct in the German book trade, such demands were a serious breach of propriety. In retaliation, publishers in other regions of the German book trade reprinted the Leipzig editions, and they did so on an unprecedented scale, attracting accusations not just of impropriety but of attacks on property, or, as it had come to be known, 'piracy'. The once placid and cosy world of the German book trade reverberated with accusations and counter-accusations so rancorous that historians have described the last third of the eighteenth century, in analogy to the contemporary literary movement, as the *Sturm und Drang* period of the German book trade. The conservative ethic of the gentleman's club had given way to the rapacious spirit of corsair capitalism.

Similar storms unsettled the book trades of other European countries. The publishing booksellers of the London Stationers' Company and those in the Paris Book Guild (*communauté des libraries*) occupied positions analogous to that of the dealers in Leipzig: like the latter, they dominated the publication of original editions, and complained bitterly—and ineffectually—of piracy. Most of the pirates, or reprint publishers, clustered on the periphery of the major book markets: in Scotland and Ireland for the English market; in the Netherlands, the Rhineland, and Switzerland for the French; and in Swabia and Austria for the German. In some of those locations, they enjoyed the protection and support of their governments. The Empress Maria Theresa, for example, decided after the Seven Years' War to build up the Austrian book trade, which until then had been largely dependent on imports. Her goal reflected the doctrine of mercantilist economics: to promote a favourable balance of trade and stimulate domestic manufactures. To that end, the empress ordered Johann Trattner, a Viennese bookseller and printer, to publish reprint editions of contemporary German literature. Trattner succeeded so well that he became one of the wealthiest book dealers in Europe.

Whether actively supported by their governments or merely tolerated, reprint publishers plied their trade unencumbered by the weight of bad conscience. The consensus against such activities—the consensus that reprinting was *ipso facto* piracy—had not yet crystallized. If anything, the situation was the reverse. Reprinting yielded so many benefits—from increased economic activity for the state to cheaper and more plentiful books for the public—that the burden lay with those who wished to ban it. On what grounds could one justify outlawing so apparently useful an enterprise? The answer was by representing it as an offence against authors. The argument in favour of what came to be known in English as 'copyright' derived that right from the creative act of authorship. And yet the agitation in support of copyright legislation came less from authors themselves than from oligarchs within the trade, such as the leading publishers of London (most of them members of the Stationers' Company) who strove to uphold what they took to be their common law right of property.

The history of copyright protection can be traced back to the traditions of the Stationers' guild and its incorporation by Royal Charter in the mid-sixteenth century. The Stationers, to whom the state devolved much power to regulate and police the book trade, claimed exclusive rights to the titles they published, and treated those claims as forms of property—in effect, therefore, as perpetual. When, as often happened in the eighteenth century, several publishers pooled resources and shared risks by coming together to publish a joint edition, the copyright was divided up like real estate. Each member of the consortium owned a part share in the enterprise. In attempting to enshrine these customs in statute in the early eighteenth century, leading London booksellers lobbied Parliament for new legislation on the book trade. What they got was not what they had lobbied for. The resulting 1710 'Bill for the Encouragement of Learning by Vesting the Copies of Printed Books in the Authors, or Publishers, of such Copies, during the Times therein Mentioned' recognized authors, or the publishers to whom the authors had ceded their manuscripts, as the proprietors of their works and accorded them an exclusive right of publication, but only for a limited term of fourteen years, plus an additional fourteen years if, at the end of that term, the author was still alive. As passed, the Act left open the question of what became of works once their term of protection had expired. In the following decades, uncertainty reigned over which editions were pirated. The Stationers' Company acted on the assumption that its underlying common law right of property was still valid, and that any works registered continued to be its property in perpetuity. Scottish booksellers, on the other hand, took the view that works whose copyright had expired fell in the public domain and could be reprinted legally. The battle came to a head in the early 1760s when the Scottish bookseller Alexander Donaldson opened a shop in London, from which he sold reprint editions of works by such famous authors as

Defoe, Fielding, Locke, Milton, Pope, Shakespeare, Swift, Thomson, and Young at 30 to 50 per cent less than the usual London prices. Donaldson's move was a flagrant provocation. A series of court cases ensued, culminating in a definitive decision by the House of Lords in 1774. That decision vindicated Donaldson's interpretation of the statute, thus establishing the modern institution of copyright as a time-limited form of protection: a compromise that balanced the property rights of authors and their publishers against the interests of the public in securing easy and cheap access to works of literature. Henceforth, books whose copyright had expired entered the public domain and could be freely reprinted.

Markets

Donaldson, Trattner, and the other reprint publishers who flourished in eighteenth-century Europe plundered what they judged to be most valuable: those books that seemed to be attracting the strongest demand. But what kind of books sold best in the age of Enlightenment? And what general trends did the literary markets of the period reveal?

The principal sources to which historians have turned in order to answer those questions yield information about markets at central sites of production and exchange such as Paris or Leipzig. They tend to omit those genres of print with a distinctively regional appeal, such as Catholic devotional tracts that circulated widely in Bavaria but were rarely if ever traded at the German book fairs. The coexistence of such regional markets with national and transnational ones makes it difficult to characterize the evolution of eighteenth-century literary markets in general terms. But it is nonetheless possible to identify at least four broad trends: the overall expansion in the volume of production; the dwindling market share of books printed in Latin; the growing importance of translations; and a shift in the nature of religious publishing.

The first of these trends stands out clearly, even if we discount for the moment the rapidly growing sector of newspapers and journals—genres of print that enjoyed increasing popularity during the last third of the century. The number of book titles entered in the Leipzig fair catalogues went up from 1,360 in 1763 to 3,719 in 1793, while the number of imprints recorded by the English Short-Title Catalogue (a compendium of surviving editions) rose, for those same years, from 2,701 to 6,801—in both cases, an increase of nearly threefold. The data for the French market do not reveal quite so sharp a rise in the decades following the Seven Years' War as occurred in the German and the English markets. In fact, the overall production of books in French may have contracted slightly following the adoption, in 1777, of new laws that limited the duration of publishers' book privileges. It certainly shrank during the early years of the Revolution, when, as we shall see, Parisian presses were occupied in turning out the political ephemera of the new revolutionary political culture—above all, pamphlets and journals. From the start of the century until the mid-1770s, however, the total volume of books printed in French exhibited sustained growth, expanding by approximately threefold, according to data compiled from administrative sources, the registers of the *dépôt légal*, and bibliographic reference works.

While markets were expanding, the percentage of books printed in Latin continued to decline. In England and France, that decline had been under way since the seventeenth century. In Germany, publication in the vernacular was somewhat slower to develop: German titles did not definitively outnumber Latin ones in the book fair catalogues until 1692. After that, however, the process accelerated. In 1740, Latin titles made up 27.7 per cent of the entries in the fair catalogues; in 1770, only 14.25; and in 1800, a mere 3.97. By then, the Frankfurt fair, once an obligatory rendezvous for the international Latin book trade, a gathering that had attracted humanist printer-publishers from beyond the Alps and across the Rhine, had dwindled into insignificance.

With the decline of Latin as the traditional cosmopolitan language of scholarly exchange, translations assumed a vastly expanded role. More translations were published in the eighteenth century than ever before, not just from ancient languages into modern ones, but also between modern languages, and in a few memorable cases—notably Galland's *Mille et une nuits*—from a non-Western into a Western language. Of those languages, one stood out as being of particular importance: French. In the age of what contemporaries called *L'Europe française*, French taste set the standard for cultural and political elites everywhere in Europe. The French language sat atop the linguistic hierarchy, and French books were sold all across the continent from Milan to Moscow. French translations, in this period, performed a role analogous to that of English translations today: they were the gateways to a wider market. *Werther*, for example, was translated three times into French in the years immediately following its publication in 1774, before it was finally translated into English five years later. Cesar Beccaria's treatise on crimes and punishments—arguably the most influential and widely discussed Enlightenment text on legal reform—reached a broad European public as *Traité des délits et des peines*, the French translation by the abbé Morellet, which appeared in 1766, two years after the Italian edition and one year before translations in English and German. In such cases, the French translations did the job of conferring recognition, endowing works of literature with the prestige of French language and culture. If the translation sold well, translations into other languages would follow, often based on the French translations rather than the originals. During the first half of the eighteenth century, German publishers typically awaited the French translations of English works before publishing German translations based on the French. They seldom had to wait very long, for more works were translated into French from English—roughly 500 during the course of the century—than from any other language. French translations did the job of conferring recognition on English works so well that eventually English literature was able to stand on its own. By the 1770s, German publishers were translating English works directly from the English, while Goethe and his fellow *Stürmer und Dränger* were lionizing Shakespeare as an alternative to the French classicism beloved of German princes. *Anglomanie*, a transnational movement of ideas mediated and spread through French translations, contributed, in the long run, to undermining French cultural hegemony in Europe.

The overall increase in the volume of book production was accompanied by a notable decline in one of the traditional mainstays of the Parisian publishing trade: religious literature. The requests of Parisian printers for authorizations to publish reveal a marked decrease during the eighteenth century in the market share of theological, liturgical, and devotional works. Such works accounted for half of the production of Paris printers at the end of the seventeenth century, and still made up a third of their production in the 1720s, but they accounted for only a quarter in the early 1750s and a tenth in the 1780s. The decline was so steep that François Furet interpreted it as evidence for the *désacralisation* of the world.

Outside of Paris, however, the situation looked quite different. Excluded from the lucrative printing contracts for Parisian first editions, printers in remote corners of the kingdom such as the Franche Comté survived by turning out Catholic devotional works (*livres d'usage* in the jargon of the trade), while booksellers in the area filled their shops with cheap, mass-produced editions of *L'ange conducteur* and *La journée du chrétien*. The notion of *désacralisation* hardly does justice to this large provincial trade in religious books. Nor does it capture what was happening in Britain and the Protestant lands of Germany. Under the influence of the Great Awakening and Pietism, various Protestant charitable societies launched ambitious campaigns to promote the dissemination of Bibles and other religious works cheaply and in large quantities—from the Kanstein Bible Institute, a Pietist-inspired organization associated with the *Waisenhaus* of Johann Francke in Halle, which printed 850,000 copies of a German Protestant Bible from standing type between 1712 and 1739, to the British and Foreign Bible Society, founded in the early nineteenth century, which arranged to have copies of the Bible mass-produced from stereotype plates for distribution across the far-flung territories of the expanding British empire. Such initiatives released vast quantities of religious literature into circulation, including cheaply produced editions of tracts by contemporary authors associated with Congregationalism, Methodism, and the Evangelical movement inside the Church of England.

Overall, religious publishing in the eighteenth century did not contract so much as it moved—down-market and out into the provinces. With its displacement, the main commercial firms of Paris, London, and Leipzig went in search of other, more secular genres of literature to fill out their catalogues.

What other genres? Surprisingly—given the oft-repeated association of the eighteenth century with the 'rise of the novel' and of the novel with England—the market share of novels does not appear to have increased appreciably in England during the eighteenth century. Individual novels, however, were among the bestselling works of the entire century both in England and on the Continent. Although the print run of each edition rarely exceeded 1,000 copies, such novels as *Robinson Crusoe, Pamela, La nouvelle Héloïse*, and *Werther* were reprinted, pirated, serialized, adapted, abridged, translated, or anthologized with greater frequency than practically any other books published in the eighteenth century. That novels were disseminated on a massive scale cannot be doubted, nor can there be any doubt about the celebrity of their authors. Showered with fan mail, Richardson, Rousseau, and Goethe became literary stars, subjects of adulation of a kind that authors had seldom, if ever, enjoyed during their own lifetimes.

Authorship

As literary markets expanded, so also did the population of authors. More men and, especially in England, more women, were publishing their works—whether under their own names, under a pseudonym, or anonymously—than ever before. Few of them, however, enjoyed anything like the celebrity of Richardson, Rousseau, and Goethe, and hardly any were able to live comfortably by their pens; publishers rarely paid enough for manuscripts to make an independent existence as an author economically viable. Even so spectacular a publishing success as *Werther* brought very little money to its author. Writing to a friend several months after *Werther* exploded onto the market, Goethe remarked tartly: 'My authorship has not yet put any fat in my soup'. ('Mir hat meine Autorschaft die Suppen noch nicht fett gemacht'.)

Not that Goethe was in any danger of starving. Scion of a patrician family in Frankfurt, he soon became a courtier in Weimar. He embodied a model of authorship that many of his compatriots envied but few could achieve: the author who wrote for the marketplace but who was also independently wealthy and the beneficiary of princely patronage. Until the age of Weimar classicism, German princes rarely bestowed their patronage on German authors. The primary beneficiaries of their support were the many expatriate French protégés and epigones of Voltaire who congregated at the princely courts and learned academies of small German states. Cut off from the sources of princely patronage, German authors who did not enjoy the benefits of inherited wealth had to enter a profession, as pastors, professors, magistrates, or government officials; otherwise, they ran the risk of falling into the ranks of the intellectual proletariat, a class of literary wage labourers that was growing up around the large publishing firms in Leipzig. In his satirical novel *Sebaldus Nothanker* (1773–6), the Berlin bookseller Friedrich Nicolai provided an—admittedly caricatured—image of the factory-like conditions in one of those firms:

> There is more than one publisher who commissions his authors to produce what he thinks he may need: histories, novels, murder stories, reliable news reports of things no one has seen...I know one such publisher who has ten or twelve authors sitting at a long table in his house, and to each he assigns a quota of work in exchange for a daily wage.

The situation was hardly any better in France. There, too, the way to financial security was not through the marketplace. It passed, rather, through what the French called *le monde*, the exclusive milieu of Parisian salons in which reputations were made, connections cultivated, and protections secured. The would-be *philosophe* who cut a smart figure in that world could aspire to the various lucrative posts, pensions, and sinecures—as editors of privileged journals, *historiographes du roi*, and academicians—that provided a secure alternative to the vicissitudes of the literary market. Those who failed to win those positions, the *philosophes manqués* whom contemporaries derided as 'poor devils' or 'Rousseaus of the gutter', survived in whatever way they could, by churning out libels, peddling prohibited books, or spying for the police. Only in England was it possible—just barely—to live comfortably by one's pen, as Alexander Pope and Samuel Johnson demonstrated. Even there, however, 'hacks' (an early-eighteenth-century neologism derived from 'hackney', a horse available for hire) were multiplying in Grub Street, the milieu of down-and-out authors satirized by Pope in his *Dunciad*.

While impecunious authors were struggling to survive, publishers were prospering, or so it appeared to contemporary observers. Actually, many publishers were struggling, too, not least because of the constant threat of piracy. But there can be no doubt that some publishing ventures yielded handsome profits in comparison to which the payments made to authors seemed paltry. *Les Moeurs* by François-Vincent Toussaint, a *succès de scandale* published in 1748, netted roughly 10,000 livres for its Amsterdam publisher Delespine, but only 500 for its author. The bestselling *Fabeln und Erzählungen* by

Christian Fürchtegott Gellert, published in the same year, made its Leipzig publisher Johann Wendler a wealthy man for life, but brought its author only a meagre one-time payment of 20 Reichstaler. These glaring discrepancies seemed all the more galling in light of the new conception of the author as original creator. This emerging view of authorship, expressed most famously by Edward Young in his *Conjectures on Original Composition* (1759), fed a growing sense of outrage over the shabby treatment of authors by booksellers. Frequently disparaged as miserly, mendacious, and untrustworthy, booksellers may have had a worse reputation in the second half of the eighteenth century than at any time since the invention of moveable type. And although some of the accusations levelled against them were unfair, individual booksellers were far from blameless. The pirate publisher Himburg in Berlin produced an edition of Goethe's complete works without paying a penny to the author, and then, as if to make amends, sent Goethe a set of porcelain dishes from the Royal Porcelain Manufactory in Berlin. In a letter to his close friend and correspondent Charlotte von Stein, Goethe made it clear what he thought of such a gesture: 'What to others is done after death,/To me was done during my life./But I do not write for porcelain or bread–/For the Himburgs I'm dead'. ('Was man anderen nach dem Tode thut,/That man mir bey meinem Leben./Doch ich schreibe nicht um Porcellan noch Brod–/Für die Himburgs bin ich todt'.)

Eventually, the outrage boiled over. Beginning in the mid-1760s, German authors organized a series of 'self-publishing' initiatives, with the goal of freeing themselves from their dependence on the professional book trade. The high point of the movement was the publication in 1774 of Klopstock's *Gelehrtenrepublik*, a work completely financed and distributed through subscriptions. Venerated as the author of *Der Messias* (an epic poem based on the Bible) and widely regarded as Germany's 'national poet', Klopstock was able to mobilize a vast network of 'collectors'. In small and large towns all across German-speaking Europe, volunteers came forward to gather subscriptions, inspired by their wish to enter into a collaborative relation with the author; and the results were impressive—more than 3,500 subscribers from 263 locations. Reproduced at the start of the published volume, the list of subscribers' and collectors' names, organized in alphabetical order by location, covered nearly seventy pages. It expressed a widely shared yearning to transcend the anonymity of the capitalist literary market and resurrect a community of authors and readers. What functioned well in the case of Klopstock, however, proved to be an impracticable model for more obscure authors. In the years following the publication of *Die Gelehrtenrepublik*, other attempts were made to replicate Klopstock's example, but with less and less success. In the end, the principal legacy of the experiments with self-publishing was the bitter realization that there was no durable alternative to the professional book trade as an intermediary between author and readers.

So what was to be done? According to the French *philosophe* Denis Diderot, the answer lay not in supplanting the commercial publishers who dominated the trade but, on the contrary, in protecting their legal position. In his *Lettre à un magistrat sur le commerce de la librairie*, written in 1763 at the behest of the Paris Booksellers' Guild, Diderot made himself the spokesman of France's publishing elite, those booksellers who owned the exclusive privileges for most of the legal literature published in France. The booksellers in the Paris guild, like their counterparts in the English Stationers' Company, had always regarded their privileges as perpetual, as a form of property that could be divided, sold, and inherited just like any other kind of property; they also feared—rightly, as it turned out—that the administration was contemplating legislation to limit the duration of book privileges and thereby revive competition in the publishing industry. Diderot made the case on behalf of the booksellers for preserving the status quo. One part of that case took the form of a straightforwardly economic argument: perpetual copyright was necessary for the commercial viability of publishing. This was so, Diderot maintained, because backlist titles generated the steady stream of profits required to offset the risks of financing new publications, and because it sometimes took several generations for even the greatest works of literature to be recognized as great and to begin yielding profits. But Diderot did not rest his case for perpetual copyright on the profitability argument alone. To the economic rationale, he joined a legal–aesthetic one. Since creations of the mind belonged to their authors, so the argument went, the latter were at liberty to sell their works to publishers, ceding full ownership to whoever purchased them; to limit the duration of that ownership would be to negate the original proprietary claim of the author. It would therefore be a form of theft.

The combination of the economic with the legal-aesthetic argument in Diderot's mémoire reflected the historical connections between the commercial interests of publishers in perpetual copyright, the proto-Romantic conception of the author as original creator, and the practical demands of authors to be fairly remunerated for their manuscripts. Seen from the standpoint of Diderot, those connections made authors and their publishers allies rather than foes in the battle against piracy. And yet, in other respects, Diderot and the Parisian guild made for odd bedfellows. One problem, as Diderot frankly acknowledged, was that he, like most of the *philosophes*, usually supported free trade and opposed the monopolies of privileged corporations. Another, even more serious problem was that the Parisian guild was closely tied to a government agency of which Diderot and his fellow *philosophes* had so frequently been the victims: the institution of censorship.

Censorship

In contrast to England, where experiments in pre-publication censorship came to an end with the lapse of the Licensing Act in 1695, the absolutist monarchy in France created a powerful apparatus for controlling the production and circulation of the printed word. A special branch of the royal administration in charge of the book trade, *La Direction de la librairie*, coordinated the labours of a growing staff of censors (roughly sixty in 1700 and nearly 180 by the eve of the Revolution), who vetted manuscripts and decided whether to allow their publication; the Lieutenant General of the Paris Police directed a team of inspectors who worked with thousands of spies (*mouchards*) to maintain surveillance over a shifting population of colporteurs, *bouquinistes*, *nouvellistes*, Grub Street hacks, and café denizens, while officials of the Paris guild inspected printing houses and examined crates of books arriving in the capital from other locations. The role of the guild was of particular importance. The regulations on the book trade, enacted through a series of edicts beginning in the late seventeenth century, were designed to shore up the position of the guild by setting strict limits on the size of its membership, by giving it a near-monopoly on the publication of new works, and by enforcing the system of exclusive book privileges. As the beneficiaries of that system,

the guild members had a built-in incentive to comply with the requirement of pre-publication censorship and to work with the police in
rooting out prohibited books, a vast category of literature that
embraced practically all of what we would today recognize as the
French Enlightenment.

It was a formidable system, one in which the administration of
censorship was inseparable from the economic regulations governing
the book trade; but it failed to prevent the publication and dissemination of prohibited books. Unable to publish their works legally inside
the kingdom, the *philosophes* turned instead to publishers located just
beyond France's eastern frontier in an area stretching from Amsterdam in the north through the German Rhineland and down to
Geneva and the Papal enclave of Avignon in the south. There, all
along what Robert Darnton memorably described as the 'fertile
crescent' of extraterritorial French publishing, printing houses turned
out editions of works that could not pass the censorship in France, as
well as pirated editions of works that had been published legally. To
get the prohibited merchandise safely to its destination inside the
kingdom was a complicated business. On some occasions, foreign
suppliers would hire smugglers to haul crates of books across the
border. Usually, however, they would send the crates through the
normal legal channels to the provincial guild halls in the cities designated as points of entry for book imports, but would conceal the sheets
of prohibited books by sandwiching them between those of legal
works. In the late eighteenth century, it was still common for books
to be transported and sold in the form of loose sheets. The hope, in
such cases, was that the guild officials in charge of inspecting the crates
would content themselves with a quick glance at the outer sheets. And
such tricks usually succeeded, for the provincial book guilds did not
have the same incentive as their Parisian counterpart to hunt out
prohibited books and enforce regulations. Once cleared through the
guild halls, the shipments could proceed to their final destinations,
often to the shops of provincial booksellers who did not belong to any
guild and whose businesses were not subject to any kind of regular
inspections.

By mid-century, prohibited books were circulating so widely that to
the Director of the Book Trade, Lamoignon de Malesherbes, the
situation had become absurd. 'A man who had read only books that

originally appeared with the formal approval of the government', Malesherbes remarked, 'would be behind his contemporaries by nearly a century'. The solution Malesherbes adopted was to expand the use of 'tacit permissions', an intermediary grade of legality that allowed works to be published in France without the government's full stamp of approval. Works published in that semi-legal fashion did not bear an official *approbation du roi* on the title page, nor, in most cases, did they indicate the correct place of publication. In general, the tacit permissions were granted on the understanding that the publisher would place a false, usually foreign, place of publication on the title page. By means of such subterfuges, the government avoided any impression that it was sanctioning the publication, but ensured that the economic benefits would accrue to printers and booksellers inside the kingdom.

The compromise embodied in Malesherbes's use of tacit permissions reflected the twofold nature of the book as a carrier of ideas and an object of economic exchange. In light of that duality, even the most conservative regimes tended to moderate somewhat the severity of their censorship policies if they feared that repression would be economically harmful. In the clerical-dominated city of Cologne, for example—the German Rome, as it was known in the eighteenth century—the resident Papal *nuncio* organized, during the 1770s, several book-burnings; large quantities of irreligious and pornographic French books were consigned to the flames in vast *autos-da-fe*. Like other port cities on the Rhine, however, Cologne derived much of its fiscal revenue from levies on trade, including the trans-shipment of books between Switzerland and the Netherlands; and the authorities had no wish to compromise that lucrative source of tax revenue. Thus, a crate of books transiting through the port of Cologne would be offloaded, weighed, and taxed, but not inspected. In the early 1770s, the Société Typographique de Neuchâtel, a Swiss publisher of prohibited books, sent hundreds of copies of *Système de la nature*, the notorious atheistic treatise by the Baron d'Holbach, through the city of Cologne to a bookseller in Cleve, a Prussian enclave in the lower Rhine. The crates took nearly three months to reach their destination, so cluttered was the Rhine with tolls, tariffs, and customs barriers. At no time, however, were they in any danger of being confiscated. Even so militantly atheistic a work as *Système de la nature* could sail through the very heart of the Catholic Rhineland without running into any obstacles.

Such examples of ideological rigour softened by economic pragmatism serve to remind us that censorship was not a uniformly repressive institution, even in a bastion of Counter-Reformation Catholicism like Cologne. It was still less uniformly repressive in the France of Malesherbes. Censorship in France had a positive as well as a repressive dimension. The censors' reports were often reprinted in books graced with privileges. Incorporated into the front matter, they functioned like the endorsements on the dust jackets of books today: they praised the book, vouched for its quality, and recommended it to readers. What mattered to the censors, moreover, was not just, or even mainly, the ideological orthodoxy of the manuscripts they examined; books that were obviously offensive to 'religion, the state, and good morals' were rarely submitted to them in the first place. Many of the censors were men of letters who regarded themselves as guardians of good taste and style. Endowed with a lofty sense of their cultural mission, they would work with authors to 'improve' their manuscripts, rather like peer reviewers and copyeditors at academic presses today.

Although the censors were generally careful and conscientious, they were not immune to slipups. The most spectacular blunder occurred in 1758 when a censor named Jean-Pierre Tercier approved the manuscript of Helvétius's atheistic treatise, *De L'Esprit*. The publication of so obviously heterodox a work with a full privilege and *approbation du roi* printed on its title page was bound to produce a scandal. And so it happened. The *parlement* of Paris, always eager to reassert its jurisdiction over the book trade, reacted with particular fury. It used the occasion to condemn not only *De L'Esprit* but also a long list of other Enlightenment works, including the first seven volumes of Diderot's *Encyclopédie*. On 10 February 1759, all those books, minus the *Encyclopédie*, were lacerated and burned by the public hangman at the foot of the great staircase of the *parlement*. To mollify his *parlementaire* critics, Malesherbes was obligated to rescind the privilege for Diderot's publication. But at the same time, he warned Diderot of an impending police raid on the headquarters of the *Encyclopédie*. Alerted in time, Diderot was able to remove his papers before the arrival of the police, depositing them for safekeeping in the house of Malesherbes! Eventually, once the storm had blown over, work on the project resumed, and the final volumes appeared quietly in 1765. The greatest publishing enterprise of the Enlightenment owed its survival to the timely intervention of France's censor-in-chief.

While it would be a mistake to view censorship as rigidly opposed to the Enlightenment, it would be equally mistaken to treat it as a benign institution. Even after the tenure of Malesherbes as director of the book trade, the police made repeated efforts to break up underground networks of production and distribution, above all when the works coursing through those networks were political libels. Purportedly based on genuine news sources, libels offered salacious exposés of moral turpitude in the royal bedchambers, the councils of state, and the corridors of Versailles. To the authorities in France, they were known as 'bad books' (*mauvais livres*), so irremediably bad that they could never qualify for a tacit permission. Such books existed entirely outside the law. And the authors who wrote them, the printers who printed them, and the pedlars who sold them continued to land in the Bastille through the 1780s. Eventually, in order to stem the tide of libels flowing into the kingdom, the French foreign secretary, the comte de Vergennes, issued an order in 1783 requiring that all book imports, regardless of their ultimate destination, travel for inspection to the guild hall in Paris. The order was so effective in disrupting the cross-border trade that it plunged the extraterritorial publishing houses into a deep crisis from which most of the firms never recovered.

The enormous efforts that the authorities made to halt the circulation of political libels in France expressed a fear that those works were dangerous. Indeed, all regimes of censorship can be said to express some degree of fear. In the Habsburg monarchy during the reign of Maria Theresa, the Austrian Censorship Commission took its fear of the printed word to such an extreme that, in 1777, it reportedly placed its own voluminous *catalogus librorum prohibitorum* containing nearly 5,000 titles on the *catalogus librorum prohibitorum*. To a north German *Aufklärer* like Friedrich Nicolai, this seemed an act of intolerance bordering on self-parody. The goal of such a move, Nicolai observed sneeringly, was to prevent 'bad people learning of bad books, and clever people learning of clever books, from the same source and then obtaining the dirty writings from smugglers at ten times the usual price'.

Recent research by Norbert Bachleitner has cast some doubt on the veracity of the oft-repeated story that the Austrian Commission banned its own catalogue of banned books. What cannot be doubted is that the Commission often bent its own rules, allowing qualified scholars to obtain prohibited books for their own use. In making such exceptions, it signalled its recognition that danger inhered less in the prohibited books themselves than in how they were read. Later, under Joseph II, a reformed and relatively liberal Austrian Censorship Commission took a similar view: although it eliminated more than 80 per cent of the titles from the old catalogue of prohibited books, it imposed stringent regulations on commercial lending libraries, institutions to which the subscribers were generally 'young and uneducated', in the estimate of the commissioners.

Both in its Theresian and its Josephist incarnations, Austrian censorship was premised on the idea that different segments of the public read differently. The challenge for the historian is how to make sense of those differences.

Reading

From the standpoint of the history of reading, the most significant difference within the populations of early modern Europe lay between those who possessed basic literacy skills and those who could not read at all. In an age before the establishment of compulsory primary education, literacy was unevenly distributed. Studies of signatures on marriage contracts, wills, court depositions, and other official documents in France, Britain, and the German lands during the eighteenth century reveal significant regional differences as well as persistently higher literacy rates in towns than in the countryside and among men than among women. Overall, however, literacy rates were increasing. They rose in France from 29 per cent of men and 14 per cent of women in the late 1680s to 48 per cent of men and 27 per cent of women a hundred years later; in England, male literacy is estimated to have doubled in the hundred years from the mid-seventeenth to the mid-eighteenth century, rising from 30 to 60 per cent with a corresponding rate for women by the later date of between 35 and 40 per cent. Comparable aggregate figures for the German lands are hard to come by, but it is clear that literacy was more widespread in western than in eastern regions. In the northwest Duchy of Oldenbourg, signature rates for men in the late eighteenth century exceeded 90 per cent in some districts.

Admittedly, 'literacy' is an imprecise term since it encompasses such a wide range of abilities. More significant than the mere ability to sign a document is the ownership of books. And, on that score, the evidence is quite clear: both the percentage of people owning books and the size of personal libraries increased markedly. Estate inventories compiled after death in Paris in the early eighteenth century record the presence of books for only 30 per cent of domestic servants and 13 per cent of journeymen workers; by 1780, those figures had risen to 40 and 35 per cent. During roughly the same period, the size of personal libraries in the possession of middle-class professionals rose, on average, from between one and twenty volumes to between twenty and a hundred; of the clergy, from between twenty and fifty to between a hundred and 300; and of nobles and magistrates, from between one and twenty to more than 300.

With the widening diffusion of print, even those town dwellers who did not own books themselves and who lacked basic literacy skills could no longer be said to live in a purely 'oral' culture. The urban landscape was littered with writing—from street signs, which began going up in Paris in the 1720s, to public notices of judicial rulings, ecclesiastical proclamations, and administrative decrees, which job printers turned out in increasingly large quantities and which were prominently displayed in squares and marketplaces, to the occasional handwritten *pasquinade* or graffiti, composed in secret and surreptitiously posted, through which public opinion found inchoate expression in moments of political turmoil.

That the posting of handwritten messages could still play an important role in politics during the eighteenth century may seem surprising. The use of urban surfaces as public bulletin boards went back many centuries, to early-sixteenth-century Rome, where citizens would post handwritten satirical verses critical of the papal government on the statue of Pasquino (hence 'pasquinade'). Yet, as late as 1776, following the supposed poisoning of the communion wine in the Zurich cathedral, a brazenly seditious pasquinade shook the Zurich republic and threatened to ignite violent civil strife. Its explosive impact provides a useful reminder that modes of communication originating in different historical epochs coexisted throughout the age of the wooden hand press.

While manuscript modes of communication retained their importance in the eighteenth century, urban institutions designed to facilitate
access to print were proliferating. Two of the most important such
institutions were the commercial lending library, established by a
bookseller, and the reading society, organized by the citizens of a
town. The former allowed subscribers to borrow books from the
bookseller's catalogue, to read periodicals on the premises of his
shop, and, in many cases, to meet with other subscribers in a room
set aside for discussions. Accessible to anyone who could afford the
annual or monthly membership fee, to women as well as men, the
commercial lending library was a relatively open institution—more
open, in any case, than the reading society, which was a civic association rather than a commercial establishment. Particularly widespread in the German-speaking lands, reading societies afforded
many of the same advantages as lending libraries: access to a common
stock of books and journals, as well as a room for discussion and
socializing. The members of the societies, however, decided collectively which works to obtain (usually periodicals and 'useful' works on
such subjects as history and geography, but no novels) and whom to
admit (usually bourgeois men but no women or workers).

A third institution in which urban residents could gather to talk
about what they had read was the coffee house, one of the principal
settings for the emergence of what Jürgen Habermas has described as
the 'bourgeois public sphere'. Unlike the lending library and the
reading society, the coffee house did not impose any formal requirements for admission. At least in theory, practically anyone could enter
such an establishment and take part in the often animated, and
sometimes raucous, debates spurred by the reading of newspapers
and manuscript news sheets circulating among the customers. Yet
despite such apparent openness, various selective filters operated to
restrict access. In London, where disputes among customers sometimes degenerated into physical violence, the reality of coffee house
culture was so far removed from the Addisonian ideal of polite
sociability that it was deemed unsuitable for women. In comparison,
the Parisian café was rather urbane. With its marble table-tops,
mirrors, silver utensils, and crystal, it exuded an air of gentility; and
because, in addition, it did not allow smoking and offered chocolate
and a range of liquors as well as coffee, it seemed more inviting to

women than the coffee houses of London. Yet, for those same reasons, it was unlikely to attract workers or the poor.

Although the lending library, reading society, and coffee house catered for different clienteles, they shared at least one point in common: they enabled men—and some women—to read a much wider range of printed material than would otherwise have been possible. In that way, such institutions contributed to the spread of 'extensive reading', to borrow a term coined by the historian Rolf Engelsing in his study of reading practices among the bourgeoisie of north German trading cities. Until the second half of the eighteenth century, Engelsing argued, most people, if they read at all, read the same small number of texts over and over. In Reformed Protestant households, for example, the Bible was read repeatedly year after year, often aloud by the head of the household at family gatherings in the evening. The object of such reading was not to discover new worlds but to recapitulate what one already knew. Extensive reading, by contrast, involved a relentless quest for novelty. The practitioners of extensive reading would rush through a text once before moving on to the next one, always with a view to broadening their intellectual horizons.

Did extensive reading in fact supplant the older style of reading in the second half of the eighteenth century? The answer to that question is undoubtedly 'no'. The history of reading cannot be adequately contained within so rigidly linear and starkly binary a framework. That extensive reading was becoming more common in the second half of the eighteenth century, however, is beyond question.

The clearest indication of its spread was the growing popularity of newspapers. No other genre of print available in the eighteenth century was more conducive to an extensive style of reading than the newspaper, each issue of which was immediately superseded by the next in an endless sequence. And during the second half of the eighteenth century, the volume of newspaper production exploded both in Europe and in European areas of settlement in the New World. In the German states, the linguistic area of Europe with the largest number of newspapers, production increased by roughly two-thirds in the space of thirty-five years, from ninety-three papers published in 1750 to 151 in 1785; by the eve of the French Revolution, the German paper with the largest circulation, the four-day-a-week

Zeitung des Hamburgischen unpartheyischen Correspondenten (*Hamburg Impartial Correspondent*), was being printed at a pressrun of 20,000 copies. In the newly independent United States, the increase was even more dramatic: there the number of newspapers rose from about twenty-five to approximately 230 in the period between the Declaration of Independence and the election of Thomas Jefferson in 1800. Of course, such aggregate data conceal a wide range of journalistic forms—from decorous and respectful court gazettes to the relatively lively, though notoriously corrupt, newspapers of England and the avowedly partisan, vituperative, *ad hominem* journalism of early republican America and Revolutionary France. Whatever their tone or content, however, all newspapers shared at least one feature: periodicity. Appearing every week on the same days, they imposed a new, distinctively modern experience of time on printing house workers and newspaper readers alike—on the workers, who had to labour according to the inflexible rhythms of production schedules and press deadlines; and on the readers, who came to expect the delivery of newspapers at regular intervals.

In addition, the typographical design of newspapers was growing more and more distinct from that of other genres of print, above all in England. While most papers on the Continent continued to be printed in either a two-column quarto or a single-column octavo format, London dailies of the 1770s adopted a new folio design: their large pages of newsprint were broken up into three or four columns, each of which contained short articles or advertisements separated from one another by printers' rules or individual titles. Such a page layout invited a particular style of reading: it directed readers to jump around within the text, to move from one item to another rather than to read the newspaper through from start to finish—precisely the kind of segmental or fragmentary reading one would expect to encounter among the distracted denizens of a crowded and noisy London coffee house.

But now, by way of contrast, consider the type of reader represented most frequently in French paintings from the second half of the eighteenth century: the solitary, usually young, female reader seated in some cosy interior space. In such paintings, the interior setting of the scene accords with the deeply private nature of the act of reading. In *La Jeune fille lisant* by Jean-Honoré Fragonard, for example, one sees a young woman comfortably installed with her back against a pillow, her body immobile and her eyes trained fixedly on the pages of the slender volume she holds daintily in her right hand; the expression on her face is one of intense mental concentration, absorption in the act of reading so thorough as to make her seem oblivious to the world around her.

Of course, artistic representations do not provide direct evidence of actual reading practices. Several aspects of Fragonard's painting, however, tally with what we know from other sources. To begin with, there is the detail of the small-format book, a volume so diminutive that it can be balanced in one hand. Although such small-format editions were not new to the eighteenth century (their origins went back to the portable editions of classical works published by the Aldine Press in Renaissance Venice), they were undoubtedly becoming more common; in the early 1780s, Louis-Sébastien Mercier, an astute chronicler of Parisian fashion, wrote of the 'mania for small formats'. Such books were ideally suited for reading in the privacy of a boudoir or bedchamber, where they could be laid on a night table or slipped under a pillow, as, in fact, occurred with the copies of *Werther* belonging to the Geneva and London suicide victims we mentioned at the start of this chapter.

Second, there is the association in Fragonard's painting of the small-format book with a female reader. That, too, seems credible in light of the fact that small formats were often used for the publication of novels, and other evidence suggests that many novel readers were women. The novelists whose unprecedented celebrity we noted earlier, above all Richardson and Rousseau, received large quantities of fan mail, much of it from female admirers who described in their letters how deeply the experience of reading had affected them. Their descriptions highlighted two things in particular: the intensely emotional nature of their reading experience and their imaginative identification with the characters of the novels. In one such testimonial, the marquise de Polignac told Rousseau of how she had broken down when she got to the deathbed scene of Julie in volume six of *La nouvelle Héloïse*:

> I dare not tell you the effect it made on me. No, I was past weeping. A sharp pain convulsed me. My heart was crushed. Julie dying was no longer an unknown person. I believed I was her sister, her friend, her

Claire. My seizure became so strong that if I had not put the book away
I would have been as ill as all those who attended that virtuous woman
in her last moments.

In comparison to the vehement passions described by the marquise de
Polignac, the emotional state of the young woman in Fragonard's
painting seems restrained; but she, too, gives the impression, by her
total absorption in the act of reading, of having transported herself
imaginatively to some fictional world.

The style of reading evoked by the marquise de Polignac and
depicted by Fragonard coincided with the heyday of the epistolary
novel. Both Richardson and Rousseau cast their novels in the form of
letters, as did Goethe and scores of other authors during the period
from the 1740s through the 1780s. Such a device enhanced the reality
effect of the fiction: it supported the illusion that the novels were not
novels at all but authentic collections of letters discovered, edited, and
published. How many readers were actually fooled is hard to say. But
clearly many *wanted* to believe in the genuineness of the letters; and in
the mid- to late eighteenth century, such a belief was not as farfetched
as would have been the case in earlier periods. That's because the rise
of the epistolary novel coincided with an actual increase in the volume
of personal correspondence and marked improvements in the quality
of postal services. Speedy, regular, and reliable mail deliveries—the
same basic communications infrastructure that made possible the
widening circulation of newspapers—formed the basis of a new epistolary culture. Correspondents, now increasingly confident that their
letters would arrive at their destination, lavished greater care on their
letters than had been common in the past. At the same time, the new
cult of sentimentality infused personal correspondence with a confessional tone, a development in which women letter-writers played a
particularly important role.

For all these reasons, the letters of fictional characters such as Julie
and Claire possessed a certain plausibility. Readers of those letters
were able to give way to the fantasy that the characters were real, and
so participate vicariously in the sorrows and joys to which the letters
bore witness. Today, such an emotional response would be described
as empathic. In the eighteenth century, it was associated with 'sym-
pathy', in the literal sense of 'suffering with', and its cultivation though

novel reading had far-reaching consequences. According to Lynn Hunt, the emotional identification of readers with fictional characters contributed to developing the sense of a common humanity, a feeling of kinship with unknown others that was a necessary condition for the emergent ideology of universal rights.

From the reading of epistolary novels to the *Declaration des droits de l'homme et du citoyen*? That connection may seem a little farfetched, but it deserves to be taken seriously because reading was such a powerful force in the eighteenth century. For some, that power was deeply unsettling. Cultural conservatives of the late eighteenth century imagined a wide range of contemporary ills that they blamed on the malign influence of untutored reading: a wave of suicides, set off by the reading of *Werther* and the writings of the *philosophes*; an epidemic of masturbation, spread through the solitary reading of erotic literature and which led its victims down a slippery slope to frailty, impotence, blindness, and insanity; and, most ominously, a growing incapacity of women afflicted with 'reading addiction' to distinguish adequately between fact and fiction and to attend responsibly to their daily chores. From such an alarming list of ills it was but a short step to blaming the outbreak of the French Revolution on the same pernicious influence, as the abbé Baruel, the theoretician of the Counter-Revolution, did when he attributed the Revolution to an evil conspiracy of *philosophes* and Freemasons. *C'est la faute à Voltaire, c'est la faute à Rousseau.* Supporters of the Revolution, however, were equally insistent on drawing that connection. The nation's representatives expressed their debt to Voltaire and Rousseau by ordering the remains of the two *philosophes* to be enshrined in the Pantheon; and after the overthrow of the monarchy in 1792, a petition was submitted to extend a similar honour to Gutenberg, the inventor of the European printing press.

That there existed a close link between the Revolution and print was a point on which both Revolutionaries and Counter-Revolutionaries could agree. But what exactly was the nature of that link?

Print and Revolution

In their determination to eliminate privilege in all its forms, the Revolutionaries destroyed the institutional and administrative infrastructure of Old Regime culture: not just learned academies and privileged journals, or the pensions, sinecures, and *gratifications* reserved for authors, but also the printers' and booksellers' guilds, the edicts on the book trade, book privileges, *La Direction de la Librairie*, and royal censorship. The destruction was so great that it catapulted the world of print into a legal void. Eventually, that void would be filled with new laws—a law on libel and sedition adopted as part of the constitution of 1791; and a law on literary property, the so-called Declaration of the Rights of Genius, passed by the Convention in 1793. In the meantime, an unprecedented situation prevailed in Europe's most populous state: a condition of near-total freedom of the press. During the first several years of the Revolution, just about anything could be printed, and anyone could set up shop as a printer or bookseller. While the members of the old Paris book guild bombarded the National Assembly with petitions and memorandums in a vain attempt to restore their privileged position, new printing and bookselling establishments were springing up all around them. Hundreds of such establishments came into existence to satisfy the public's insatiable thirst for political pamphlets and newspapers. And the Revolution generated huge quantities of both. At least 2,600 pamphlets were published between January and the opening of the Estates General on 5 May 1789. Nearly 250 newspapers appeared during the six months after the storming of the Bastille, and more than 500 between 14 July 1789 and the overthrow of the monarchy on 10 August 1792. The revolutionary experiment with a free market in ideas produced an explosive growth in the volume of print.

Nearly all that growth, however, was in the field of political ephemera. Book publishing—the kind of serious, large-scale, capital-intensive activity associated with the Paris guild—went into steep decline. Various factors lay behind that decline. One was simply that political ephemera were the genres of print most in step with the revolutionary experience of time: its sense of rupture with the past and rapid, dizzying change in the present. Newspapers, in particular, were of crucial importance in helping citizens to comprehend the meaning of rapidly unfolding events. And some of the men who wrote and edited those papers—Brissot, Desmoulins, Marat, and Hébert—enjoyed a degree of fame and visibility such as journalists had never before enjoyed. The most famous 'authors' of the Revolution wrote newspapers and pamphlets, not books. And yet book publishing would not have declined as steeply as it did had it not been for a second, even more important factor: the lack of an adequate regulatory framework. In effect, the revolutionary crisis in publishing vindicated the position Diderot had defended in his mémoire on behalf of the Paris guild: commercial book publishing was not viable without the security of legally guaranteed copyright protections. The Convention sought to provide those protections through the Declaration of the Rights of Genius, but that law was not enough in itself to place book publishing on a stable economic foundation. The term of protection afforded by the law was too short (just ten years after the death of the author); the enforcement mechanisms were too weak; and the protection did not, in any case, extend to books published before 1789. Those books were deemed the property of the nation, and so passed into the public domain. The entire literary inheritance of France was merged into a vast cultural commons, no part of which could be fenced off and enclosed.

The Triumph of the Book

Ultimately, it fell to the Napoleonic state to create the conditions in which book publishing could flourish anew. Following a wave of bankruptcies that shook the Parisian book trade in the early years of the new century, the French authorities took steps in 1810 to re-establish a comprehensive regulatory framework. The *règlement* of 1810 created a new organ of government, the Direction générale de l'imprimerie et de la librairie, to superintend the administration of the book trade, and a corps of inspectors and police officials to monitor the trade; it re-imposed limits on the number of printing houses in Paris and required of all printers and booksellers that they obtain a licence (*brevet*) from the Direction générale; and it lengthened the term of copyright protection to twenty years following the death of the author, his widow, and their children.

Most important from the standpoint of book publishing, the *règlement* mandated that one deposit copy of each new publication be submitted to the *dépôt* at the Bibliothèque nationale, and all new publications registered with the Direction générale. With a general system of registration and legal deposit in place, it became possible for the first time to compile a reliable and exhaustive catalogue of books in print—*La Bibliographie de l'empire francais ou Journal de l'imprimerie et de la librairie*, which the Direction générale published and updated periodically beginning in 1810. The information contained in that catalogue allowed publishers to survey the entire literary market and plan their publishing strategies accordingly. In addition, the requirement of registration for all editions made it possible for publishers to exploit the public domain effectively. The Direction générale would grant authorization for the re-edition of works belonging to the public domain provided that the editions were different from others on the market. In such cases, the protection conferred by the state applied not to the text, which at least in theory remained part of the cultural commons, but to what the literary scholar Gérard Genette has dubbed the 'paratext'—all those aspects of an edition (format, notes, introduction, illustrations, and so on) that distinguish it from other editions of the text. So attractive did the re-edition of classic works now become that it threatened to tip the balance in the world of publishing, from the production of *nouveautés* to the reproduction of cultural patrimony.

Of course, the revival of book publishing was not the only goal that the architects of the 1810 *règlement* had in view. Their overriding concern was to control the circulation of ideas; and to that end, the *règlement* reintroduced pre-publication censorship. But the principal mechanism of control in the new system was surveillance, not censorship, which, in any case, applied more to pamphlets and periodical literature than to books. Decades of political agitation stretching back to the 1770s had demonstrated that the most incendiary genres of print were the shortest—from Tom Paine's *Common Sense*, which set the North American colonies on a course towards independence from Great Britain; to the abbé Sièyes's *Qu'est-ce que le tiers état?*, which fixed the terms of political debate in the crucial period before the meeting of the Estates General; to Hébert's *Père Duchesne*, the unofficial organ of the Parisian Sans-Culottes during the Terror. Compared to such pamphlets and journals, longer works now seemed benign, as the liberal political philosopher Benjamin Constant explained in 1814:

> All enlightened men seemed to be convinced that complete freedom and exemption from any form of censorship should be granted to

longer works. Because writing them requires time, purchasing them requires affluence, and reading them requires attention, they are not able to produce the reaction in the populace that one fears of works of greater rapidity and violence. But pamphlets, handbills, and newspapers are produced quickly, you can buy them for little, and because their effect is immediate, they are believed to be more dangerous. (Benjamin Constant, *De la liberté des brochures, des pamphlets et des journaux* (Paris, 1814), p. 1.)

Eventually, in accordance with Constant's reasoning, the restored Bourbon monarchy would exempt works containing more than nineteen sheets from the requirement of pre-publication censorship; then, following the Hundred Days, it would eliminate book censorship altogether, even while it maintained strict control over the periodical press and preserved other aspects of the system established by the law of 1810. In that way, it encouraged what Carla Hesse has described as an 'elite civilization of the book' in contrast to the more popular print culture of pamphlets, newspapers, and handbills.

A similar bias against popular print culture can be seen in the censorship policies of other regimes during the Restoration era. Under the influence of the Austrian chancellor Metternich, the newly created German Confederation adopted the Karlsbad Decrees in 1818, draconian censorship laws that were designed to stifle political opposition but that exempted works of twenty or more sheets from the requirement of censorship: 'Nineteen sheets are dangerous, but twenty make [a work] honourable ... [A work of] twenty sheets one doesn't buy', joked the satirist and poet Robert Prutz. ('Neunzehn Bogen sind gefährlich, aber zwanzig machen ehrlich ... Zwanzig Bogen kauft man nicht'.)

While the Confederation displayed considerable zeal in censoring publications of fewer than twenty sheets, it was slow to adopt a ban against book piracy—much to the disappointment of Germany's leading publishers, who had hoped that the meeting of the new Federal Diet in 1815 would lead to a copyright law valid for all member states. The following year, when the Diet gave no sign of taking action, the Hamburg publisher Friedrich Perthes issued an anonymous appeal to its deputies in the form of a pamphlet with the portentously Kantian-sounding title, *The German Book Trade as the Condition for the Existence of a German Literature* (*Der deutsche Buchhandel als*

Bedingung des Daseins einer deutschen Literatur). Only with the legislative
support of the Confederation, Perthes argued, could German booksellers perform their exalted mission—to confer material existence on
the products of the German Spirit (*Geist*). His appeal, however, fell on
deaf ears, not least because piracy continued to be a lucrative branch
of the publishing industry in Austria. It was not until 1835 that the
Diet finally adopted a general prohibition against piracy, and not until
the establishment of the Reich in 1871 that the German book trade
was subject to a uniform copyright law.

  Nor did piracy disappear from the world of the English-language
book trade, notwithstanding the decision of the House of Lords in
favour of Donaldson. In the nineteenth century, as the threat of piracy
from Scotland and Ireland receded, a new pirate nation arose on the
other side of the Atlantic: the United States. In the nineteenth century,
American publishers practised piracy on an industrial scale, and they
did so, moreover, with the full support of the US government, which
was not a signatory to international copyright agreements.

  And yet, as the age of the wooden hand press gave way in the
second quarter of the nineteenth century to the industrial age of the
steam-powered rotary press, book publishing unquestionably rested
on a more stable economic foundation, and authors enjoyed greater
bargaining power in their negotiations with publishers than had been
the case a half-century earlier. At that time, as we saw, the spectacular
international success of *Werther* had yielded practically no economic
benefit for its author. By the 1820s, when Goethe prepared the final
edition of his collected works—his 'intellectual bequest to the nation
and his financial bequest to his descendants', in the words of Reinhard
Wittmann—the author once decried as a corrupter of youth and an
apostle of suicide had been elevated to the rank of national hero. So
celebrated was Goethe, in fact, that all thirty-nine member states of
the German Confederation agreed to protect the edition of his collected works against piracy, the first time that any publication had
enjoyed such protection in German-speaking Europe. Whoever won
the competition to publish Goethe's works would be assured of a
monopoly. And the competition in such a high stakes game was
ferocious. Leading publishers in Germany sought to outbid each
other, raising the price until, finally, Goethe accepted the offer of
Johann Friedrich Cotta in Stuttgart, 'the Bonaparte of the book trade'

as he was known to his contemporaries. The price was 65,000 Taler! Goethe's experiences in the literary market were, of course, no more typical at the end of his career than they had been at the beginning. But the difference between his early and late experiences provides a measure of just how much had changed in the world of print. By the end of the *ancien régime typographique*, the literary author had been enshrined at the centre of a civilization of the book mediated through the book trade and increasingly supported by the power of the modern state.

10

South Asia

Graham Shaw

Between 1907 and 1912, the Pashupati Press in Calcutta (modern-day Kolkata) printed five little books which at first sight look exactly like South Asian manuscripts, comprising a series of long, narrow palm-leaves, the traditional surface over many centuries for making copies of texts. The deception is heightened by the books being held together by a cord threaded through a central hole in each leaf. These editions of the *Devi-mahatmya*, the Sanskrit poem glorifying the goddess Durga's victory over the buffalo demon Mahishasura, were not produced to be read silently in private but to be recited and heard at public gatherings during the great Durgapuja festival held in Calcutta every autumn. In their use and materiality, these books symbolize the interplay between oral, manuscript, and print which characterizes the history of the book in South Asia (modern India, Pakistan, Bangladesh, Nepal, Sri Lanka, and Afghanistan). Each new mode of textual transmission did not entirely supplant the old: they overlapped, coexisted, and influenced each other. Manuscript and print have never completely displaced orality and public performance as the principal channels through which a religious or literary work is experienced. A simplistic binary view equating orality (or manuscript) with tradition, and print with modernity, does not apply. The history of the book in South Asia is more a narrative of continuities than revolutionary changes.

The time spans of the different modes of textual transmission as major 'cultural carriers' demonstrate this dramatically: oral transmission and public performance persisting for three and a half millennia from 1750 BCE; the production of manuscripts continuing for more than twenty-four centuries from the fifth century BCE; print featuring prominently for a mere 200 years from the early nineteenth century onwards. Texts in South Asia, both religious and secular, have been received through oral channels rather than through the printed or even the handwritten word. The region has, until relatively recently, exhibited a listening culture rather than a reading one.

Important languages and their book histories straddle the modern geopolitical entities. For example, Urdu, Panjabi, Kashmiri, and Sindhi are common to India and Pakistan; Pashto to Pakistan and Afghanistan; Nepali, Maithili, and Bhojpuri to India and Nepal; and Bengali and Assamese to India and Bangladesh. It is necessary, therefore, to take a supranational—not a national—approach to the history of the book in South Asia. Before Nepal's first printing press was established in the 1860s, Nepali books had been published for almost half a century in India, at Varanasi, Darjeeling, and Calcutta. Presses in Indian cities such as Amritsar and Peshawar had issued works in Pashto before Munshi 'Abd al-Razzaq from Delhi trained the first lithographers at Kabul in the 1870s. Some languages are also shared with countries outside the subcontinent proper, such as Balochi between Pakistan, Afghanistan, and Iran, and Arakanese between Bangladesh and Myanmar.

This trans-regional feature is even more evident in the case of the classical languages that have been current in South Asia. In ancient India, Sanskrit occupied a position akin to that of Latin in medieval Europe, becoming the primary vehicle not only for religious and literary works but also scholarly compositions of all kinds across the sciences and humanities. As Hinduism spread into Southeast Asia, the Sanskrit 'cosmopolis' extended into Myanmar, Thailand, Cambodia, and Java. Likewise, Mahayana Buddhism took Sanskrit into Tibet and China. About 1000, as political power in South Asia devolved to new regional kingdoms, a parallel change in literary culture occurred. In this process of 'vernacularization', the regional languages gradually replaced Sanskrit as vehicles for literary creation. New versions of the Sanskrit *Ramayana* epic, for instance, were composed in all the major vernaculars. As a result of successive Muslim invasions of north India, the Persian 'cosmopolis' which covered much of Central Asia also extended to that part of the subcontinent. Such was Persian's cultural prestige that even rulers whose mother tongue was Turkish (such as the Khilji and Tughluq dynasties of Delhi) made it their court language. Remarkably, more works in Persian—both poetry and prose—

were composed in South Asia than in Iran itself. Persian's dominance reached its height under the Mughal dynasty, with 170 Persian poets said to have flourished during the emperor Akbar's reign (1556–1605) alone. In 1582 Persian was made the official language for administering both justice and taxation. With the establishment of the British Raj in India from 1757 to 1947, the subcontinent subsequently became part of the English 'cosmopolis', paving the way for the enormous contribution to modern English literature made by authors of South Asian origin.

Oral Transmission and Public Performance

In South Asian cultural history, the oral has never been regarded as inferior to the written. On the contrary, textual meaning has been held to be fully realized only through the application of oral skills that bring the correct timbre, pitch, and rhythm to each individual word. The most remarkable example of the efficacy of oral transmission in South Asia concerns Hinduism's holiest books, the *Vedas* (literally 'knowledge'). These collections of hymns, prayers, and ritual invocations, composed between 1500 and 1000 BCE, were preserved orally with remarkable accuracy over more than a millennium by generations of the Brahmin priestly caste. The Buddhist pilgrim Yijing, one of many Chinese monks to visit his faith's holy sites in India, observed this memory culture during his stay between 671 and 695: 'The *Vedas* have been handed down from mouth to mouth, not transcribed on paper or leaves. In every generation there exist some intelligent Brahmans who can recite the 100,000 verses...This is far from being a myth, for I myself have met such men' (*A Record of the Buddhist Religion...by I-Tsing*, trans J. Takakusu (Oxford, 1896), p. 182). Person-to-person transmission was ideally suited to protecting Brahmins' monopoly on sacred knowledge and continued in widespread use even after the introduction of writing. Indeed, manuscripts of the *Vedas* were essentially by-products of the oral tradition, produced as aids to the memorization of text. In many handwritten copies of the *Vedas*, accents were added above the words to indicate the correct ritual intoning of the text.

The oral tradition survives to this day—albeit on a very limited scale—in the Vedic schools conducted for the training of Hindu priests by the Nambudiri Brahmin community of Kerala. To mem-orize all 432,000 syllables of the oldest text, the *Rigveda*, takes four and a half years. The pupil repeats the text syllable by syllable as recited by the teacher who uses an elaborate system of hand gestures (*mudras*) to aid memorization. As he recites, the teacher also manipulates the pupil's head into various positions to ensure correct pronunciation, so vital for the spiritual effectiveness of each verse when intoned in ritual situations such as sacrifices. It was essential that the exact sounds of the original divine revelation were faithfully recreated. Writing the text down had no place in this process, and such action could even be regarded as blasphemous. The *Mahabharata* epic warned that whoever polluted the *Vedas* by mispronouncing them—*or* by writing them down—was bound for hell.

If oral transmission of the *Vedas* was restricted to the Brahmin caste as a means of ensuring their privileged social position, so too was the reception of these texts. The words were too sacred and too powerful to be widely shared: women and members of the lowest castes (*shudras*) were forbidden to hear them. But the social role of text changed dramatically from the seventh century onwards. Hinduism switched from focusing on Vedic sacrificial rites to an emphasis on personal devotion (*bhakti*) to individual gods and goddesses, notably Shiva, Vishnu in his incarnations as Rama and Krishna, and Devi in her manifestations as Kali and Durga. Rama's story was told in the *Ramayana* epic, while other deities were celebrated in a series of Sanskrit texts called *Puranas* ('old stories'). Both of ancient India's epics, the *Mahabharata* and the *Ramayana*, were for centuries transmit-ted and transmuted orally.

Devotional poets (*sants*) also composed hymns of praise in all the major regional languages, beginning with the Alvars in Tamil. The works of these *sants* were and still are performed in group recitations known as *kirtana* ('tellings'). The lead narrators (*kirtanakars*) possessed handwritten notebooks, but these functioned as prompts for their performance rather than as archives of fixed compositions, indicating that the writing down of standard text was subservient to dynamic recitation. The textual variances found in handwritten copies of the *Puranas* equally indicate the influence of orality on the manuscript tradition more than mere scribal carelessness. Texts were not fixed and stable, but fluid and open-ended. They changed over time, manipulated by individual reciters in different contexts through processes of revision, addition, excerption, and reinterpretation. Thus, South Asia exhibited two types of oral transmission: the 'tight', absolutely precise mode required for the *Vedas* which brooked no deviation from tradition, and the 'loose' mode associated with other Hindu religious texts that allowed variation and innovation.

Hindu devotional works were imparted to a largely illiterate population through recitations performed during the annual cycle of festivals and ceremonies. Such a text was the *Ramcharitmanas*, the sixteenth-century reworking by the Hindi poet Tulsi Das of the life of Rama. Tulsi's text still plays a prominent part in the *Ram-Lila*, the dramatic re-enactment of Rama's exile and victory over the demon-king Ravana, widely performed every autumn across north India. The *Lila's* most spectacular manifestation takes place at Ramnagar near Varanasi, which is transformed into a series of large-scale, open-air theatre sets. Episodes from the life of Rama are performed over thirty-one consecutive evenings, actors and audience moving from one location to the next, while hundreds of holy men known as *Ramayanis* recite the appropriate sections of the *Ramcharitmanas*. As Tulsi emphasized, reciting the holy name of Rama (aka Raghunayak) confers spiritual benefit on both performer and listener: 'Singing the virtues of Raghunayak yields all blessings; reverently listening, one crosses the ocean of existence without a boat'.

As well as public performances, recitation of the *Ramcharitmanas* traditionally formed part of private family worship every morning and evening. Among the most popular practices have been the reading aloud of the complete text over one month (*mas parayan*), and the nine-day reading (*navah parayan*) in which four to six hours were devoted to reciting 120 stanzas each day. The greater circulation of copies which printing facilitated only served further to popularize ritualized recitation, not to replace it with silent reading. Similarly, recitation featured strongly among devotees of Krishna, whose life was recounted in the Sanskrit *Bhagavata-purana*. Speaking the words of its text would earn both reciter and hearer as much spiritual merit as the most elaborate and costly sacrifices performed by Hindu kings: 'That house in which the recitation of the *Bhagavata* occurs daily, becomes itself a holy place, destroying the sins of those who dwell there; he who recites daily one-half or one-quarter of a verse of the

Bhagavata, secures the merit of a *rajasuya* and an *ashvamedha* sacrifice'
(Philip Lutgendorf, *The Life of a Text* (Berkeley, CA, 1991), p. 58). The
central cultural importance accorded to oral transmission in Hinduism meant that it spread to other religions in South Asia. For several
centuries in Indian Buddhism, the *Vinaya*, the rules for righteous living
laid down by the Buddha himself for monastic communities, were
passed on orally from generation to generation. The Chinese Buddhist monk Faxian, who spent some fourteen years from 399 travelling
through Central Asia, India, and Sri Lanka in search of *Vinaya*
manuscripts, reported that 'in all the kingdoms of north India he
found masters transmitting the Rules from mouth to mouth, without
ever reducing the text to writing'. Oral transmission was also initially
adhered to by Jainism, a breakaway movement from orthodox Brah-
manical Hinduism like Buddhism, with regard to its sacred texts. The
sermons of its twenty-four teachers known as *tirthankaras* ('ford-
makers'—that is, Saviours) culminating in the historical Mahavira, a
close contemporary of the Buddha, were memorized and passed on
orally for perhaps as much as a millennium before being written
down. Later, Sikhism was also influenced by the Hindu emphasis on
oral reception of text with its tradition of the 'unbroken reading'
(*akhand path*) of its holiest book, the *Guru Granth Sahib*. The entire text
is recited by a relay of readers called *granthis*, from either a manuscript
or a printed copy. This forty-eight-hour ritual is still performed on
special occasions or on a weekly basis in some Sikh temples.

Beyond religious texts, the practice of oral transmission also played
a significant role in Hindu education. In traditional schools (*pathasha-
las*), pupils routinely learnt works on Sanskrit grammar by heart, and
to be regarded as a specialist in any field of learning meant committing
key texts to memory. In pre-modern India, public reception of literary
texts was also primarily through performance. In towns and villages
across the subcontinent, the principal entertainment was folk theatre,
performed by itinerant troupes of actors. Its themes were romantic
tales and stories from Hindu mythology. This theatrical tradition was
known by various names: Nautanki in north India, Khyal in Rajasthan, Tamasha in Maharashtra, Bhavai in Gujarat, Mach in Madhya
Pradesh, Jatra in Bengal, Assam, Bihar, and Odisha, Kutiyattam in
Kerala, and Terukkuttu in Tamil Nadu. The *Chaitanyabhagavata*, a
biography of the Bengali Vaishnava reformer Chaitanya, recorded an

all-night performance datable to 1507 of *Rukminiharan* ('The abduction of Rukmini'), an episode from the life of Krishna. But inscriptional evidence from western India suggests that such performances under royal patronage date much further back, to at least the first century under the Satavahana dynasty.

How much of South Asia's oral literature has been lost, for never having been preserved in written form, is unknown. But the tradition of oral textual transmission has been so strong that some can still be recovered from performers today. A well-known example is the epic of Pabuji, originally a medieval Rajput prince but now worshipped as a deity by nomadic herdsmen in Rajasthan. The entire text is recited to music by itinerant singers called *bhopos*. A large painting of the story serves as a guide to the narrative and a backdrop to the performance, which may typically total forty hours of recitation over five consecutive nights. Oral versions of another folk epic telling the story of the love of Chanda, a married Rajput princess, for Lorik, a humble cowherd, have been collected in at least eight different Hindi dialects (including Avadhi, Bhojpuri, Chattisgarhi, and Magadhi). It was transmitted orally for centuries before forming the basis of Maulana Da'ud's mystical romance, the *Chandayana*, written in 1379, and is still recited today by otherwise illiterate Ahir cowherds as their tribal epic. As the Indian cultural historian Kapila Vatsyayan has commented: 'There is no question of making demarcation between the literate and the illiterate in this sphere, for many times a seeming illiterate will know the story and the words better and with a greater understanding of its value than one who reads it only as an intellectual exercise' (Kapila Vatsyayan, *Traditional Indian Theatre* (New Delhi, 1980), p. 111). A high cultural value has consistently been placed on oral composition of literary works throughout South Asia. In Bengal, for instance, *kabigana* ('poets' singing') were important cultural events in which participants vied with each other to compose and chant verses extempore, often with musical accompaniment. These compositions were not usually written down but the most popular were memorized by the audience, a process of oral rather than written preservation. In south India, major public events known as *arankerram* ('debuts'), sometimes lasting weeks or even months, saw poets reciting new works for the first time. The famous nineteenth-century Tamil poet Minatch-ichuntaram Pillai is reputed to have composed most of his works orally, dictating them to a scribe—oral and manuscript traditions again commingling.

From the seventeenth century onwards, Telugu literature contained a strong tradition of freestanding verses called *catu*, full of social comment, often erotic or subversive, and displaying their creators' linguistic prowess. These were transmitted exclusively by word of mouth among ordinary people, swapped, quoted, discussed, and recontextualized. As the Telugu literary historians Velchuru Narayana Rao and David Shulman have noted: 'to reduce them to writing, in a collection contained between two covers, is to displace them from their living, collective context into a strangely silent medium'. But formal oral recitation performances achieved their most central and important form in Urdu literature. These *mush'airas* ('symposia'), frequently fuelled by literary rivalries, were enormously popular and remain a prominent cultural feature, not only in the subcontinent itself but also among the Indo-Pakistani diaspora.

The oral reception of text also featured prominently in medieval Islamic culture in the subcontinent. When the Mughal emperor Humayun returned to India from Iran in 1555, artists and poets followed him, escaping the illiberal atmosphere of the Safavid Shah Tahmasp's court. They brought with them the tradition of reciting elaborate stories (*dastans*) featuring, among others, Hatim Ta'i, the ideal of Islamic generosity and virtue, and the heroic deeds of the Prophet Muhammad's uncle, Amir Hamza. The emperor Akbar, reputedly illiterate himself, loved to listen to these stories and employed a professional narrator of tales, a *dastango* or *qissah-khvan*, at his court. The *dastan* of Amir Hamza became the most popular in South Asia, with several new versions being created. The seventeenth-century *Bostan-e khiyal*, which filled fifteen large volumes, was widely circulated in manuscript to be rerecited by *dastangos* all over north India. A *dastango*'s talent was measured not by his ability faithfully to deliver a fixed text, but to extemporize and elaborate the story's narrative, showing a clear emphasis on oral dexterity. From Persian, the *dastan* tradition passed into Urdu, and public recitations were regularly held in places such as the famous Qissah-khvani Bazar ('Narrators' Market') in Peshawar. *Dastangos* attended fairs and festivals catering to mixed Muslim-Hindu audiences. The Muslim reformer Syed Ahmad Khan described such events in 1847 at the

Jama Masjid, the principal mosque in Old Delhi: 'In the evening a *qissah-khvan* arranges a reed stool, sits down, and narrates the *dastan* of Amir Hamzah. To one side the *qissah* of Hatim Ta'i is being told, and somewhere else the *dastan Bostan-e khiyal*. Hundreds of men gather to hear the performances'. The famous nineteenth-century Urdu poet Mirza Ghalib arranged weekly *dastan* performances in his own house. The most celebrated *dastango* was Mir Baqir 'Ali Dihlavi, who knew thousands of verses by heart and continued to perform until his death in 1928. When Munshi Nawal Kishore, the most successful commercial publisher in nineteenth-century north India, decided to issue a *Hamza-nama* series from 1881 onwards, he hired three leading *dastangos* of Lucknow to recite their versions which he had scribes write down. The result was monumental: forty-six printed volumes averaging 900 pages each.

While Christian missionaries in South Asia in the nineteenth century were ardent advocates of print, they nevertheless recognized the people's predilection for hearing rather than reading text. The 1811 British and Foreign Bible Society Report recommended embracing this tradition:

> The Mahometans have everywhere appointed readers of the Koran, who read aloud the book from beginning to end. The Hindoos have Poranees, who perform the same office in reading the Shasters, and no offence has been given or taken by either. In the same manner, the Christian Scriptures might be read publicly, without incurring the smallest opposition. The Mahometans rank our Scriptures among 'the heavenly books', and the Hindoos are disposed to tolerate every religion. It will be easy for the chaplains and others to employ and superintend several public readers at each station, and the expense will be inconsiderable.
>
> (*Reports of the British and Foreign Bible Society ... for 1811,*
> *1812 and 1813* (London, 1813), p. 161)

For missionaries, this oral tradition was ideal for overcoming the low literacy rate among Indians. In 1892, the Wesleyan missionary Henry Haigh in Mysore experienced its effectiveness for himself. Questioning a village headman, he learnt that the *Vrttanta Patrike*, his weekly newspaper in Kannada, reached a far greater audience than the number of copies circulated would indicate:

I asked him if anyone in the village could read. 'Only one man,' was his reply; 'I have engaged a Brahman to teach the boys of the village . . . Every Friday evening, about this time, a newspaper comes to our village . . . When it comes I take it to the schoolmaster and a boy goes round to tell the neighbours. After a while they all come together and sit down under that great tree, as many as thirty or forty . . . There is an almanac every week, and we always see what are the market prices in Mysore and Bangalore. Then it explains all that the Sirkar [Government] is doing, and sometimes tells the Sirkar that it is making mistakes . . . It says a great many things about our customs. It is always telling us that idolatry is false and we have great talks about that; and every week there is something about a Great Guru, called Jesus Christ.

    (Alfred Manwaring, ed., *Report of the Third Decennial Missionary Conference held at Bombay, 1892–93* (Bombay, 1893), 2: 735–6)

In South Asia, the tradition of oral communication could be harnessed to expand the reach of print.

The Invention of Writing and Manuscript Production

South Asia has one of the world's largest manuscript heritages, estimated at some thirty million volumes in both public and private collections. This huge figure is not fanciful, given that the National Mission for Manuscripts (established by the Government of India in 2003) has already identified over 50,000 different repositories and detailed over four million manuscripts. Libraries were formed in the subcontinent from an early date. In the seventh century, for instance, the library of the great centre of Buddhist learning at Nalanda in Bihar is reputed to have contained several hundred thousand volumes. This is matched in the modern era by the Jaina libraries in western India known as *jnana-bhandars* ('storehouses of knowledge'). That at Koba in Gujarat possesses alone an estimated quarter of a million manuscripts. The vastness of this manuscript heritage can be attributed in no small measure to the region's multi-religious history: Hinduism, Buddhism, Jainism, Islam, Sikhism, and Christianity each developed their own textual traditions. The multiplicity of languages as vehicles for religious, literary, and scholarly expression also added to this manuscript richness, Sanskrit above all. Both the paper and non-paper surfaces used for writing in South Asia have been very vulnerable to the region's monsoon climate and the depredations of insects and rodents, which have combined to take a massive toll. All this attests incontrovertibly to the massive scale of manuscript production throughout the subcontinent.

As noted in Chapter 2, the invention of writing in South Asia is still debated by scholars. It was long believed to have originated with the Indus Valley Civilization, the subcontinent's earliest urban culture extending from Afghanistan to Gujarat between the fourth and second millennia BCE. Over 4,000 objects, mostly clay and stone seals, have been excavated with inscriptions on them, sometimes accompanied by images of deities or ritual scenes. Four hundred distinct signs have been identified in this Indus Valley script, variously interpreted as encoding an early Dravidian or Indo-Aryan language. But the script has not been satisfactorily deciphered, and scholarly opinion increasingly regards these signs as non-linguistic. They may, for instance, denote the affiliations of families, clans, or cities to specific gods, and may have been worn as amulets or badges. But their most likely purpose was commercial, as a mechanism for labelling and tracking items traded internationally by the Indus Valley Civilization, perhaps attached as ownership tags to bales of goods.

On more reliable evidence, the invention of a South Asian writing system can be dated to the reign of the Mauryan Emperor Ashoka, *c.*268 to 232 BCE. The need for writing arose from the emperor's desire to promote Buddhism throughout his kingdom stretching from Balochistan in the west to Assam in the east and as far south as Karnataka. Edicts proclaiming Ashoka's allegiance to the Buddha's teachings were carved into rock faces or onto stone pillars using various scripts: Greek, Aramaic, Kharoshthi (a short-lived Indian script), and—most commonly—Brahmi. Probably derived from a Semitic script model, Brahmi developed in the north Indian heartland, and gradually spread from the Mauryan capital of Pataliputra (near modern Patna) into the Deccan and southernmost India. Its arrival in Sri Lanka was traditionally associated with the spread of Buddhism to the island by Ashoka's son Mahinda, as told in the ancient Sinhalese chronicles, the *Dipavamsa* and *Mahavamsa*. Archaeological excavations since the 1990s, however, have revealed that Brahmi was in use a couple of centuries before Ashoka's reign, as a language of commerce at least, if not of administration, literature, or religion.

At Porunthal and Kodumanal (in Tamil Nadu), hundreds of potsherds have been unearthed bearing Brahmi inscriptions, some in strata radiocarbon-dated back as early as 490–450 BCE. Similar finds at the ancient Sinhalese capital Anuradhapura have been firmly dated to *c*.400 BCE. The inscriptions mostly denoted ownership of the pots on which they were scratched, and their contents. These finds indicate that Brahmi's diffusion was due to trade rather than religion, since all these sites had well-established mercantile links with the script's birthplace in north India. If the use of Brahmi had reached south India well before the middle of the fifth century BCE and Sri Lanka at the beginning of the fourth, then its invention in north India must be pushed back before the Mauryan empire into the sixth century BCE, the era of its predecessor, the kingdom of Magadha. Over many centuries and in different regions of the subcontinent, various adaptations of Brahmi emerged, and from it evolved all of South Asia's major scripts. Furthermore, through trans-regional cultural influence, it was the ancestor of scripts in Central and Southeast Asia such as Tibetan, Burmese, Thai, and Javanese.

This earlier date for Brahmi's invention chimes with the first literary references to writing from South Asia, which are found in two distinct sources: parts of the Buddhist canon and Greek writers dating back to the fifth and fourth centuries BCE. Initially, writing was regarded as a purely utilitarian device, fit only for making lists or keeping commercial accounts. No doubt under the influence of the Hindu tradition, writing was considered inappropriate for the transmission of religious or literary texts. The region's native flora dictated the choice of writing surfaces: birch-bark (*bhurjapatra*) in the western and aloe-tree bark (*sanchi*) in the eastern Himalayas, and palm-leaf in all regions below the mountains from the Indo-Gangetic plains to Sri Lanka. Sections of the inner bark of the birch tree were flattened, glued together into long sheets, sometimes stitched at the edges for further strengthening, and folded flat or rolled into a scroll. The text was then written on in ink using a reed pen. In 1931 a large cache of birch-bark manuscripts was found in a Buddhist stupa at Gilgit (in north Pakistan) dating from *c*.400–600.

More recently, birch-bark manuscripts dating from the first and second centuries have been discovered, Buddhist texts from the kingdom of Gandhara (straddling Pakistan and Afghanistan). Although prone to splitting, birch-bark continued to be widely used in Kashmir until the seventeenth century. The preparation of palm-leaves was more complicated. They were boiled in water, dried, and cut into long, narrow strips. Both sides of the leaves were then polished with pumice to provide a smooth writing surface. Leaves from two palm species were used: first the talipot and later the palmyra. The talipot was not native to north India and only became known there once the Mauryan empire expanded into the south during the third century BCE. Prior to that, leaves or wood from other trees must have been used in the north, but no examples survive. Like birch-bark, talipot leaves were written on in ink using a reed pen. The oldest surviving talipot manuscripts from north India are Buddhist texts dating from the tenth and eleventh centuries; the earliest from the south is a Jain text dated 1112. In the sixteenth century the palmyra palm was introduced to India, probably from East Africa. A hardier species than the talipot, it could be cultivated in north as well as south India, and was economically more attractive, supplying other products such as fruit and the palm-wine, toddy. The palmyra quickly supplanted the talipot as a writing surface, although inferior because it did not take ink well. Instead, the text was incised using a metal stylus, and ink rubbed into the grooves afterwards to highlight the text.

As writing surfaces, neither parchment nor paper were extensively used in ancient South Asia. The use of animal skin would have been totally anathema to Hindus, Buddhists, and Jains alike. Although the raw materials were readily available, paper-making in the Chinese manner was not widely practised in the subcontinent. There is some evidence of small-scale paper manufacture in the western Himalayas as early as the sixth century, since paper as well as birch-bark manuscripts were discovered at Gilgit. Knowledge of the craft may well have come across the Karakoram mountains from China, but the product was technically inferior to Chinese paper. In Nepal, by contrast, paper-making became well established, from at least the twelfth century onwards. Paper was not suited to the more tropical climate of the subcontinent proper and could not replace palm-leaf and birch-bark sanctified by centuries of tradition. Besides, high-caste Hindus probably feared pollution from contact with paper made from recycled rags which replaced mulberry bark in the process as learnt by Arabs after their conquest of Samarqand in 751. Manuscripts on paper from South Asia dating from before 1500 are rare, although its widespread adoption in the subcontinent can be traced back to the Turkish dynasties who conquered north India during the early thirteenth century. Initially supplies of paper must have been imported from Iran and elsewhere in the Muslim world, but from the sixteenth century onwards centres of paper-making developed in South Asia itself such as Ahmedabad, Daulatabad, Lahore, and Kashmir, producing high-quality, durable papers capable of being burnished and decorated.

From the thirteenth century onwards, paper also gradually supplanted palm-leaf for manuscript production among Jains and Hindus, although it initially retained the long, narrow proportions of the palm-leaf format. The earliest illustrated Jain paper manuscripts are copies of the *Kalpasutra*, the biography of Mahavira, from the mid-fourteenth century; the oldest illustrated Hindu paper manuscript is a *Vasantavilasa*, a poem on Krishna's dalliances with the female cowherds, dated 1451. In some areas, however, such as Orissa and Sri Lanka, the use of palm-leaf persisted up to the nineteenth century. In Orissa not only was the text incised using a stylus, but illustrations were, too, with colouring sometimes also being added.

The greater durability of metals, especially copper, led to their long use in the subcontinent for recording legal or political texts where permanence was paramount, such as title deeds to land or diplomatic treaties. The earliest surviving copper-plate land grants date to the Pallava dynasty of fourth-century south India. The largest known, comprising eighty-six sheets held together by a copper ring and dated 1053, records the donation of eight villages to Brahmins by the Chola king Rajadhiraja. The issuing of copper-plate charters was also adopted by some Muslim rulers. Persian-language examples were issued by the Bahmani dynasty of Bidar in the Deccan from the sixteenth century onwards. In 1691 and 1711 the treaties concluded between the Dutch East India Company and the Zamorin of Calicut, a Hindu ruler in Kerala, were engraved on narrow strips of gold and silver, respectively.

With the writing down of sacred texts alien to orthodox Hinduism, it was Buddhism and Jainism which provided the initial stimulus for the production of manuscripts. At the core of both religions was the fundamental importance of recording the *exact* words spoken by their respective founders, the Buddha and Mahavira. Following the Hindu practice of oral transmission, over time accounts of their teachings had begun to differ, and both Buddhist and Jain monks held a series of councils to establish standard, canonical texts. Once writing had been accepted as a proper means of preserving sacred words such as the Buddha's own discourses (*suttas*), religious literature seems to have rapidly expanded. In 645, for example, the Buddhist pilgrim Xuan-zang was able to take back to China no less than 657 Buddhist texts. In the case of Hinduism, writing seems to have replaced the dominant oral tradition only much later, when the armies of Muhammad of Ghor swept through north India in the 1190s. With the wholesale destruction of temples and monasteries, writing was the last resort against the threat that Hindu culture might be totally obliterated. But for Hindus, the writing down of text continued to operate within a primarily oral tradition. One consequence was that, except for royal and other deluxe commissions, little importance was attached to the visual and aesthetic aspects of manuscripts. No Hindu traditions of calligraphy developed comparable to the Islamic, and the Uzbek polymath Al-Biruni, visiting India in the early eleventh century, commented further:

> The Indian scribes are careless, and do not take pains to produce correct and well-collated copies. In consequence, the highest results of the author's mental development are lost by their negligence, and his book becomes already in the first or second copy so full of faults that the text appears as something entirely new, which no one could any longer understand. (Qeyamuddin Ahmad ed., *India by al-Biruni*
> (New Delhi, 1983), p. 8)

It was not until the seventeenth century that Hindu scribes—in Kashmir at least—treated calligraphy as a serious art for the first time.

Manuscript illustration in South Asia also owed its origin to Buddhism and Jainism. Since they embodied the teachings of the founders of those faiths, there was a strong impulse to beautify manuscripts through fine calligraphy and the addition of images. In Buddhist Nepal, for example, a vogue developed for writing sacred texts in gold ink on paper dyed blue-black. The illustration of palm-leaf manuscripts started among Buddhists in eastern India and Nepal about 1000 and was quickly imitated by Jainism, the oldest decorated

Jain manuscript dating from 1060. In both Buddhist and Jain manuscripts, the earliest images—gods and goddesses, bodhisattvas and
monks—did not illustrate the texts they accompanied. Their purpose
was talismanic rather than narrative: to provide an auspicious or
protective presence. Manuscripts quickly became objects of veneration in themselves, bestowing religious merit (*punya*) on those who
commissioned their copying and embellishment. Manuscripts of Jain
scriptures were mass produced at centres such as Patan and Ahmedabad specifically for the pious purpose of donation to temple libraries.
Buddhist manuscripts were exhibited to lay worshippers during an
annual *pustakapuja* ('book worship') day when their covers were ritually
anointed with sandal-paste. This cult of the book had been ordained
by the Buddha himself in the *Prajnaparamitasutra* ('The Sutra of the
Perfection of Wisdom'):

> After it has been well written in a great book with very clear letters
> through the sustaining power of the Buddha, it must be honoured,
> treated as guru, highly esteemed, worshipped, adored, venerated with
> flowers, incense, perfumes, garlands, unguents, aromatic powders,
> clothes, music, covers, umbrellas, flags, bells, banners, and garlands
> of lamps all round with many forms of worship.
>
> (Jinah Kim, *Receptacle of the Sacred* (Berkeley, CA, 2013), p. 1)

This practice continues today among Nepalese Buddhists. At the
Golden Temple (Kwa Baha) in Lalitpur, a lavish thirteenth-century
manuscript of the *Prajnaparamitasutra* is displayed to worshippers on
major ritual occasions throughout the year, when Buddhist priests
invoke the goddess of wisdom's presence within the book itself. Likewise, in Jainism, copies of the *Kalpasutra*, containing the biography of
Mahavira, feature prominently in the Paryushana festival celebrated
during the monsoon. The oral and written traditions meet when the
monks recite the entire text and carry the manuscript in public
procession, allowing the congregation a viewing of the holy scripture.
The copying and illustration of Buddhist manuscripts under the Pala
dynasty in eastern India at the great monasteries such as Nalanda,
Vikramashila, and Uddandapuri disappeared with Muhammad of
Ghor's incursions at the end of the twelfth century. In western India,
the illustration of Jain manuscripts continued, with images beginning
to follow a narrative rather than talismanic purpose as the thirteenth

century closed. This change may well have been prompted by the example of Persian illustrated manuscripts, marking the first example of the Islamic world's influence on the South Asian book.

Very few Arabic or Persian manuscripts survive from early Muslim rule in India during the thirteenth and fourteenth centuries. But the scholars and *littérateurs* who flocked to the courts of Delhi and elsewhere from across the Muslim world must have brought manuscripts with them, which undoubtedly served as models for the production of copies locally. The Khalji sultans of Malwa, for example, brought to their capital Mandu artists from Afghanistan and Iran who produced between 1490 and 1510 copies of the *Bustan* of Sa'di, illustrated in the Herat style, and the *Ni'matnam*a, a book of recipes, imitating the Shiraz style. The Islamic book in South Asia reached its apogee under the Mughal emperors. It was Akbar in the mid-sixteenth century who established the imperial studio (*tasvir-khana*) on a grand scale. Its output of illustrated manuscripts far surpassed that of the studio of Shah Tahmasp of Iran. The most ambitious manuscript project Akbar commissioned was the *Hamza-nama* in fourteen volumes containing a hundred paintings each, which took fifteen years to complete, from 1562 to 1577. It is estimated that Akbar employed hundreds of calligraphers and artists in his studio. Their names indicate that they came from many different parts of the subcontinent, including Kashmir, Gujarat, and the Deccan. About 70 per cent of the calligraphers and artists were Hindu, such as two master illustrators, Dashvant and Basavan. Calligraphy, the highest Islamic art, was especially prized, with Muhammad Husayn al-Kashmiri honoured with the title *Zarin Qalam* ('Golden Pen').

The artists in Akbar's studio evolved a more naturalistic style through a synthesis of Iranian and Indian elements. To this in the 1590s were added European elements such as perspective, learnt from European religious prints presented by Portuguese Jesuits from Goa. In his efforts to break down barriers between different religious communities in his empire, Akbar established a translation bureau (*maktab-khana*) to prepare Persian versions of Hindu Sanskrit works, resulting in illustrated manuscripts of *inter alia* the *Mahabharata* (renamed the *Razmnama*) and the *Ramayana*. Instead of large, heavily illustrated manuscript projects, Akbar's son Jahângîr favoured assembling fine examples of calligraphy and painting into an album

(*muraqqa*'), showing his exquisite taste as a collector. The more orthodox Aurangzeb condemned manuscript illustration, but did patronize
calligraphy and in old age made copies of the Qur'an by his own hand.
In 1739 the imperial Mughal library, reputedly containing some
24,000 manuscripts, was looted by Nadir Shah and many of its
treasures carried off to Iran.

The Mughals were the first indigenous power in South Asia to come
into contact with the European printed book. In 1580 a Jesuit dele-
gation from Goa presented the emperor Akbar with a copy of Christopher Plantin's magnificent Polyglot Bible, one of the greatest
products of the Renaissance. But it stirred no interest in the technology behind its production. There was no request for a printing press to
be installed in the imperial studio. Mechanical composition could not
compete with the exquisite calligraphy of Akbar's scribes. The Mughals maintained a well-developed information and knowledge network,
based on the large-scale production and dissemination of manuscripts
by professional scribes (*katibs*), and underpinned by regular newsletters
(*akhbars*) compiled by news-writers in every corner of the empire.
Contemporary Hindu kingdoms operated a similar system, with hereditary castes of scribes (*kayasths*) fulfilling the roles of information
providers and circulators. Printing with moveable metal types failed
completely to replace traditional book production methods at the
court or any other level of Indian society. Pero Luis was the first
Indian to be involved with the press, assisting in printing Tamil
Christian texts in the 1570s, but as the first Indian Jesuit, he did not
represent traditional society. The first Indian to request a European
printer and press was the wealthy Gujarati merchant Bhimji Parak,
broker to the East India Company at Surat, but his plan in 1670 to
print 'ancient Braminy writings' in 'Banian characters' came to nothing. The first royal press in South Asia was established by Sarabhaji II,
Maratha ruler of Tanjore, only in 1805.

The Mughal style influenced manuscript illustration in almost every
part of the subcontinent. Rajput princes who became powerful figures
during the reigns of Akbar and Jahângîr established court studios of
their own. One of their finest products was the magnificent *Ramayana*
manuscript prepared for Maharana Jagat Singh of Mewar between
1649 and 1655 containing some 500 large paintings. As in the Mughal
studio, both Muslim and Hindu artists were involved, Sahib Din

alongside Manohar. A later Maharana, Sangram Singh II initiated a huge new programme of illustrated manuscripts, including a *Bhagavadgita* with 710 illustrations, one for each verse. After the Mughal conquest of Assam in 1681, Delhi artists influenced the manuscript painting style favoured by the Ahom rulers, as seen in the 1734 *Hastividyarnava*, a treatise on the care of elephants.

With the gradual break-up of the Mughal empire, *littérateurs* and artists migrated to the newly independent states in the Deccan, Bengal, and Avadh to secure fresh patrons. In the later eighteenth century, the Nawabs of Avadh, Shuja' ud-Daula and his son Asaf ud-Daula, especially favoured the production of *Ragamalas* ('Garlands of Ragas'), sets of texts and paintings describing the various musical modes. At the same period, Europeans began to collect South Asian manuscripts, albeit with great difficulty in the case of sacred texts. But in 1789 Colonel Antoine Polier returned to France with the first copy of the *Vedas* ever to leave the subcontinent.

The Impact of Printing Technologies

Xylography, typography, and lithography all had an impact on South Asia in different ways. On present evidence, xylography was practised in Tibet and Nepal but not in sub-Himalayan South Asia itself, although Indians must have known the technology. Buddhist pilgrims from China and Central Asia would surely have brought woodblock-printed texts with them on their visits to India; and Hindu merchants trading in Chinese ports would have seen woodblocks being carved with text at first hand. This non-adoption of xylography has been interpreted as Hinduism's active 'resistance' to print, perhaps regarding it as tainted because of its association with Buddhism. But the reaction was probably a more passive one of simple indifference, since the textual needs of Hindus were effectively met by oral transmission, performance, and widespread manuscript circulation. It was impracticable for Indian Buddhist teachers visiting Central Asia and China to carry a large number of manuscripts with them. For centuries the teachers relied instead on their powers of memory for the transmission of texts in the course of their teaching. Always greatly revered, memorization as a technique has remained to this day central, for instance, to traditional monastic education in Tibet.

The earliest known example of Sanskrit in print is a *dharani* found at the Central Asian oasis of Turfan in Xinjiang, dated between 650 and 670. *Dharanis* were short prayers often intoned as magic or protective spells. In Tang-dynasty China, Sanskrit, the language of the Mahayana Buddhist texts, and the Siddham script in which they were written, both acquired a sacred status from at least the eighth century onwards. Since so few people could write the Siddham script, these small texts were block-printed on single sheets, often spiralling around a central image of the Boddhisattva Avalokiteshvara to form a mandala. *Dharanis* were regularly used in imperial rituals, for example, to invoke rainfall or snow, with instances known as early as 708 and 711. They were also worn for personal protection inside amulets on the arm or round the neck, and examples continue to be excavated in tombs in China. In 758 the Chinese emperor was reputedly cured of an illness by a *dharani* given him by a Buddhist monk. The consecration ritual for Buddhist *stupas* (pagodas) also included placing *dharanis* inside. Prominent centres of Sanskrit woodblock printing were Chang'an, Chengdu, Shaoxing, and Dunhuang. Not only short prayers but also entire texts of various Buddhist Sutras were xylographed in Sanskrit, to increase the number of copies that could be distributed to Buddhist monasteries throughout China for teaching and study purposes. This multiplication of copies by means of xylography also accelerated the process of translation of Buddhist Sanskrit texts into Chinese. An edition of the popular Heart Sutra (*Prajnaparamitahridayasutra*) found at the Tangut city of Karakhoto in Inner Mongolia shows that Sanskrit texts were regularly recited in Buddhist rituals. The finely calligraphed Sanskrit text is printed vertically in the Chinese fashion syllable by syllable, accompanied by the Chinese equivalent not of the meaning but of the pronunciation, thus enabling a non-scholar of Sanskrit to recite the words perfectly as the ritual demanded. Xylographed editions of Buddhist Sanskrit works continued to be produced at least until the fourteenth century under the Mongol Yuan dynasty at Central Asian sites such as Kocho (modern Gaochang).

Printing with moveable metal types was an example of European technology transfer to South Asia. The lateness of typography's arrival in South Asia can be judged by observing that Tamil literary culture, for instance, had by then already flourished for well over a millennium, the early corpus of Sangam-era poetry dating between the third centuries BCE and CE. In 1556 a printing press was set up by Jesuit missionaries in the Colégio de São Paulo at Goa, the capital of the Portuguese empire in Asia. This issued mostly religious works in Portuguese and Latin, such as India's earliest surviving imprint, the works of St Bonaventure (1559). The focus of Roman Catholic conversion in the subcontinent had, since St Francis Xavier's mission in the 1540s, been the Tamil-speaking Paravar fisher community in the far south. In 1574 Alessandro Valignano, as Jesuit Visitor, boosted printing in the regional languages. He released the linguistically talented Henrique Henriques from pastoral duties to prepare works for the press in Tamil for the Paravars—catechisms, a confessionary, and lives of the saints. Tamil types were first cast at Goa in 1577 and then improved at Quilon (modern Coulam) a year later. This marked the beginning of Indian type design and its domination by Europeans, which would persist into the early nineteenth century with British commercial type founders such as Vincent Figgins. Such influence could have malign consequences, as with Konkani, the language of the Goan region. From 1616 onwards, Konkani works, such as those of the first English Jesuit in India, Thomas Stephens, were printed using only Roman types, inaugurating a trend that persists until today. When the first Protestant mission press was established in the Danish East India Company enclave of Tranquebar (modern Tharangambadi) on the Coromandel coast in 1712, the scope of South Asian Christian publishing widened to include Biblical translations. A Tamil edition of the Gospels and Acts was issued in 1714. The year before, a virulently anti-Hindu polemic *Akkiyanam* ('Ignorance') had also been printed in Tamil, setting the aggressive tone that would characterize much Christian literature until the middle of the nineteenth century and provoke a backlash in print from the subcontinent's other faiths.

Until 1800, the scale of printing facilities in South Asia remained very limited. All presses were under the control of European colonialists and missionaries and confined to a few coastal locations. They did not affect the overwhelming majority of the subcontinent's population. These facilities could not even meet all the information and leisure-reading needs of the small expatriate European population. Books were regularly imported from Britain from the 1730s as part of the private cargoes allowed to captains of East Indiamen, and were eagerly bought up by houses of agency and subscription libraries. Novels rapidly became all the rage in India: the 1793 will of Mrs Patty LeGallais, the wife of a Calcutta tavern-keeper, listed thirty titles, including *The Nabob* and *Dangers of Coquetry*.

Britain was the last of the colonial powers to embrace printing, after the Danes at Tranquebar (1712), the Dutch at Colombo (1737), and the French at Pondicherry (1758). The English East India Company was content to rely on its own manuscript culture through the corps of 'writers' recruited from Britain. Furthermore, the Company's first printing press was not imported from Europe, but seized as booty at the siege of Pondicherry in 1761. Even then it became only a part-time official press, used also for religious purposes by the two German missionaries at Madras entrusted with its superintendence. During the last quarter of the eighteenth century, Calcutta became the first centre of commercial publishing in India, outstripping both Madras (modern-day Chennai) and Bombay (modern-day Mumbai) in quantity as well as variety of products. Newspapers proliferated in all three cities; at Calcutta in the 1790s it was possible to read a different title every day of the week. From the publication of the very first newspaper in India, *Hicky's Bengal Gazette* in 1780, the press came into conflict with the East India Company, which was reluctant to brook any criticism. The libertarian James Augustus Hicky, who compared himself with John Wilkes, wickedly lampooned Warren Hastings as 'The Great Mogul'. In 1781 Hicky was put on trial for libel, imprisoned, and had his press confiscated a year later. Another newspaper editor, William Duane, was deported in 1794 after just eleven weeks of publishing *The World*. In 1799 the Governor-General Marquess Wellesley introduced the first press censorship in India which required all copy to be approved by government before publication. During the entire colonial period, government oscillated between loosening or tightening restrictions on the press, culminating in the draconian 1910 Press Act promulgated in the wake of 'seditious' publications provoked by the Partition of Bengal.

Despite its introduction three and a half centuries earlier, print only had a significant impact in the nineteenth century in South Asia. In every major regional language there was an 'explosion' of all forms of publishing: books, journals, newspapers, and ephemera, creating a new public space for discourse of all kinds—religious, cultural, social, economic, and political. From now on, the balance of print's exploitation shifted from the European minority to the indigenous majority. It was the more liberal Press Act of 1835 which led to widespread ownership of presses in the subcontinent. But there were earlier examples of local ownership, such as the royal press of the Nawab of Avadh, Ghaziuddin Haidar at Lucknow (1817), and commercial presses such as that of Fardunji Marzban at Bombay (1812) and the Khidirpur press, Calcutta, opened by Babu Ram (1807). Even earlier, a highly significant event in South Asian publishing history had occurred at Bombay. In 1796 Gujarati types had been cast to print the East India Company's official notices in translation in the *Bombay Courier* newspaper. Two years later, Parsee compositors at the Courier Press used those same types to print a prayer-book—the *Khordeh Avesta*—for the benefit of their community, representing the first successful initiative in print by Indians for Indians without any direct European involvement. Alongside print in regional languages, the demand for English-language materials rose dramatically following Thomas Babington Macaulay's *Minute on Indian Education*, notorious for its sweeping dismissal of Indian traditions of knowledge. Under the resulting English Education Act of 1835, the East India Company transferred funding from traditional Hindu and Muslim schools teaching in Sanskrit and Persian to new English-medium schools teaching a curriculum of only European knowledge. Education had also been the stimulus for the earliest English-language printing in South Asia, an edition of Thomas Dyche's *A guide to the English tongue* (Tranquebar 1716). The switch to English as the medium of instruction provided a lucrative opportunity for British educational publishers such as Oxford University Press and Macmillan to exploit the huge Indian market.

After educational works, the largest publishing sector in nineteenth-century South Asia was created by Christian missionaries who valued the press as an essential arm of their conversion project. On average, twenty-five mission presses were in operation annually in the region. In one decade alone (1852–61), no less than 7,776,533 books and tracts were issued. By 1870 over 4,000 Christian titles had been prepared in thirty languages, more than 1,000 in Tamil alone. By 1900 over 1,100 editions of the Bible, whole or in part, had been printed in sixty languages and dialects. Funding was often provided by the British and Foreign Bible Society in London, just as the Religious Tract Society regularly subsidized the printing of smaller pamphlets. An infrastructure of Christian book depositories and bookshops was formed, facilitating an aggressive programme of circulation pursued by foreign missionaries and paid local colporteurs. Religious fairs and festivals were especially targeted, presenting opportunities for distribution to large numbers of people from different parts of the subcontinent. Inevitably, this flood of Christian material provoked a backlash among the region's other religions which felt themselves under attack. Unwittingly the Christian missionaries contributed to South Asia's cultural renaissance, at the forefront of which was religious revival. To defend themselves, Hinduism, Islam, and Buddhism turned the missionaries' own weapons against them: promoting their own religious tenets in print as well as preparing anti-Christian material; founding presses; forming tract societies; publishing journals; and deploying their own colporteurs. Arumuga Navalar, for instance, translated Christian tracts into Tamil for the Wesleyan Mission and the Jaffna Bible Society before establishing his own Vidyanubalana Press in 1850 issuing works in praise of Shiva. In Madras, R. Sivasankara Pandiah set up the Hindu Tract Society in 1887, sending his own evangelists all over south India with anti-Christian tracts. In Sri Lanka in 1862, the Society for the Propagation of Buddhism was formed to counter the virulent anti-Buddhist literature circulated by Wesleyan Methodist missionaries. Christian mission presses were also channels for the transfer of printing expertise to South Asians. For example, Gangakishor Bhattacharya trained at the Baptist Mission Press, Calcutta before founding the Bengal Gazette Press, and Javji Dadaji worked at the American Mission Press, Bombay before opening his Indu-Prakash Press.

The one printing medium that did strike an immediate cultural chord was lithography, introduced to South Asia in the 1820s. Lithography became a mainstream, rather than a marginal technology, appealing especially to Muslim communities. The reason was that it enabled the printed book to imitate the characteristics of the manuscript which still held cultural authority in the Islamic scholarly tradition. Lithography made an apparent paradox a reality: the mass-produced manuscript. Whereas Buddhists had earlier xylographed Sanskrit *dharanis* to imitate manuscript amulets, so Muslims had

Qur'anic verses lithographed for the same purpose. It was printed letter-forms, not calligraphy, which presented problems of legibility in South Asia. As late as the 1830s, for instance, Baptist missionaries in Orissa paid local scribes to copy Biblical texts onto palm-leaves, a practice begun by the Danish missionaries at Tranquebar in the early eighteenth century. Traditional scribes readily embraced the new profession of lithographic writer and became so skilled that at Lucknow they mastered 'mirror-writing'—that is, copying entire texts in reverse directly onto lithographic stones. As well as Muslims, lithography was also used by Hindus. Many Sanskrit works were lithographed at Bombay, Poona, and Benares, adhering to the manu-script *pothi* format and including a colophon rather than a title page. In South Asia, both xylographed and lithographed texts 'hovered' as it were midway between manuscript and print, showing features of both while also exhibiting differences, but clearly emphasizing the import-ance and persistence of the manuscript tradition in both Hindu and Muslim culture.

The nineteenth century provides examples of South Asia's import-ance in spreading printing to other parts of Asia and in creating an international book market around the Indian Ocean from East Africa to Indonesia. The Serampore Mission Press in Bengal founded by the Baptist William Carey in 1800 was not only a pioneer in evangelical publishing in the languages of South Asia; in the wake of the East India Company's expanding interests in Asia, Serampore became the continent's hub for Christian printing and publishing in Burmese, Vietnamese, Malay, Javanese, and Chinese. It was a 'safe haven' for missionaries working in more dangerous areas such as Vietnam and China, where no Christian press could safely be established. Seram-pore's innovative type founding was also crucial, casting, for instance, the first Chinese moveable metal types of the modern era in 1812. In 1816 Serampore sent a second printing press to Burma for the use of American Baptists (the first, sent to the Burmese court in 1813, had sunk in the Irrawaddy river). Nathaniel Moore Ward, trained by his uncle, the Serampore printer William Ward, was sent to Sumatra in 1818 with a press and types to serve the Governor Sir Stamford Raffles. Commercial publishers also exploited South Asia's pivotal geographical position, none more so than Nawal Kishore from his press at Lucknow. Beyond British India, he was able to access a vast market in Afghanistan, Iran, and those Islamic countries of Central Asia which had yet to develop their own printing and publishing industries. From the 1880s onwards, books in Persian, Pashto, and Arabic, especially editions of the *Qur'an*, were sold through local agents and also to visiting traders from cities such as Bukhara (in Uzbekistan) and Yarkand (in Xinjiang), with its Muslim Uighur population.

Although printing in Vietnam, Laos, Myanmar, Cambodia, and Thailand fully developed only in the mid- to late nineteenth century, for several centuries before that different book production and printing materials and practices had intermixed. Some Qur'ans in Indonesia and nearby regions, for example, were copied on palm-leaves, while printing in Indonesia, Malaysia, and the islands of Southeast Asia developed from earlier European missionary activity, but also with interesting amalgams of practices. The first book printed in the Philippines (in 1593) resulted from the Chinese manner of woodblock printing, but with the first letterpress printing in the Philippines swiftly following in 1602. Much later, the first official English-language newspaper in Malaysia (1806) was printed by Andrew Burchett Bone, who had previously worked as a commercial printer in both Calcutta and Madras—another example of India as a hub for the diffusion of printing technology. Even so, the ancient and diverse manuscript book culture of South Asia exerted a further, profound influence on manuscript book production across all of Southeast Asia—and a far greater influence than that of East Asian woodblock printing. Some authors, intent on restricting the readership of their work to friends or members of the social elite, continued to circulate their writings in manuscript. Hand-copying Buddhist sutras also remained an act of devotion, and of particular devotion if copied in one's blood. This was a practice which the prominent Chinese scholar Hu Shih (1891–1962) condemned as the 'Indianization' of China in the nineteenth century, even though Chen Shuling (陳叔陵), the Prince of Changsha, is recorded as copying the *Nirvana Sutra* in his own blood as early as 579 CE. For some scholars, Vietnam has offered a further difference in that some notable texts here were printed in Chinese from woodblocks well before the introduction of mechanized moveable type. While this woodblock printing has contributed to a consideration of Vietnam as an East Asian culture, the more significant change was actually one of the adopted script—the replacement of printing in Chinese characters (*chu nom*) by an accented form of the Roman alphabet (*chu quoc ngu*) under French colonial rule from 1910.

Meanwhile, from the 1860s onwards, Bombay capitalized on its pre-eminence as a major port to supply works all around the Indian Ocean. The few presses that were in operation in the Middle East were either government or missionary; the Bombay commercial presses shrewdly exploited the gap in the market for more popular literature, such as legends and stories of Muslim saints. Islamic printing in Bombay became a multi-lingual business, embracing Gujarati, Urdu, Persian, Arabic, Malay, Javanese, and Swahili. The city became the hub of a transnational Persian book trade via the shipping routes to Bushire and Bandar Abbas. Many editions of popular classics, such as Jalal al-Din's celebrated *Masnawi* or Firdawsi's national epic, the *Shah-nama*, were published. Munshi Karim's press printed works in Arabic and Swahili specifically for the Zanzibar market where he employed a local agent. As well as across the Arabian Sea, Arabic books found a ready market throughout Southeast Asia. Urdu books were shipped to the expatriate Indo-Muslim community in South Africa, and books in Javanese to Indonesia. Most remarkably, for several decades, from the 1870s Bombay became the Malay world's chief source of Islamic religious texts and popular ballads printed in Malay in the *Jawi* variant of Arabic script.

By the turn of the twentieth century, probably more Arabic-script Malay books were being produced in Bombay than Singapore. Its presses produced works of better quality both in terms of print and paper, causing the Singapore presses to decline. Printing machinery was also exported: about 1875, Sultan Sayyid Barghash bin Said of Zanzibar purchased a typographic press at Bombay and later, Bombay Parsee entrepreneurs set up their own presses on Zanzibar. Bombay itself attracted entrepreneurs from outside South Asia into its book trade, eager to exploit its nexus of steamship routes. In 1868, for example, the Iranian Mirza Muhammad Shirazi opened one of the city's most important bookshops and publishing houses. The prestige of the Bombay presses drew authors from around the Muslim world, anxious to enhance their scholarly reputation through print. Safi 'Ali Shah, a Muslim cleric from Isfahan, printed his first work, *Zubdat al-asrar* ('The Essence of Secrets'), at Bombay in 1872, and Sayyid Ibrahim Saif al-Din al-Qadiri, descendant of the celebrated medieval saint of Baghdad 'Abd al-Qadir Jilani, had a collection of religious poems printed in Arabic, Persian, and Urdu while visiting followers in Bombay in 1912. Even works on numerology and letter magic by the long-dead Nigerian Muslim mystic al-Kishnawi were printed at Bombay in the 1880s.

Although print has been the primary mode of textual transmission for only some two centuries, this has coincided with a tumultuous period in South Asia's history, the transition from colonialism to independence. Throughout the Indian Freedom Movement, print nurtured and sustained the spirit of nationalism, not least through posters, broadsheets, and collections of patriotic songs circulated among Mahatma Gandhi's non-violent protesters (*satyagrahis*). Independence in 1947 ended the domination of British publishers, enabling more locally owned enterprises to flourish. Despite the advent of digital media, print remains immensely popular. Six of the world's twenty newspapers with the largest circulations are published in India. But the contemporary Indian book world poses dangers as religious pressure groups impose censorship and make death threats against authors and publishers alike.

11

Industrialization

Marie-Françoise Cachin

In Europe and the United States, publishing could not remain unaffected by the development of new techniques and the newly industrialized economy. Late-eighteenth- and early-nineteenth-century innovations in printing, paper-making, typesetting, binding, and illustration, presaged far-reaching technical progress that hugely increased production and reduced its cost.

At the beginning of the nineteenth century, Lord Stanhope developed a printing press made of metal with a large platen allowing large-format printing. He also contributed to the commercial success of the stereotyping process—that is, printing from a solid plate of type-metal cast from plaster. The technique was widely adopted and used for reprinting throughout the nineteenth and the early twentieth centuries. The stereotype plate was first used in the United States in 1813 and remained one of the most distinctive aspects of American book production.

Throughout the century, the manufacture of new mechanical printing presses advanced on both sides of the Atlantic as American press builders adapted ideas from Europe and vice versa. Early on, George Clymer, a printer in Philadelphia, produced the Columbian Iron Press in 1807, soon available and used in Britain and other European countries. A steam-driven cylinder press created by Friedrich Koenig in 1811 printed *The Times* in 1814, its first important application; in 1826, the Leipzig publisher F.A. Brockhaus adopted the Koenig press for books. An early rotary press was designed by Richard Hoe in the 1840s, and destined mostly for newspaper work. The rotary press allowed the printing of whole sheets of paper and consequently increased the speed of production.

European and American paper-making techniques also improved, although problems now concerned materials more than machinery. Printers tried different plant fibres, such as ferns, nettles, or straw. In the 1840s, experiments were made with wood pulp, and in the 1860s, esparto grass was largely used in Britain. Mechanization also concerned paper-making, with the first commercially successful machine invented by the Frenchman Nicholas-Louis Robert in 1798. His water-driven invention, commercialized and built in London by the Fourdrinier brothers, revolutionized paper-making, transforming it into a large-scale industry. Consequently, the production of paper increased significantly. In the United States, it passed from 1,000 tons per year in 1800 to 2.8 million at the beginning of the next century. In Britain, it grew from 96,000 tons in 1861 to 648,000 tons in 1900.

Typesetting remained a long, complicated process, and solutions to improve it came only later in the century. The first Linotype machine, invented by Ottmar Mergenthaler, an American engineer of German origin, served to print *The New York Tribune* in 1886 before being introduced into England in about 1890. The American Tolbert Lanston first produced the Monotype system in 1889, encouraging book printers to modernize their composing rooms. Typesetting had many advantages: apart from accelerating the task of composition and reducing its cost, it improved the appearance of books thanks to the use of various fonts. Newspaper production similarly benefited from it. Numerous improvements also transformed binding techniques over the same period. Around 1820, cloth began to be used instead of leather. But the mechanization of binding proper only came about after the invention of the embossing machine by the American Sheridan company in 1838. Finally, several innovations appeared in the field of illustration. Thomas Bewick developed new techniques in wood engraving in the 1790s and, as described in Chapter 9, Alois Senefelder invented lithography in Germany at the end of the eighteenth century, a technique introduced to England in 1801. The daguerreotype followed around 1830, and photoengraving some fifty years later.

As printers appreciated the progress of mechanization and new processes, they invested in them in order to increase output. In 1814, the French printer François-Ambroise Didot sent his son to England to acquire information about new inventions, eventually buying the recently invented Stanhope press. Didot was an early adopter of steam power and, in 1823, he built a new factory outside Paris to print larger editions. The same kind of development existed in the other two main publishing centres of the time, London and Leipzig, and later on in the United States. In Germany, Brockhaus built a factory in Leipzig in 1843 to accommodate his new mechanical presses; he owned nine by 1850, twenty-two by 1872. The new technology allowed printers to run off thirty-two pages at a time. The availability of cheap paper and the use of mechanical printing made much larger print runs possible, and consequently publishers developed new strategies to respond more quickly to market demands.

Such changes in the printing business led to an overhaul of printing buildings and to the creation of a new workforce with new working practices. Factories started to combine the various activities needed to publish a book, including paper-making, type-setting, printing, and binding. Each stage required its own specialist workforce and enough space for machinery. Proprietors confronted problems of safety and hygiene, heating, lighting, and ventilation. In addition to the machine rooms, it became necessary to set up different specific offices for correspondence, accounting, and other secretarial tasks, as well as ever larger storage spaces to stock the printed works ready for retail. In the 1850s, in Thomas Nelson & Sons' Edinburgh printing, publishing, and binding establishment, a total of nineteen machines and seventeen presses worked constantly. Other rooms were used for the letter-press, book-binding, and lithographic departments, requiring a well-oiled system of division of labour. Rationalizing work to increase output transformed traditional printing houses into industrial factories, sometimes called 'book factories' or 'literary factories', where book production was carefully planned and organized.

Consequently, working conditions also changed: some tasks fell by the wayside, replaced by fresh ones. The new machines required qualified workers to operate them, and so the need for other categories of workers developed. Printers increasingly employed women to cut up and prepare rags collected in the streets to make paper or, later, when this new technique came into use, to process wood-pulp. New factory management systems organized workers according to the duties allotted to them. The general system was later dubbed Taylorism after the American industrial engineer Frederick Winslow Taylor

(1856–1915), whose 1911 book *Principles of Scientific Management* advocated large-scale manufacturing through assembly-line factories. The new working practices forced workers at every stage to increase their hours and shifts for the sake of profit, so as to keep machines in operation all day. The various stages of book production were now carried out one after the other, and workers no longer had an overview of the whole process. The new organization led to the development of a clear hierarchy, from the lowest unskilled workers to the managers and directors at the head of the whole structure. Even so, some firms continued to be in the hands of 'gentlemen publishers' like Louis Hachette in France, the Macmillan family in Britain, and the Harper brothers in the United States.

Unsurprisingly, especially in Europe, the transformation of the manufacture of printed works, and the changes in working practices gave rise to various protest movements. In France, for example, in 1848, typographers protested against the decline in their working conditions brought about by technological progress. The conflicts culminated in 1862 with a strike by Parisian typographers, which led to the 1867 foundation of the Société typographique parisienne to fight for higher wages and better working conditions. Although generally employed for the humblest tasks, women sometimes suffered hostility from their male counterparts because their wages were lower, meaning some employers preferred to hire them. In Boston, a union was founded in December 1848 to guarantee workers decent wages and to ban women from working as typesetters. In November 1849, Boston printers started a strike which lasted into December. By 1857, the Boston Typographical Union accepted female typographers, and advocated equal pay.

From Printing Firms to Publishing Houses

The industrialization of the book trades and its impact on the various sectors of national economies developed gradually. Many firms remained family businesses, but large and well organized, and employing a great number of workers. This was so in the case of the German printer Brockhaus, with successive generations inheriting the management of the firm and ensuring its cohesion and continuity. Across the Rhine in France, François-Ambroise Didot was in charge of his Paris printing house, his brother Pierre-François was a printer and the manager of the Essonne paper-making factory, while his youngest son Firmin ran the engraving and typographical foundry sections. The American house of Harper continued in the hands of four brothers, James, John, Wesley, and Fletcher; in Britain, the house of Macmillan was created by Alexander and his brother Daniel, whose eldest son Frederick inherited the firm in 1890.

These family firms progressively adopted industrial methods, but smaller printers could not always afford to acquire new machinery. Heavy investments were necessary to develop new buildings and to modernize printing processes. The financing of these investments took place within the family whenever possible, thanks to inheritances and dowries, often in the form of property. Another solution was to find partners by purchasing printing houses or bookshops. Until the turn of the century, most European firms were reluctant to borrow from banks. In France, for example, Flammarion preferred to borrow money from relatives or friends rather than turn to the banks. By the early twentieth century, however, more and more publishers with increased industrial capacity relied on bankers to finance the development of their businesses. Even so, moving from a modest family business to a large business enterprise took some time.

The process of industrialization in the United States was somewhat different. There, the late-eighteenth-century book trade consisted of small, non-specialist shops producing books for the local market. By the 1850s, numerous specialist firms of variable size served the various branches of book production. Some of these companies suffered from undercapitalization. In the long run, however, most publishers had enough capital to manufacture their books without taking too many risks. A few businesses combined printing and publishing, which required a higher level of capital investment. American firms like Harper and Appleton in New York and Lippincott in Philadelphia followed this model, while in Britain publishers such as the Murray family gradually focused mostly on publishing, keeping the different functions of book production separate. In Germany some firms preferred to adopt a vertical structure. As the book trade became a full-fledged industry, it expanded even more beyond national frontiers and in many cases took on a major international dimension.

The Circulation of Books and the Internationalization of Publishing

The industrialization of publishing took place in line with other technological advances, particularly in transport and communication, which definitely transformed and facilitated the circulation of printed material. After 1830 and especially during the 1840s and 1850s, railways developed rapidly in many countries, first of all in Britain. By 1830, 375 miles of line had been built; by 1840, London was connected with Birmingham, Manchester, and Brighton. The railway boom culminated with 1,500 miles of railway in 1840, 2,400 miles in 1845, and 6,000 in 1850—five times the length of the French railway system. By 1848, it was possible to travel by rail from Paris to Leipzig, Berlin, and Vienna. In the United States, the expansion of railroads was so considerable that by the end of the century, the American rail network was one of the most extensive in the world.

Other transportation improvements concerned roads, particularly in France, where the state invested in the extension of the network. In Britain, also, country roads—often in poor repair—had to be mended and new ones built. Development was assured by revenues gained from the extension of turnpike roads, with some 8,000 toll gates working in England and Wales by 1840. The advent of steam also revolutionized river, coastal, and ocean transport. In Britain, canals had transformed transport from the mid-eighteenth century, but new ones were dug throughout the next country. Moreover, the opening of the American company Cunard's first line between Liverpool and the United States gave an important boost to the cross-Atlantic book trade in 1840. The construction of the Suez Canal in 1869 made the Indian subcontinent and the Far East more accessible, facilitating the export of industrial goods, including printed material. Agents grew accustomed to delivering orders where needed rapidly, and transport costs and deadlines shrank progressively. This was particularly significant for the delivery of time-sensitive material such as newspapers: by 1851 the London morning papers were available in Bristol at 11 o'clock.

Across Europe and North America, improved transport links led to a more reliable postal service. Wholesalers, retailers, and even private customers could easily receive books by mail. In the United States, the postal system was a means of reaching customers directly, without relying on booksellers. In England, where the Post Office already played an important role at the end of the seventeenth century and throughout the eighteenth century, the Post Office and the railway companies worked together after a Parliamentary Act of 1838 obliged the railway companies to convey mail by special carriages. One further invention in the field of communication technology that had a major impact on the book trade was the telegraph, which enabled orders to be placed far faster than before. Britain created an Electric Telegraph Company in 1846, quickly followed by other European countries including France, Prussia, and Austria, where the telegraph was a state monopoly. Together with the Post Office, in Europe as in America, the telegraph could be used not only to send packages of printed material, but also orders and bills.

The new modes of transport hugely boosted the international expansion of the book trade. Colonization demanded the export of print and books to support overseas communities in their own languages, and both France and Great Britain enjoyed captive markets in their territories. Huge quantities of volumes were exported to the American colonies from the mid-eighteenth century onwards, as well as to the Caribbean and India. In France, 8 per cent of all books produced in 1821 were exported to Asia and Africa—a proportion that grew to 27 per cent by the end of the century. As Jeffrey Freedman showed in Chapter 9, significant international trade had flourished for several centuries. The French book trade in particular exported to its French-speaking neighbours Belgium and Switzerland, as well as to countries such as Russia, Spain, and Italy, where French remained the language of the cultural elite.

The desire for international expansion led to the creation of export departments in the larger publishing companies, a development originating from the late eighteenth century and the overseas sales activities of employees such as Christopher Brown, working for Longmans of London. Exports consequently increased, in spite of market fluctuations. Exports of French books to South America tended to decline, while they increased for Canada, the third-largest French-speaking market outside France, after Belgium and Switzerland. Unsurprisingly, Britain became the leading exporter of books worldwide, especially for the United States and the countries of the British empire. The emergence of trade journals facilitated exports. In France, the *Journal de la Librairie* first appeared in 1811, while in Germany, the *Börsenblatt für den deutschen Buchhandel* started in 1834. International booksellers like Bossange used such publications to advertise their books and offer their services as book-trade middlemen. Similarly, Treuttel and Würtz started to publish monthly newsletters in London in 1817.

Following the development of export departments, the largest publishing companies set up branches in the great cities of the world. British publisher Thomas Nelson established an American operation in 1854 which considerably expanded under the supervision of its second manager James Robertson. After their arrangement with Oxford University Press for the marketing of Bibles was cancelled in 1896, Nelson's American branch took over the manufacturing of Bibles for the American market. Macmillan's expansion overseas started only in the 1870s, when Frederick Macmillan went to America, while his brother, Maurice, explored possibilities in Australia and India in the mid-1880s. A New York branch opened in 1869, while the Macmillan Company of Canada started in Toronto at the end of 1905, and the Macmillan Company of New York created its own subsidiary office in Chicago at the beginning of 1907. Longmans opened a branch in New York and developed in India, in particular with an educational sector which produced books for Indian students. Leipzig publisher Brockhaus had their first branch in London in 1831, followed by Paris in 1837 and Vienna in 1864. Another German publisher, Deubner, was present in Moscow from 1842 and founded other branches in Odessa and St Petersburg in 1878. The increase in printed material circulating worldwide is clear evidence of the internationalization of exchanges of printed materials as one of the consequences of the industrialization of the book trade. The increasing global reach was enabled by export departments and overseas subsidiaries, particularly in the latter half of the century.

Libraries and Literacy

Increased literacy represented an important consequence of and a further stimulant to industrialization. Manufacturers needed workers capable of reading job-related printed materials, and more and more people felt the same need for reading skills for both personal and professional reasons. As a result, increasing literacy in most industrialized countries during the nineteenth century greatly boosted the demand for books. Given that most books were relatively expensive, various kinds of libraries were created to enable access to reading for different sections of the population.

Until the development of the 'public library movement' in many cities (and especially in Britain) during the second half of the nineteenth century, free libraries remained exceptionally rare and largely unavailable to general readers. Many countries did establish or reorganize their national libraries at an early date, but a general reading audience was not admitted to these grand and imposing (and often contrasting) institutions such as the National Library of Spain or the National Library of India in Kolkata, both founded in 1836. The National Library of South Africa was founded as a 'public library' in 1818 by the Cape Colony's first civil Governor Lord Charles Somerset to 'lay the foundation of a system, which shall place the means of knowledge within reach of the youth of this remote corner of the Globe'. The National Library of Brazil was officially founded in 1810, incorporating large collections from the Royal Library in Lisbon; the National Library of Mexico was founded in 1833. The Imperial Public Library in St Petersburg dates from 1795, and was refounded as the National Library of Russia with a continuing emphasis on its apparent 'publicness' after the Revolution in 1917.

Such libraries were not built and did not develop their structures in isolation. Models were important, both as ideals and as warnings. The British Museum Library, inaugurated in the eighteenth century, greatly expanded during the next century, while established and celebrated university libraries, from those of Oxford and Cambridge to those of Harvard and Yale, reserved the reading of their rich and fast-growing collections to scholars and students. Many European libraries, of distinguished lineage, changed character according to local pressure (and in some cases according to political exertions and military occupations). Leipzig University Library opened in 1542, with a permanent librarian appointed in 1616. From 1833, the library maintained daily opening hours. Warsaw University Library, established in 1816, also became known as a 'public library', but the operation of this proved strictly limited. Public viewings of university and national libraries did take place but, even here, visitors were vetted, and the privilege was often closely guarded.

Consequently, private, charitable, and commercial clubs and libraries offered the most effective means of satisfying readers' growing demands for books, magazines, and newspapers. By 1900, hundreds of commercial circulating libraries flourished in Britain and North America (in France *cabinets de lecture*) or reading societies (*Lesegesellschaften* in Germany). Some, together with many grander subscription libraries and 'library societies', originated in the eighteenth century, but many of the new commercial libraries (and certainly those in the burgeoning towns and cities of South America, and colonial southern Africa and Australia) were products of the second half of the nineteenth century. Many such libraries took advantage of the growing production of books, buying many of the newly published novels as well as instructional manuals and moral self-help essays to attract readers. British mechanics' institute libraries or other 'popular' libraries such as the Bibliothèques des Amis de l'Instruction in France of the 1860s allowed workers and artisans access to books at a reasonable cost. Some allowed borrowing, others kept reading rooms. All these institutions stimulated the demand for books, which in turn stimulated the publishing industry.

General access to books still remained limited until the creation of free public libraries. A British Parliamentary Select Committee, established in 1849, enquired into the nature and availability of libraries and notably in comparison to what already existed in France, Italy, and Germany. Numerous testimonies confirmed the lack of public library facilities and—as phrased in a small pamphlet written by Edward Edwards—the 'paucity of libraries freely open to the public'. In 1850, a British Public Library Act allowed the creation of public libraries in major towns. In the United States, similar lobbying to develop public libraries followed from complaints about the expense of books and the limited access to reading materials. More than a decade before the iconic British Library Act, the first fully tax-supported library was established in 1833 in Peterborough, New Hampshire. The first large public library in the United States opened as the Boston Public Library in 1848. It was not until after the American Civil War, however, that local committees and benefactors established public libraries throughout the country. Pre-eminent was the role played by Andrew Carnegie, the great steel magnate of Scottish origin and a renowned philanthropist. Through his foundation, the Carnegie Corporation, he began to give grants for the establishment of public libraries. The first Carnegie library was built in Dunfermline, Scotland—Carnegie's hometown—in 1883. The first Carnegie library in the United States opened in Braddock, near Pittsburgh, the place of Carnegie's Steel Company. Such an expansion of public libraries worldwide could not but contribute to the spread of reading and the increase of publishing, even though the budget for books of most public libraries remained limited, and the choice of books for the readers controlled by institutional committees and civic guardians of moral worth and education.

Newspapers and Magazines

The advance of literacy was also enabled by the profusion of newsprint and magazines and periodicals published in a variety of styles, formats, and regularity during the nineteenth century. The ability to print larger sheets supported the increase in the number of newspapers and magazines, which became an essential part of a publisher's output, in Europe as well as the United States. The industrial press supported both daily and weekly newspapers, primarily intended to provide information as well as general commercial advertising and weekly or monthly magazines, many illustrated and destined for leisure reading. Newspapers originated in the seventeenth century and flourished in both capital cities and provincial towns in the eighteenth century, but new mechanization, financing, and new market support offered fresh and vast opportunities. In France, two new and very influential daily papers were launched in 1836, Emile Girardin's *La Presse* and Armand Dutacq's *Le Siècle*. Both papers achieved a daily circulation of 80,000 to 180,000 copies between 1836 and 1847. By the 1850s, six morning dailies and three evening papers were issued in London, with a print run of 60,000 copies for *The Times*. In the United States, Benjamin Day created *The Sun* in 1833, retailing at 1 cent per copy, with more readers than the London *Times* after two years. In 1841, Horace Greeley launched *The New York Tribune* which reached a circulation of 200,000 copies in the 1860s. In Italy, the industrialization of printing led to the launch of newspapers like *Il Corriere della Sera* in Milan in 1876 and *Il Messagero* in Rome in 1878.

Many publishing companies became involved in general or literary periodicals that were also frequently used as advertising for publishers who considered them as a normal part of their activities. Advertising in and by periodicals proved very useful for promoting the publisher's writers and informing readers of the firm's publications. In his history of the House of Macmillan, Charles Morgan accounts for the Macmillan brothers' decision to launch a periodical, considering it as an integral part of their business. Fletcher Harper saw *Harper's New Monthly Magazine,* launched in June 1850, as a 'tender to our business'. Each national market across Europe and North America had an array of periodicals catering to various sectors of the readership. For instance, Harper started *Harper's Magazine* in 1850, *Harper's Weekly* in 1857, *Harper's Bazaar* in 1867, and *Harper's Young People* in 1879. A sort of magazine mania spread everywhere, with periodicals for every kind of occupation, such as educational papers for teachers or technical papers for a specific trade. Between 1850 and 1865, America could reckon some 2,500 separate titles, though most of them did not last very long. Germany had its literary journals like the *Literarisches Wochenblatt* and illustrated weeklies such as *Über Land und Meer* and the *Leipziger Illustrierte.* In France, *La Revue des deux mondes* first came out in 1831, and publishers like Hachette and Larousse issued numerous periodicals for children. Many publishers brought out periodicals bearing their own name, such as *Macmillan's Magazine* and *Longman's Magazine* in Britain and *Scribner's Monthly* and *Putnam's Monthly* in the United States, turning them into brand names. The production of magazines went increasingly together with that of books which could be advertised or even published in parts in their pages. Books and periodicals mutually helped each other. The magazines were a means to support the trade in books, their success dependent on the great expansion of serialized fiction and the readership they attracted. The number of serial titles increased massively between 1800 and 1900 owing to the multiplication of periodicals and to the presence of two, sometimes even three, serials overlapping in the same magazine. Great profits could be gained from successful serials as they would increase the number of readers. Another undeniable advantage was that the practice allowed publishers to test novels before publishing them in book form.

The Variety of Book Production

The tendency to increase and diversify production can be largely explained by rising literacy rates, greater leisure opportunities, and, in some regions, the influence of the evangelical religious revival. Industrialization in Europe and North America had an indirect impact on the growth of literacy, which in turn had a definite effect on the book trade. While literacy was a basic social skill for the middle class, economic circumstances gradually made it a necessity for workers. Although we cannot always assume that literacy went hand-in-hand with economic progress, illiterate workers were increasingly considered as an obstacle to modern industry, and social aspiration was a definite incentive to reading. In North America, illiteracy declined sharply in the first half of the nineteenth century, although literacy rates varied considerably between the northern and southern states. Enslaved African Americans were forbidden to read until after the Civil War, when African American literacy increased to an estimated 30 per cent in 1880 and 55 per cent by 1900.

Religious activity also continued to improve literacy rates, particularly in Protestant countries. The evangelical revival in English-speaking countries undoubtedly contributed to the development of a mass publication market, with many religious associations and Sunday Schools taking an active part in the teaching of reading in Britain and America. Religion comprised the largest single book category in Britain during the first half of the nineteenth century, reaching around 20 per cent of overall book production, but falling to 15.6 per cent during the 1870s owing to the challenge to orthodoxy and the development of free thinking. To a lesser extent, religion also proved a major publishing sector in North America, although secular publication gained ground towards the end of the nineteenth century. The market for religious works included not only Bibles, sold in their millions worldwide, but also prayer books and hymn books, catechisms, and lives of saints in Catholic countries not only in Europe, but also in South America, as well as other religious texts. Foreign missions and religious societies like the Religious Tract Society and the British and Foreign Bible Society in England, and the Philadelphia Bible Society and the American Tract Society in the United States, printed and distributed them on a large scale. In North America, the

Bible represented more than 20 per cent of religious book sales in some years. In France, the Tours-based publishers Mame brought out the new, unified Catholic prayer book. In the second half of the century, religious publishing evolved, with books more focused on questions of faith, some of which were highly successful, like *La vie de Jésus* by Ernest Renan, published by Hachette in 1863, which became an overwhelming bestseller, translated and distributed throughout Europe.

Educational and Children's Publishing

The advance of basic education brought important consequences for another significant publishing sector across the Western world and especially in English-, French-, and Spanish-speaking colonies. An entirely new field of mass publishing opened up for textbooks and the printing of huge quantities of educational texts not only in European but also indigenous languages. In Britain, following the 1870 Education Act which imposed compulsory elementary education, elementary textbooks became an important part of the output of publishers such as Longman and Macmillan. In France, schoolbooks became a major market for publishers like Hachette, Masson, and Armand Colin. Fernand Nathan, one of the market leaders in this sector, owed much of his success to Jules Ferry's laws making schooling compulsory in the 1880s. In the United States, schoolbooks came to be published in large quantities, supplanting British efforts. Estimates of book production in dollars reveal the spectacular expansion of school books, from $750,000 in 1820 to $5,500,000 in 1850. Twenty years later, the American textbook business was worth some $8 million, with huge quantities of new texts and reference books launched, and others revised by publishers like Houghton Mifflin in order to bring them up to date.

Much more extensive publishing for children developed alongside textbooks, particularly because of new illustration techniques. Building on the pioneering work of eighteenth-century publishers such as John Newbery of London, who issued books with a style and presentation perfectly suited to young readers' tastes, publishers became aware that children's books could be a profitable part of their business. This was particularly so because children's books could be produced cheaply, even when well illustrated. Many children's books drew on traditional fables, nursery rhymes, and fairy tales, as well as classics and stories from the Bible. In Britain, simplified versions of famous books first intended for adult readers, such as *Robinson Crusoe* and *Gulliver's Travels*, appeared in new editions adapted for the youth market. Similarly, French publishers offered adaptations of Molière's plays and La Fontaine's *Fables* in shorter formats for children. However, books specially written for young readers increasingly represented a significant proportion of publications, aided by the international circulation and translation of bestsellers. Highly successful titles could appear from anywhere: Hans Christian Andersen's *Fairy Tales*, published in Denmark in the 1830s, were available in no fewer than three English translations by 1846. American novelists like James Fenimore Cooper, Harriet Beecher Stowe, Mark Twain, Maria Cummins, and Louisa May Alcott wrote the first truly world-famous children's books and contributed to the success of the sector.

Specific series and periodicals for young readers was another characteristic of publishing as it developed from the 1830s. The French Catholic publisher Alfred Mame launched various series, such as the Bibliothèque de la jeunesse chrétienne and the Bibliothèque illustrée des petits enfants, in small inexpensive formats. Mame was also one of the first publishers of a typically French product, the *livre de prix*, a book rewarding hard-working pupils at the end of the school year. Following his example, Pierre-Jules Hetzel decided to specialize in works for children and launched his *Nouveau Magasin des enfants* in 1843, followed in the 1860s by the Bibliothèque d'éducation et de récréation and a periodical called the *Magasin d'Éducation et de récréation*. In the meantime, Hachette had entered the field and launched his famous series the Bibliothèque rose illustrée in 1856, for which he had taken on the Comtesse de Ségur, who contributed many volumes. He also started a periodical entitled the *Semaine des enfants* in 1867. Children's publishing developed similarly in Germany, where it expanded rapidly with famous writers like Christoph Schmidt, author of moral tales, and in Italy with best-sellers such as Carlo Collodi's *Avventure di Pinocchio* in 1886. In Britain, children's fiction amounted to 16 per cent of publishing output between 1814 and 1846, but nearly doubled at the beginning of the twentieth century. Macmillan published the worldwide bestseller *Alice in Wonderland* in 1865, while some of their earlier titles like *Tom Brown's Schooldays* by Thomas Hughes (1856) and Charles Kingsley's *The Water-Babies* (1863) were also successful. Adventure stories for boys, particularly those by Captain Mayne Reid published in Britain by several publishers, reached international fame in translation. By the end of the century, many British publishers like Routledge, Cassell, and Nelson had developed this sector. Children's fiction could be serialized in children's periodicals, as was the case for R.L. Stevenson's *Treasure Island*, which first appeared weekly in *Young Folks*.

Practical Books and Guidebooks

New readers needed new books; people with more leisure time wanted more books. The development of a significant new readership and changes in lifestyle clearly boosted the output of printed material, whether periodicals or books. This was particularly so, given that the readership was now segmented into specific categories, each of them requiring texts to meet specific needs. Publishers readily understood that they had to diversify their production to take account of fresh social and cultural circumstances. Leisure continued to support new markets in the book trade, and the fall in working hours for skilled and unskilled labourers alike freed up leisure time to devote to reading for this social category. Two genres developed rapidly: practical books and guidebooks. Practical books and books of manners had proved popular with European publishers and readers for centuries, but the demand now greatly increased. In France, the firm of Nicolas-Edmé Roret (active from the 1820s) regularly reprinted more than a hundred guides to all sorts of trades and occupations. In English-speaking countries, how-to books, particularly books of manners and medical works, met with equal success. In Britain, *Mrs Beeton's Book of Household Management*, originally published in twenty-four monthly parts in 1859–61, was a publishing phenomenon, with 60,000 copies sold in the first year alone. In France, Hachette, Charpentier, and Flammarion, among other publishers, developed series set at various prices to reach as many social categories as possible. Cookbooks for teaching girls or for women supervising domestic staff were particularly successful, not only in France but also in Canada and in the United States.

The modernization of the transport network and the extension of leisure time contributed to the expansion of tourism and travelling, and the promotion of guidebooks. In France, *Galignani's Travellers' Guides* was one particularly successful series published by the Galignani Brothers in the early nineteenth century. Later, between 1860 and 1909, the *Collection des Guides Joanne*, published by Hachette, featured some 300 titles relating to France and other countries. In 1836, John Murray III wrote and published *A Handbook for Travellers on the Continent*, providing accurate, practical information and followed by other titles covering all English counties. His greatest rival was the famous German publisher Karl Baedeker, whose guidebooks were published not only in German, but also in English and French. By mid-century, the market for guidebooks expanded worldwide, with American publishers launching profitable travel guide series such as *Appleton's Railroad and Steamboat Companion* (1847). These sorts of books, destined to be carried along by travellers, soon became standardized by publishers in terms of format and colour—red hardbacks from Murray and Baedeker, blue from Joanne—and were increasingly referred to by their brand names.

Publishing for a Mass Readership

Improved literacy across Europe and North America created new working-class readerships. However, as the price of books remained relatively high, publishers saw the necessity to produce works at a lower cost. The best-known means to this end was the cheap series, one of the characteristics of late nineteenth-century American publishing. Reprint series were also an essential production of the British publishing industry and a prominent feature of the book trade. Similar series existed in France thanks to Gervais Charpentier, who sparked a publishing revolution in 1838 when he began to reprint successful works of fiction and non-fiction, in a one-volume format that later became known as 'the Charpentier', at the fixed price of 3.5 francs. Such reprint series paved the way for similar cheap collections elsewhere in Europe: the Leipzig-based publisher Philip Reclam launched his Universal Bibliothek in 1867 at 20 pfennigs a volume, which met with immediate success. In Britain, between 1827 and 1832, cheap books were issued in series such as Constable's *Miscellany* and Murray's *Family Library*, soon imitated in the United States by a non-fiction series published by the Harper Brothers, Harper's Family Library at 45 cents a volume. The expansion of train travel created another new market, first in England, where W.H. Smith set up bookstalls in most railway stations. One of the earliest publishers associated with this new mode of publishing was George Routledge, who launched his Railway Library in 1848, soon imitated by competitors like Smith Elder and Sampson Low. Such cheap volumes, known as yellowbacks owing to their yellow covers, were often—but not always—reprints of well-known novels. France also had its own railway reading material, in particular, Hachette's Bibliothèque des Chemins de Fer, begun in 1853.

Another possibility for reducing the cost of reading matter was part-publication, a long-standing tradition for non-fiction which developed in the nineteenth century for novels. The Dickens Household Edition, for example, could be bought in weekly 6-penny instalments with a blue cover. John Cassell used this format for his Cassell's *Popular Educator*, at 1 penny a number, a kind of publication aimed at a readership keen on self-improvement. In the same way, the arrival on the market of new volumes in paper covers reflects the publishers' search for cheaper printed material. This is best illustrated with the famous American dime novels which first appeared in 1860, published by Erastus and Irwin Beadle. These volumes had soft-paper covers and sold mostly for a dime (10 cents) and told tales of life on the frontier, adventures at sea, or 'rags to riches' stories. Other countries produced similar types of lowbrow fiction: France had its *romans à quatre sous*, and England its 1-shilling books. Italian readers could buy 1-lira titles, and Germans could obtain books for 10 or 20 pfennigs.

Fiction

Fiction—often considered for respectability's sake as light reading matter for women—often appeared in the form of serials, which proved another means of reducing the price of books. The upsurge of periodicals and the craze for novels facilitated serialization and offered many advantages to publishers who could adjust their output according to recent sales. It was also possible to reprint and sell back numbers. As pioneers in the eighteenth century had found, serial publication had many other advantages. The sales of one part financed the production of the next; at the end of the serial, and sometimes even earlier, the whole novel could be published in various formats and editions; and significant revenue could be gained from advertising on the coloured wrapper of each number.

Serials took up increasing space in periodicals and were a publishing asset in many countries. In France, Emile de Girardin published the first serial, Honoré de Balzac's *La vieille fille*, in *La Presse* in October 1836, and Eugène Sue's *Les Mystères de Paris* was serialized in *Le Journal des débats* in 1842–3. Sue's other serial, *The Wandering Jew*, increased the circulation of *Le Constitutionnel* from 3,600 to 25,000 copies. In Britain, novelists like Wilkie Collins and Mary Elizabeth Braddon favoured serial publication for their novels. In the USA, Harriet Beecher Stowe's novel *Uncle Tom's Cabin* first appeared as a serial in *The National Era* in 1851–2, while other serials appeared regularly in *Harper's New Monthly Magazine* and *Putnam's Monthly Magazine*. Various categories of readers consumed serial fiction, depending on the type of periodicals in connection with their target audience, whether, for example, a family readership or a female one, while cheap weeklies were aimed at a working-class audience. These magazines, known as 'penny dreadfuls' in Britain (later largely directed towards children) and Groschenhefte in Germany, could spin out serial narratives for years. One of the most popular in Britain was *Black Bess*, issued over the course of almost five years, while G.W.M. Reynolds's *Mysteries of the Court of London*, inspired by Sue's *Mysteries of Paris*, ran from 1849 to 1856. The penny dreadful market existed throughout Europe and contributed to the expansion of reading habits among the lower classes.

Retail

The diversification of production and publishing formats required a transformation in retail operations. Publishers had long printed and distributed catalogues listing their works, with information about their formats, prices, and so on, and, as we have seen, even earlier such catalogues were produced for early modern book fairs such as those at Frankfurt and Leipzig. By the nineteenth century, much-refashioned book fairs flourished in other European countries. In the United

States, book fairs based on the model of the great German fairs developed during the first decade of the nineteenth century, first in New York from 1802, followed by other cities. The fairs reappeared after the Civil War, with what was heralded as the first Book Fair of the American book trade in New York in 1875. Nonetheless, the fairs soon decreased in favour of trade sales, which had already flourished in the 1850s as a means of distribution and played a significant financial role before themselves declining in the 1890s. Organized for the book-trade business around sales, orders, and the exchange of information, the new style book fairs contributed to the development of commercial relationships not only between publishers, but also between printers and binders. Fairs also hosted displays of new machinery and technologies.

Trade catalogues continued to be used by wholesalers, retailers, and, in some cases, customers. They provided information on what books were available and advertised new books. Publishers issued them regularly, particularly at Christmas when books were in greater demand. Special issues of professional periodicals drew lists of numerous seasonal titles, especially for children. Publishers also publicized their books in the trade journals. In Britain, the first number of *The Publishers' Circular* came out in 1837. *The Bookseller* followed some twenty years later in 1858, while in the United States, *Publishers' Weekly* was founded in 1872, following the *Norton's Literary Gazette and Publishers' Circular* (1854–72).

Publishers and booksellers distributed their books in various ways. In Europe, readers bought most of their books in stores which might sell a whole variety of other goods, like stationery, patent medicines, perfumes, purses, or wallets. Readers could also order their books by mail to be delivered at their home. By the end of the nineteenth century, new retail outlets selling mostly newspapers, periodicals, and cheap books developed. Besides, postal services facilitated subscriptions. In France, a dense network of bookshops developed across the country between 1850 and 1880. In Germany, the number of bookshops grew considerably during the century. In the United States, book retailing was in most cases combined with other trades in a variety of outlets, though bookstores selling only books were common in New England.

In Britain, W.H. Smith opened the first railway bookstalls at Euston station in 1848, after negotiating an exclusive contract with the

London and North Western Railway. These stalls which stocked different sorts of literature at various prices soon proved popular. Following Smith's example, Hachette signed a contract with the French railway Compagnie du Nord in 1853. Railway bookstalls spread to Germany, but there the most striking innovation was the invention of book vending machines by the publisher Anton Philipp Reclam for his *Universal Bibliothek* at the beginning of the twentieth century.

Besides these modern undertakings, pedlars continued to ply their trade late into the century in most countries and particularly in rural areas in European countries like Poland, Italy, Spain, and northern Scandinavia, where they were the only means of reaching potential readers. In France, the golden age of book peddling spanned the decades between 1820 and 1880, after which the practice declined. Another kind of itinerant bookseller used by publishers was the travelling salesman. In Britain the use of travellers became well established by the 1830s. In the United States, the largest publishing houses could have as many as four travelling salesmen, covering huge areas of the country. American publishers relied increasingly on commercial travellers after the Civil War. At the turn of the century, however, they had come to prefer provincial wholesalers to sell their output, which speeded up the distribution of books. Finally, books could be sold by mail, particularly in countries where modern postal systems improved methods of distribution. In 1848, Britain established the 'book post'— that is, special cheap postal rates for book parcels.

Advertising

Advertising, a major incentive to the industrialized book trade, greatly profited from mail services. Postal advertising became the most direct way to reach readers, in the form of catalogues, brochures, and prospectuses. Publishers' catalogues listed new titles as well as backlist material, while prospectuses summarized the contents of a particular work accompanied by a few remarks on its key selling points. Publishers increasingly relied on the placement of advertisements in newspapers and periodicals destined for the general reading public, as well as in the professional trade papers. Reviewing books in periodicals prior to publication was a practice associated with unscrupulous early nineteenth-century publishers, such as Henry Colburn, nicknamed 'the Prince of Puffers' by the British press. He printed favourable reviews of his own books in the *Literary Gazette*, a magazine he had launched precisely for that purpose. Another way of advertising was to showcase other publications from the same list in the blank pages at the end of a book or even on the covers of popular editions like yellowbacks. In the mid-nineteenth century, some advertisers considered that newspapers afforded the best opportunities to reach large audiences, while others preferred publishers' monthly magazines, like *Putnam's* or *Scribner's*, read by the more prosperous and educated classes of society. But such publicity was not limited to the publisher's publications, and book covers could advertise all sorts of products such as soap, medicines, furniture, or even clothes.

Advertising became a significant part of the cost of a book, particularly in case of a specific campaign for a particular book or series. In Britain, advertising contracts could be passed with railway advertising offices in provincial locations such as Newcastle-upon-Tyne in Britain. In France, publishers displayed posters publicizing new titles on the walls of railway stations. In the 1860s, Hachette appointed one of his employees to oversee advertising for the company's publications. Publishers also sent circulars advertising their lists to the retailers they worked with. In America, what little advertising there was by the 1830s generally consisted only of show-cards or posters put up in store windows. Later, modern advertising techniques came into use. Peterson is said to have spent $6,000 on advertising in 1854 prior to the publication of Mrs E.D.E.N.'s novel, *The Lost Heiress*, contributing to its rapid success. In 1886, George Bentley, proprietor of the London publishing house which his father Richard had started with Henry Colburn in 1829, drew up a long précis of advertising procedures 'for Office Use only'. These were in four parts: (1) the sending out of advertisements; (2) the recording of advertisements; (3) the paying for advertisements; (4) the literature of advertisements, suggesting its importance for the company. Sometimes, book advertising caused controversy between authors and publishers, with writers accusing publishers of not doing enough to promote their work while publishers complained of the costs of publishing. The industrialization of publishing undoubtedly modified the relations between the different participants in the book trade.

Relations Between Authors, Publishers, and Printers

Publishing company archives are rich sources of information on the strategies of the different firms. For instance, the Macmillan archive in the British Library holds the incoming and outgoing letters exchanged between various participants in the publishing process, including publishers' readers, authors of fiction and non-fiction, editors, literary agents, illustrators, printers, journalists, and so on, which shed light not only on the individuals involved, but on the wider business. Surviving archives also include material recording the publishing process itself, including the stages from the submission and selection of manuscripts, the publishers' professional readers' advice, the marketing of the completed product at home and abroad, the cost of advertising, discussions about binding and illustrations, and the pricing of books. The most significant aspect of such archives, however, is the light they shed on author–publisher relationships and financial negotiations.

Copyright remained a central concern. Traditionally, most writers seeking commercial publication received a lump sum on handing over their manuscript to the publisher, and in return for the financing publisher taking the risk, gained no income from subsequent sales of their books. As industrialization led to larger print runs, however, and publishers came to depend increasingly on the success of their authors, writers began to demand payment on terms that reflected subsequent market success. The eventual result was a royalty system where writers accepted a proportion (usually small) of market profits. As arrangements developed during the mid- to late nineteenth century, writers could sign three main kinds of contracts: publishing on commission, profit-sharing (usually half-profits), or outright sale of copyright. Commission publishing, mostly used for poetry and non-fiction, meant that the writer paid the costs of bookmaking and gave the publisher a commission. According to Walter Besant, the practice of paying part of the publisher's expenses for novel publishing lasted until the end of the century. The half-profits system consisted of dividing the money earned from sales between publisher and author after deducting costs. Perhaps surprisingly, the third possibility—outright sale of copyright— remained commonplace during the Victorian period, probably because writers were often in immediate need of money.

In the United States the same three kinds of payment existed, but the half-profits system was less common than in Britain. The most frequently used contract was the percentage system, granting the author 10 per cent of the retail price for a specified number of copies or of all copies sold except those sent out either for review or for publicity. In most countries, the full royalty system became progressively more widespread throughout the second half of the nineteenth century, and contracts began to be standardized. In France, in the 1850s, the average royalty percentage varied between 4 and 14 per cent. Each writer's level of earnings therefore depended on the contracts signed with the publisher, the relative degree of efficiency devoted to the promotion of his/her works, and his/her own reputation. Mutual respect and trust between the two parties were essential.

Authors frequently had little choice but to find other means of increasing their earnings, such as writing articles for various periodicals, although it is difficult to know exactly how much money writers could earn from them. North American magazines sometimes boasted of paying their contributors very well. But all of them competed to attract the most famous writers, writers' names being now considered as 'valuable commodities' in their own right that could increase sales considerably. Authors could also get royalty payments from the sales of their books abroad, but only at the very end of the century did publishers in the United States agree to stop printing pirated works without giving the author a single cent. While the Berne Convention, signed in 1886 by several European countries—the first step towards the institution of international copyright—created a 'Union for the protection of the rights of authors over their literary and artistic works', it took long and difficult negotiations before the United States accepted international copyright with the passing of the Chace Act in 1891. Prior to this vote, however, some American publishers such as Harper paid nominal fees to foreign writers thanks to a system called 'courtesy of the trade', which guaranteed publishers exclusive publication rights. As the years passed, relationships between authors and publishers became more and more complicated and business-like, as is clear from their correspondence. Money matters came frequently to the foreground, with writers asking for advances on the publication of their next book, especially if they were well established but short of money. The British novelist Margaret Oliphant is said to have used her publishers Blackwood and Macmillan as bankers, drawing credit from them for yet unwritten works.

Relations between publishers and authors were undeniably central to the trade, with authors trying to improve their status and conditions and publishers seeking to increase their profits. Writers made various attempts to found organizations destined to defend their rights against publishers. The first of these associations was the Société des Gens de Lettres founded in France in 1838 with the support of several leading novelists of the day, including Balzac, Victor Hugo, and George Sand. Britain followed suit with the Incorporated Society of British Authors in 1883, which soon became known as the Society of Authors, taking an active part in negotiations between authors and publishers and the defence of literary property. In 1890, the Society launched a monthly magazine, *The Author*. Several authors' organizations emerged in quick succession in the United States, including the Society of Authors in 1884, the Society of American Authors in 1891, and the Syndicate of Associated Authors in 1892, all with the aim of helping authors in their dealings with publishers.

Slightly later, publishers and booksellers formed trade associations. In France, the Cercle de la Librairie for booksellers and printers began as early as 1847, with Ambroise Firmin-Didot as its president. The creation of the Syndicat des libraires détaillants and the Syndicat national des éditeurs took place only in 1892. The Associated Booksellers of Great Britain and Ireland began in 1895, and the Publishers' Association the following year. The American Booksellers' Association started in 1900 and the American Publishers' Association in 1901, but local organizations of the same kind had existed earlier in Boston and New York.

The development of such organizations reflects growing difficulties in negotiations between authors and publishers, and led to the creation of the literary agent, whose role was and still is to represent and protect authors' rights and financial interests. The first British literary agent seems to have been A.P. Watt, a self-taught former bookseller in Edinburgh, who worked as secretary, reader of manuscripts, and head of advertising for the publisher and magazine owner Alexander Strahan. When Strahan's business fell into decline around 1875, Watt became a literary agent: his first client was George MacDonald, Strahan's chief author, and he later represented Rudyard Kipling and Conan Doyle, among others. It is less clear when literary agents first appeared in the United States: in the late nineteenth century, literary bureaus working on behalf of authors, such as the Athenaeum Bureau of Literature and the New York Bureau of Literary Revision, were in business, but it seems their role consisted more of correcting writers' manuscripts than in finding publishers for them. The first recorded American literary agents proper were Elisabeth Marbury who represented many theatrical performers in the 1880s, and Paul Revere Reynolds who established his literary agency in New York in 1893. France has remained unenthusiastic about, if not hostile to, literary agents until the present time.

After all the technological progress and transformations undergone in book production, the literary agent contributed further to the transformation of publishing. The family firms of the beginning of the nineteenth century evolved into an international capitalist industry; publishers seemed more like managers and enterprising businessmen, while many authors became more aware of their significance in the book trade and their own new status as professionals. Like many other sectors of the economy, at the turn of the nineteenth century, publishing had become a modern entrepreneurial capitalist business.

12

Modern China, Japan, and Korea

Christopher A. Reed and M. William Steele

For over 1,000 years, cultural and political elites in China, Japan, and Korea maintained a strong respect for the knowledge, power, and authority to be gained from reading books, especially the Confucian Classics. In the nineteenth century, all three countries began the transition from woodblock printing of books to Internet- and digitally produced books. Each nation has since emerged as an active participant in the information explosion that characterizes our world today.

The history of the book in China, Japan, and Korea from the nineteenth century to today invites important but problematic questions. What role have books and print culture in general played in the transition to modernity? More specifically, what is the connection between the printed word and attempts to construct national and individual identities? All three countries had sophisticated printing, publishing, and marketing systems in place well before the introduction of Western printing technologies, complicating the story of modern and contemporary developments. Further, whereas China, Japan, and Korea shared centuries of cultural interaction, differing experiences of imperialism, war, and ideological conflict in the twentieth century were particularly divisive. In the past, books served to unite the three countries; it remains to be seen whether their evolving print cultures will help to restore that unity.

China

Between 1966 and 1969, the People's Republic of China (PRC) is said to have printed and published over one billion copies of the motivational *Quotations from Chairman Mao Zedong* (known colloquially as 'The

Little Red Book'), making it the most widely reprinted book in world history after the Bible. During the decade of the Cultural Revolution (1966–76), 2.2 billion portraits of Mao and 120 million sets of Mao's *Selected Works* were also reputedly printed and distributed.

Printing and publishing on this titanic scale reflected Chinese party-state ambitions before Mao's death in 1976. Relatively little could have been published, however, if not for the ever-expanding industrialization of Chinese printing and publishing methods under way since approximately 1800.

China's modern media revolution is divisible into: a preparatory phase (*c.*1800–80s), when traditional Chinese printing technologies (chiefly xylographic) still prevailed; and a print-capitalist phase (1890s–1949), when Western industrial printing and publishing methods were adapted by Chinese to their own objectives, chiefly for privatized profit; and the current print-communist stage (1949–present). In this third period, industrialized printing and publishing have been subordinated to Communist Party-led objectives. Since the 1980s, however, these goals have been modulated by privatized profit-seeking and evolving degrees of government control.

China had been printing texts for far longer than the nations of the Westerners who arrived in the 1800s determined to change China with religion and technology. China's xylographic technology had stimulated early printing in both Korea and Japan and had also fostered China's own three publishing sectors: governmental; non-governmental and non-commercial; and commercial. Although historians debate late imperial literacy rates, as many as a hundred million literates, more than the combined reading publics of early modern Europe, Japan, and Korea, consumed China's printed matter between 1700 and the mid-1800s. Included were the millions who competed via written examinations for civil service qualifications until 1905, when the system ended.

Already in the early 1800s, woodblocks, combined with two other ancient Chinese inventions—paper and ink—had enabled the Chinese to print more books more cheaply than could be found in any other of the world's bookmaking civilizations. For these historical reasons, the Chinese embrace of Western methods was not inevitable. Media with relief (letterpress), planographic (lithography), and intaglio (gravure printing, etching, and engraving) surfaces were initially applied experimentally to Chinese-language book production. Chinese themselves most often used the first two of these three, but in a sequence that reversed the familiar Western narrative.

The first stage of what we might term Gutenberg-style printing in China was led by Western Christian missionaries between 1800 and the 1880s, initially in defiance of China's 1724 proscription of Christianity. Gradually, though, Westerners were superseded by Chinese. Chinese efforts to adapt Western printing methods to local publishing goals accelerated from the 1870s and became irreversible (but not all-encompassing) in the 1890s. Anticipating China's 1911 revolution, publishers disseminated ideas that helped shape the Republic of China (ROC, 1912–49). Ever since, Chinese publishing has never been far from politics.

The first significant modern Western-style book produced in China using cut-metal Chinese characters was Robert Morrison's bilingual *Dictionary of the Chinese Language* (1815–23), a project sponsored by the British East India Company. Morrison's dictionary owed much to China's *Kangxi Dictionary* (1716). Morrison used its 214-radical system (still found in many Chinese dictionaries today) to organize his text and included approximately the same number of entries.

The American Presbyterian Mission Press (APMP) and French Jesuits took the next steps. Both stimulated Chinese investment in Western printing technologies. Chinese choices built on Western technology, but adapted them to explicitly Chinese objectives. Far more secular than those of the Western missionaries, these Chinese ambitions initiated China's Gutenberg revolution. Richard Cole founded the APMP in Macao in 1844, when the United States concluded its unequal Treaty of Wangxia, modelled on the 1842 Anglo-Chinese Treaty of Nanjing. The French soon signed a similar treaty. Among the benefits that now accrued to Britain, America, and France was the opening of the first treaty ports to their nationals. Christian printers were no longer outlaws.

In 1858, William Gamble brought APMP the equipment and skills needed to begin electrotyping Chinese types. Electrotyping produced a fine, durable imprint and could also be used to print halftone pictures, recommending it to book printers. Gamble's method produced type more quickly than cutting or casting; type size could now also be more easily modified. Gamble also relocated the APMP's print shop to Shanghai, already the 'monarch of the treaty ports'. APMP was then printing eleven million pages per year. Gamble left for Japan in 1869, promoting his methods there as well. Western printing and publishing methods boomed in Shanghai until 1937. Just as important, the three traditional sectors of Chinese publishing mingled and industrialized there.

By 1876, APMP matrices became available in five sizes of Chinese type, five varieties of Japanese type, one of Manchu, and two of English. Just as important, both Chinese government and Western printing offices purchased them. China, if not yet the Chinese, now retailed Western-style type.

First, however, lithographic printing claimed the limelight. Lithography was the most important Western alternative to techniques derived from Gutenberg. By the 1830s, it was a fully developed national industry in France and was being used in China to print the earliest modern Chinese periodicals (which still resembled Chinese books with thread bindings and floppy bamboo paper). In 1876, French Jesuits brought the process to suburban Shanghai, where it rapidly spread to secular, commercial, Chinese investors.

Two years later, a high Qing official promoted the reprinting of books in danger of being lost forever. He deemed 'preservation printing' more useful than the publication of new books. It was a spirit that has motivated many Chinese publishers ever since. Lithography fit these publishing goals. Chinese preference for it altered the conventional Western narrative, in which cast moveable type are taken to mark the first extended stage of printing while other methods—including lithography—play only a later and supporting role.

Lithography soon displaced both Chinese woodblock publishers and missionary letterpress ones. During Shanghai's lithographic 'golden age', nearly one hundred firms competed for both texts and readers. With one big exception—Dianshizhai—such firms were Chinese-owned and operated. In addition to books, lithography advanced industrial production of newspapers such as the reformer Liang Qichao's *China Progress*. The Shanghai newspaper *Shenbao* (Shanghai journal) began buying type fonts from APMP in the mid-1870s. At the same time, however, it also opened the Dianshizhai Litho-Publishing House. One early publication was a miniaturized reprint of the *Kangxi Dictionary*. Three pages of the original were printed on a single page, one above the other.

Dianshizhai also published reprints of the Confucian Classics, literary encyclopaedias, novels, travelogues, maps, stele rubbings, painting manuals, and occasional Western books. Then, in 1884, Dianshizhai commenced its landmark magazine, the *Dianshizhai Pictorial*, presenting humorous and satirical commentary on treaty-port life. In the meantime, letterpress expanded through newspaper coverage of the events of the First Sino-Japanese War (1894–5).

Thus, by the 1890s, at least four communities—Western Protestant and Catholic printers along with secular Chinese book and newspaper publishers—had laid the foundation for what is termed Chinese print capitalism. Chinese publishers had industrialized both lithography and letterpress. Soon, Chinese manufacturers began copying or adapting earlier technologies to new purposes. As in the West and Japan, large publishers established printing plants to harness all of these technologies even as China's first modern censorship law was promulgated in 1898 to limit their impact.

In the mid-1880s, APMP had contributed again to the advance of Chinese-language, Western-style printing and publishing when it apprenticed three Shanghai missionary-school students. In 1897, after mastering the Western-style printer's trade, Xia Ruifang and two classmates started the Commercial Press. It began life as a job-printing operation but grew, over the next four decades, into East Asia's largest comprehensive publisher.

Anticipating the textbook market that soon dominated modern Chinese publishing and supplied modern schools, the Commercial Press first printed a pirated English-language primer. By 1904, it cornered the educational market formerly dominated by the lithographers. When the government issued its first official list of primary school textbooks, over half bore the Commercial Press imprint. That proportion remained stable down to 1937 as public education broadened beyond China's cities.

If preservation of rare works and textbook publishing were powerful dynamics, so too was the production of what were called 'Western Studies'. Western-style encyclopaedias merging Western and Chinese genres and information had started to appear in the 1830s, but peaked between the 1880s and 1930s. The Commercial Press published well-regarded translations of Mill, Montesquieu, Spencer, Huxley, and some 140 Western literary works. Still further works on politics, law, and modern administration, among others, introduced large readerships to Western modernity. Even books banned by the Qing court could be issued from the Western-dominated treaty port, which followed different censorship rules.

Chinese print capitalism, the industrialized system that printed and published textual commodities for privatized profit, blazed red hot between 1912, when the first Republic, its capital in Beijing, replaced the Qing dynasty, and 1928, when the Nationalist Party (GMD) established a new Republican government and capital in Nanjing. In savage competition with each other, China's modern publishers produced a vast spectrum of books, journals, magazines, and newspapers. After 1928, Chiang Kai-shek and the GMD imposed a new ideology derived from Sun Yat-sen's 1924 landmark ideological text *Three Principles of the People* (nationalism, popular sovereignty, and social democracy). Now, many publishers sought accommodation rather than confrontation with the government.

Shanghai, meanwhile, became the polestar of market-driven modern Chinese publishing, thanks in part to its publishers' successes in hiring employees from both governmental and commercial backgrounds and in attracting foreign investment. Again, the Commercial Press provides an illustration. In 1903, founder Xia had approached Zhang Yuanji, a former high official and imperial tutor, to direct his editorial office. Xia also persuaded the leading Japanese textbook publisher Kinkōdō to invest in his company, making it a Sino-Japanese firm until 1914.

Journal publishing was another important market for the Commercial Press. Capitalizing on the growing anxiety that many Chinese felt about their country's place in the world, *Diplomatic News* first appeared in 1902 and was followed by *Eastern Miscellany* in 1904. By 1910, the latter was the most widely read journal in China. Other major journals hinting at newly targeted readerships followed, including *Short Story Monthly* (which, in 1927, issued Ding Ling's landmark 'Diary of Miss Sophie', launching modern heroine-centred, sexualized fiction), *Educational Review*, *Youth Magazine*, *Ladies Journal*, and *Children's World*. The Press eventually brought out eight major journals and no fewer than forty smaller ones, each aimed at new readerships.

Acknowledging that Chinese publishing could not make its own way until it controlled its technology, the Commercial Press also experimented with printing techniques. Foreigners, including Japanese, were hired as instructors. Collotype was added, followed by three-colour printing and manufacturing of type and other printing equipment; advanced printing technology of all sorts now flowed to the publisher. At the same time, Zhang Yuanji collected rare works for the Commercial Press's editorial reference library. The library enabled the firm to complete a Qing court commission on constitutionalism that also signalled the editors' support for constitutional monarchy. Editors used the library to create innovative reference works such as the *New Dictionary* (1912), China's first major one since the *Kangxi Dictionary*. The *Encyclopaedic [Classical Phrase] Dictionary* (*Ciyuan*) followed in 1915.

In 1916, Zhang Yuanji interviewed Shen Yanbing, one of many prominent cultural figures whose careers intersected with the Commercial Press. Shen later published important fiction such as *Spring Silkworms* (1932) and *Midnight* (1933) under the pseudonym Mao Dun. Inspired by the Bolshevik Revolution, Shen joined China's Communist Party (CCP) shortly after its founding in Shanghai in 1921. He also doubled as an undercover intermediary between the Press's editorial offices, where he ran *Short Story Monthly*, and the firm's 4,000 radicalized printing workers. In Shanghai, Shen met Mao Zedong, a former Changsha journal editor, bookstore operator, and printing industry organizer, and also found an editorial job for Chen Duxiu, the first CCP secretary.

Chen himself had earlier founded the radical magazine, *New Youth*. It helped initiate the New Culture Movement (1915–21), which attacked Confucian traditionalism and called for progress, science, and democracy. Among its readers was Mao Zedong, who found inspiration in its iconoclastic message. In 1918, the magazine published the vernacular story, 'A Madman's Diary', for which the author first used his later-famous penname Lu Xun. In the view of many, modern Chinese literature dates from the New Culture Movement.

Ex-Qing officials and Communists were not the only groups represented at the Commercial Press. On 1 May 1919, Zhang Yuanji met Hu Shi, the liberal Beijing University philosophy professor, *New Youth* editor, and future high-ranking GMD official and ambassador to the

United States. Hu had already begun revision of the Chinese literary canon by praising vernacular novels such as *Water Margin* (*c.*1400) and the eighteenth-century *Story of the Stone*. Hu also promoted language reforms intended to create a national vernacular and align the written and spoken languages.

Now, just three days before the 4 May 1919 demonstrations against the perceived sell-out of China's national interests at Versailles refocused the New Culture Movement in a political and eventually communist direction, Zhang tried to hire Hu. Instead, Hu recommended his former teacher, Wang Yunwu. Wang joined the Press in 1921 and almost immediately steered it in a new direction. Experimenting with serial reprints of well-known titles for a mass audience, Wang's *Miniature Encyclopaedia*, summarizing current Western thought across a range of topics, sold well. Later, Wang directed production of the *Universal Library Series* and *Collection of Collections*. For sales, all relied on Wang's close ties with the GMD, necessary, he lamented, because the ROC was simply not a nation of readers.

Zhang Yuanji's influence continued to be felt through high-quality photo-lithographic reprints. The *Sibu congkan* (*Four Branches of Literature*, 1919–36), a collectanea of 504 historic titles, echoed the earlier call to reprint rare works. A supplement, the *Baina* edition of the *Twenty-Four Standard Dynastic Histories*, accompanied it. The *Sibu* was followed by a reprint of the Daoist Canon (1923–6, reprinted again after 1949). Thousands of other, non-religious titles were also reprinted between 1929 and 1941.

Paradoxically, after 1932, when Japanese bombers deliberately targeted the Commercial Press plant during the Shanghai War, the publisher prospered anew. To avoid vigilant government officials enforcing restrictive GMD censorship laws, the Commercial Press now concentrated on apolitical reference works, library series, and collections. From 1927 to 1936, the Press published nearly 18,000 titles, just under half of China's 42,718 total in that same period.

While the Commercial Press concentrated on the heights of both modern and traditional book culture, hundreds of smaller publishers issued more innovative or experimental works. Many took inspiration from the New Culture Movement. Shanghai's Taidong Press issued journals and book series for the Creation Society before the latter left to form its own publishing company. In 1923, Xinchao published Lu

Xun's famous collection, *Call to Arms*. It included 'A Madman's Diary', considered China's first modern short story, and 'Kong Yiji', a satire of Confucian pedantry. Also printed was 'The True Story of Ah Q'. Like much modern Chinese literature, 'Ah Q' had been serialized in a literary supplement before appearing in book form. Kaiming Press crowned the list of small publishers; founded in 1926 by former Commercial Press editors to advance social reform, it soon became China's fifth-largest modern publisher. Ye Shengtao, a Commercial Press editor and writer, joined Kaiming to initiate its much-honoured children's publishing programme.

Zhonghua Books, Republican China's second-largest publisher, also emerged directly, if not amicably, from the Commercial Press. Established in 1912, Zhonghua took the Chinese name of the new republic to signal its political ideals. Founder Lufei Kui, a committed revolutionary, moved straight from his old office at the Commercial Press, where he had edited textbooks and a journal, to his new one at Zhonghua. Other early employees also had Press links and suggest why Zhonghua's backlist soon resembled that of the Press.

Like the Commercial Press, Zhonghua, too, allied with the Republican government in pursuit of sales. Imitating Zhang Yuanji at the Commercial Press, Lufei brought in a roster of political notables. They ranged from a former minister of education to a past and a future premier and included the late-Qing publicist Liang Qichao. Even Charles Jones Soong, Bible publisher and father of future GMD government minister T.V. Soong and the famous Soong sisters (one would marry Sun Yat-sen and another Chiang Kai-shek), was an investor and board member. Starting with a textbook series decorated with the new Republican flag to contrast sharply with the yellow dragon adorning the Commercial Press's pro-dynasty ones, Zhonghua quickly grabbed 30 per cent of the national textbook market. Between 1919 and 1926, 'Eight Big Journals' also began to appear, complemented by the profitable *Great Zhonghua Dictionary*.

Shenbao was briefly linked to Zhonghua's fortunes in 1917 when the newspaper initiated a hostile, but temporary, takeover. Talks were even conducted about merging Zhonghua with the Commercial Press. In 1918, Zhonghua's board was reorganized. Lufei was temporarily side-lined, and Sun Yat-sen's brother-in-law and GMD financier H.H. Kung entered the firm. Soon, Zhonghua even began to print government securities and currency. Zhonghua remained dependent on this cosy relationship with the GMD government until 1949.

In 1936, Zhonghua's editorial department answered the Commercial Press's *Ciyuan* with its landmark *Ocean of Words* (*Cihai*). Both phrase dictionaries were found in Mao Zedong's library along with Republican-era reprints of *Records of the Grand Historian* (100 BCE) and *Comprehensive Mirror for Aid in Government* (1050). Today in China, the latter works are still read in scholarly, ordinary, and even comic-book editions along with the ever-popular military romance *Tale of Three Kingdoms* (1400). Between the founding of the Republic in 1912 and 1937, Zhonghua published well over 5,000 titles, both popular and scholarly. Included among the latter was the *Sibu beiyao* (*Essentials of the Four Branches of Literature*, 1920–37), a collectanea with 351 titles printed with Zhonghua's own type design. In 1934, Zhonghua also produced *New Atlas of Republican China*, the nation's first completely Chinese-surveyed, -drafted, and -printed modern map, for *Shenbao*.

The 'third leg of the tripod' of Republican publishers was World Books, whose name announced its global market ambitions. One commentator calls its founder Shen Zhifang 'the outstanding oddity' of the Shanghai publishing world. Throughout his career, Shen operated more than ten publishing ventures, but only World had a major impact. In 1900, Shen started as a street peddler for the Commercial Press. He then established his own firm to pirate Press titles. As the law closed in, the Press invited him back. Shen now started another venture to print anti-Qing literature. The Press soon bought it out. Another firm reprinted rare and even proscribed works, activities for which Shen was praised in progressive circles. Next, he started an outfit to reissue Ming- and Qing-dynasty essays and novels, many of which were quite rare. Thanks to their anti-Qing content, they sold very well. When the 1911 Republican revolution succeeded, Shen allied with Lufei to form Zhonghua. Six years later, Shen left Shanghai just ahead of a lawsuit charging him with counterfeiting medicine. Fleeing to nearby Suzhou, Shen issued his own obituary before sneaking back to Shanghai. Now, he marketed polite publications under one name but indecent titles under others, one of which was World Books.

By 1921, World set out to make a killing in the trade-book market by publishing mass-market literature, including works by the middlebrow 'Mandarin Ducks and Butterflies' novelist Zhang Henshui and detective-fiction writer Cheng Xiaoqing. Racing to keep up with its competitors' lists of 'eight big journals', World issued five aimed at the readership consuming its pulp fiction. Then, in 1925, World invented the name 'serial-picture books' for its comic-book-style presentation of the famous sixteenth-century novel *Journey to the West*. Ever since, myriad classic and popular novels have appeared in this format.

Only in 1923 did Shen enter the textbook business. Hiring celebrity editors and, like the Commercial Press and Zhonghua, advertising widely, Shen also curried favour with the government by bribing officials. Further, he focused on markets that his competitors had neglected, particularly in rural areas. In response, Zhonghua formed a united front with the Commercial Press to drive World Books out of business. The alliance made no headway before the two abandoned it in 1927. The three firms' textbooks now competed to advance New Culture goals as well as GMD political agendas.

The previous year—1926—Shen Zhifang had hedged his bets by printing radical GMD propaganda that no other Shanghai publishers would touch. Once the GMD established its new government at Nanjing, World hired a GMD stalwart to revise its old textbooks. Later, from 1934 onwards, a GMD elder effectively ran World Books, dominating World and Shen with government-allied capital just as Lufei and Zhonghua had been curbed in the 1920s. Between 1921 and 1937, World published more than 4,000 titles, most popular rather than scholarly.

In that same period, of course, Communists could be found throughout the Shanghai media worlds, positioning them to critique Shanghai's 'Big Three' capitalist publishers. The CCP itself tried out alternate publishing models while issuing banned or hard-to-find titles. In the early 1920s, its publishing wing issued a reprint of the first (1920) complete Chinese translation of *The Communist Manifesto* and also Lenin's *State and Revolution*. To keep up with the Party's own editorial and publishing output, a Communist-owned underground printing house was opened in Shanghai.

In 1926, both publisher and printer relocated up the Yangzi River to Wuhan, where they issued party journals, Bukharin and Preobraz-hensky's *The ABC of Communism*, translations of Marx and Lenin, and

Mao Zedong's landmark *Report on the Hunan Peasant Movement* (1927). An independent ranking of China's 1927 bestsellers listed Sun Yat-sen's *Three Principles of the People* first (the GMD distributed it free), *The ABC of Communism* second, and the suggestive *Sex Histories* third.

By the mid-1930s, government surveillance and market forces brought most Chinese publishers to heel. The GMD, seeking ideological conformity, rewarded compliance and penalized independence, sometimes placing its agents on corporate boards of directors but also founding quasi-governmental publishing companies to compete with the private sector. The marketplace, dependent on GMD educational policies, and the Second Sino-Japanese War (1937–45) did the rest, emasculating China's print capitalists. In 1937, Japan's invasion and occupation of China's eastern half, including Shanghai, destroyed the treaty port's supremacy in market-centred Chinese publishing. Further, the ultimate failure of the GMD state, which evacuated Nanjing for western China until 1946, provided the CCP an opportunity for expansion.

The next chapter in China's Gutenberg revolution turned out to be Communist-led, first from Yan'an, the northwestern stronghold to which the Communists withdrew in 1937, and then, after 1949, from Beijing. The Long March, which took the CCP to Yan'an, began in 1934. Some used the year-long odyssey to catch up on their reading. Others lugged printing presses and lithographic machinery along the 6,000-mile route. Despite Yan'an's rustic conditions, the Communists now proved more successful there at printing, publishing, and distribution than they had been in either Shanghai or Wuhan.

New China News Agency was founded in 1937 to unify news and propaganda work. The New China Bookstore followed in 1939. The latter published seven different periodicals in its first year and distributed 113,000 copies of books and 900,000 pages of newspapers; today, it is China's largest book-distribution chain. Liberation Agency issued Marxist–Leninist works, including *History of the Communist Party of the Soviet Union (Bolsheviks): Short Course.* This textbook guided Mao's sinification of Marxism–Leninism. Edgar Snow's biography of Mao, extracted from his classic *Red Star over China* (1937), was translated and widely circulated, confirming to the outside world that Mao was still alive. When necessary, printers laboriously carved type or cut woodblocks; grass was often used to make a coarse, dark paper.

As suggested by the Cultural Revolution's publishing scale mentioned earlier, Western printing methods reached a crescendo after the establishment of the PRC in 1949. Print communism—that is, party-dominated, centrally planned publishing to advance proletarian revolution—has also provided a framework for both the post-1980s recommoditization of Chinese publishing and the digital/Internet revolutions. Canadian scholar Yuezhi Zhao has characterized this latter era as one in which publishers operate 'between the party line and the bottom line'.

By 1947, when the Communists left Yan'an in the midst of civil war and two years prior to proclaiming the PRC at Beijing's Tian'anmen, the party had been printing books, periodicals, and even currency on a large scale for a decade. Even more important, the CCP had perfected the model for print communism it would implement on a national scale after 1949. Rejecting Republican-era, government-dependent, market-driven publishing paradigms, the CCP had thrived over an extended period in which patriotism and ideology were tied into non-commercial distribution systems.

The first of October 1949, when the PRC was proclaimed, changed everything. Politics and technology now gave the CCP unprecedented hegemony over China's print media. Beijing emerged as China's new national publishing centre, even as advanced equipment was redistributed from older coastal publishing locations to newer inland ones. World Books was long gone, a victim of politics and the marketplace. The Commercial Press and Zhonghua were soon nationalized; unlike countless other pre-1949 publishers, both retain their names today amidst the PRC's nearly 600 publishers (61 per cent of them based in Beijing). Commercial Press branches are found in Hong Kong, Taipei, and Singapore.

When the PRC was established in 1949, China's national literacy rate was about 32 per cent, a figure that prevailed until the 1980s. Today, it is approximately 95 per cent, thanks to increased education, publishing, and leisure. Before 1949, only a few thousand copies of major novels had been printed; now, new printings numbered in the tens to hundreds of thousands, still a small number given China's population. Between 1949 and 1966, however, only ten new literary titles appeared annually, compared to 1912–49 averages of between 135 and 270. The leading socialist-era bestseller *Red Crag* (1961) was reprinted 126 times for a total of only 6.8 million copies, which pales in comparison with Cultural Revolution publishing. During and just after the Cultural Revolution, readers often resorted to hand-copying out-of-print books.

Still, reading and literature had become an essential part of life for many. In 1979, when PRC publishers issued 11,000 book titles, one-sixth concerned literature or art. 1,100 periodicals now reached 165 million readers. With the development of the socialist market system, the problem was now neither printing nor publishing nor censorship (streamlined through a 'responsible-editor' system) per se. Rather, the stodgy command economy lacked the agility needed to meet changing demands. In response, an unofficial 'second channel' opened. No one exploited it more successfully than Wang Shuo (b. 1958), who earned millions writing 'hooligan literature'. In the 1990s, popular fiction by writers such as the Hong-Kong-based 'kung-fu' novelist Jin Yong (Louis Cha, 1924–2018), the most widely read Chinese writer today, and the apolitical, pre-1949, novelist Zhang Ailing (Eileen Chang, 1920–95), author of *The Golden Cangue*, surged in popularity. Although newspapers still report that most readers prefer hard copies, many writers jumped onto the Internet. Romance, fantasy, sex, crime, biography, history, reference, educational guides, and self-help all returned as topics for both fiction and non-fiction publishing.

Simultaneously, state-owned enterprises revived 'preservation publishing'. *Dictionary of the Chinese Language*, today's foremost China-published comprehensive dictionary of Chinese (surpassed only by Morohashi Tetsuji's Chinese–Japanese dictionary discussed in the next section), was commissioned in 1975. Shanghai's Cishu Publishers, inheritor of Zhonghua's pre-1949 editorial library, brought it out from 1986 to 2010. From 1984 to 1996, Zhonghua produced the Buddhist Tripitaka in 106 large volumes; slightly later, a 232-volume reprint of the Tibetan Tripitaka was completed. In the past thirty years, some 62 million Christian Bibles have been published officially. All publications contribute to the sense that the present government is China's greatest sponsor of religious publishing in several centuries. The numerical output of Qu'rans, however, remains hazy; like other books, it is available online.

In the same period, China became the world's digital printing plant. After unsuccessful attempts by the Qing (1899) and Republican

Chinese (1915, 1928) governments to implement enforceable copy-right legislation, the PRC issued its copyright law in 1990 while preparing to join the Berne Convention and World Trade Organization (WTO). China now offers discount services to international publishers in their languages of choice. Thus, in one of world history's great ironies, early Western missionary efforts to create a Chinese Christian empire via the printing press appear to have backfired. By re-energizing China's centuries-old indigenous printing and publishing traditions, they actually helped to fortify China's late-Qing, Republican, Maoist, and post-Maoist revolutions and print media systems.

Japan

Although early modern Japan maintained only limited contact with the Western world, its publishing activities made it one of the world's most dynamic print cultures. Especially from the eighteenth century, the book became a commercial artefact, produced and sold in a national market. By the early nineteenth century, there were more than 917 publishing houses in Edo (the former name of Tokyo), with sizeable numbers in Kyoto, Osaka, and other major provincial cities. The variety of publications is impressive: the Confucian and Buddhist classics and other highbrow works, but also cartoons, illustrated novels and *ukiyoe* prints, farmer almanacs, travel guides, and school primers intended for a popular audience. Nearly all publications used wood-block printing, or xylography.

Increasing contact with Europe and the United States in the middle of the nineteenth century brought knowledge of Western printing technology. In 1848, Motoki Shōzō, an interpreter at the Dutch trading post in Nagasaki, experimented with a hand press and a Dutch-made set of lead type. Even more opportunities for the intro-duction of Western technology emerged after 1868, when a newly formed government with the Meiji emperor as its head embarked on a policy of radical Westernization. When William Gamble, the printer associated with the APMP in Shanghai, arrived in Japan in 1869, Motoki was quick to seek his help in producing Chinese-character typefaces by means of electrotyping. In 1872, Motoki moved to Tokyo and set up Japan's first moveable-type foundry in Tsukiji, the birth-place of Japan's modern printing revolution.

Among the first publications using letterpress technology was *An Encouragement of Learning*, a series of seventeen booklets published between 1871 and 1876, by Fukuzawa Yukichi, Japan's foremost promoter of Western ideas. The first booklet proclaimed bold new ideas for the modern era, including equality, independence, and freedom. But the publication technology was equally startling. Although the booklets used Japanese-style *washi* paper and traditional Chinese-style binding, Fukuzawa had managed to obtain a set of moveable metallic type to print the text. *An Encouragement of Learning* proved to be an enormous bestseller, with each booklet selling around 200,000 copies. Long recognized as a seminal event in modern Japanese social and intellectual history, the publication of *An Encouragement of Learning* was also a milestone in the history of the modern book in Japan.

Despite the extraordinary popularity of this book and other books in Western format, existing technologies and literary styles were not easily abandoned. In the 1880s, typeset translations from Western languages existed alongside woodblock reprints of Japanese classical literature. Nevertheless, the introduction of the printing press coupled with the spread of compulsory education from the early 1870s created the infrastructure for a new industrialized print culture. Specialized publishers, printers, distributors, and retailers emerged. Maruzen, founded in Tokyo in 1869, was Japan's first Western-style bookstore and publisher. The new capital quickly established itself as the centre of modern publishing. Shūeisha, founded in 1876, published Japan's first true Western-style book, a revised translation of *Self-Help* by Samuel Smiles (published in 1859). In 1877, the number of new books published was 5,441; by 1890, this number had risen to 18,720, and by 1910, to 41,620. The growing availability of books and magazines made Japan into a nation of readers.

The mass production of books and other printed materials not only encouraged literacy but changed patterns of reading and writing and attitudes towards books themselves. The shift to moveable type, for example, resulted in a sort of 'visual revolution' in which novels and other writings depended less on illustrations and more on descriptive prose. New printing technologies also led to the replacement of communal reading aloud with solitary and silent reading. Moreover, the easy-to-read print plus the introduction of uniform punctuation speeded up the reading process. Diaries and books with blank pages intended for personal writing were also published in the 1890s. The Hakubunkan publishing house, for example, began publishing pocket diaries from 1895. This industry grew rapidly, turning Japan into a nation of solitary writers as well as readers.

The growth of reading and writing as a national pastime in the late 1890s and the early 1900s created a public space for political and cultural debate. In 1887, for example, the journalist Tokutomi Sohō established the Minyūsha publishing house and printed Japan's first general-interest magazine, *The Nation's Friend*. Its advocacy of British-style democracy and populism played a role in the composition of Japan's 1889 constitution. The abundance of books empowered a vastly expanded reading public, but it also left some vulnerable to information exploitation. Books, magazines, and newspapers contributed to the creation of a national imagined community and, as Japan won the Sino-Japanese War (1894–5) and the Russo-Japanese War (1904–05), many people became willing agents of nationalism and imperialism.

In the opening decades of the twentieth century, Japan emerged as an information-based, cosmopolitan society. The range of issues discussed by opinion leaders in Japanese books, journals, and newspapers broadened. Readers looked to general-interest magazines such as *The Sun, Central Review*, and *Reconstruction* for political, economic, and social commentary. Literature also served to make people aware of events and changes taking place around them. Japan's most famous novelist of the modern era, Natsume Sōseki, portrayed Japan's painful break with its past in his novel *Kokoro* ('The Heart'). Serialized in the *Asahi* newspaper in 1914, the novel was subsequently published as the maiden work of the newly established Iwanami Shoten, set up in Jinbōchō, the area that became Tokyo's book town. Iwanami published works on philosophy and liberalism and continues today as Japan's foremost academic press.

Kōdansha, a Tokyo publishing house established in 1909, took aim at a different, but equally modern, readership. Promising books and magazines that would be both interesting and cheap, Kōdansha evolved into Japan's largest publishing house. In 1914, Kōdansha issued a new magazine, *Youth Club*, filled with stories of adventure and mystery, often in the form of serialized manga comics. Magazines targeting girls and women followed, as well as *King*, a general-interest magazine put out by Kōdansha in 1925. As a result of massive advertising, *King* became the first publication in Japan to sell over a million copies.

The Great Kanto earthquake that devastated Tokyo and Yokohama in 1923 ironically consolidated Tokyo's position as the centre of Japanese publishing. The earthquake not only destroyed millions of books, creating a seller's market, but it also provided an opportunity to modernize the book printing industry and expand distribution and retailing networks. At the same time, entrepreneurs founded new, spacious bookstores, including Kinokuniya, established in 1927 in Shinjuku and now the headquarters of Japan's largest chain of bookstores.

In 1926, Kaizōsha began the publication of a sixty-three-volume *Collected Works of Modern Japanese Literature* that answered the aspirations of Japan's rising middle class. The series was sold on a subscription basis at the attractive price of 1 yen per volume, and some 340,000 persons signed up to receive one book a month over a five-year period. Other '1-yen' book series followed, including a fifty-seven-volume anthology of world literature issued by the publisher Shinchōsha that was even more successful in sales. Iwanami's pocketbook (*bunko*) series, begun in 1927, also made good books available at inexpensive prices. Iwanami Shigeo, the founder of Iwanami Shoten, was convinced that an educated citizenry was the best defence against autocratic rule. His paperback series, modelled on the German Reclam's Universal-Bibliotek, offered mass access to life-transforming classics of world literature. Many publishers quickly followed Iwanami's model.

The concern to educate coupled with a desire to amuse meant that the number of books published in Japan increased dramatically. In the 1920s, a popular book could sell 500,000 copies in one printing. The number of new titles issued grew from 43,153 in 1911 to 74,464 in 1931. Although the economic depression that followed the collapse of world markets in 1929 brought widespread hardship and contributed to the military takeover of the Japanese government in 1932, it failed to dampen the book publishing industry. Some 85,357 new titles were published in 1932, and as many as 121,949 in 1934. Publication numbers thereafter declined: to 97,268 in 1938; 73,152 in 1940; and 42,211 in 1943. In 1945, the last year of the Second World War, a mere 878 new books were published.

From the late 1930s, the Japanese government strengthened long-standing publication controls. It imposed censorship on all forms of mass media, requiring writers and journalists and cartoonists to cooperate with the war effort. Perhaps the most popular novelist of the war years was the master of historical fiction, Yoshikawa Eiji. His *Miyamoto Musashi* (1935), *Tale of Three Kingdoms* (1940), and other historical tales provided escapist literature while also affirming the glories of war and the strength and martial spirit of the Japanese fighting man. Rivalling Yoshikawa for sales was Hino Ashihei, who used first-hand observation in China as the basis for his trilogy on the daily lives of soldiers published in 1938 and 1939. The trilogy sold over a million copies. The government also engaged in direct propaganda. In 1937, the Ministry of Education issued *Cardinal Principles of our National Policy* in order to unify understanding of Japan's unique characteristics; it distributed nearly two million copies throughout Japan and its empire. School textbooks similarly served to indoctrinate Japanese youth. In 1942, just after the attack on Pearl Harbor, a fourth-grade reader proclaimed: 'We came to know that Japan, blessed with the Emperor, is the most respected country in the world'.

Some authors and publishers, nonetheless, found ways of presenting counter-narratives. In 1938, for example, Iwanami inaugurated a series of short paperbacks (modelled on the British Penguin series) called *shinsho* or 'new books', designed for 'the contemporary education of contemporary people'. The first book of the series was a translation of *Thirty Years in Moukden, 1883–1913*, written by Dugald Christie, a medical missionary stationed in Manchuria. The text detailed the terrible sufferings experienced by Manchurian people at the time of the Russo-Japanese War in 1904–5. Among other subtle forms of resistance, the denunciation of British imperialism in the wartime mystery novels of Oguri Mushitarō could be read as a critique of all colonial ventures, including Japan's. In 1945, just before the end of the war, the photographic news magazine *Asahi Graph* sent a subversive message by juxtaposing the photograph of the emperor on one page with images of air-raid survivors on the opposite page; when the magazine was closed, the faces of the suffering masses rubbed against the emperor's face.

After Japan's surrender in August 1945 ended years of intellectual starvation, people lined up, sometimes for days, to buy books as they were issued. In response to this widespread hunger for words, the publishing industry revived. In 1946, 3,466 new books were published; ten years later the number exceeded 14,000. New novelists such as Mishima Yukio and Abe Kōbō produced serious literature alongside pre-war giants such as Tanizaki Junichirō and the Nobel-Prize-winning Kawabata Yasunari. A vast array of pulp publications sold alongside hardback editions of serious academic scholarship. The sinologist Morohashi Tetsuji's monumental Chinese–Japanese dictionary, *Dai Kan-Wa jiten*, begun in the 1920s, was finally published in 1955. Iwanami produced its hundred-volume *Anthology of Classical Japanese Literature* between 1957 and 1967. In the 1960s, the post-war baby boom opened a new market for children's literature and the weekly magazine and manga industries took off amid a period of rapid economic growth. At the same time, businessmen devoured the world's longest novel, Yamaoka Sōhachi's fictional biography of Tokugawa Ieyasu, founder of Japan's last shogunate. Published in twenty-three volumes from 1963, Yamaoka's epic was touted as a guide to successful business strategy.

The 1970s and the 1980s proved to be the golden years of Japanese book publishing. The number of new titles rose from 18,745 in 1970 to 40,576 in 1990. Major presses offered pocket-sized paperback editions in quantity to a general readership. They also published the collected works of well-known authors along with large multi-volume canons of primary texts in literature and thought. Iwanami issued a sixty-seven-volume *Anthology of Japanese Thought* between 1970 and 1982. Shōgakukan issued a twenty-volume Japanese equivalent of the *Oxford English Dictionary*, the *Nihon kokugo daijiten*, between 1972 and 1976. In 1981, Kuroyanagi Tetsuko, a popular television personality, published *Totto-chan* (*The Little Girl at the Window*), the story of her unconventional education during the war years. Ostensibly a children's story, *Totto-chan* became an instant bestseller. With total sales of some eight million copies domestically, it became Japan's all-time bestseller. In translation, it also proved popular in China and Korea; an English translation appeared in 1984. Three years later,

Murakami Haruki published his fifth novel, *Norwegian Wood*, to wide acclaim. As translations in English, Chinese, and other languages appeared, Murakami secured his position as a major figure in modern world literature.

Perhaps the most distinctive feature of contemporary Japanese print culture is the relative decline in the importance of the written word and, by contrast, a renaissance of visual media, particularly manga. One year after the end of the Second World War, Hasegawa Machiko, one of Japan's first female manga artists, introduced *Sazaesan*, a light-hearted story of post-war family life in Japan. In 1952, Tezuka Osamu created *Mighty Atom*, the story of a robot boy that presaged a peaceful world indebted to the advance of science. Both *Sazaesan* and *Mighty Atom* enjoyed widespread popularity as long-running manga series and as animated cartoons on television. From the 1960s, weekly manga magazines, some of them over 200 pages, were eagerly consumed by young boys and girls. Shūeisha's *Weekly Shōnen Jump*, begun in 1969, was particularly successful. In 1994, thanks to such hits as *Dragon Ball* (1984–95), *Slam Dunk* (1990–5), and the long-running *Kochikame* (1976–2016), *Weekly Shōnen Jump* claimed a weekly circulation of 6.2 million. Although circulation has since declined, *Shōnen Jump* is Japan's biggest-selling periodical. Manga account for 25 per cent of all books published in Japan today and have attracted a substantial international audience, especially in Asia.

Korea

During the long Joseon period (1392–1910), publishing in Korea generally was confined to large government-sponsored Confucian and Buddhist projects, which were produced and consumed largely outside the market economy. By the early nineteenth century, however, more commercial book production began to aim at a commoner audience. Cheap woodblock editions of popular tales such as *The Romance of Chunhyang* were sold in bookshops and rented out in circulating libraries. These and other less-than-sacred books, published in the Korean phonetic script (*hangeul*), flourished in the shadows of official celebration of the Chinese classics. Although commoners were not encouraged to read vernacular fiction, these humble books nurtured commoner literacy, widened circles of readers, and helped to cultivate Korean national identity.

During the nineteenth century, the Korean court attempted to maintain an isolationist policy in the face of growing pressure from the West. In 1876, however, Japan assumed the initiative in forcing Korea to sign a treaty of trade and international relations; Western nations followed in the 1880s. In 1881, the first Western-style printing press entered Korea when a group of Japanese merchants in Busan published the short-lived Japanese-language *Korea News*. In 1883, a reformist group within the government began a Korean-language newspaper, *Seoul News*, with the aim of bringing the benefits of Western civilization to Korea. The necessary printing equipment was purchased in Nagasaki by Gim Ok-gyun (Kim Ok-kyun) who had sought the advice of Fukuzawa Yukichi during a study mission to Japan; a former student of Fukuzawa served as editor. Although the press was destroyed by anti-Japanese conservatives in 1884, replacement equipment from Japan was used to publish a new paper, *Seoul Weekly*. It offered articles written entirely in *hangeul*, making the news accessible to ordinary Koreans for the first time.

During the 1890s, a series of reforms promoted *hangeul* as Korea's national language, abolished the traditional civil service examination system, and established a new national educational system with a focus on practical learning. At the same time, the commercialization of the printed word and the availability of new types of reading materials spurred the expansion of the Korean reading public. *The Independent*, founded in 1896 and published entirely in *hangeul*, played a seminal role in the development of Korean civil society. Other newspapers followed, including *Imperial Post* and the more political *Imperial Capital Gazette*, both begun in 1898. Christian missionaries imported printing presses to publish Korean translations of the Bible and other religious literature. By the turn of the century, easy-to-read typeset editions of traditional tales joined newspapers, magazines, and books in creating a new print culture based on *hangeul* that had become a symbol of national identity as well as a means of communication.

In the opening decades of the twentieth century, a new generation of Korean writers expanded the range of literary genres, following trends that were becoming established in Japan. The Japan-educated I Injik (Yi In-jik) published what he called 'new fiction', novels written in *hangeul* that dealt with contemporary social and political issues. His best-known work, *Tears of Blood* (1906), explored the conflict between 'enlightened daughters' and their more old-fashioned mothers, a problem common to modernizing Japan and Korea. As in Japan (and China), novels were often first serialized in periodicals, blurring the distinctions between fact and fiction. In 1908, Choe Nam-seon, poet, journalist, and nationalist, used his education in Japan and his fascination with Western print media to establish the Sinmungwan (New Culture Press). With the aim of inspiring the creation of a 'new Korea', Choe established Korea's first popular magazine, *Boys*, which included one of his own poems, 'From the Sea to the Young'. Credited as the first poem written in the vernacular, it urged the youth of Korea to abandon the old continent and look to new horizons—to Japan and the West.

Another emerging trend was the publication of *hangeul* versions of Korean literary classics and books on Korean history that encouraged a broad segment of the population to think in terms of national identity. In 1908, the historian Sin Chae-ho published his *A New Reading of History*. Rejecting the traditional focus on the rise and fall of dynasties, Sin envisioned the linear development of a unique Korean nation formed through struggles with neighbouring Japan and China.

Annexation by Japan in 1910 had immediate repercussions on Korea's publishing industry. Privately owned newspapers were closed and a rigorous system of publication permits and pre-publication censorship was introduced. Moreover, changes in the educational system and the establishment of new civil service examinations increased government control over the flow and content of printed information. Within this new legal and ideological framework, however, the number of publishers grew from twenty-eight in 1910 to fifty in 1920, reaching a peak of sixty-two in 1926. Moreover, the replacement of private newspapers by one government-controlled paper, *The Daily Post*, resulted in increased newspaper readership. In 1913, thanks to the installation of a new rotary press, daily circulation topped 50,000.

The Daily Post also attracted aspiring writers. In 1912, I Haejo (Yi Hae-jo) serialized *Flower in Prison*, a modern retelling of the traditional *Romance of Chunhyang*. In book form, the novel was reprinted in ninety-seven editions before 1945. In 1917, while a student at Waseda University in Tokyo, I Gwangsu (Yi Kwang-su) serialized *Heartless*, often identified as Korea's first modern novel. *Heartless* used the archetypical love triangle to depict Korea's struggles with modernity, encouraging comparisons with Natsume Sōseki's *Kokoro* (The Heart). While Sōseki's protagonist faces a bleak future, however, the hero of *Heartless* resolves to 'cast aside the old Korea and make a new Korea, transformed by modern civilization'.

Students and other activists led a major protest demanding freedom from Japanese colonial rule on 1 March 1919. The publisher Choe Nam-seon authored the Declaration of Independence that was read aloud throughout the country. Although the movement was ruthlessly suppressed, it forced Japan to change its approach to colonial administration. In 1920, Governor-General Saitō Makoto inaugurated a new era of 'cultural rule', which aimed to co-opt Korean elites by encouraging their active participation in the cultural and even political affairs of the colony. A relaxation in publication controls resulted in a rush of new publications. In 1920 alone, 409 magazines and three private newspapers were granted publications permits. Korean poetry and fiction also experienced a renaissance: between 1920 and 1929, some 356 permits were issued for poetry titles, and 10,801 permits for works of prose fiction.

Despite the reality of everyday censorship, the publishing boom of the 1920s significantly widened the spectrum of Korean print culture. Literary and general-interest magazines, such as *Creation*, *The Ruins*, and *White Tide*, published articles on topics hitherto unimaginable. In 1922, for example, the novelist Yi Kwang-su published a master plan for the reconstruction of Korea, focusing on advances in education that would strengthen national identity and economic autonomy. Reading books and magazines, both in Korean and Japanese, became a middle-class phenomenon. By 1931, Seoul boasted more than thirty bookstores, including branches of Japanese bookstores such as Ōsakayagō, Maruzen, Sanseidō, and Kinbudō. The diary of Yu Chin-o, a university student at the Keijō (Seoul) Imperial University, provides good evidence of the colonial modernity that characterized Korea in the 1920s. Yu devoted himself to the 'boundless reading' of books in non-Korean languages, primarily Japanese and German. He subscribed to a Korean left-wing journal, *The Light of the Peninsula*, and

316 Christopher A. Reed and M. William Steele

the Japanese *Reconstruction*, also left of centre. He frequented Maruzen and Ōsakayagō bookstores. Although a colonial subject, his education and fluency in Japanese allowed him to participate in a broad realm of intellectual debates.

Despite the onset of economic woes, Korea's print industry continued to expand into the 1930s. Publishing was profitable so long as censorship limits were not overstepped. The circulation of newspapers and general-interest magazines, many imported from Japan, steadily increased. Between 1927 and 1939, the number of Japanese newspapers and magazines imported into Korea rose from 1,200 to over 550,000 copies. Specialty magazines, such as *New Woman*, flourished. Advances in art lithography and photography were reflected in beautiful books and eye-catching advertising.

Korean publishers used marketing strategies to make Korean authors more attractive to the Korean reading public. In 1935, advertisements for a retelling of the popular *Romance of Chunhyang* by Yi Kwang-su championed the fundamental 'Korean-ness' of the tale, claiming that only Korea's foremost author could transform it into a literary masterpiece. In 1938, the Joseon (Chosŏn) Film Company announced that its first feature film would be an adaptation of Yi's bestselling *Heartless*. That same year, Hangsong Publishing House released Yi's latest novel, *Love*—the first Korean novel to appear in book form before being first serialized in a newspaper or literary journal.

Japanese military expansion on the Chinese mainland from 1937 and war against the United States from 1941 led to harsher Japanese control of Korean affairs. Censorship of the publishing industry was strengthened, eliminating loopholes that had allowed relative freedom of the press in non-political areas. Privately operated newspapers were once again disbanded, leaving only the Japanese-controlled *Daily Post* written in Korean. Interestingly, its circulation surged to nearly 200,000 copies a day. Novels written in Korean were published only if they accorded with Japanese colonial goals in Korea. In such conditions, many Korean writers began to publish in Japanese, allowing them to access the expanding reading market of the Japanese empire. In 1940, Kim Sa-ryang (Gim Saryang) a Korean novelist writing in Japanese, was nominated for Japan's highest literary honour, the Akutagawa Prize, for his short story 'Into the Light'.

On 15 August 1945, the streets of Seoul were filled with Koreans celebrating liberation from Japanese control. Overcoming difficulties, the publishing industry began to recover. In December 1945, a collection of poems, *The Liberation Commemorative Anthology*, celebrated Korea's newfound freedom. Novels, essays, and works for children were equally animated by hopes for a better future. The jubilation, however, did not last long. While Japan under Allied occupation experienced democratic reforms and the rekindling of economic growth, Korea soon suffered catastrophic civil war that tore the country in two, encouraging autocratic rule and delaying economic recovery.

With the outbreak of the Korean War in 1950, the period of apparent liberation that had emerged after the end of Japanese colonial rule disappeared for decades in the south and is yet to resurface in the north. During the Korean War, Seoul was occupied, and most printing facilities were destroyed. Only fifteen books were published in 1950, and 778 in 1951. United States aid made new printing equipment available, but even the pro-growth reforms initiated from 1961 by the government of General Bak Jeonghui (Park Chung-hee) had only modest impact on the publishing industry. Between 1960 and 1970, the number of new titles published rose from 1,618 to only 2,633.

Despite political repression and economic slowdown in the 1970s, the emergence of an aspiring middle class increased the demand for Korean-language books and other publications. New progressive publishing houses emerged, including Munhaksasang in 1972 and Hangilsa in 1976. In 1977, Hangilsa began a series on contemporary thought, *Thinkers of Today*, that had great social impact. A separate series, *Understanding Before and After Liberation*, begun in 1979, inspired student political activists. Harsh restrictions on media content that followed the 1980 political takeover by General Jeon Duhwan (Chun Doo-hwan) failed to dampen popular enthusiasm for books. New titles rose from 20,985 in 1980 to over 30,000 by 1984. Korea's most famous bookstore, the Kyobo Book Centre, was founded in 1981 with the slogan 'People create books; books create people'.

After massive demonstrations forced Jeon to step down in 1987, government restrictions on the publishing industry were relaxed and the number of new titles expanded rapidly. Unrestricted commercialization meant that publishers could give priority to books that would sell. Even more than fiction, self-help literature and educational manuals dominated. Korea's first million-seller was the 1989 autobiography of the now-disgraced business tycoon, Gim U-Jung (Kim Woo-jung), the founder of Daewoo Conglomerate, who urged Korean youth to work hard and dream of success. The Korean translation of Japanese author Saisho Hiroshi's *Morning Person*, a call for early rising as a path to success issued in 2003, achieved sales ten times greater than the original. The range of genres broadened from the late 1990s, when the laws restricting the entry of Japanese popular culture were lifted. In 2013, new titles totalled 43,146, of which translations accounted for 22 per cent; over 60 per cent of the translated titles came from Japan. In addition to Japanese manga, bestselling authors from Japan, including Murakami Haruki and Yoshimoto Banana, are today displayed prominently in major Korean bookstores.

The Future of the Book in China, Japan, and Korea

Since the 1990s, the publishing industries in China, Japan, and Korea have faced challenges from the growing global power of the Internet, e-books, and online sales, even as publishers, writers, and readers have generally embraced new opportunities.

China has been connected to the Internet since the mid-1990s and today is the world's second-largest book market after the United States; even with restrictions on access and changing tastes, the reading public is growing. Publishers seek new markets both domestically (aided by the Internet, digitization, twenty-four-hour bookstores, and genres aimed at youthful readers like graphic novels, espionage novels, and SciFi) and internationally (as active exhibitors, retailers, and buyers of copyrights at world book fairs such as Frankfurt and London). Even as a recent newspaper article reported on fifty contemporary Chinese writers, each of whom earned royalties of more than US$165,000, China's 2012 Nobel Prize-winning novelist Mo Yan, ranked thirteenth, has found his sales stalling. Some argue that literature has lost the prestige it held earlier and has been replaced by other forms of diversion. Novelist Zhang Jiajia, who topped the list with more than US$3 million in earnings, disagrees, observing, 'I think readers now are tired of being lectured by books, they crave relaxation and relief by reading'.

Meanwhile, both Japan and Korea are experiencing low birth rates and the reality of population decline. While the number of first titles has grown, total sales of books and magazines have decreased, and the number of conventional bookstores has shrunk precipitously. Even more significantly, at the individual level, reading print media as a pastime appears to be on the decline. Beginning in 2012, the e-book market in Korea went into a downturn. According to the *Korea Times* of March 2013, 'Koreans don't read books and don't read newspapers. They flock to the movies, however'. And, ominously, a 2017 survey of university students in Japan reported that more than 50 per cent of the nearly 10,000 respondents spent 'zero hours' reading books. The demand for educational books and cram-school study guides, however, continues. And, as part of Japan Cool and the Korean Wave, Japanese and Korean manga are eagerly consumed at home and abroad, spurring sales at discount retail chains, such as Book Off in Japan, Aladdin in Korea, and on Internet-based Amazon. As the print industry goes digital and global, debates are under way on the future of the book.

13

Globalization

Eva Hemmungs Wirtén

By the end of the nineteenth century it was clear to promoters and concerned governments alike that authors, publishers, and readers were international by default and that the texts they wrote, published, and read moved with ease across national and linguistic borders. As earlier chapters amply illustrate, nothing was new in that. For centuries, cross-border movements were simply part of the way books behaved. What was new was the recognition that these flows had now reached a level which required the governance of an international legal regime. Bilateral agreements had been around for some time, but the arrival of a multilateral instrument of regulation represented a critical juncture in the history of the book as a global phenomenon.

On 9 September 1886 in Berne, Switzerland, representatives of Belgium, France, Germany, Great Britain, Haiti, Italy, Liberia, Spain, Switzerland, and Tunisia signed the world's first multilateral treaty on copyright. It was a turning point in the history of the book. As they boarded their trains or steamers back home, some of these men—and they were all men—felt both relieved and elated at having achieved what their governments wanted. Other participants felt weary, perhaps even disappointed, that they had been unable to sign the Berne Convention for the Protection of Literary and Artistic Works. That document allowed access to the Berne Union, a completely new international arena for the book.

The regulation introduced by the 1886 Berne Union and Convention resulted from the advance of new technologies, better means of communication, and the expanded reading public described in the previous chapter. New communication networks and technological advances influenced literacy and education, ideas of authorship and piracy, and the concept of the book itself. If these changes brought on a first wave of globalization in the history of the book, a second wave gained momentum in the thirty-year period following the Centennial of the Berne Convention in 1986.

Globalization, when understood as a process of information technology associated with the arrival of the Internet, e-books, cloud services, streaming, and smartphones, is only a few decades old, a very post-1986 event. Even so, such contemporary considerations are constraining. A broader history of globalization originates with the Berne Convention after which we can think about globalization and the book as a continuum, one that reveals a number of long-standing relationships between the material object and all those invested in its fate. Many influences affecting twentieth-century books resulted from an increasing internationalization, and later, a globalization produced by an increased interconnectedness across ever greater distances. Such dependencies and relationships were enabled by more efficient transportation and communication networks and set within fast-moving economic and cultural change.

Copyright and Censorship

Copyright and censorship are central to questions of ownership and control, authorship and creativity, as well as to the ongoing question of where the boundaries of cultural work are drawn. Such questions have been and continue to be intrinsic to the history of the book, especially in an age of globalization. Copyright mediates social relations, and the Berne Convention addressed several of the most important relationships we identify within the orbit of the book— between authors and readers, between new technologies and the stability and instability of the work, between publisher and market, and between the global North and the global South.

Victor Hugo's keynote speech on the need for an international copyright regime at the Congrès Littéraire Internationale in Paris 1878 set things in motion. As a bestselling author, Hugo had suffered widespread piracy. In the next few years, a number of organizations, led by the French, worked intensely to forge a treaty for authors' rights that reflected the huge contemporary increase in multilateral treaties, conventions, and agreements. The first such multilateral organization of note, Union internationale des telecommunications, dated from 1865, and the Union Postale Universelle from 1874. Another Convention, however, signed in Paris in 1883, served as the more direct inspiration of the Berne Convention. The objective of the Paris Convention on the Protection of Industrial Property was the regulation of patents, trademark, and design—all crucial to industry—and it had been successfully concluded at a time when innovation and applied science held the keys to future wealth and prosperity.

But what was the broader situation for the book like towards the end of the nineteenth and into the twentieth century? The novel had triumphed, printing technology was sophisticated enough to facilitate large-scale piracy, the reading public displayed an appetite for foreign works, and European authors and publishers operated within a highly uneven market. Censorship remained a global phenomenon, enacted by local and specific variation and policing. As the previous chapter noted, China's first modern censorship law of 1898 presaged strict controls during the next century and up to the present, while from the late 1930s, Japan increased its own rigorous censorship regulations. In Europe and the Americas, and in independent democratic countries as well as colonies, censorship ranged from court injunctions to local pressure group interventions (as Graham Shaw observed above in Chapter 10 on South Asia). Notably in Russia, late nineteenth-century 'golden age' literature flourished at the same time as rigid censorship of publishing. Following a certain relaxation after the 1917 Revolution, a state censorship office, Glavlit, was established in June 1922, and is usually regarded as marking the official reintroduction of general censorship. Glavlit was joined in the following year by Glavrepertkom, the Main Repertory Commission. In Germany in 1933, the Reichstag Fire Decree of President von Hindenburg suppressed freedom of the press, a move consolidated by Joseph Goebbels's Ministry of Public Enlightenment and Propaganda, resulting in the routine imprisonment of authors and publishers.

After the Second World War, the 1948 United Nations Declaration of Human Rights asserted that 'everyone has the right to freedom of opinion and expression; this right includes freedom to hold opinions without interference, and to seek, receive, and impart information and ideas through any media regardless of frontiers'. But across the world,

breaches of this Declaration have been more notable than obser-
vances, and some regions have rarely been free of draconian state
intervention. In South America and even more so in Africa, authori-
tarian and volatile regimes have banned books and imprisoned
authors, publishers, and librarians, and have also imposed religious
interdictions with a regularity that belies claims to modernity and
toleration. The government of Nigeria, for example, detained Wole
Soyinka, the country's first Nobel laureate. In Apartheid South Africa,
the 1975 Publications Act extended the range of 'undesirable' books
and writings and seizable before and after publication. In the United
States, in the 1956 film *Storm Center*, Bette Davis's local librarian
struggles with county commissions and their ban on Communist
literature. The film reminds us of Hollywood's response to 1950s
McCarthyite censorship in a nation founded on the principles of
free speech, independent thought, and the equality of man. With
respect to official information and publications, governments around
the world continue to determine which materials are public or protected from disclosure in the national interest, even if some of the
more democratic states are now also subject to 'sunshine laws' or
freedom of information legislation used to define the limits of national
interest.

Authorship and Piracy

Twentieth-century political and religious interference in publishing
always proved striking and disruptive, suppressing literature and
silencing authors and publishing firms, but also creating underground
literature and notable resistance. The broader campaign to ensure the
voice of author and the security of publishing rights, however, continued to be critical. At the close of the nineteenth century, the
interconnectedness of sophisticated communication networks meant
that it was essential to create an international infrastructure securing
protection for these assets, assets that were prone to cross-border
competition. The Paris and Berne Conventions and Unions sought
to regulate flows of knowledge, to stem piracy, and to ensure national
supremacy in industries that were becoming increasingly important.
The treaties regulated different things in different ways, but both were
about *intellectual* property and both evidenced the professionalization

of categories such as inventors and authors, who now knew that international collaboration and organization was the only way forward.

Crystallized around the narrative superpowers, Great Britain and France, was a core group of exporting nations and a very large group of importing ones. It is one of the more persistent structural facets of the book that we, from the very beginning of the Berne period, can trace the book trade along certain distinct flows of export and import. Exporting nations of the time, especially France, were highly invested in securing the Berne Convention and implemented its tradition of authors' rights internationally, whereas importing nations of the time, the Scandinavian countries chief among them, were to resist such expansion. Historically and in the present, this scenario spawned its winners and its losers, and it is worth keeping in mind as this history approaches our own times that the geopolitics of the book were to remain central, not only to many of the controversies in making the Berne Convention in 1886, but throughout the lifespan of the Convention.

It is indicative of the book's inherent international potential that no question during the years leading up to the 1886 Convention was as controversial as translation. That the author's exclusive right of translation, the author's right to authorize translations of his or her work, as well as the right of the translator to his or her translation, warranted the label of *the* international question *par excellence* is not surprising. Translation was the most obvious vehicle by which authors became *international* authors. It still is. Not only did it enable an accelerating diffusion of the work, but it also provided for an accelerating growth in the number and range of readers. This was the upside of the translation process. On the downside, it was unclear to the diplomats negotiating the first multilateral copyright agreement how to accommodate translation within the distinction between original and copy.

When the negotiations began for the Berne Convention in two diplomatic conferences in 1884 and 1885, translation pitted France against Sweden, the first an exporter and the second an importer of books. The interchange between the two nations revealed fundamentally contradictory views of reading publics and translation. On the one side stood the argument for assimilation, on the other, freedom of translation. For the French, the interests of the public and the author went hand in hand. Only protection and control over the work by the author ensured a text faithful enough to the original. The Swedish position was just the opposite. If the extension of the author's control over his or her text limited reader's access, then the public was the victim. In the end, this would be detrimental also to the author's ideas, now corrupted by a substandard authorized translation standing in the way of a superior, but legally questionable, unauthorized one.

The French view prevailed at the 1886 Convention, and until 1904 (when revised national laws allowed the country to adhere to the Union), Sweden was judged a pirate nation by the international copyright community (especially the French) for its advocacy of the freedom of translation. Sweden was of only peripheral interest, however, in comparison to the pre-eminent pirate nation at the time, the United States, a country represented at the Berne diplomatic conferences but not a signatory to the Convention until 1989, more than a hundred years after its establishment.

Few authors have been as associated with the piracy problem during the nineteenth century as Charles Dickens, who issued anti-piracy declarations during his American lecture tour in 1842. Some claim that the American tour did him and the cause more harm than good. In following decades, American authors such as Mark Twain, Harriet Beecher Stowe, James Fenimore Cooper, Joseph Conrad, and Walt Whitman all took an interest in the promotion of international copyright. But the views on international copyright were divided in the United States. Those in favour spoke of fairness and emphasized how cheap imports hurt the chances of developing an American literature and contributed to the import of foreign ideas. Those against rewarding authors, and especially foreign authors, at the expense of domestic printers and publishers, championed the dissemination of texts to the benefit of the reading public. British and American authors engaged energetically with transatlantic piracy and in many cases lobbied for securing United States compliance with international copyright.

Authors and nations debated the question of copyright in a new international arena, but the culture of reprinting and the culture of translation were equally present in the piracy scenario. Piracy in the culture of reprinting was perhaps the most lucrative and easy. Transmission involved no middle-man—or-woman for that matter, given that the translator historically often has been represented as female.

Although the culture of translation diverged in many ways from the culture of reprinting, there were also similarities in how the question of public interest in the dissemination of knowledge covered up a protectionist policy favouring printers and publishers. The shared English language made the reprinting culture possible, but translation also remained crucial to the dissemination of literature within a country such as the United States, where large immigrant groups depended on access to reading material in a wealth of other languages. Piracy within the same language—for instance, in the American–British reprinting culture—was clearly the site of controversy and conflict. Translation, however, generated a set of different and even more acute concerns in the relationship between authors and readers. Translation made new works out of old ones. A prerequisite for the continued circulation of texts, translation continued to be the primary vehicle by which authors multiplied their works, but even more significantly, produced new readers. Yet, translation was a double-edged sword, a problem in search of a legal solution. On the one hand was the promise of new markets and readers. On the other hand, without proper regulation, the transformation of a text by translation into a new language could result in substandard or corrupt texts that also alienated the author from his or her work. And in this transmission between text and reader appeared another author: the translator.

The question of how the law should view the translator and the translated work was officially solved in 1908, when the Berne Convention implemented something of a paradox, or a double ownership. When the Convention was revised at the 1908 Diplomatic Conference in Berlin, it was decided that the translator was no longer simply a tool for the original author, but an independent creator in her or his own right. From 1908, translations were also to be protected as original works *without prejudice* to the underlying work. Translation crucially tests the perceived stability of cultural works—including new media forms that soon outran the book-bound rationale behind the 1886 Berne Convention. Moreover, while translation was an early example of the transformative use of cultural works and its treatment in international copyright, it was not the last. New technologies have forced the international copyright community, the Berne Convention, and the book itself to adapt.

New Book Technologies

To twenty-first-century media consumers, radio is old technology. So are cinematic films, vinyl records, television sets, and gramophones, all of which have changed the consumption and production of culture. While books increasingly competed with new media, they seemed safe in at least one respect. In material terms, books appeared to have reached an evolutionary apex: their ease of use could hardly be improved. Nonetheless, during the twentieth century, publishers and entrepreneurs introduced important changes to the format of books, most notably perhaps in 1935, when Allen Lane launched the Penguin paperback book.

It was an incremental and modest transformation in the physical appearance of the book, but this minor change in format represented by the Penguin paperbacks heralded a major change in dissemination and access, one that was to change the book landscape forever and make the paperback ubiquitous. Costing no more than a packet of cigarettes, cheap Penguins were available outside traditional retailers, and cleverly designed to ensure instant recognition by readers. What had arrived was a branded book. The colour-coded Penguin or Puffin or Pelican immediately told consumers that they could expect very affordable, high-quality content. Of itself, the branding of books was nothing new. Branding had been a key to the 'library' series of John Bell and many others in the eighteenth century, but the scale of production and the insistence of the design and its promotion was unprecedented. This development underwent a further step change after the Second World War. Penguin and other paperback publishers were established before the war, but the paperback revolution most obviously occurred in the 1960s, a new era in the history of the book for which the function and form of the paperback seemed tailor-made.

Books had proved themselves a highly adaptable commodity that prospered in the booming market conditions of mass production as early as Charles Dickens and Victor Hugo, but international book publishing came late into modernity. Penguin not only produced a new kind of book, but a new kind of publishing experience. Although major firms like Longman and Macmillan developed major overseas branches and trading by 1900, it was not until after the Second World War that publishing became part of the large corporate sector and adopted the practices of publicity and marketing characteristic of monopoly capital. In many quarters, the publishing industry had long regarded itself as a business not quite like others, driven by love of books rather than love of profits. Now, that industry was transformed. The integration of publishing into larger media conglomerates began in the 1960s and continued in three stages to the early twenty-first century. Integration began with the buying of textbook publishers by companies with little or no previous experience of publishing, continued with larger media corporations buying independent trade publishers, and ended with the buying-out of competitors and, increasingly, the buying-into of the supply chains of the full-blown media corporation.

In the first phase, during the 1960s, the acquisition of textbook publishers by corporations like IBM, ITT, Westinghouse, and Xerox was prompted by an anticipation that control over content, in combination with the hardware, was strategically wise given the then-widely perceived market potential of teaching and education. Computers and photocopiers were the core business of these companies. Together with trade and professional books, education proved one of the most important segments of the publishing industry. Much discussion of the changing characteristics of publishing has centred on trade publishing, and mostly for its cultural rather than financial significance. Yet the impact and importance of professional and educational publishing can hardly be discounted in an era where globalization is increasingly about the access and control of information and knowledge.

The second wave of corporate inroads into publishing occurred when corporations such as CBS and Gulf and Western began to purchase trade publishing houses in the 1960s. The story of Random House—the world's largest trade-book publisher in 2020—is a good example of the buying and selling pattern typical of this consolidation. Bought by RCA for $40 million in 1966, Random House had already purchased Knopf in 1960 and Pantheon in 1961. Sold to the Newhouse group (Advance Publications) in 1980, the group in turn traded Random House to the German company Bertelsmann for $1.4 billion in 1998. By 2015, Penguin Random House acted as the corporate umbrella for over a hundred publishing houses in nineteen countries, owning imprints such as Knopf, but also Ballantine Books and

Bantam Dell in the United States, Plaza and Janes in Spain, and Goldman in Germany.

The third stage of the transformation of modern publishing was in many respects a consolidation of stage two, in that the further developments operated in a distinctly transnational media market. Publishing left behind its traditional family-run businesses and became integrated into transnational media conglomerates, conglomerates that look very much like a Russian *Babushka* doll.

These developments, sometimes labelled as 'conglomerization', give us, nevertheless, only one side of the story of publishing under globalization. Even if a corporation like Random House consists of publishers in many countries, its acquisitions retained a certain Anglo-American slant. In addition, the publishing landscape continued to comprise many independent, small publishers, who actually promoted and built authorships in a tradition associated with the logic of a different kind of book market. Nonetheless, conglomerization denotes a structural realignment in the way publishing as a business was conducted and represents the emergence of a new kind of book economy. For instance, the literary agent knew how to negotiate and promote the deals that some authors now expected. The subsidiary-rights race that began in the wake of a truly successful book started with paperback publishing, but soon branched out into major licensing deals. Other, less public developments impacting on the book industry were breakthroughs represented by standardization and computerization. The increasing presence of technology paved the way for inventory control and the standardization of information such as the International Standard Book Number (ISBN) of 1970. The book was and is increasingly labelled and tracked by new gadgets of surveillance.

Thus trade publishing during the 1960s transitioned from its well-established identity as an independent business to a segment of larger media corporations, but at the same time independent bookshops faced similar challenges from the consolidation of giant book chains. Already in 1941, Barnes & Noble had designed their flagship store on 105 Fifth Avenue in New York, influenced by the logic of supermarket sales. They used the retail space in a way that facilitated customer traffic through the store. Again, business strategies were largely driven by the influx of students and the booming educational textbook

market. Such changes in the space of bookshops were visible in the
United States by the Second World War; things would change later in
Europe. Experiences from a Stockholm bookshop during the 1960s
speak of a different world. The shop was predominantly staffed by
men who were required to wear suits to work. Books were stacked
behind counters or simply shelved so high that customers were unable
to reach them. This was bookselling as cordoned-off expertise, not as
something best left to the independent perusal of consumers.

Three decades later, the tension between the temple bookshop and
the supermarket bookshop had become familiar enough to merit a
film of its own. In an adaptation of Ernst Lubitsch's 1940 classic *The
Shop Around the Corner*, a 1998 film, *You've Got Mail*, recast the original
love story as one between the owner of a small and financially
challenged children's bookshop and the owner of monolith megastore.
The film suggested that the demise of the small bookshop was
as inevitable as the changing dating behaviour brought about by
e-mail and chat rooms.

For all these changes in publishing and bookselling during the
1960s, the book endured. But it would soon find itself challenged by
the success of a somewhat unexpected technology: the photocopier. It
might seem counterintuitive to think of the photocopier as a technology that fundamentally transformed the conditions of the book, and
yet that is exactly what the machine of a particular company—
Xerox—did. The arrival of the photocopier opened up a market
that nobody knew existed, and the surging demand for copies took
everybody by surprise. Copyright lawyers were especially surprised.
The copier opened up endless opportunities for the dissemination of
information, and in ways that were to be intimately associated with
the history of the book.

The highly successful television commercials that Xerox launched
under the concept of 'Brother Dominic', were telling examples of how
the copier was marketed by drawing on a very long history. The
commercials featured a monk—Brother Dominic—who, when Father
Superior wants him to produce 500 more sets of the manuscript he has
been toiling with, has an epiphany, exits through a heavy wooden
door, and arrives in a corporate office equipped with a Xerox 9200.
His prayers are answered (and not for the first time, it seems), when
Brother Dominic returns with his 500 perfect sets. Father Superior

looks to the sky and utters, 'it's a miracle!'. These prize-winning commercials showed how texts—from the meticulous copying by monks to the modern information society—depended on reproduction. Indeed, it was one of the long-standing selling points for Xerox that their machines made copies 'as good as originals'. Today, it is impossible to distinguish digital copies from the original. Copies are virtually one and the same. In the analogue era, however, such an idea was something new, and the point was driven home by using books as an example of what could and should be copied.

In 1966, at the peak of Xerox's success, Marshall McLuhan stated that xerography represented the most startling and upsetting electrical innovation to date. In his discursive style he went on to describe why what he later called 'every man's brain-picker' posed such a tremendous challenge to the status quo. He claimed that this technology destabilized both authorship and readership, and suggested that a revolution had taken place in the old Gutenberg sphere when anyone could take a book apart and make a new one.

McLuhan was obviously concerned about the arrival of xerography and the copier because he expressly singled them out, but he was even more focused on the consequences of this new technology, especially as it related to print culture and authorship. He was not the first to worry. In 1935, the same year as Penguin was launched, Walter Benjamin famously questioned the modern machine's ability to strip the work of art of its aura. Just as Marshall McLuhan discussed the upheaval of tradition, so did Benjamin predict that the mass market and commodity capitalism would sever the ties between the author and the public, mapping out a new territory in which the reader was about to turn into writer at any moment. By extension, this also meant a dramatic revolution in the ordering of intellectual property, as copyright law really had not foreseen nor accommodated the possibility of the photocopier. Both McLuhan and Benjamin used the machine to suggest that such a reversal of roles was imminent; Xerox relied on commercials and print advertisements to illustrate the outcome of their prophecies. Thanks to a machine that instantaneously reproduced texts, *anyone* could become author and publisher by bypassing the traditional functions of print culture. The copier and its new users colluded to demystify and to question the roles previously assigned to producer, distributor, and consumer in a 'print culture'. In addition, these roles had, until the 1960s, mostly been occupied by men.

The photocopier operates as a printing press of sorts, but it is still a far cry from actually producing new *books*. In fact, the function of the copier is precisely the reverse: it negates the book and offers a perfect description of both a material and an immaterial transformation. You need only to visualize the process. Place a book or a journal under the lid of a copier and press a button. The light turns on inside the machine and a few seconds later something comes out not remotely resembling what was originally placed there. Smudged and unintelligible at times, the photocopied pages containing the information you need can be, and often are, too dark or too light—with insufficient or too much enlargement or reduction. The copied pages might be screwed up, having been released from a jam in the machine, or they are simply not forthcoming at all because the machine is broken. The copier is the perfect machine for its time and challenged the established book order because it emphasized not form but content. It also placed authorial power in the hands of the person using the machine. The photocopier was not only a new technology that offered the possibility of new authors and new books, but it was a technology that was to affect certain institutions more than others. In libraries, corporate research units, and universities, the copier responded to and helped accelerate an upsurge in information, education, and knowledge as both political and monetary resources. For the law, however, the photocopier was an unknown. And as the photocopier became part of the corporate, educational, and public landscape it was also a lawsuit about to happen. When it finally did, research and education were primarily implicated, once again demonstrating how intimately aligned these domains were with the increased dissemination of books. Much of this dissemination concerned textbooks for the so-called 'developing world', and, again, the photocopier was to play an important part in a further aspect of the globalization of the book in the 1960s: decolonization.

UNESCO and Decolonization

Immediately after the Second World War, the stage was set for international cultural collaboration with the founding of a host of organizations devoted to the international management of culture and education. Among the most important and controversial of these organizations was the United Nations Educational, Scientific, and Cultural Organization (UNESCO), an organization that has played an important role in trying to redress what in copyright terms was a post-war split between two entirely separate and independent parts of the world. The two superpowers of the approaching Cold War—the United States and the Soviet Union—did not adhere to the Berne Union. Many years after the 1886 *Puck* caricature of the American Pirate Publisher, a number of formalities and legal differences still stood in the way of the accession by the United States to the European-dominated Berne Convention.

Alongside the consistent defeat of pro-international copyright supporters in the United States Congress, it was not until after the Second World War that the stalemate would cease, when the United States once and for all moved from being an importer to becoming a prominent exporter of cultural works. UNESCO anchored its copyright policy in the Declaration on Human Rights from 1948, observing how copyright functioned as a barrier to the free flow of culture among all the peoples of the world. In the next few years, UNESCO instigated a number of copyright initiatives, culminating in the 1952 Universal Copyright Convention. It was a Convention to which both the United States and the Soviet Union *were* signatories.

The first Berne diplomatic conference after the Second World War, convened in Brussels in 1948, agreed that Stockholm and Sweden—a country unscathed after the war—would host the next revision conference in 1967. By 1948, the Convention had reached seventy years and had survived numerous challenges. Following the initial controversies over translation was work to accommodate the legal conundrum of new technologies, and the negotiating hiatus brought on by the two World Wars. In the 1960s, however, the international copyright community was about to meet one of its most serious challenges: decolonization. Over the decade, new technologies really began to destabilize and challenge the book, and the practices of publishing and bookselling undeniably began to follow the logic of the market. But it was also a time when the world of the book began to expand as a result of a large number of countries gaining political independence from former colonial powers. In this respect, the Berne Convention was a particularly contentious site for the conflicts that emerged when the old book world order contended with a new, decolonized world map. The control that copyright afforded moved to the fore in the international agenda.

During the 1960s, newly independent states sought to replace colonial legal regimes with new laws that were sensitive to the new circumstances and flexible in relation to an embryonic knowledge economy. Although barriers that frustrated the influx of culture and science were barely appreciated, copyright controls could encourage local production of culture and knowledge. This tension reverberated into the substratum of the Berne Union, and came to a head with the so-called colonial clause, which had extended the reach of the Convention by incorporating by proxy the dominions and colonies of the original European signatories. Following decolonization, newly independent states had to affirm (or alternatively denounce) their loyalty to the Union by declarations of 'continued adherence'. Several meetings with African nations in the early 1960s voiced concerns over the injustices of the copyright system. The meetings concluded that international copyright conventions were deeply unfair and benefited only exporting nations.

Such conflicts surfaced during the Stockholm revision conference in 1967, which was poised to deal with the repercussions of this new geopolitical landscape. Remembered as one of the most controversial conferences in copyright history, it turned on one main point: what sort of concessions could be made for developing countries in terms of copyright? Developing nations argued that they failed to see why they should comply with levels of protection that hindered, rather than facilitated, development. Developed nations were disinclined to give exceptions that they argued would damage their publishing industry and authors. Furthermore, pro-copyright developed nations encouraged developing nations to consider the well-being of their own national authors given how minimal was their protection. The pro-copyright advocates argued that while lower copyright levels would clearly harm foreign authors, they would more greatly injure ambitions to foster authorship in developing nations. Such an argument deflected the copyright question away from access and reading and towards investment and incentives, predicated on the universal plight of authors. If authors were disenfranchised in developed nations, how could the disenfranchising of authors in developing nations be the answer to the copyright problem?

This argument was matched by a similar debate about publishing. Supporting and building a national publishing industry was a cornerstone of the pro-copyright lobby, and commentators regarded a failure to protect copyright as a direct threat to the promotion of a local publishing industry serving growing educational needs. Yet, the statistics and experiences from the African market were discouraging. Post-independence African publishing houses were often small and heavily state-subsidized, and more to the point, dependent on an infrastructure set in place during colonial rule. British presence was not diminished but rather reinforced by the setting up of joint ventures that provided know-how and training while offsetting some of the local costs. Colonial presence and dependency was thereby retained largely intact. Even *The Times* worried that the best markets of British publishers included nations that were likely to take advantage of the Protocol and the 'legalized piracy' it afforded in the educational sector. Given the additional and destabilizing potential of the photo-copier, support for use-rights of copyrighted works for educational purposes became particularly contentious.

Controlling knowledge was big business already in the mid-1960s. With educational publishing a profitable sector, British publishers had invested heavily in markets now becoming independent. What took place in Stockholm threatened to undermine an industry that paid lip-service to the necessity of indigenous publishing and authorship. At the same time, British publishers were highly reluctant to abandon a possibly lucrative future market in which they already had secured a foothold. Book production in Africa certainly appeared negligible and even on the verge of non-existence. African book output averaged at six titles per million inhabitants and only twenty of the then thirty-four African countries produced books at all. This represented a per capita estimation of one-thirtieth of one book per person, per year. For all its insignificance in monetary terms, Africa remained an important textual territory.

One particular dimension of the Stockholm Conference was how it framed—explicitly and implicitly—books within a familiar triangulation of aid, hunger, and food. Participants spoke of 'book hunger' and 'book famine'. Not texts, not readers, but *books* were in short supply.

Perhaps this framing was a counterreaction to the fact that texts now circulated quite easily independently of the book, in part because of machines such as photocopiers. Because, as McLuhan noted, books could be taken apart and the copier could facilitate new combinations of ideas as well as their dissemination, even if in a less attractive format. The subtext of the scarcity problem led to an almost fetishistic preoccupation with the book rather than with the inaccessibility of content or the dangers of illiteracy. To name and measure the great divide between the haves and the have-nots as one of abundance versus shortage corrobo-rated the standard narrative of flows of knowledge from a source in metropolitan centres outwards to the peripheries of the colonies.

History has come down hard on the Stockholm Conference: defective, objectionable, a complete failure. Nobody seemed happy with what the resulting Stockholm Act and Protocol was to mean for developing nations. For the first time, the Union had become politicized, and its continued survival was uncertain. British pro-copyright proponents talked about Berne as a copyright club and insisted that if you wanted to join then you had to play by the rules. Framing international collaboration as dependent on a shared spirit of sportsmanship was far from how African states interpreted the situation. For them, Berne membership was reserved for the wealthy and initiated. The question now was what rules the club was supposed to set for the future and who would be allowed to join it. More importantly still, was there to be a 'club' at all?

Global Books and Readers

To capture the many facets of globalization and the book is a daunting task. Several major trajectories supported the overall premise that the book from 1886 to the present has been and will continue to be crucially implicated in so-called 'globalization', not least as a commodity circulating in a global trade system. First- and second-wave globalization have several key changes in common. The Berne Convention operated as a critical node in this undertaking because it encompasses so many of the conflicts that have earmarked this history in a decidedly international and later global arena.

Translation has always been essential to the international flows of books. From the very beginning, translation called into question the nature and stability of texts. Translation set in motion a contradictory and ongoing expansion of authorship. Translators, editors, and indexers are now authors, and because they are, they help destabilize the traditional view of authorship and the fixity of the work. At the same time, they expand the scope of what copyright protects, which creates as many problems as it solves. Highlighting the interdependency between old and new works, translation was a contentious issue at the first diplomatic conferences leading up to the Berne Convention in 1886 and remains one of the contentious issues in the present framework of copyright and digitization. Two current cases of appropriation, an activity with a long and illustrious history, are 'mashing up', or the taking of digital media files of text, images, and audio from preexisting sources in order to create a new derivative work, and 'sampling', or the taking of a sample of a sound recording and reusing it as an instrument or sound. Borrowing, adapting, abridging, translating, appropriating, and even copying—these transformative practices are historically, linguistically, and legally situated. The book is as affected by these changes as other media forms are. But to think of digital works as inherently unstable and the book as somehow always stable is a misconception. The codex is still with us, but we have grown accustomed to discussions on its imminent death because of the proliferation of devices that carry the book and remove it as a material object at the same time. The fact that we seem to have a certain difficulty separating *reading* from *the book* is certainly a current dilemma, but the same question was present during the discussions in Stockholm in 1967.

Indeed, the 1960s has in many ways been a key period in the globalization processes described in this chapter. One aspect of 'West meets the Rest' was the international copyright system. Conflicting interests and intense negotiations in Stockholm 1967 did not cause the undoing of the Convention. On the contrary, the Berne Convention went on to prosper, in part by abolishing itself. One of the concrete outcomes from the Stockholm Conference was the decision to dissolve the administrative framework of the Berne Convention in existence since 1886 and construct a new one. In 1970, the World Intellectual Property Organization (WIPO) was born, and a year later the Convention revised once more in Paris. The dust had settled, and a new era in the history of the Berne Convention began.

Yet, for all its current importance in the global economy, the concept of 'international copyright' remains something of an oxymoron. Copyright was and still is national law. Copyright was and still is a powerful instrument in the hands of nation-states. Despite all these caveats, international copyright exists, and by and large is associated with the Berne Convention. At the end of the nineteenth century, a European diplomatic and aristocratic elite articulated the concerns of vested stakeholders like authors and publishers. In 1967, fifty-seven states and more than 400 non-governmental organizations (NGOs) were present in Stockholm to try and expand and update the Convention so that newly decolonized nations would be able to join the Union. At the time of writing, 2018, 184 member nations and over 250 NGOs burn the midnight oil debating the minutiae of intellectual property rights at WIPO negotiations in Geneva. In fact, as the numbers show, the presence of civil society in these global arenas has only accelerated and the nation-state is no longer the most obvious negotiating partner. An amorphous consumer base, mobilized around shared interests that cut across borders, has shifted the stakeholder perspective and makes it less dependent on the perimeters of the nation-state. While French interests and the French language led the nineteenth-century movement towards Berne, the present trade-based intellectual property regime appears substantially driven by US interests and speaks English.

At a geopolitical level, tensions between centre and periphery, between importers and exporters, and between users and producers were present in 1886 and remain central to the negotiations in WIPO to this day. Decolonization and the power-relation tensions of the 1960s in the dissemination of knowledge are important parts of the history of the book under globalization. They are also often forgotten. The merits and disadvantages of being an 'importer' as opposed to being an 'exporter' should be weighed with great care. The idea that cultural trajectories work in only one direction is refuted by strong local and regional cultural flows that cut across sweeping geopo-litical assumptions of sender and receiver. One of the more contentious discussions in Stockholm concerned the question of knowledge in relation to imports and exports. The question tended to situate developing nations as importers and therefore as recipients of a knowledge ultimately produced elsewhere. This discussion continues today in the Access to Knowledge (A2K) and Open Access movements.

The A2K movement represents in many ways a continuation of the discussion from the 1960s, albeit shifted to debates about digitization. Open Access, or the parallel movement to make research freely available on the Internet is an obvious contempo-rary disseminator of information and knowledge, but it is also a critical tool in redressing past wrongs concerning access and bridging the very real and con-tinuing digital divide. And while an organization such as UNESCO seemed ready to challenge the old copyright system in the 1960s, the situation had changed radically in 1995. That year, UNESCO named 23 April—the death date of Cervantes and Shakespeare—as the annual World Book and Copyright Day.

Another proof that the 1960s represented a watershed moment in the globalization of the book comes not only in the new shape and form of the paperback and the challenges brought on by the photo-copier's potential to make new 'books'. Standardization and mass merchandizing made the book easier to classify, track, order, and sell, all according to the principles of the supermarket. The emergence and consolidation of publishing into larger media conglomerates must be seen against the backdrop of the growth of transnational corpor-ations in all types of businesses. On the one hand, this period appears to be one in which the market for books expands and becomes truly global; on the other hand, the control and ownership of publishing through the media conglomerates become ever more concentrated. Such concentration is not only limited to publishing; it increasingly affects bookselling.

It was in 1994 that 'the world's largest bookstore' was born, a title almost exactly reproducing the claim of James Lackington in 1794, but offering a very different experience and a vastly greater dimen-sion. Twenty years later, in 2014, Amazon.com was still a bookstore, but it was primarily a giant online retailer, selling anything under the sun and branching out into French, German, Brazilian, Chinese, and Mexican platforms. It is also the producer of hardware, primar-ily the Kindle reader, which represents only one of many formats the late modern consumer can choose from as she or he decides what to read.

Readers, in fact, are hard to think of as global, but they do congregate around global publishing phenomena. Few books have been as successful as the Harry Potter titles, books that have come to epitomize the global reach of conglomerate publishing and how an adaptation industry then diversifies literary content into movies and merchandizing. But the Harry Potter books are also a typical example of how readers and fans produce new stories on the basis of characters and settings in which they feel highly invested. In some cases, such practices have been labelled piracy, in some cases they are seen as crucial narrative reworkings that operate in symbiosis with publishers. The instability of cultural works and their relationship to authors and readers, or, in a more updated terminology, 'users', is one of the baseline relationships in the history of the book, and it has changed with the arrival of the Internet and new technology. Today, the Pirate Publisher attacked by a collective of disgruntled authors is not American, but Chinese. Having signed the Berne Convention in 1992 and become a member of the WTO in 2001, China is also generally seen as the world's number one pirate country.

Digitization is an essential dimension of globalization, and it is therefore quite appropriate to end this chapter by drawing attention to the turbulence around Google Book Search, first launched by Google in 2004. What started out as a service to provide snippets of text snowballed in the next few years into a major legal controversy. Initially hailed for making available public domain books that suddenly experienced a new lease of life in digital format, vocal criticism soon ensued, and on two fronts. Authors and publishers accused Google of copyright infringement. Librarians and academics pointed out the dangers of having such massive digitization being controlled by a corporation and argued that the whole project reeked of cultural imperialism. We do not yet know what will happen to Google's digitization initiatives, but it is worth noting that what Google ended up promoting was the idea of a truly global *library*, the ultimate utopia of the digitization/globalization matrix. And that vision, of truly global access and use, is alive in many places: Europeana and the Digital Public Library of America (DPLA) are but two examples of the work cultural heritage institutions continue to do in order to digitize and globalize their collections. In a future wave of globalization, the regulation of cultural flows, the arrival of new technologies, the tensions between being an exporter and an importer of works, and the instability of categories such as author and reader will surely all continue to transform the material forms and intellectual influences of books as they travel and are deployed around the world.

14

Books Transformed

Jeffrey T. Schnapp

If by books you are to be understood as referring to our innumerable collections of paper, printed, sewed, and bound in a cover announcing the title of the work, I owe you frankly that I do not believe (and the progress of electricity and modern mechanism forbids me to believe) that Gutenberg's invention can do otherwise than sooner or later fall into desuetude as a means of current interpretation of our mental products.

> (Octave Uzanne, 'The End of Books', *Scribner's Magazine* 16 (1894): 223–4)

Because books have been many things over the course of their history, the question of their future remains an abiding feature of that history.

Printing was never a single or monolithic technology or industry. It could be employed in the service of everything from playing cards or posters designed to endure for weeks to massive tomes destined for centuries of consultation. And within the shifting universe of printed things, books have always been perceived as too available or unavailable, too controlled or uncontrolled, too large or small, too cheap or luxurious. This pendulum of concerns, shaped by shifts in the landscape of media and communications, has informed every scenario for a bookish end game from the era of newsprint to that of the paper-like digital display technology known as e-ink. The book has ended time and again. On every such occasion the book has given birth to new kinds of books.

In the case of the bibliophile Uzanne, a prodigious innovator in the design of contemporary editions as unified art works, the event that prompted his ruminations on the end of the book was a visit to

Thomas Edison's laboratory in Orange Park, New Jersey. There Uzanne encountered a wide array of tools and technologies wedding electricity to what he called 'modern mechanism', from phonograph cylinders to the kinetograph. The visit opened up Uzanne's eyes to a future when, just as 'the elevator has done away with the toilsome climbing of stairs; phonography will probably be the destruction of printing': authors will become recording artists, tomes will become registering cylinders 'as light as celluloid penholders', libraries will become 'phonostereoteks', and readers will be transformed into listeners carrying their 'pocket phono-operagraphs' with them on hikes in the canyons of Colorado ('The End of Books', p. 224). Notably, Uzanne, a prolific writer on bibliography and the book trade, edited and published the Paris review *Le Livre moderne; Revue du monde littéraire et des bibliophiles contemporains*, founded in 1890 and dedicated to the analysis of contempo-rary trends in the publishing industry.

Like most such entries into the fool's game of media prophecy, Uzanne's is both prescient—he forecasts the advent of radio, television, and mobile media devices—and blinkered—within decades registering cylinders would be gone. But his musings on the disruptive powers of 'electricity and modern mechanism' are indicative of shifting perceptions of print over the course of the twentieth and twenty-first centuries, as paper pages become increasingly entangled with screen pages (and vice versa).

At the turn of the twentieth century, daily newspapers and the periodical press seemed to be both eclipsing and infecting books. Instead of periodicals being understood as a medium for the stable long-term storage of vetted information, retrieved within the serene and sober confines of a library or study, print seemed to be evolving into something akin to a 'live' medium whose value was measured on the basis of informational freshness and immediate impact, designed to be consumed distractedly and on the move in public places. The signs of the new fast-paced culture of print were many: the widespread use of telegraphy for the transmission of news stories; the proliferation of cheap, industrially produced publication series for semi-literate readers; a growth in short, compressed forms of communication; the advance of vignettes and cartooning as well as advertising; and the emergence of publishing channels devoted to sensationalist scandal, crime, and disaster shouted out in the form of banner headlines.

Jeffrey T. Schnapp

To some, it seemed as if the codex itself was about to explode into an ever more volatile and vulgar cloud of information.

How then did critics address this crisis of the industrial-age book? Two responses, distinct but intertwined, arise around the turn of the twentieth century that shape the subsequent history of what are referred to here as 'books transformed'.

The first response was articulated by the French symbolist poet Stéphane Mallarmé in his 1896 essay 'Le livre, instrument spirituel' ('The Book, A Spiritual Instrument') and informed a century-long lineage of artists' and experimental books, reinvigorated in recent decades thanks to a budding revolt against the supremacy of screen culture as well as a sense of excitement regarding the potential for new and innovative approaches to print under digital conditions. Mallarmé summoned up the spectre of the entire universe flowing into a 'total', contemporary book: a book, material and metaphysical, in time and outside time, that transcended the revolution inaugurated by Johannes Gutenberg. Much like Uzanne's modern hand-crafted luxury volumes, Mallarmé's codicological dream implied a turn away from the industrialization of book production and the standardization of print formats. Instead, Mallarmé sought to plumb the expressive depths of the book's material condition in a forward-looking fashion: to animate the theatre of the page through the play of punctuation, spacing, and word placement and the meticulously choreographed drift of meanings and typographical arrays; also to privilege the feel and fold of quality papers, the texture of covers, the binding as physical presence as well as metaphysical metaphor. The resulting Book, conjured up in the autograph layout of his masterpiece *Un coup de dés* (but never realized during Mallarmé's lifetime), was to stand at the opposite, enduring, 'spiritual' end of the evolutionary scale from an all-too-evanescent product of the past century: the daily newspaper.

In the eyes of Mallarmé, the newspaper was as paradoxical as the e-book would become one century later—at once primitive and a harbinger of the future, at once too palpable and immaterial:

> Everything, into the present, that printing discovered under the rubric of the Press assumes an elementary form in the newspaper—the sheet itself, crudely stamped, exhibits, to the first degree, the flow of text.

No doubt, the practice, proximate or previous to the product's completion, tenders the writer advantages: posters hinged end-to-end, proofs,
invitations to improvise. Thus, the daily unfurls, rigorously, bit by bit,
before the eyes—whose eyes?—as a meaning laid out, charmed like a
popular magic show. ('Le livre, instrument spirituel', p. 34)

The magic show for the masses is none other than a *féerie populaire*: a
phantasmagoria composed of fleeting fast-paced illusions produced by
means of state-of-the-art electrified media machinery. That's the very
kind of spectacle upon which the second response to the *fin de siècle*
crisis of the book was modelled: the electric book or, as it has been
called, 'The Book of the Now'—the book that fulfils the promise of
near-instantaneity tendered by newspapers.

The democratic promise of the electric book or Book of the Now
was to be fulfilled only gradually in the course of the long transition
from page to screen, and then back again, from screen to page. In this
respect, the electric book was neither an invention of the television nor
of the Internet eras. Rather, its lineage extends back to the aspir-
ational, electrified, and avant-garde experimental books of the 1910s
and 1920s, forward through the electric information age paperbacks
of the 1960s and 1970s, the Dynabook of computer pioneer Alan Kay
and experiments with new screen-based page architectures carried out
at the Massachusetts Institute of Technology (MIT) by the Architecture
Machine Group and the Visual Language Workshop, and forward
again into today's proliferation of reading devices and web-inspired
forms and formats. At each of the stages of this century-long evolution,
there were significant shifts in the ways that books were understood,
read, performed, produced, experienced, shared, and disseminated.
There are also significant continuities.

The Italian Futurist movement, led by the poet (and Mallarmé
translator) Filippo Tommaso Marinetti, marked, on the eve of the
First World War, a key moment in the reconceptualization of the
codex as an almost live, interactive, electric medium, addressed to a
mass audience. Futurist books embraced the fairy of electricity as their
muse and modelled their poetics ('words in freedom', 'telegraphic
imagination', 'multilinear lyricism', 'typographical revolution') after
the design of the front page of Europe's dailies. Futurist books made
newsprint their paper of choice and were conceived as scripts for
live performances in settings such as rallies and mass assemblies.

They assumed the form of throwaway industrial paperbacks, as much books as they were magazines, made up of sequences of typographically active visual and verbal tableaux, statements regarding the movement, and listings of movement personnel. In literary efforts like Marinetti's 1914 war poem 'Zang Tumb Tuuum', the poem was redacted on the basis of the poet's telegraphic dispatches from the Balkan front, where he had served as a war correspondent for the Parisian daily, *Gil Blas*.

'Zang Tumb Tuuum' combines the ambitions of a tumultuous, real-time reportage delivered live from the front and a work of experimental poetry, typography, and book design that is the worthy double of Mallarmé's *Un coup de dés*.

Marinetti's call to overcome conventional models of bookishness was sharpened less than a decade later by El Lissitzky (Lazar Markovich Lissitzky), the Russian Constructivist artist and designer. In a brief 1923 manifesto entitled 'The topography of typography', El Lissitzky listed eight attributes of the future book:

1. The words on the printed surface are taken in by seeing, not by hearing.
2. One communicates meanings through the convention of words; meaning attains form through letters.
3. Economy of expression: optics not phonetics.
4. The design of the book-space, set according to the constraints of printing mechanics, must correspond to the tensions and pressures of content.
5. The design of the book-space using process blocks which issue from the new optics. The supernatural reality of the perfected eye.
6. The continuous sequence of pages: the bioscopic [cinematic] book.
7. The new book demands the new writer. Inkpot and quill pen are dead.
8. The printed surface transcends space and time. The printed surface, the infinity of books, must be transcended. THE ELECTRO-LIBRARY (*Merz* 4 (July 1923), p. 47)

El Lissitzky, who described himself as a 'book builder' rather than a 'book designer', underscored the crafting of books as *visual* artefacts. But as revealed by his design work on Vladimir Mayakovsky's *Dlya Golosa* (*For The Voice*) during the very same year, the Constructivist electro-library, like its Italian Futurist predecessor, proved a hybrid space: at once architectural, made up of 'process blocks' (or graphical building blocks), and a score always on the verge of being vocalized by a poet-orator.

El Lissitzky's page layouts were made entirely out of materials from the compositor's type-case. Two-colour printing was employed throughout, with frequent recourse to overlays, orthogonal compositions, and pages engaged in a visual dialogue across the gutter. A thumb index built around mini-icons (akin to the so-called 'favicons' used in contemporary web design for the bookmarking of websites) grants accelerated access to the poems for purposes of staging and declamation. As El Lissitzky described it: 'My pages stand in much the same relationship to the poems as an accompanying piano to a violin. Just as the poet unites concept and sound, I have tried to create an equivalent unity using the poem and typography'. In this important essay on 'Our Book' in 1923, El Lissitzky also argued that

> perhaps the work inside of the book is not yet at the stage of exploding the traditional book-form, but we should have learnt by now to recognize the tendency [. . .] The book is becoming the most monumental work of art; no longer is it something caressed only by the delicate hands of a few bibliophiles; on the contrary, it is already being grasped by hundreds of thousands of poor people.
>
> (*El Lissitzky—Life, Letters, Texts*, ed. Sophie Lissitzky-Küppers, London 1980, pp. 359–60)

The Futurist-Constructivist electro-library's migration from page to screen was further marked by the work of the Hungarian *Bauhäusler* Laszlo Moholy-Nagy. Well acquainted with Futurist and Constructivist precedents, Moholy-Nagy was among the first to articulate a comprehensive media theory based upon the interlacing of the textual and the visual, the static and the dynamic. In seminal writings, such as his 1925 treatise *Painting Photography Film*, he argued that:

> Only quite recently has there been typographic work which uses the contrasts of typographic material [. . .] in an attempt to establish a correspondence with modern life. These efforts have, however, done little to relax the inflexibility that has hitherto existed in typographic practice. An effective loosening-up can be achieved only by the most sweeping and all-embracing use of the techniques of photography,

zincography, the electrotype, etc. The flexibility and elasticity of these techniques bring with them a new reciprocity between economy and beauty. With the development of photo-telegraphy, which enables reproductions and accurate illustrations to be made instantaneously, even philosophical works will presumably use the same means, though on a higher plane, as the present day American magazines. The form of these new typographic works will, of course, be quite different typographically, optically, and synoptically from the linear typography of today.   (trans. Janet Seligman; Cambridge, MA, 1969, p. 39)

The emphasis here on the role performed by near-instantaneous reproductions and illustrations cemented a claim already explicit in the 'continuous sequence of pages' featured in El Lissitzky's ideal 'bioscopic book'. If properly designed, it was asserted, the suite of pages that make up a contemporary codex can become the precise equivalent of the succession of visual frames that make up a film.

The equation became explicit in Moholy-Nagy's *Dynamik der Gross-stadt*, a layout experiment variously described as a 'cinematic frame of the dynamics of a big city', an 'outline for a film script', and a 'sketch for a film that is also typophotographic'. *Dynamik der Gross-stadt* first came about as the script for a film to be realized in collaboration with Carl Koch. When the film proved too costly, it evolved into a kind of *paginated movie* in which Moholy-Nagy figured less as an author, tasked with laying down words on the page, than as a director-designer, tasked with setting frame rates, sequencing cuts, juxtapositions, and crosslinks. The result was a fluid, multimedial concept of the codex, playable like the reel of a film.

As Moholy-Nagy's allusion to 'present-day American magazines' suggests, the 'loosening up' of the media contours of the page was hardly limited to the *avant-garde*. Such loosening was the shared undertaking of multiple media categories and generations of practitioners. Some of those involved were professional designers and artists, others were journeymen. Many worked in commercial printing houses; others for illustrated newspapers or reviews. Few agreed on the terminology for the new and emerging concept of the book. Moholy-Nagy coined the neologism 'typophotography' to designate the flexible, typographically inventive, photo-driven book production of the future. In 1928, Jan Tschichold opted instead for the phrase 'the new typography' with the understanding that 'we see in photography exactly the factor that distinguishes our typography from everything that went before' (*The New Typography*, trans. Ruari McLean, 1928; repr. Berkeley, CA, 1998, p. 92).

Although a wide range of labels came and went over the course of the twentieth century, the belief remained that offset lithography, photography, telegraphy, telephony, radio, moving pictures, television, video, and digital media had disrupted the printed book and created the prerequisites for a communications revolution. A gulf had opened up between the nineteenth century printed page with its standardized typographic geometries, subordination of image to text, and cognitive linearity, and contemporary life, with its simultaneity, accelerated cadences, and overabundance of distractions and sensory stimuli. The solution was to re-establish what Moholy-Nagy refers to as 'a correspondence': to bridge the gulf between literature and life through a faster, freer, more compact, and attention-grabbing mode of bookish communication, a mode better suited to the requirements of the era of popular sovereignty—an era in which the multitudes were history's masters. In short, the aim was to build a new concept of the book around a new vernacular that weaves together the visual and the verbal.

If we fast-forward to the late 1960s when, under the spell of critical works like Marshall McLuhan's *Understanding Media* (1964), a new generation of books was variously understood as 'televisual', 'cinematic', or of the 'electric information age'. The most celebrated of these books was the first of Jerome Agel's 'comprehensive contractions' of the work of a contemporary thinker carried out by the graphic designer Quentin Fiore: McLuhan's mischievously titled *The Medium is the Massage* published in 1967. Signed by McLuhan and Fiore, 'coordinated' by Agel, accompanied by *The Medium is the Massage with Marshall McLuhan*, 'the first spoken arts record you can dance to', the book's title puns on a key aphorism from *Understanding Media*: 'the medium is the message' (with message becoming massage). It was also published in a boxed/deconstructed version as an issue of *Aspen*, which described itself as 'the first three dimensional magazine' and 'an unbound magazine in a box'. Published by former *Advertising Age* editor Phyllis Johnson, the magazine appeared between 1965 and 1971.

By means of a playful Pop-flavoured mix of visual materials assembled by Fiore and verbal excerpts from McLuhan, *The Medium is the*

Massage formulates a narrative of reassurance regarding the socio-cultural upheavals of the first cybernetic age. It argues that anxiety and perplexity are understandable responses to what McLuhan called the 'allatonceness' associated with contemporary media oversaturation. Because everything is moving at such a rapid pace, he argued, models of communication and cognition, and, by extension, *books* must all undergo a process of redesign. As his co-author Fiore explained in a 1992 interview:

> In view of the great changes that were taking place, I felt that utilizing humor would be the most effective way to reach our audience. The book was intended to be *A Guide for the Perplexed*. It had to convey the spirit, the populist outcry of the time in an appropriate form. The lineality of the text in an average book wouldn't do. The medium, after all, was the message.
>
> (interviews with Quentin Fiore, http://inventorypress.com/ product/the-electric-information-age-book-supplement)

Cast in the language of television, catchy and polished like an advertisement, *The Medium is the Massage* sought to entertain while offering a process of cognitive retooling. To this end, the book demanded of its readers an active, participatory, non-linear approach to reading, based upon the forms of verbal and visual pattern recognition that McLuhan believed to be essential to survival and success in the electric information age.

As indicated by his important collage essay 'The Future of the Book', Fiore had more than a passing interest in the history of the book. A self-taught graphic designer and calligrapher, Fiore studied painting with George Grosz and Hans Hoffman, worked briefly with Moholy-Nagy at the Chicago Bauhaus, and then moved to New York, where he served as a lettering artist for Lester Beall. In subsequent years, he became engrossed in the history of manuscripts, typography, and paper-making, contributing a technical study of handmade paper to the review *Industrial Design*. To these historical interests Fiore brought a strong commitment to the field of telecommunications. He directed industrial training films for Bell Labs and collaborated on the development of a television-based facsimile system that anticipated videotext. Consequently, he was entrusted with the design of an electronically distributed newspaper.

The world of telecommunications into which Fiore was venturing in the 1960s and 1970s hosted new modes of textual and visual transmission as well as new architectures of the page. These included early imaginings of twenty-first-century laptops, tablets, and electronic reading devices, such as Alan Kay's prescient Dynabook. Born in 1968 as the KiddiComp 'teaching machine', the Dynabook (as fully formulated at Xerox Parc in 1972) was, in its founder's words, designed to:

> provide us with a better 'book,' one which is active (like the child) rather than passive. It may be something with the attention grabbing powers of TV, but controllable by the child rather than the networks. It can be like a piano: (a product of technology, yes), but one which can be a tool, a toy, a medium of expression, a source of unending pleasure and delight ... and, as with most gadgets in unenlightened hands, a terrible drudge!!
>
> ('A Personal Computer for Children of All Ages,' Aug. 1972, p. 1; http://mprove.de/diplom/gui/Kay72a.pdf)

The Dynabook was said to be 'better' because its design was shaped around insights into human cognition, psychology, and learning associated with the work of Jean Piaget, Seymour Papert, and Jerome Bruner. Although its desktop might appear crude to us today, the Dynabook sought to equal print in its typography, visual contrast ratios, and graphics. (Kay's illustrations of his experimental loadable character generator at work feature the opening of Irving Stone's *The Agony and the Ecstasy* in fonts that resemble Bodoni, Times Roman, and Lydian Cursive.) The Dynabook aspired to exceed print in its speed, flexibility, and storage capabilities. Most of all, it tendered the promise of new means of access, proliferation, and exchange on the scale of a personal, hand-held device rather than a room-sized computer. As Kay wrote in 1972:

> 'Books' can now be 'instantiated' instead of bought or checked out. One can imagine vending machines which will allow perusal of information (ranging from encyclopedias to the latest adventures of wayward women), but will prevent file abstraction until the fee has been paid. The ability to make copies easily and to 'own' one's information will probably not debilitate existing markets, just as easy xerography has enhanced publishing rather than hurting it as some predicted, and

as tapes have not damaged the LP record business but have provided a
way to organize one's own music. Most people are not interested in
acting as a source of bootlegger; rather, they like to permute and play
with what they own.

('Personal Computer for Children of all Ages', p. 6)

Permutation and play, Kay insisted, encompassed the sharing of files
across devices, collaborative learning, interaction at a distance, and
practices of social reading. Similar principles were to inform other
pioneering efforts such as Doug Engelbart's 'oN-Line System' (a
virtual collaboration platform built at the Stanford Research Institute's Augmentation Research Center) and the Hypertext Editing and
File Retrieval and Editing Systems that Andries Van Dam developed
at Brown University.

What the Dynabook envisaged on the scale of a personal device and
oN-Line conceived as a 'hyper collaborative knowledge environment
system', others imagined as room-sized environments. After all, why
not explode the codex and transform the world into an immersive
informational landscape given that even a hand-held reading device
now had the potential to store and deliver entire libraries of text,
image, and sound? And why not displace rigid conventions of pagination with a fluid, screen-based approach to information that featured
resizable 'pages', flexible data chunks, and the ability to zoom in and
out of the page? Such was the ambition of the Spatial Data Management System (SDMS), known as Dataland, developed by the Architecture Machine Group at MIT. Led by the future founder of the
MIT Media Lab, Nicholas Negroponte, Dataland comprised an array
of devices surrounding an instrumented Eames lounge chair that
allowed for the spatialized navigation of sound, visual, and tactile
interfaces. Although the media files involved include everything
from eight channel recordings to satellite maps to videodisks, the
environment was modelled after a home library on the principle
that space trumps word-based indexing. When retrieving a book,
one scans not so much titles as the relative place of a book within
the physical structure of a bookcase.

Books are just one data type within the expanded universe of media
that make up Dataland. Here, as in *The Medium is the Massage*, a switch
has been thrown. No longer the rulers of the data kingdom, books

become metaphors. They are approached with an estranged gaze, zoomed in on as if approaching an extra terrestrial landscape. As Negroponte explained in his *Spatial Data Management* of 1979:

> Our notion of perusal includes a class of 'data types' which, when addressed, prove to be unusually rich in motion, color, and sound. One of these new data types is yet an old and familiar one: the 'book'. The user zooms in on what appears from afar to be simply a rectangle. At close enough range, the color patch gains detail in the form of some horizontal black rows of 'characters' implying a printed title. Upon even yet nearer approach, the black figures give way to readable text, giving the title of the item, which is now clearly seen as implying a 'book-like' image. The user, of course, knows that the rectangle is a 'book,' having put it there in the first place. However, if he is a subscriber to a computer-network-based 'book of the month' service, and has perhaps requested or has a standing order for books, the book may be one he has yet to see, having just appeared on the Dataland surface in a certain area on the data plane serving as a 'book drop' for incoming communications which are book-like.   (p. 28)

In addition to being dropped frictionlessly onto virtual desktops, Dataland books can be illustrated with movies, animated diagrams, and sound files. They can be accompanied by written or auditory annotations and hyperlinked across media. Such affordances apart, scroll formats are eschewed with the aim of maintaining the codex's stable sense of 'knowing where you are in the material'. The Dataland book can still be 'paged through' by use of a touch pad and joystick, a striking example of attendant skeuomorphism—that is, how a derivative object retains original but no longer essential design elements, on the assumption that familiarity makes devices easier to use (despite sometimes taking up more screen space and making interfaces more difficult to learn).

As Dataland was undergoing development, Negroponte and his collaborator, long-time MIT Press design and media director, Muriel Cooper (1925–94), also began to think of the project in terms of 'books without pages'. In a paper bearing this very title presented at the July 1978 IEEE congress, Negroponte and Cooper argued that, although 'in many regards the old fashioned book remains the best random access information resource we have', the time had come to investigate 'new opportunities [which] include: personalization, sound synchronization, spatial data access'. These were among the themes that Cooper's Visible Language Workshop explored between 1973 and 1985 alongside domains such as remote digital printing, 3-D interface design, concepts of authorship encompassing making and design, visual and verbal hybridities, and the linking of static and dynamic media. Within the Visible Language Workshop, questions regarding the datalands of tomorrow were, however, rigorously grounded in work centred on printing and the (re)design of analogue books. In such ways, the experimental ideas of Mallarmé and Marinetti about the book were renewed to serve the communication needs and possibilities of the digital age.

Muriel Cooper was not a programmer, but a book designer. She was associated with works like the first MIT Press edition of *Learning From Las Vegas* by Robert Venturi, Denise Scott Brown, and Steven Izenour, remembered for its glassine wrappers, cinematic page sequences, as well as for the controversy that it stirred up. (Though now a highly prized collector's item, the authors found the design 'modish' and 'inappropriate'.) More indicative as regards Cooper's generative approach to book design is *The Bauhaus: Weimar, Dessau, Berlin, Chicago*: the expanded American edition of Hans Maria Wingler's 1962 German tome. Massive in scale ($14.1' \times 10' \times 2.5'$), encyclopaedic in scope, *The Bauhaus* is a book that aspires to become an archive, but in the expansive, playful, multimedial spirit of Dataland's information landscapes. *The Bauhaus* weaves together vast amounts of text (in Helvetica, the typeface invented in 1957 but little known in American printing until 1968), handwritten letters, printed documents, drawings, photographic sequences, galleries of portraits, and catalogues of industrial design objects and tools. Spaces are used rhythmically and type strategically to differentiate these categories of material and pace the eye. The argument zooms in on small details and zooms out for macro views of the Bauhaus as a whole, inviting readers to dip in and out midstream, to jump, to speed up and slow down the pace of page-flipping.

Cooper didn't stop there. In the 1980s and early 1990s she reworked the contents of *The Bauhaus* into an exhibition, a set of posters, even a one-minute film in which nearly 700 pages of layouts dance across the screen—each set of facing-pages equals three frames—much like the geometries of an experimental abstract film from the 1920s. The notion of the page sequence as frame sequence cemented an increasingly cinematic and televisual understanding of the codex that encouraged a wide range of interpretations in the twentieth and early twenty-first centuries. At one end of the spectrum came a long line of artist's books like Bruno Munari's 1953 *An unreadable Quadrat-print*, an early specimen of his long series of 'illegible books' (*libri illegibili*), in which page sequences operate much like animations, but animations consisting as much in the play of folds, cuts, tears, transparencies, and textures, as they do in the movement of geometrical forms. Sometimes even physical threads pierce the surface of Munari's pages in order to materialize possible pathways of 'reading'. At the other end of the spectrum stand an equally long line of documentary photo-driven books from Erskine Caldwell and Margaret Bourke-White's *You Have Seen Their Faces* (1937) through more recent hybrid analogue and digital photo-essays like Brandon Stanton, *Humans of New York* (2010): books that approach text and image as 'coequal, mutually independent, and fully collaborative'.

So it is less Cooper's continuation of the 'book as film strip' equation than her generative shuttling back and forth between page and screen that makes her such an appropriate transition figure to the contemporary scene. For, far from being locked in a battle for primacy or survival, analogue and digital book forms have been caught up in a procreative embrace at least since the 1970s, with influence flowing in *both* the analogue-to-digital and digital-to-analogue directions. Media revolutions are rarely reducible to narratives of displacement and substitution. Rather, they provoke dynamic realignments between the old and the new, a reshuffling of existing hierarchies and imitative play across media. In the process, they assign to once-dominant media narrower, more specialized roles. Earlier chapters in this volume have described many examples of this development, including scrolls enduring as juridical documents and illuminated manuscripts continuing to be produced in the sixteenth century as luxury pocket editions.

The book's passage into the digital age is no exception to this process. While a certain understanding of the industrial codex, as well as the industries that supported its production, distribution, and consumption came under ever increasing pressure as the dialogue between paper and electric books intensified in the late twentieth century, new expressions of bookishness and bookish culture began to form and flourish. In charting these expressions, it is important to underscore that, historically speaking, the changes have been rapid and began even when the digital innovations were at early stages of development. The oldest surviving digital documents date back to the 1960s. The World Wide Web (WWW) is 30 in 2019, and smartphones about half as old. E-readers reached the mass market only in the 2000s, as did the low-cost printing technologies and instant book machines that supported the growth of print-on-demand and self-published books. In short, many of the key agents of disruption in contemporary publishing are still in their infancy.

Any scan of the present universe of 'analogue' books must grapple with two factual considerations as a point of departure: first, that more books have been printed during the past decades than ever before in the history of the book and, even if current long-term growth trends in the publishing industry appear flat, the levelling in sales *preceded* the initially explosive (but now modest) growth trends in e-book sales; second, that books, strictly speaking, have not been analogue objects since the late 1960s. The digital mutations undergone by books have been masked by continuities in their external form that are mirrored in many, if not most, digital surrogates and descendants of books. Despite the transformative impact of digital tools, media, networks, and knowledge forms on nearly every aspect of contemporary society, what Negroponte and Cooper wrote in 1978 remains plausible today: that 'in many regards the old fashioned book remains the best random access information resource we have'.

Beneath the surface, however, the book's ontology has shifted. Thanks to machines like the IBM 2680 and Linotron 202, character-by-character, computer-aided phototypesetting started coming into its own in North America by the 1970s, succeeded by stand-alone, digital image-setting systems in the 1980s. Next came freestanding minicomputer and desktop publishing solutions, complete with an increasingly sophisticated array of software that included mark-up (QuarkXpress, PageMaker), standardized printer control languages including graphics capabilities (PostScript), as well as expanding libraries of both analogue-derived and digitally native typefaces and fonts. By the 1990s, specialist typesetting companies, once responsible for the bulk of tasks associated with book production, faced extinction throughout the world—displaced by in-house teams and even authors. Authors increasingly became word-processors and typesetters, as the labour of once distinctive composing and designing professionals was displaced by integral components of text-editing packages. Digital camera-ready copy became the norm, with resulting files directly shared as a ready-at-hand publishing and distribution operation. Whether physically printed, distributed in digital form for screen reading, or produced by home or on-demand printing, the resulting books were born as MARC (Machine-Readable Cataloguing) records long before they found their way onto bookshelves.

If the great majority of books continue to look and feel like their pre-digital predecessors, the same can also be said of the e-book. As already shown, the history of e-books, both experimental and conventional, extends back to the late nineteenth century. The triumph of e-books as a mass market commodity derived from e-ink devices like the Kindle (Amazon, 2007) and the Nook (Barnes and Noble, 2009), together with tablets like the Apple iPad and the distribution systems that support them. E-books have, thus far, proved the ultimate skeuomorphic device, fulfilling the Dynabook's dream of compressing an entire library into a portable device, but not its ambitions of revolutionizing the nature of reading, information retrieval, and learning. E-readers have thus done battle among themselves by striving to emulate the precise attributes of physical books: the whiteness of paper; rapid page-turning speeds; paper-like contrast ratios; features like easy bookmarking, highlighting, and note-taking; and a need for recharging so occasional that it's 'almost as simple as reading an analogue book'.

The layout conventions of the vast majority of e-books remain those of the conventional industrial-era book. The same is true of the vast libraries of e-pub documents readable in WWW libraries like Project Gutenberg, the volunteer-led digital archive of cultural works founded in 1971 to 'encourage the creation and distribution of eBooks'. Reading consists of the act of successively paging forward and backward, with position markers substituting for physical indications of location or depth. The page remains the standard informational unit, and the design conventions continue to be those of print. Experiments with sound files and interactive features found in some of the pioneering HyperCard and CD-ROM editions of the 1990s remain the

·exception. As a result, e-books became the perfect way to take a
library of bestsellers on vacation, but not graphic and photography-
intensive works such as travel guides. As the Dutch author and
inventor Haje Jan Kamps noted in 2016, the technology to do much
more is readily available: 'using platforms such as the *iBooks Author* or
Amazon's own publishing guides, there is a lot of technology and
features available to publishers—much of which is very rarely used.
And that, ladies and gentlemen, is a tiny tragedy'.

Tragedy or not, the ways in which these codex-inspired digital
artefacts circulate and are read have altered significantly over time.
Vast virtual communities of readers assemble routinely on sites such as
Goodreads.com to share opinions and suggested further readings.
Buyer ratings systems encroach upon many of the functions once
performed by critics and bestseller lists. Readers engage in hybrid
analogue–digital reading and annotation practices as when they blend
screen reading with scribbling in Moleskine notebooks. They also read
strategically, equating specific genres of textual information with
specific devices: long forms with e-readers; news and messaging with
smartphones; magazines with tablets. The contents of books migrate
back and forth across the analogue-to-digital divide, with readers
generating digital paratexts before, during, and after the act of reading. Public interpretation, annotation, and collaborative writing flourish. Digital authors become active and accessible presences, with both
local and global readerships, in ways unimaginable in the epoch of
Uzanne. The very data trails created by this buzz of readerly and
writerly activity become an integral feature of the lives of books,
hovering about them in something that might be described as a
socio-electrostatic field.

Such alterations of the compass of social reading are flanked by
developments in the design and production of books that exploit new
technology-enabled possibilities or explore the potential for convergence or divergence between analogue and digital forms of publishing. Instead of striving to replicate the familiar (in the mode of
conventional e-books and e-pubs), they seek out the novel, the polem-
ically or playfully anachronistic, the hybrid, and/or the medium-
specific whether analogue or digital.

On the analogue side of the divide, the publishing industry has
attempted to give greater material form to commodities like art books,

magnifying the glossy physicality of works like Phaidon's 16½-×12⅝-inch *Andy Warhol 'Giant' Size*. This volume weighed in at over 15 lb and comprised 600 black-and-white and 1,400 colour illustrations. A parallel urge (though with sharply divergent aims) animated the explosive growth of handmade 'fanzines', serving as protest platforms against the ubiquity of screen culture and localized bulwarks of resistance to globalization. Likewise, the popular success of annual events like the New York, Berlin, and Melbourne art book fairs dedicated to artists' books and the continuing maturation of a niche market for letterpress editions both confirm a larger trend: namely, that even as he travels the world with eyes fastened upon his cellphone, *homo digitalis* harbours longings for more encompassing sensory experiences. Books that are not mere neutral conveyors of data; books that deliver local, situated experiences of touch, smell, and sight; books that are oversize or undersize, too slick or too rough; irreducible books thrive in the digital age precisely as conventional books struggle to hold their own against other channels of information and entertainment.

On the digital side of the divide, a new generation of designers like Tokyo-based Craig Mod have long been engaged in charting the distinctive affordances, information architectures, and forms of organization that characterize born-digital textual forms. Mod's work began with a spin-off of the online magazine *Hitotoki* entitled *Hi.co*, a smartphone-based storytelling platform, that led in turn to the creation of the *Pre/Post* publishing umbrella in 2010, where he began building complex, non-linear bridges between 'books that should be made' and electronic editions designed to exploit the graphic capabilities of e-readers. Then came a period working on the Flipboard app, accompanied by writings on such topics as web typography, context-sensitive adaptive reading devices, the tablet as medium, the need to rethink the page as graphic and informational unit, the form of digital books, collaborative authorship, and the desirability of what Mod called 'post-artefactual' books. Others, like the New York designer David Reinfurt, have sought to critique the publishing industry's assembly-line methods, replacing them with the sort of inexpensive, on-demand, integrated, modular approaches embodied by *The Serving Library*: 'a cooperatively-built archive that assembles itself by publishing' and transgresses the analogue–digital boundary.

Attempts to categorize contemporary innovation and experimentation with book forms can never be exclusive. Falling between categories is Waldek Węgrzyn's *Electrobiblioteka*, a book with a built-in USB interface that translates page-turning into the turning of virtual pages on an accompanying website, thereby fulfils El Lissitzky's dream of the electro-library. The same hybridity characterizes works of experimental poetry like Amaranth Borsuk's and Brad Bouse's epistolary *Between Page and Screen*, in which the abstract geometric glyphs printed on the book's pages metamorphose into text only under the friendly gaze of the reader's webcam.

Even scholarly books have joined in the fun, like Matthew Battles's and my own *The Library Beyond the Book*: a design-driven essay about the future of libraries, complete with an accompanying card deck, whose final chapter assumes the form of a database documentary. Such productions increasingly find themselves in the company of learned works such as the Instituto Nacional de Antropología e Historia's interactive edition of the Codex Boturini, also known as the *Tira de la Peregrinación* (Pilgrimage Strip). This publication is a philologically impeccable replica of the sixteenth-century hand-drawn pictographic Mexican codex, printed on *papel amate* (paper made from the bark of the Ficus tree). The replica is accompanied by an app that allows the reader to decode the flow of pictographs without compromising the integrity of the original document.

As new waves of 'books transformed' wash up on future shores, it seems that the codes of the codex will remain supple and mutable, just as the 'phonostereoteks' and the 'pocket phono-operagraphs' of today become ever more entangled with more conventional 'collections of paper, printed, sewed, and bound in a cover announcing the title of the work'.

Abbreviations and Glossary

abjad a consonantary: a type of writing system where each symbol or glyph stands for a consonant, leaving the reader to supply the appropriate vowel

AH Anno Hegirae, or 'in the year of the Hijra', the Islamic dating of years

aljamiado Arabic script used to transcribe European languages, especially Romance languages such as Spanish, Mozarabic, Portuguese, and Ladino

ancien régime typographique typography in the age of the manual printing press

BCE Before Common Era; synonymous with BC

bestiary (or *bestiarum vocabulum*) a descriptive or anecdotal compendium or morality treatise on various kinds of animal, usually medieval; its predecessor was the Greek *Physiologus*

biblical concordance an alphabetical index of the principal words of the Bible

bibliography the history or systematic description of books, their authorship, production, printing, publication, editions, dissemination, and reception (as distinct from the common meaning of bibliography as a reference list of publications)

bibliometrics the counting and statistical presentation of book production

bifolio large, single sheet of parchment or paper folded in half to make two leaves

black letter (also known as Gothic script, Gothic minuscule, or textura), a western European script (from *c.*1150) and then type face from *c.*1450), and used to print in English into the seventeenth century (see also 'Fraktur' and 'Schwabacher')

black mouths black columns at the upper and/or lower outside edges in some pre-modern Chinese texts

blanks forms, usually printed, with spaces left for further, usually scripted, insertions and additions

book eyebrows commentaries printed in the upper margin of a page of a pre-modern Chinese text

book hand (also book-hand or bookhand) a script used especially for the copying of literature in Europe, and often contrasted to documentary hand, aimed primarily at clarity, regularity, and impersonality; more generally, any of several deliberately stylized handwriting scripts intended for legibility and often used in transcribing official documents

Book of Hours Christian devotional collection of texts, prayers, and psalms, often with decorations and images, popular from the thirteenth to the sixteenth centuries CE

book press an early European form of freestanding bookcase or chest, usually with sloping tops on which books (sometimes chained) could be read (usually while standing)

bukan Japanese; literally 'mirrors of the military': directories of *daimyō* and shogunate officials produced by commercial publishers in the Tokugawa period (1600–1868)

bulla (pl. bullae) a hollow lump of clay originally used to store accounting tokens, often sealed

Cairo Geniza (or Genizah) a collection of some 300,000 Jewish manuscript fragments, mostly in Hebrew, Arabic, and Aramaic on parchment, paper, papyrus, and cloth, found in the *geniza* or storeroom of the Ben Ezra Synagogue in Fustat or Old Cairo, Egypt

calligraphy design and execution of lettering with a brush, pen, or other instrument; beautiful writing typically on a supple support

case see 'type-case'

CE Common Era, synonymous with AD

ce a Chinese fascicle, often bound separately and roughly corresponding to a volume of a Western book

chain-lines the wide-spaced, parallel lines in the laid paper of both manuscripts and printed books; by the second century CE, Chinese moulds had thin strips of rounded bamboo laid side by side, tied by threads of flax, silk, or animal hair, and leaving the equivalent of a chain-line mark; in more modern times, chain-lines were left by the wire mesh used in paper manufacture (see also 'watermarks' and 'wire-lines')

chained book/chained library books attached to a bookcase or book press by a chain long enough for the books to be moved to be read, but preventing their removal from the library

chapbook a small pamphlet, often of twenty-four pages, containing tales, ballads, or tracts, and often sold by pedlars

chase a frame of wood or steel used to hold type in a letterpress; in addition to type, most space in the chase not occupied with type was filled with blocks of wood called furniture, which, like the type, was held in place by quoins (see 'quoin')

chrysography writing in gold, either by attaching gold leaf to letters written in glair, or gum, or by writing in powdered gold suspended in gum Arabic

codex (pl. codices) papyrus, parchment, or paper folded into a book-like object

collectanea a series of passages, remarks, and other pieces of texts, often reprints, published in a collection

colophon a brief statement containing information about the publication usually at the end of a book, in comparison to an early-page *subscriptio* (see '*subscriptio*')

composing stick a tool used to assemble individual pieces of type into words and lines, before they are then transferred to a galley, locked into a forme, and printed

compositor person who arranges type on a composing stick or keys text into a composing machine

congshu Chinese; literally 'thicket book' or collectanea (see 'collectanea'), a collection of writings in one series, often treating a single subject or representing the best of a collector's library

cuneiform literally 'wedge-shaped': describes a number of different writing systems used in the ancient Middle East, *c.*3200 BCE–100 CE, made by incising wedge-shaped characters into the surface of clay, stone or metal. Some cuneiform scripts were complex systems of syllables, ideograms, numerals, and punctuation, while others were simple alphabets

cursive penmanship creating characters joined together

daimyō Japanese military lords controlling large hereditary domains and serving as vassals to the shogun, the de facto ruler of Japan for much of the period between the twelfth and nineteenth centuries CE

deckle the removeable wooden frame or 'fence' used in manual paper-making; deckle edge paper is industrially produced paper with rough cut edges

dhāranī Sanskrit; literally 'that which holds', an incantation used as a talisman or protection against evil or as an aid to concentration

doublure the interior lining of a book cover

ears small boxes at the upper right or upper left of pages, sometimes containing titles or chapter numbers, in early Chinese texts

edition the particular form or version of a published text; the total number of copies of a book, newspaper, or other published material issued at one time

ehon Japanese illustrated book

emaki Japanese illustrated narrative hand scroll

endpapers leaves of paper at the beginning or end of a book, especially one fixed to the inside of the cover

ephemera cheap, short, and unbound publications originally expected to have only short-term usefulness or popularity; often used as a category in collections

epigraphy   the study and interpretation of ancient inscriptions on hard, non-supple surfaces

etching   traditionally the process of using strong acid or mordant to cut into the unprotected parts of a metal surface to create (incise) a design in intaglio in the metal

al-Fātiḥa   the opening chapter of the Qur'an, often recited as a prayer

fishtails   bracket-like markings at the outer edges of pages in Chinese texts

flexography   a rotary technique for relief printing on paper, fabrics, and impervious materials such as plastics, using rubber or plastic plates and fluid inks or dyes

florilegium (pl. florilegia)   literally 'a gathering of flowers': a collection or anthology of literary extracts (European, usually medieval, and often collections of extracts taken from the writings of the Christian Church Fathers arranged under alphabetical headings)

foliation   the numbering of folios (leaves) with numbers or other indicators

font   'A fount of type was a set of letters and other symbols in which each sort was supplied in approximate proportion to its frequency of use, all being of one body- [or point-] size and design' (Philip Gaskell, *A New Introduction to Bibliography* (Oxford, 1972), p. 33). In US English, 'font' has also been used to mean a set of types of the same design cast on the same body at the same time. In modern, more general—and seemingly universal—usage, 'font' means digital simulations of a set of types (or 'sorts') of the same design

forme   a body of type arranged and secured in a chase (see 'chase') for printing

fount   see 'font'

Fraktur   a calligraphic hand of the Latin alphabet and any of several derivative blackletter type faces used especially in German contexts; its forms are angular as compared to the curves of the Antiqua type faces modelled after antique Roman square capitals and Carolingian miniscule; 'Fraktur' or 'Gothic' is sometimes applied to *all* blackletter type faces (also known as *Gebrochene Schrift* or 'broken script')

frame   see 'chase'

gathering   normally, two or more leaves, sewn or otherwise joined together, made from one folded sheet (or a fraction of it) or two or more sheets 'nested' one inside another (see also 'signature'); and with variants in Islamic and Asian regions (see also 'quinion')

Gothic letter   see 'blackletter' and 'Fraktur'

grapheme   the smallest meaningful unit in a writing system

ground   the resin covering the plate on which etching is done

halftone or mezzotint   a method to obtain different tones in engravings through the use of different instruments. The lighter parts of the engraving are created by scraping and polishing down areas of the plate so that they hold less ink in printing. Also a reprographic technique simulating a continuous tone imagery by using only two colours

***hangeul* (*hangŭl*)**   the Korean alphabet, developed in the fifteenth century CE by King Sejong as a vehicle for popular moral education

hieroglyphic script   literally 'sacred writing': describes any writing system of pictographic logograms (signs that represent whole words, both semantically and visually); most often used to refer to ancient Egyptian script, but also several ancient Mesoamerican scripts including Aztec and Maya

ḥijāzī   literally 'from the Hijaz', site of the holy cities of Mecca and Medina within the region of western Arabia where the Qur'an was revealed; name used for a distinctive early Arabic script in which the verticals slant to the right

homograph   a letter sharing the same basic shape

hornbook   a leaf or page displaying the alphabet, numbers, the Lord's Prayer, and other items for basic instruction, covered with a transparent sheet of horn or mica and usually with a handle attached for easy (and often shared) reading and teaching

humanism/humanist   a European intellectual movement of the fourteenth to sixteenth centuries CE based on reviving and extending the cultural, literary, and artistic legacy and moral philosophy of classical antiquity

hypotext   an originating text serving as a source for the current text

ideogram   a character of script representing an idea or a concept rather than a particular sound in a language; some ideograms are pictographic, but others are entirely abstract

imprint   a printer's or publisher's name or names, addresses, date, and other details in a book or other publication, and in modern times, a brand name under which books are published, typically the name or trademark of a publishing house

incunable (pl. incunables) or incunabulum (pl. incunabula)   a European printed book, pamphlet, or broadside printed before the year 1501

indulgence   a means in the Western medieval and Catholic Church of reducing the punishment for sin after death; printed indulgences were among the earliest items created by moveable type

intaglio   printing techniques in which the image is incised into a surface and the incised line or sunken area holds the ink, and is therefore the direct opposite of relief printing

interleaving   the insertion of leaves, often blank ones, between the leaves of a book

italic   a cursive font based on a stylized form of humanist calligraphic handwriting; normally slanting to the right and used in modern print for emphasis or formulaic distinction (such as title names or words in different languages to the main text)

Jianben   publications from Jianyang in northern Fujian province, China, an important publishing centre from the eleventh to the mid-seventeenth century CE

jobbing   the printing of small items which are not books but forms, contracts, decrees, and the like, rapidly produced and sold to generate cash flow

justification   a line of type or piece of text in which letter- and word-spacing is adjusted so that the text is flush with both margins; in each paragraph or block of text all words in all lines are spaced so that the first word aligns with the left margin and last word with the right margin

juz' (**pl.** *ajza'*)   one of thirty parts of varying lengths into which the Qur'an is often divided

kana   syllabaries representing all the sounds of the Japanese language and used with Chinese characters to write Japanese

kaozheng   'evidential research' and usually referring to an eighteenth-century CE scholarly movement promoting exacting textual analysis of ancient Chinese texts

khipu (**or** *quipu*)   a knotted string record of the Andean Incas, the earliest known dating from the tenth century

kinetograph   an early motion-picture device, creating the illusion of movement by conveying a strip of perforated film bearing sequential images over a light source with a high-speed shutter

kokugaku   'national studies'; an eighteenth-century CE movement promoting study of classical Japanese works in reaction to the near-exclusive focus in Tokugawa scholarship on Chinese texts

kufic   literally 'from Kufa'; name applied in modern times to a block-like rectangular form of writing Arabic script used in early Islamic times

kunten   'reading marks' inserted into classical Chinese texts to aid Japanese readers, specifically by indicating how to convert the Subject-Verb-Object syntax of Chinese into the Subject-Object-Verb syntax of Japanese

laid paper   paper with a ribbed structure, usually created (laid) sheet by sheet by a vatman using a mould with a ribbed structure of wire-lines and chain-lines running perpendicular to the former; from the nineteenth century onwards, it was largely replaced by machine paper or wove paper (see 'wove paper')

letterpress   technique of relief printing using a printing press, and by which copies are produced by repeated direct impression

ligature   joined graphemes or letters in writing or typography creating a single glyph (as in æ but also, especially typographically, other conventionally joined letters, such as fl)

lithography/lithographer a relatively inexpensive process of printing based on the resistance of oil and water to mix in solution; printing is from a flat surface—a stone or metal plate—treated so as to repel the ink except where it is required for printing; invented in 1796 by German author and actor Alois Senefelder

logogram a character of script representing a whole word, rather than just a single syllable or phoneme; some logograms are pictographic but others entirely abstract

majuscule calligraphic capital, uppercase, or large letter in most alphabets, in contrast to the minuscule (below)

manga Japanese books of disconnected cartoons first appearing in the early nineteenth century CE

Masha editions texts published in Masha, a township in Jianyang, China, and notorious from the eleventh to the thirteenth century CE for shoddy production qualities and error-ridden contents

mashq literally 'extension'; in Arabic script, the horizontal elongation of a letter for visual effect

matrix the mould, usually made of copper, used to cast a letter of metal type (also known as a sort used in letterpress printing); in print-making, the matrix is whatever is used with ink to hold the image, whether a plate in etching and engraving or a woodblock in woodcut (see also 'punch')

metrology system or study of weights and measures

mezzotint see 'halftone'

minuscule calligraphic lowercase, or small letter in most alphabets

missal a Christian liturgical book containing all the instructions and texts for the celebration of Mass throughout the year

mono no aware 'sorrow at evanescence'; the melancholy awareness of the transience of things; a term used in analysis of Japanese literature and art since the eighteenth century CE

ostrakon (**pl.** *ostraka*) in an archaeological or epigraphical context, an inscribed piece of pottery, usually broken off from a vase or other earthenware vessel

palimpsest a reused manuscript or piece of writing material, often parchment, on which the original writing has been effaced to make room for later writing; the original writing can be read through traces that remain or by the application of special lighting

paratext images and textual elements which surround, or are secondary to, the main body of a published work and are created by authors, editors, printers, and publishers, such as title pages, subtitles, tables of contents, notes, bound-in advertisements, indexes, covers, and the like

parchment   writing material made from specially prepared untanned skins of animals, primarily sheep, calves, and goats (see also 'vellum')

periodical   a magazine, newspaper, review, or digest published at regular intervals

petroglyph   images created by many peoples worldwide by removing part of a rock surface by incising, picking, carving, or abrading, as a form of rock art

phonography   the use of devices for the mechanical recording and reproduction of sound

phonostereoteks   idealized cylinders of recorded sound containing all human knowledge to be stored in libraries and reminiscent of ancient scrolls in ancient libraries

phono-operagraphs   early twentieth-century anticipated mobile receptacles of recorded sound to instruct and entertain

pictogram/pictography   a character of script that represents a word or idea through visual similarity to that word or idea

polyglots/Polyglot Bibles   books that contain side-by-side versions of the same text in several different languages; Polyglot Bibles present parallel texts in Hebrew, Greek, Latin, and other ancient languages

pouncing   a Western medieval method of reproducing images by poking holes along the edge of the original and transferring the outline onto a blank space by sprinkling coloured dust through the holes

print run   the number of copies of a book, magazine, and other publications printed at one time

printer's device   the mark, emblem, or insignia used as a trademark by early printers from the fifteenth century CE

psalter   a copy of the biblical Psalms, especially for liturgical use

punch   the hard metal base in which letters were carved to produce pieces of letterpress type of the same shape when cast in a mould or matrix (see 'matrix')

quaternion   quire composed of four bifolios; standard for Greek and Latin manuscripts

quinion   quire composed of five bifolios; the most common form of codex in the Islamic lands

quire   four sheets of papyrus, paper, or parchment folded to form eight leaves, notably in medieval manuscripts; but generally, any collection of leaves one within another in a codex; and can also refer to twenty-five (and earlier, twenty-four) sheets of paper that comprises one twentieth of a ream (see also 'quaternion' and 'quinion')

quoin   a wedge or expanding mechanical device used for locking a letterpress forme into a chase (see 'chase')

Rangaku Japanese; literally; 'Dutch learning' the body of knowledge, particularly of Western medicine and technology, developed by Japanese scholars through their contacts with Dutch merchants and texts in the late eighteenth and nineteenth centuries CE

relief printing printing from raised images, as in letterpress and flexography (and therefore the opposite of intaglio; see 'intaglio')

Republic of Letters (or *respublica literaria*) a common expression for the Western intellectual community from the sixteenth century onwards; communicating by manuscript letters and printed matter

rubrication/rubricator the addition of written text, headings, lines, or initial characters usually in red ink; the person who specialized in making such additions in a manuscript or early printed book

Sagabon Japanese; literally 'books from Saga' used between the late sixteenth and early seventeenth centuries CE to describe high-end works, with colour illustrations, published by a wealthy merchant in the Saga area of Kyoto; wooden moveable type was used to produce text in *kana*

scholasticism the system of theology and philosophy taught in medieval European universities, based on Aristotelian logic and the writings of the early Christian Fathers

Schwabacher a specific blackletter type face derived from Gothic textura

scriptio continua script in which words were written without spaces between them—typical of much ancient writing in Greek and Latin

scriptorium (pl. scriptoria or scriptoriums) the shared practices or physical site of the copying, writing, or illuminating of manuscripts and records, within a community, usually monastic

Shāhnāma 'Book of Kings'; the Persian national epic compiled by the author Firdawsi in the early eleventh century CE and recounting the mythical history of Iran from creation to the coming of Islam; the most popular text in the Persian-speaking world

shangtu xiawen Chinese; literally 'picture above, text below'; a page format with illustration on the top third of the leaf and text below

shunga Japanese; literally 'spring pictures'; erotic prints or paintings

shupeng Chinese; a portable Chinese book rack used by book pedlars to display their wares in market towns and villages

signature/signature mark an alpha-numeric indicator for the bookbinder of a gathering (see 'gathering') or pairs of conjugate leaves to identify its or their place in a sequence of gatherings; a 'signature' can also more generally refer to a group of printed or part-printed pages from a single sheet of paper that once folded, trimmed, bound, and cut, become a specific number of pages depending on the page size and the size of the press sheet

skeuomorphism the mimicking by a software object of its real world counterpart, such as the digital 'page'; a skeuomorph is a derivative object that retains ornamental design cues

stereotyping printing from a solid plate of type-metal cast from plaster

stylus (pl. styli or styluses) a writing tool for marking on parchment or paper or incising clay and wax (etc.)

subscriptio an inscription usually at the beginning of a manuscript book, indicating the place and/or the date of making the book and/or the name of a scribe or of a person who ordered the book

sura a chapter of the Qur'an

sutra a traditional religious and ethical instructional text particularly in Hinduism, Buddhism, and Jainism; in Hinduism, sutras are a distinctive compilation of short aphoristic statements; in Buddhism, sutras, also known as *suttas*, are canonical scriptures (see 'Tripitaka'), many accepted as the oral teachings of Gautama Buddha; in Pali, *sutta* refers only to the scriptures of the early Pali canon

tranche files extra chain-lines resulting from wires in the paper mould close to and parallel to both shorter deckle edges used to reinforce the structure during paper-making; see also 'deckle'

Tripitaka Sanskrit; literally 'Three Baskets'; the Buddhist canon, consisting of the sutras or the teachings of the Buddha, the rules of the monastic order, and philosophical discourses on Buddhist teachings

type a piece of metal (usually) used in letterpress printing, with a raised letter or character on its upper surface; also known as a 'sort' (see also 'font')

type-case a multi-compartmentalized wooden box used to sort and store the many different pieces of moveable type used in letterpress printing

typophotography a neologism of the early twentieth century for a flexible and typographically inventive, photo-driven book production in the future

ukiyoe Japanese; literally 'pictures of the floating world'; a genre of popular woodblock prints (and some paintings) produced between the seventeenth and nineteenth centuries CE and depicting life in the pleasure quarters, beautiful women, *kabuki* actors, as well as famous tourist sites, fauna, and flora

vellum often referring to a quality parchment made from the skins of young animals such as lambs and young calves and where the surface is particularly smooth and thin, but sometimes used more generally for parchment as a writing surface

vernacular the language spoken as a mother tongue rather than as a learned or imposed second language; the 'mother tongue' also originally meaning the language spoken by illiterates in a domestic setting

watermarks faint designs, typically identifying the makers and general dates of manufacture, made in some paper during its manufacture and which is often only visible when held against the light (see also 'chain-lines' and 'wire-lines')

weiqi 'Chinese chess', a strategy board game for two players

wire-lines in hand-laid paper, lines set a millimetre or less apart, running parallel to the longer edge of the paper mould (see also 'chain-lines' and 'watermarks')

wove paper paper with a uniform surface and not ribbed or watermarked, for which the paper-making mould's wires run parallel to each other; first produced *c.* 1747

xylography printing from woodblocks, a technology developed in China in the seventh or eighth century CE and eventually employed throughout East Asia; a text or illustration is cut in relief on a prepared wooden block, the block is inked, and a sheet of paper laid and gently pressed over it

Further Reading

Chapter 1

Alexander Bevilacqua, *The Republic of Arabic Letters: Islam and the European Enlightenment*. Cambridge, MA, 2018.

Cynthia Brokaw and Kai-wing Chow (eds), *Printing and Book Culture in Late Imperial China*. Berkeley, CA, 2005.

Robert Darnton, 'What is the History of Books?' *Daedalus*, 111 (Summer, 1982): 65–83.

Caroline Davis and David Johnson (eds), *The Book in Africa: Critical Debates*. Basingstoke and New York, 2015.

Elizabeth Eisenstein, *The Printing Press as an Agent of Change: Communications and Cultural Transformations in Early-Modern Europe* 2 vols. Cambridge, 1979; and *The Printing Revolution in Early Modern Europe* 2nd edn, Cambridge, 2005.

Elizabeth Eisenstein, *Divine Art, Infernal Machine: The Reception of Printing in the West from First Impressions to the Sense of an Ending*. Philadelphia, 2011.

Lucien Febvre and Henri-Jean Martin, *The Coming of the Book: The Impact of Printing 1450–1800*, trans. D. Gerard. London, 1976; originally published 1958.

Gérard Genette, *Paratexts: Thresholds of Interpretation*, trans. Jane E. Lewin. Cambridge and New York, 1997.

Jan Loop (ed.), special issue of the *Journal of Qurʾanic Studies on The Qurʾan in Europe*. Edinburgh, 2018.

Joseph P. McDermott, *A Social History of the Chinese Book: Books and Literati Culture in Late Imperial China*. Hong Kong, 2006.

D.F. McKenzie, *Bibliography and the Sociology of Texts*. London, 1985.

Philip Gaskell, *New Introduction to Bibliography*. Oxford, 1972.

James Raven, *What is the History of the Book?* Cambridge, 2018.

Henry Woudhuysen and Michael Suarez (eds), *Oxford Companion to the History of the Book, 2* vols. Oxford, 2010.

Chapter 2

General and Thematic

Peter D. Damerow, 'The Origins of Writing as a Problem of Historical Epistemology', *Cuneiform Digital Library Journal* 2006:1. Online: http://cdli.ucla.edu/pubs/cdlj/2006/cdlj2006_001.html

Joshua Engelhardt (ed.), *Agency in Ancient Writing*. Boulder, CO, 2012.

Marcus Hilgert (ed.), *Understanding Material Text Cultures: A Multidisciplinary View*. Berlin, 2017. Open access online: http://degruyter.com/view/product/455268

Kathryn E. Piquette and Ruth D. Whitehouse (eds), *Writing as Material Practice: Substance, Surface and Medium*. London, 2013. Open access online: http://ubiquitypress.com/site/books/detail/7/writing-as-material-practice/

Christopher Woods (ed.), *Visible Language: Inventions of Writing in the Ancient Middle East and Beyond*. Chicago, 2010. Open access online: https://oi.uchicago.edu/sites/oi.uchicago.edu/files/uploads/shared/docs/oimp32.pdf

China

Paola Demattè, 'The Origins of Chinese Writing: the Neolithic Evidence', *Cambridge Archaeological Journal* 20 (2010): 211–28 doi:10.1017/S0959774310000247.

Mark Edward Lewis, *Writing and Authority in Ancient China*. Albany, NY, 1999.

Li Feng and David Prager Branner (eds), *Writing and Literacy in Early China*. Seattle and London, 2011.

Edward L. Shaughnessy, *Rewriting Early Chinese Texts*. Albany, NY, 2006.

Tsuen-hsuin Tsien, *Written on Bamboo & Silk: the Beginnings of Chinese Books & Inscriptions*, 2nd edn. Chicago, 2004.

Tsuen-hsuin Tsien, *Collected Writings on Chinese Culture*. Hong Kong, 2011.

Wang Haicheng, *Writing and the Ancient State: China in Comparative Perspective*. Cambridge, 2014.

The Middle East and Mediterranean

Roger S. Bagnall (ed.), *The Oxford Handbook of Papyrology*. Oxford, 2009.

Thomas E. Balke and Christina Tsouparopoulou (eds), *Materiality of Writing in Early Mesopotamia* (Berlin, 2016). Open access online: http://degruyter.com/view/product/467525

Chris Eyre, *The Use of Documents in Pharaonic Egypt*. Oxford, 2013.

Wouter F.M. Henkelmann, 'Administrative Realities: The Persepolis Archives and the Archaeology of the Achaemenid Heartland', in Daniel T. Potts (ed.), *The Oxford Handbook of Iranian Archaeology*. Oxford, 2013, pp. 528–46.

George W. Houston, *Inside Roman Libraries: Book Collections and Their Management in Antiquity*. Chapel Hill, NC, 2014.

Jason König, Katerina Oikonomopoulou, and Greg Woolf (eds), *Ancient Libraries*. Cambridge, 2013.

André Lemaire, *Levantine Epigraphy and History in the Achaemenid Period* (539–332 BCE). Oxford, 2015.

Christopher Rollston, *Writing and Literacy in the World of Ancient Israel: Epigraphic Evidence from the Iron Age*. Atlanta, GA, 2010.

Pierre Tallet and Gregory Marouard, 'The Harbor of Khufu on the Red Sea Coast at Wadi al-Jarf, Egypt', *Near Eastern Archaeology* 77 (2014): 4–14.

The Americas

Elizabeth H. Boone and Walter D. Mignolo (eds), *Writing Without Words: Alternative Literacies in Mesoamerica and the Andes*. Durham, 1994.

Elizabeth H. Boone and Gary Urton (eds), *Their Way of Writing: Scripts, Signs and Pictographies in Pre-Columbian America*. Washington, DC, 2011.

Candace S. Greene and Russell Thornton (eds), *The Year the Stars Fell: Lakota Winter Counts at the Smithsonian*. Lincoln, NB, 2007.

Maarten Jansen and Laura Broekhoven (eds), *Mixtec Writing and Society: Escritura de Ñuu Dauzi*, Amsterdam, 2009. Open access online: https://openaccess.leidenuniv.nl/handle/1887/14164

Maarten Jansen and Gabina Aurora Pérez Jiménez, *The Mixtec Pictorial Manuscripts: Time, Agency and Memory in Ancient Mexico*. Leiden, 2010.

Jeffrey Quilter and Gary Urton (eds), *Narrative Threads: Accounting and Recounting in Andean Khipu*. Austin, TX, 2002.

Kathryn E. Sampeck (ed.), *Colonial Mesoamerican Literacy: Method, Form, and Consequence:* Special Issue of *Ethnohistory* 62:3 (2015).

Gary Urton, *Signs of the Inka Khipu: Binary Coding in the Andean Knotted-String Records*. Austin, TX, 2003.

Gabrielle Vail. 'The Maya Codices', *Annual Review of Anthropology* 35 (2006): 497–519.

Chapter 3

Charles Barber, *Figure and Likeness: On the Limits of Representation in Byzantine Iconoclasm*. Princeton, NJ, 2002.

Michelle Brown (ed.), *In the Beginning: Bibles to the Year 1000*. Washington, DC, 2006.

Barbara Crostini and G. Peers (eds), *A Book of Psalms from Eleventh-Century Byzantium: the Complex of Texts and Images in Psalter Vat. gr. 752, Studi e Testi*. Vatican City, 2016.

Casey Dué, *Recapturing a Homeric Legacy*. Washington, DC, 2009.

Eusebius, *Life of Constantine*, ed. and trans. A. Cameron and S.G. Hall. Oxford, 1999.

Maria Evagelatou, 'Word and Image in the Sacra Parallela (MS *Paris. gr.* 923)', *Dumbarton Oaks Papers* 62 (2008): 113–97.

Harry Y. Gamble, *Books and Readers in the Early Church: A History of Early Christian Texts*. New Haven, CT, 1995.

George Houston, *Inside Roman Libraries: Book Collections and their Management in Antiquity*. Chapel Hill, NC, 2014.

John Lowden, *The Octateuchs: A Study in Byzantine Manuscript Illustration*. University Park, PA, 1992.

John Lowden, *The Jaharis Gospel Lectionary: The Story of a Byzantine Book*. New York, 2009.

Hugo Lundhaug and Lance Jenott, *The Monastic Origins of the Nag Hammadi Codices*. Tübingen, 2015.

Roy MacCleod (ed.), *The Library of Alexandria, Centre of Learning in the Ancient World*. London and New York, 2000, repr. 2005.

M. McCormick, 'The Birth of the Codex and the Apostolic Life-Style', *Scriptorium* 39 (1985): 150–8.

Reviel Netz, William Noel, Natali Tchernetska, and Nigel Wilson (eds), *The Archimedes Palimpsest*, 2 vols. Cambridge, 2011.

Carl Nordenfalk, *Die spätantiken Kanontafeln. Kunstgeschichtliche Studien über die eusebianische Evangelien-Konkordanz in den vier ersten Jahrhunderten ihrer Geschichte.* Gothenburg, 1938.

Eva Nyström, *Containing Multitudes: Codex Upsaliensis Graecus 8 in Perspective.* Uppsala, 2009.

Lidia Perria, *Γραφίς. Per una storia della scrittura greca libraria (secoli IV a.C.—XVI d.C.).* Rome and Vatican City, 2011 (English trans. forthcoming).

I. Pérez Martin and J. Signez Codoñer (eds), *Textual Transmission in Byzantium: Between Textual Criticism and Quellenforschung.* Turnhout, 2014.

James Raven (ed.), *Lost Libraries: The Destruction of Great Book Collections since Antiquity.* Basingstoke, 2004.

I.M. Resnick, 'The Codex in Early Jewish and Christian Communities', *Journal of Religious History* 17 (1992): 1–17.

Colin H. Roberts and T.C. Skeat, *The Birth of the Codex.* Oxford, 1983.

John L. Sharpe III and Kimberly Van Kampen (eds), *The Bible as Book: The Manuscript Tradition.* London, 1998.

P.L. Tucci, 'Galen's Storeroom, Rome's Libraries, and the Fire of AD 192', *Journal of Roman Archaeology* 21 (2008): 133–49.

Kurt Weitzmann and Massimo Bernabò, *The Byzantine Octateuchs.* Princeton, NJ, 1999.

Kurt Weitzmann and George Galavaris, *The Monastery of Saint Catherine at Mount Sinai: The Illuminated Greek Manuscripts. I. From the Ninth to the Twelfth Century.* Princeton, NJ, 1990.

Websites

http://sinaipalimpsests.org/technologies

https://ancientlives.org

http://pinakes.irht.cnrs.fr

http://ngv.vic.gov.au/essay/illuminating-words/

Chapter 4

China

Cynthia Brokaw, *Commerce in Culture: The Sibao Book Trade in the Qing and Republican Periods.* Cambridge, MA, 2007.

Lucille Chia, *Printing for Profit: The Commercial Publishers of Jianyang, Fujian (11th–17th Centuries).* Cambridge, MA, 2002.

Lucille Chia, 'Of Three Mountains Street: The Commercial Publishers of Ming Nanjing', in Cynthia Brokaw and Kai-wing Chow (eds), *Printing and Book Culture in Late Imperial China.* Berkeley, CA, 2005, pp. 107–51.

Kai-wing Chow. *Publishing, Culture, and Power in Early Modern China.* Stanford, CA, 2004.

Sören Edgren. 'Southern Song Printing at Hangzhou'. *Bulletin of the Museum of Far Eastern Antiquities* 61 (1989): 1–212.

Ronald Egan, ' "To Count Grains of Sand on the Ocean Floor": Changing Perceptions of Books and Learning in Song Dynasty China', in Lucille Chia and Hilde de Weerdt (eds), *Knowledge and Text Production in an Age of Print, 900–1400*. Leiden, 2011, pp. 33–62.

Yuming He, *At Home and the World: Editing the 'Glorious Ming' in Woodblock-Printed Books of the Sixteenth and Seventeenth Centuries*. Cambridge, MA, 2013.

Robert Hegel, *Reading Illustrated Fiction in Late Imperial China*. Stanford, CA, 1998.

Philip K. Hu, *Visible Traces: Rare Books and Special Collections from the National Library of China*. New York and Beijing, 2000.

Joseph P. McDermott, *A Social History of the Chinese Book: Books and Literati Culture in Late Imperial China*. Hong Kong, 2006.

Tsuen-hsuin Tsien, *Paper and Printing*. Vol. 5, Part I: *Science and Civilisation in China*. ed. Joseph Needham. Cambridge, 1985.

Jiang Wu and Lucille Chia (eds), *Spreading Buddha's Word in East Asia: The Formation and Transformation of the Chinese Buddhist Canon*. New York, 2016.

Korea

Young Jung Ok, *Early Printings in Korea*. Seongnam, 2013.

Young Kyun Oh. *Engraving Virtue: The Printing History of a Premodern Korean Moral Primer*. Leiden, 2013.

Peter H. Lee and Wm. Theodore de Bary (eds), *Sources of Korean Tradition*. Vol. 1: *From Early Times through the Sixteenth Century*. New York, 1997.

Beth McKillop, 'The History of the Book in Korea', in Michael F. Suarez and H.R. Woudhuysen (eds), *The Oxford Companion to the Book.* 2 vols. Oxford, 2010, pp. 366–73.

Pow-key Sohn, 'Early Korean Printing', *Journal of the American Oriental Society* 79.2 (April–June 1959): 96–103.

Suyoung Sun, 'Transmitting *Haoqiu zhuan* in Eighteenth-Century Chosŏn Korea', *East Asian Publishing and Society* 3:1 (2013): 3–30.

Boudewijn Walraven, 'Reader's Etiquette, and Other Aspects of Book Culture in Chosŏn Korea' in Wilt L. Idema (ed.), *Books in Numbers: Seventy-Fifth Anniversary of the Harvard-Yenching Library Conference Papers*. Cambridge, MA, 2007, pp. 237–65.

Japan

Mary Elizabeth Berry, *Japan in Print: Information and Nation in the Early Modern Period*. Berkeley, CA, 2006.

Jack Hillier, *The Art of the Japanese Book*. 2 vols. London, 1987.

Roger S. Keyes, *Ehon: The Artist and the Book in Japan*. New York, 2006.

Peter Kornicki, *The Book in Japan: A Cultural History from the Beginnings to the Nineteenth Century*. Leiden, 1998.

Chapter 5

Bernhard Bischoff, *Manuscripts and Libraries in the Age of Charlemagne*. Cambridge, 1994.

Michael Camille, *Images on the Edge: The Margins of Medieval Art*. Cambridge MA, 1992.

Joyce Coleman, *Public Reading and the Reading Public in Late Medieval England and France*. Cambridge, 1996.

Christopher De Hamel, *A History of Illuminated Manuscripts*, 2nd edn. London, 1994.

Christopher De Hamel, *Scribes and Illuminators*. London, 1992 (reissued as *Making Medieval Manuscripts*. Oxford, 2017).

Rosamond McKitterick, *The Carolingians and the Written Word*. Cambridge, 1989.

M.B. Parkes, *Their Hands before Our Eyes: A Closer Look at Scribes*. Aldershot, 2008.

Pamela Robinson and J. Roberts (ed.), *The History of the Book in the West: 400 AD–1455*. London, 2010.

R.H. Rouse and M.A. Rouse, *Manuscripts and their Makers: Commercial Book Producers in Medieval Paris, 1200–1500*. Turnhout, 2000.

Kathryn Rudy, *Piety in Pieces: How Medieval Readers Customised their Manuscripts*. 2016: http://openbookpublishers.com/product/477/

Don Skemer, *Binding Words: Textual Amulets in the Middle Ages*. University Park, PA, 2006.

R.S. Wieck, *Time Sanctified: the Book of Hours in Medieval Art and Life*. Baltimore, MD, 1988.

Chapter 6

Guy Bechtel, *Gutenberg et l'invention de l'imprimerie. Une enquête*. Paris, 1992.

Barbara Bieńkowska and Halina Chamerska, *Books in Poland: Past and Present*. Wiesbaden, 1990.

Roger Chartier, *The Order of Books: Readers, Authors and Libraries in Europe Between the 14th and 18th Centuries*, trans. Lydia G. Cochrane. Stanford, CA, 1985.

Roger Chartier, *The Cultural Uses of Print in Early Modern France*, trans. Lydia G. Cochrane. Princeton, NJ, 1987.

Melissa Conway, *The* Diario *of the Printing Press of San Jacopo di Ripoli 1476–1484: Commentary and Transcription*. Florence, 1999.

Martine Delaveau and Yann Sordet (eds), *Édition et diffusion de l'Imitation de Jésus-Christ (1470–1800). Études et catalogue collectif*. Paris, 2011.

Elizabeth Eisenstein, *The Printing Revolution in Early Modern Europe*, 2nd edn. Cambridge, 2005.

Lucien Febvre and Henri-Jean Martin, *The Coming of the Book: The Impact of Printing 1450–1800*, trans. D. Gerard. London, 1976; originally published 1958.

Alexandra Gillespie, *Print Culture and the Medieval Author: Chaucer, Lydgate, and their Books 1473–1557*. Oxford, 2006.

Anthony Grafton, *Commerce with the Classics: Ancient Books and Renaissance Readers*. Ann Arbor, MI, 1997.

Anthony Grafton, *The Culture of Correction in Renaissance Europe*. London, 2013.

Antony Griffiths, *The Print Before Photography: An introduction to European Printmaking 1550–1820*. London, 2016.

Wytze Gerbens Hellinga, H. de la Fontaine-Verwey, and G.W. Ovink (eds), 2 vols. *Copy and Print in the Netherlands: An Atlas of Historical Bibliography*. Amsterdam, 1960–2.

R.A. Houston, *Literacy in Early Modern Europe: Culture and Education 1500–1800*, 2nd edn. Harlow, 2002.

Rémi Jimenes, *Les caractères de civilité. Typographie & calligraphie sous l'Ancien Régime. France, XVIe–XIXe siècles*. Paris, 2011.

Albert Kapr, *Johann Gutenberg: The Man and His Invention*, trans., D. Martin. Aldershot, 1996.

Jeffrey Todd Knight, *Bound to Read: Compilations, Collections, and the Making of Renaissance Literature*. Philadelphia, 2013.

David McKitterick, *Print, Manuscript and the Search for Order, 1450–1830*. Cambridge, 2003.

Ian Maclean, *Scholarship, Commerce, Religion: The Learned Book in the Age of Confession, 1560–1630*. Cambridge, MA and London, 2012.

Paul Needham, *The Printer and the Pardoner: An Unrecorded Indulgence Printed by William Caxton for the Hospital of St. Mary Rounceval, Charing Cross*. Washington, DC, 1986.

Angela Nuovo, *The Book Trade in the Italian Renaissance*, trans. Lydia G. Cochrane. Leiden and Boston, MA, 2013.

Joran Proot, 'Converging Design Paradigms: Long-Term Evolutions in the Layout of Title Pages of Latin and Vernacular Editions Published in the Southern Netherlands, 1541–1660', *Papers of the Bibliographical Society of America*, 108:3 (Sept. 2014): 269–305.

James Raven, Naomi Tadmor, and Helen Small (eds), *The Practice and Representation of Reading in England: Essays in History and Literature*. Cambridge, 1996.

James Raven, *The Business of Books: Booksellers and the English Book Trade 1450–1850*. London and New Haven, CT, 2007.

Brian Richardson, *Printing, Writers and Readers in Renaissance Italy*. Cambridge, 1999.

Margaret M. Smith, *The Title-Page: Its Early Development, 1460–1510*. London and New Castle, DE, 2000.

Hendrik D.L. Vervliet, *Sixteenth-Century Printing Types of the Low Counties*. Amsterdam, 1968.

Hendrik D.L. Vervliet, *French Renaissance Printing Types: A Conspectus.* London and New Castle, DE, 2010.

Hendrik D.L. Vervliet, *The Palaeotypography of the French Renaissance: Selected Papers on Sixteenth-Century Typefaces,* 2 vols. Leiden, 2008.

Eric White, *Editio princeps: A History of the Gutenberg Bible.* Turnhout, 2017.

Chapter 7

Luigi Balsamo, *Bibliography: History of a Tradition,* trans. A. Pettas. Berkeley, CA, 1990.

Wolfgang Behringer, 'Communications Revolutions: A Historiographical Concept', trans. Richard Deveson, *German History* 24:3 (2006): 333–74.

Ann Blair, *Too Much To Know: Managing Scholarly Information Before the Modern Age.* New Haven, CT, 2010.

Peter Burke, *A Social History of Knowledge: From Gutenberg to Diderot.* Cambridge and Malden, MA, 2000.

Liesbeth Corens, Kate Peters, and Alexandra Walsham, *The Social History of the Archive: Record-Keeping in Early Modern Europe. Past and Present Supplement* 11 (Oxford, 2016).

Hilde De Weerdt, *Information, Territory, and Networks: The Crisis and Maintenance of Empire in Song China.* Boston, MA, 2016.

James Delbourgo and Staffan Müller-Wille, 'Listmania: How Lists Can Open Up Fresh Possibilities for Research in the History of Science', *Isis* 103:4 (Dec. 2012): 710–52.

Juliet Fleming, William Sherman, and Adam Smyth (eds), a special edition of the *Journal of Medieval and Early Modern Studies* 45:3 (2015) on 'Renaissance Collage: Towards a New History of Reading'.

John-Paul A. Ghobrial, *The Whispers of Cities: Information Flows in Istanbul, London, and Paris in the Age of William Trumbull.* New York and Oxford, 2013.

George Hoffman, *Montaigne's Career.* Oxford, 1998.

Sachiko Kusukawa. *Picturing the Book of Nature: Image, Text, and Argument in Sixteenth-Century Human Anatomy and Medical Botany.* Chicago, 2012.

Michael Lackner, 'Diagrams as an Architecture by Means of Words: The *Yanji tu*' in Francesca Bray, Vera Dorofeeva-Lichtmann, and George Métailié (eds), *Graphics and Text in the Production of Technical Knowledge in China: The Warp and the Weft.* Leiden, 2007, pp. 341–77.

David McKitterick, *Print, Manuscript and the Search for Order, 1450–1830.* Cambridge, 2003.

Robin Myers, Michael Harris, and Giles Mandelbrote (eds), *Books For Sale: The Advertising and Promotion of Print since the Fifteenth Century.* New Castle, DE, and London, 2009.

Brian Ogilvie, *The Science of Describing: Natural History in Renaissance Europe.* Chicago, 2006.

Andrew Pettegree, *The Book in the Renaissance.* New Haven, CT, 2010.

Andrew Pettegree, *The Invention of News: How the World Came to Know about Itself*. New Haven, CT, 2014.

Daniel Rosenberg and Anthony Grafton, *Cartographies of Time*. Princeton, NJ, 2012.

Chad Wellmon, *Organizing Enlightenment: Info Overload and the Invention of the Modern Research University*. Baltimore, MD, 2015.

Chapter 8

General

George Atiyeh (ed.), *The Book in the Islamic World: The Written Word and Communication in the Middle East*. Albany, NY, 1995.

Sheila Blair, *Islamic Calligraphy*. Edinburgh, 2006.

Sheila Blair and Jonathan Bloom (eds), *By the Pen and What They Write: Writing in Islamic Art and Culture*. London, 2017.

Early Manuscripts of the Qurʾan

François Déroche, *The Abbasid Tradition: Qurʾans of the 8th to the 10th Centuries*. London, 1992.

François Déroche, *La transmission écrite du Coran dans les débuts de l'islam. Le Codex Parisino-petropolitanus*. Leiden, 2009.

François Déroche, *Qurʾans of the Umayyads: A First Overview*. Leiden, 2014.

François Déroche et al., *Islamic Codicology: An Introduction to the Study of Manuscripts in Arabic Script*. London, 2005.

Adam Gacek, *Arabic Manuscripts: A Vademecum for Readers*. Leiden, 2009.

Alain George, *The Rise of Islamic Calligraphy*. London, 2010.

David James, *Qurʾans and Bindings from the Chester Beatty Library*. London, 1980.

Gregor Schoeler, *The Oral and the Written in Early Islam*. London, 2006.

Gregor Schoeler, *The Genesis of Literature in Islam: From the Aural to the Read*. Edinburgh, 2009.

The Transition to Paper

Jonathan Bloom, *Paper before Print: The History and Impact of Paper in the Islamic World*. New Haven, CT, 2001.

Konrad Hirschler, *The Written Word in the Medieval Arabic Lands: A Social and Cultural History of Reading Practices*. Edinburgh, 2012.

David James, *The Master Scribes: Qurʾans of the 10th to 14th centuries AD*. London, 1992.

Ibn al-Nadim, *The Fihrist of al-Nadim*, trans. B. Dodge. New York, 1970.

David Storm Rice, *The Unique Ibn al-Bawwāb Manuscript in the Chester Beatty Library*. Dublin, 1955.

Houari Touati, *L'Armoire à sagesse. Bibliothèques et collections en Islam*. Paris, 2003.

The Illustrated Book

Martin B. Dickson and Stuart Cary Welch, *The Houghton Shahnameh*. Cambridge, MA, 1982.

Oleg Grabar and Sheila Blair, *Epic Images and Contemporary History: The Illustrations of the Great Mongol Shahnama*. Chicago and London, 1980.

Thomas W. Lentz and Glenn D. Lowry, *Timur and the Princely Vision: Persian Art and Culture in the Fifteenth Century*. Los Angeles, CA, 1989.

Marianna S. Simpson, *Sultan Ibrahim Mirza's Haft Awrang: A Princely Manuscript from Sixteenth-Century Iran*. New Haven, CT, 1997.

Eleanor Sims, *Peerless Images: Persian Painting and its Sources*. London, 2002.

Wheeler M. Thackston, 'Treatise on Calligraphic Arts: A Disquisition on Paper, Colors, Inks, and Pens by Simi of Nishapur', in Michael M. Mazzaoui and Vera B. Moreen (eds), *Intellectual Studies on Islam: Essays Written in Honor of Martin B. Dickson*. Salt Lake City, UT, 1990, pp. 219–28.

Other Forms and Formats

Oleg Akimushkin, *The St. Petersburg Muraqqa: Album of Indian and Persian Miniatures from the 16th–18th Centuries and Specimens of Persian Calligraphy of Imad al-Hasani*. Lugano, 1996.

M. Uğur Derman, *Letters in Gold: Ottoman Calligraphy from the Sakip Sabanci Collection, Istanbul*. New York, 1998.

Eva-Maria Hanebutt-Benz, Dagmar Glass, and Geoffrey Roper (eds), *Middle Eastern Languages and the Print Revolution: A Cross-Cultural Encounter*. Westhofen, 2002.

Shamil Jeppie and Souleymane Bachir Diagne (eds), *The Meanings of Timbuktu*. Cape Town, 2008.

Chapter 9

Norbert Bachleitner, *Die literarische Zensur in Österreich 1751–1848. Literaturgeschichte in Studien und Quellen*, vol. 28. Vienna, Cologne, and Weimar, 2017.

Raymond Birn, *La censure royale des livres dans la France des Lumières*. Paris, 2007.

T.C.W. Blanning, *The Culture of Power and the Power of Culture: Old Regime Europe 1660–1789*. Oxford, 2002.

Simon Burrows, *The French Book Trade in Enlightenment Europe*. London, 2018.

Pascale Casanova, 'The Invention of Literature', chap. 2 in *The World Republic of Letters*, trans. M.B. Debevoise. Cambridge, MA, 2004, pp. 45–81.

Roger Chartier, 'Urban Reading Practices', in *The Cultural Uses of Print in Early-Modern France*, trans. Lydia G. Cochrane. Princeton, NJ, 1987, pp. 183–239.

Roger Chartier, *The Cultural Origins of the French Revolution*, trans. Lydia C. Cochrane. Durham, NC, and London, 1991.

Roger Chartier and Henri-Jean Martin (eds), *Le livre triomphant 1660–1830*, vol. 2: *Histoire de l'édition française*. Paris, 1984.

Mark Curran, *The French Book Trade in Enlightenment Europe I: Selling Enlightenment.* London, 2018.

Marcus Daniel, *Scandal and Civility: Journalism and the Birth of American Democracy.* Oxford, 2009.

Robert Darnton, *The Business of Enlightenment: A Publishing History of the Encyclopédie 1775–1800.* Cambridge, MA, 1979.

Robert Darnton, *The Literary Underground of the Old Regime.* Cambridge, MA, 1982.

Robert Darnton, *The Forbidden Best-Sellers of Pre-Revolutionary France and The Corpus of Clandestine Literature in France, 1769–1789*, 2 vols. New York, 1995.

Robert Darnton, *The Devil in the Holy Water or the Art of Slander from Louis XIV to Napoleon.* Philadelphia, 2010.

Robert Darnton, 'Bourbon France: Privilege and Repression', in *Censors at Work: How States Shaped Literature.* New York, 2014, 23–86.

Elizabeth Eisenstein, *Grub Street Abroad: Aspects of the French Cosmopolitan Press from the Age of Louis XIV to the French Revolution.* Oxford, 1992.

Markman Ellis, *The Coffee-House: A Cultural History.* London, 2004.

Rolf Engelsing, 'Die neuen Leser', in *Der Bürger als Leser. Lesergeschichte in Deutschland 1500–1800.* Stuttgart, 1974, pp. 182–215.

Marie-Claude Felton, *Maîtres de leurs ouvrages. L'édition à compte d'auteur à Paris au XVIIIe siècle.* Oxford, 2014.

Jeffrey Freedman, *A Poisoned Chalice.* Princeton, 2002.

Jeffrey Freedman, *Books Without Borders in Enlightenment Europe: French Cosmopolitanism and German Literary Markets.* Philadelphia, 2012.

François Furet, 'La librarie du royaume de France au 18e siècle', in G. Bollème et al. (eds), *Livre et société dans la France du XVIIIe siècle.* Paris and The Hague, 1965, pp. 3–32.

Dena Goodman, *Becoming a Woman in the Age of Letters.* Ithaca, NY, 2009.

Brean S. Hammond, *Professional Imaginative Writing in England, 1670–1740: 'Hackney for Bread'.* Oxford, 1997.

Christine Haug, Franziska Mayer, and Winfried Schröder (eds), *Geheimliteratur und Geheimbuchhandel in Europa im 18. Jahrhundert.* Wiesbaden, 2011.

Carla Hesse, *Publishing and Cultural Politics in Revolutionary Paris.* Berkeley, CA, 1991.

Carla Hesse, *The Other Enlightenment: How French Women Became Modern.* Princeton, 2001.

Lynn Hunt, '"Torrents of Emotion": Reading Novels and Imagining Equality', in *Inventing Human Rights: A History.* New York, 2007, pp. 35–69.

Adrian Johns, 'The Piratical Enlightenment', in Clifford Siskin and William Warner (eds), *This is Enlightenment.* Chicago and London, 2010, pp. 301–22.

Helmuth Kiesel and Paul Münch, *Gesellschaft und Literatur im 18. Jahrhundert. Voraussetzungen und Entstehung des literarischen Markts in Deutschland.* Munich, 1977.

François Moureau, *La plume et le plomb. Espaces de l'imprimé et du manuscrit au siècle des Lumières.* Paris, 2006.

Jeremy Popkin, *Revolutionary News: The Press in France, 1789–1799*. Durham, NC, and London, 1990.

James Raven, 'Historical Introduction: The Novel Comes of Age', in James Raven and Antonia Forster (eds), *The English Novel 1770–1829: A Bibliographical Survey of Prose Fiction Published in the British Isles*, vol. 1: *1770–1799*. Oxford, 2000, pp. 15–121.

James Raven, *The Business of Books: Booksellers and the English Book Trade*. New Haven, CT, and London, 2007.

Thierry Rigogne, *Between State and Market: Printing and Bookselling in Eighteenth-Century France*. Oxford, 2007.

Thierry Rigogne, 'Readers and Reading in Cafés, 1660–1800', *French Historical Studies* 41:3 (August 2018): 473–94.

Mark Rose, *Authors and Owners: The Invention of Copyright*. Cambridge, MA, 1993.

Pamela Selwyn, *Everyday Life in the German Book Trade: Friedrich Nicolai as Bookseller and Publisher in the Age of Enlightenment, 1750–1810*. University Park, PA, 2000.

Will Slauter, 'The Rise of the Newspaper', in Richard R. John and Jonathan Silberstein Loeb (eds), *Making News: The Political Economy of Journalism in Britain and America from the Glorious Revolution to the Internet*. Oxford, 2015, pp. 19–46.

Geoffrey Turnovsky, *The Literary Market: Authorship and Modernity in the Old Regime*. Philadelphia, 2010.

James van Horn Melton, *The Rise of the Public in Enlightenment Europe*. Cambridge, 2001.

Reinhard Wittmann, 'Der gerechtfertigte Nachdrucker? Nachdruck and literarishes Leben im achtzehnten Jahrhundert', in *Buchmarkt und Lektüre im 18. und 19. Jahrhundert. Beiträge zum literarischen Leben 1750–1880*. Tübingen, 1982, pp. 69–92.

Reinhard Wittmann, *Geschichte des deutschen Buchhandels. Ein Überblick*. Munich, 1991.

Martha Woodmansee, 'Genius and the Copyright' in *The Author, Art, and the Market: Rereading the History of Aesthetics*. New York, 1994, pp. 35–55.

Websites

Norbert Bachleitner and Daniel Syrovy. Verpönt, Verdrängt—Vergessen? Eine Datenbank zur Erfassung der in Österreich zwischen 1750 und 1848 verbotenen Bücher. http://univie.ac.at/zensur/info.php

Simon Burrows and Mark Curran, The French Book Trade in Enlightenment Europe Database, 1769–1794. http://fbtee.uws.edu.au/stn/interface/, 6 May 2014.

Robert Darnton, A Literary Tour de France: Publishing and the Book Trade in France and Francophone Europe 1769–1789. http://robertdarnton.org/

Mapping the Republic of Letters. http://republicofletters.stanford.edu/index.html

Chapter 10

Christopher A. Bayly, *Empire and Information: Intelligence Gathering and Social Communication in India, 1780–1870*. Cambridge, 1996.

Rimi Barnali Chatterjee, *Empires of the Mind: A History of the Oxford University Press in India under the Raj*. New Delhi, 2006.

Robert Fraser and Mary Hammond (eds), *Books Without Borders... Vol. 2: Perspectives from South Asia*. Basingstoke, 2008.

Anindita Ghosh, *Power in Print: Popular Publishing and the Politics of Language and Culture in a Colonial Society*. New Delhi, 2006.

B.N. Goswamy, *The Word is Sacred; Sacred is the Word: The Indian Manuscript Tradition*. New Delhi, 2006.

Jan E.M. Houben and Saraju Rath, 'Manuscript Culture and Its Impact in "India": Contours and Parameters', in Saraju Rath (ed.), *Aspects of Manuscript Culture in South India*. Leiden, 2012, pp. 1–53.

Jinah Kim, *Receptacle of the Sacred: Illustrated Manuscripts and the Buddhist Book Cult in South Asia*. Berkeley, CA, 2013.

Jeremiah Patrick Losty, *The Art of the Book in India*. London, 1982.

Miles Ogborn, *Indian Ink: Script And Print in the Making of the English East India Company*. Chicago and London, 2007.

Francesca Orsini (ed.), *The History of the Book in South Asia*. Farnham, 2013.

Francesca Orsini and Katherine Butler Schofield (eds), *Tellings and Texts: Music, Literature and Performance in North India*. Cambridge, 2015.

Sheldon Pollock, 'Literary Culture and Manuscript Culture in Precolonial India' in Simon Eliot, Andrew Nash, and Ian Willison (eds), *Literary Cultures and the Material Book*. London, 2007, pp. 77–94.

Anant Kakba Priolkar, *The Printing Press in India: Its Beginnings and Early Development*. Bombay, 1958.

Ulrike Stark, *An Empire of Books: The Naval Kishore Press and the Diffusion of the Printed Word in Colonial India*. Ranikhet, 2007.

A.R. Venkatachalapathy, *The Province of the Book: Scholars, Scribes, and Scribblers in Colonial Tamilnadu*. Ranikhet, 2012.

Dominik Wujastyk, 'Indian Manuscripts', in Jørg B. Quenzer, Dmitry Donarev, and Jan-Ulrich Sobisch (eds), *Manuscript Cultures: Mapping the Field*. Berlin, 2014, pp. 159–81.

Chapter 11

Louis André, *Machines à papier. Innovation et transformations de l'industrie papetière en France, 1798–1860*. Paris, 1997.

Frédéric Barbier, 'The Publishing Industry and Printed Output in 19th Century France', in Kenneth E. Carpenter (ed.), *Books and Society in History*. New York and London, 1983.

Laurel Brake, *Print in Transition 1850–1910: Studies in Media and Book History*. London, 2003.

Annie Charon and Elisabeth Parinet, *Les ventes de livres et leurs catalogues XVIIe–XXe siècles*. Paris, 2000.

D.C. Coleman, *The British Paper Industry 1495–1860: A Study in Industrial Growth*. Oxford, 1958.

H. Curwen, *A History of Booksellers, the Old and the New*. London, 1873.

Simon Eliot, *Some Patterns and Trends in British Publishing 1800–1919*. London, 1994.

Lee Erickson, *The Economy of the Literary Form: English Literature and the Industrialisation of Publishing 1800–1850*. Baltimore, MD, 1996.

John Feather, *A History of British Publishing*. London and New York, 1988.

James Hepburn, *The Author's Empty Purse and the Rise of the Literary Agent*. Oxford, 1968.

Elizabeth James (ed.), *Macmillan: A Publishing Tradition*. London, 2002.

Helmut Lehmann-Haupt, *The Book in America: A History of the Making and Selling of Books in the United States*. New York, 1952.

Martyn Lyons, *Books: A Living History*, London, 2011.

David McKitterick (ed.), *The Cambridge History of the Book in Britain*, vol. 4. Cambridge, 2009.

Frank L. Mott, *A History of American Magazines*, vol. 2. Boston, MA, 1938.

Isabelle Olivero, *L'invention de la collection*. Paris, 1999.

Donald Sassoon, *The Culture of the Europeans from 1800 to the Present*. London, 2006.

Catherine Seville, *Literary Copyright Reform in Early Victorian England: The Framing of the 1842 Copyright Act*. Cambridge, 1999.

S.H. Steinberg, *Five Hundred Years of Printing*. Baltimore, MD, 1955.

Michael Winship, 'The Rise of a National Booktrade System in the United States, 1865–1916', in Jean-Yves Mollier and Jacques Michon (eds), *Les mutations du livre et de l'édition dans le monde du XVIIIe siècle à l'an 2000*. Laval, 2001.

Chapter 12

China

Cynthia Brokaw and Christopher A. Reed (eds), *From Woodblocks to the Internet: Chinese Publishing and Print Culture in Transition, circa 1800 to 2008*. Leiden, 2010.

Alexander C. Cook (ed.), *Mao's Little Red Book: A Global History*. New York, 2014.

Jean-Pierre Drege and Hua Chang-ming, *La révolution du livre dans la Chine moderne. Wang Yunwu, éditeur*. Paris, 1979.

Man-ying Ip, *The Life and Times of Zhang Yuanji, 1867–1959*. Beijing, 1985.

Shuyu Kong, *Consuming Literature: Best Sellers and the Commercialization of Literary Production in Contemporary* [1990s] *China*. Stanford, CA, 1995.

Leo Ou-fan Lee, *Shanghai Modern: The Flowering of a New Urban Culture in China 1930–1945*. Cambridge, MA, 1999.

Daniel Leese, 'The Little Red Book', in Leese, *Mao Cult: Rhetoric and Ritual in China's Cultural Revolution*. New York, 2011, ch. 5.

Perry Link, *The Uses of Literature; Life in the Socialist Literary System* [1970s–1990]. Princeton, NJ, 2000.

Christopher A. Reed, 'Re/Collecting the Sources: Shanghai's *Dianshizhai Pictorial* and Its Place in Historical Memories, 1884–1949', *Modern Chinese Literature and Culture* 12:2 (Fall 2000): 44–71.

Christopher A. Reed, *Gutenberg in Shanghai: Chinese Print Capitalism, 1876–1937*. Vancouver, Toronto, and Honolulu, 2004. Hong Kong, 2005.

Christopher A. Reed, 'Modern Chinese Print and Publishing Culture: The State of the Discipline II', *Book History*, 10 (2007): 291–316.

Fei-Hsien Wang, *Pirates and Publishers: A Social History of Copyright in Modern China*. Princeton, NJ, 2019.

Endymion Wilkinson, *Chinese History: A New Manual*, 4th edn. Cambridge, MA, and London, 2015.

Yuezhi Zhao, *Media, Market, and Democracy in China; Between the Party Line and the Bottom Line*. Urbana, IL, 1998.

Xiaoqing Ye, *The* Dianshizhai Pictorial: *Shanghai Urban Life, 1884–1898*. Ann Arbor, MI, 2003.

Japan and Korea

Vipan Chandra, *Imperialism, Resistance, and Reform in Late Nineteenth-Century Korea: Enlightenment and the Independence Club*. Berkeley, CA, 1988.

Anne M. Cooper-Chen, *Cartoon Cultures: The Globalization of Japanese Popular Media*. New York, 2010.

David C. Earhart, *Certain Victory: Images of World War II in Japanese Media*. Armonk, NY, 2008.

Man-nyun Han, 'Publishing in Korea, An Historical Survey', *Transactions Royal Asiatic Society Korea Branch*, 45 (Seoul) (1969): 51–85.

James L. Huffman, *Creating a Public: People and the Press in Meiji Japan*. Honolulu, 1997.

Insatsu Hakubutsukan (Printing Museum, Tokyo), *Insatsu toshi Tōkyō to kindai Nihon* (Tokyo—The Printing Capital and Its Role in Modern Japan). Tokyo, 2012.

Insatsu Hakubutsukan (Printing Museum, Tokyo), *Mirion seraa tanjō-e: Meiji-Taishō no zasshi media* (The Birth of a Million Seller: Magazines as Media in the Meiji-Taishō Era). Tokyo, 2008.

Wilt L. Idema (ed.), *Book in Numbers: Seventy-Fifth Anniversary of the Harvard-Yenching Library*. Cambridge, MA, 2007.

Andrew T. Kamei-Dyche, 'The History of Books and Print Culture in Japan: The State of the Discipline', *Book History*, 14 (2011): 270–304.

Kyung Hyun Kim (ed.), *The Korean Popular Culture Reader*. Durham, NC, 2014.

Peter Kornicki, *The Book in Japan: A Cultural History from the Beginnings to the Nineteenth Century*. Leiden, 1998.

Peter Kornicki, 'Japan, Korea, and Vietnam', in Simon Eliot and Jonathan Rose (eds), *A Companion to the History of the Book*. Oxford, 2007, pp. 111–25.

Ann Sung-hi Lee, *Yi Kwang-su and Modern Korean Literature: Mujong*. Ithaca, NY, 2005.

Edward Mack, *Manufacturing Modern Japanese Literature: Publishing, Prizes, and the Ascription of Literary Value*. Durham, NC, 2010.

Young Kyun Oh, *Engraving Virtue: The Printing History of a Premodern Korean Moral Primer*. Leiden, 2013.

Barbara Sato, *The New Japanese Woman: Modernity, Media, and Women in Interwar Japan*. Durham, NC, 2003.

Chapter 13

Sarah Brouillette, *Postcolonial Writers and the Global Literary Marketplace*. London, 2007.

Sarah Brouillette, *Literature and the Creative Economy*. Stanford, CA, 2014.

Robert Darnton, *The Case for Books: Past, Present, and Future*. New York, 2009.

Daniel Fuller and DeNel Rehberg Sedo, *Reading beyond the Book: The Social Practices of Contemporary Literary Culture*. London and New York, 2013.

Eva Hemmungs Wirtén, *No Trespassing: Authorship, Intellectual Property Rights and the Boundaries of Globalization*. Toronto, 2004.

Eva Hemmungs Wirtén, *Cosmopolitan Copyright: Law and Language in the Translation Zone*. Uppsala 2011. Available in full-text (pdf) from: http://urn.kb.se/resolve?urn=urn:nbn:se:uu:diva-161978

Laura J. Miller, *Reluctant Capitalists: Bookselling and the Culture of Consumption*. Chicago, 2006.

Simone Murray, *The Adaptation Industry: The Cultural Economy of Contemporary Literary Adaptation*. New York and London, 2011.

Sydney Shep, *Books without Borders: The Cross-National Dimension in Print Culture*. Houndmills, 2008.

Claire Squires and Ray Murray Padmini, 'The Digital Publishing Communications Circuit', *Book 2.0*, 3:1 (2013): 3–24. http://hdl.handle.net/1893/17181

Ann Steiner, 'The Global Book: Micropublishing, Conglomerate Production, and Digital Market Structures', *Publishing Research Quarterly*, Nov. 2017. Online: https://doi.org/10.1007/s12109-017-9558-8

Ted Striphas, *Late Age of Print: Everyday Book Culture from Consumerism to Control*. New York, 2009.

John B. Thompson, *Merchants of Culture: The Publishing Business in the Twenty-First Century*. Cambridge, 2010.

Chapter 14

Thierry Bardini, *Bootstrapping—Douglas Englebart, Coevolution, and the Origins of Personal Computing*. Stanford, CA, 2000.

Elizabeth Eisenstein, 'The Newspaper Press: The End of Books?', in *Divine Art, Infernal Machine—The Reception of Printing in the West from First Impressions to the Sense of an Ending*. Philadelphia, 2011, pp. 198–214.

Eileen Gardiner and Ronald G. Musto, 'The Electronic Book', in Michael Felix Suarez and H.R. Woudhuysen (eds), *The Oxford Companion to the Book*. Oxford, 2010, pp. 164–6.

Paul Ginisty, *La Féerie*. Paris, 1901.

Vivien Greene (ed.), *Italian Futurism, 1909–1944—Reconstructing the Universe*. Simon R. Guggenheim Museum. New York, 2014.

Haje Jan Kamos, 'E-books Are More Than Just Digital Facsimiles, and Publishers Need to Realize That, Pronto', *Techcrunch*, 26 March 2016. Online: http://techcrunch.com/2016/03/26/will-nobody-think-of-the-trees/

Alan Kay, 'A Personal Computer for Children of All Ages' (Aug. 1972, 1). Original paper available at: http:// mprove.de/diplom/gui/Kay72a.pdf

Giovanni Lista, *Le livre futuriste. De la libération du mot au poème tactile*. Modena, 1984.

Stéphane Mallarmé, 'Le livre, instrument spirituel', *La Revue blanche*, 1 July 1895: 33–6.

John McCormick, *Popular Theatres of Nineteenth-Century France*. London, 1993.

Hugh McGuire and Brian O'Leary (eds), *A Futurist's Manifesto*. Sebastopol, 2012.

Marshall McLuhan, *Understanding Media: The Extensions of Man*. New York, 1964.

Marshall McLuhan and Quentin Fiore. Coordinated by Jerome Agel. *The Medium is the Massage*. New York, 1967 (the title puns on 'medium is the message').

Craig Mod, http://craigmod.com/sputnik/; http://craigmod.com/journal/post_artifact/; and http://craigmod.com/journal/ebooks/.

Laszlo Moholy-Nagy, *Painting Photography Film*, trans. Janet Seligman. Cambridge, MA, 1969.

Nicholas Negroponte, *Spatial Data Management*. Cambridge, MA, 1979.

Geoffrey Nunberg (ed), *The Future of the Book*. Berkeley, CA, 1996.

Andrew Piper, *Book Was Here—Reading in Electronic Times*. Chicago, 2012.

Claudia Salaris, *Marinetti editore*. Bologna, 1990.

Jeffrey Schnapp with Adam Michaels, *The Electric Information Age Book (McLuhan/Agel/Fiore and the Experimental Paperback)*. Princeton, NJ, 2012.

Jan Tshichold, *The New Typography: A Handbook for Modern Designers*, trans. Ruari McLean. 1st edition 1928; repr. Berkeley, CA, 1998.

Robert Venturi, Denise Scott Brown, and Steven Izenour, *Learning From Las Vegas*. Cambridge, MA, and London, 1972.

Robert Wiesenberger, 'Muriel Cooper and the Book as Interface', in Nanni Baltzer (ed.), *Before Publication: Montage in Art, Architecture, and Book Design*. Zurich, 2016.

Index